W9-CND-653

Success at Last!

Helping Students with Attention Deficit (Hyperactivity) Disorders Achieve Their Potential

Edited by

Constance Weaver

Western Michigan University

Heinemann
Portsmouth, NH

HEINEMANN
A division of Reed Elsevier Inc.
361 Hanover Street
Portsmouth, NH 03801–3912
Offices and agents throughout the world

Copyright © 1994 by Heinemann. All rights reserved. No part of this book may be reproduced in any form or by electronic or mechanical means, including information storage and retrieval systems, without permission in writing from the publisher, except by a reviewer, who may quote brief passages in a review.

Editor: Philippa Stratton
Production: J.B. Tranchemontagne
Text design: Mary Cronin
Cover design: Mary-Lynne Bohn

Every effort has been made to contact the copyright holders for permission to reprint borrowed material where necessary. We regret any oversights that may have occurred and would be happy to rectify them in future printings of this work.

The authors and publisher are grateful to the following for permission to reprint previously published material:

Portions of Chapter 1, "Understanding and Educating Students with an Attention Deficit Hyperactivity Disorder" by Constance Weaver, are reprinted from *Alternatives in Understanding and Educating Attention-Deficit Students* by Constance Weaver, NCTE Concept Paper Series No. 3, 1991.

Figure 1–2: PET Scan Images from "Cerebral Glucose Metabolism in Adults with Hyperactivity of Childhood Onset" by A. J. Zametkin et al. Reprinted by permission of *The New England Journal of Medicine* (323:1361-366, 1990). Also appeared in the Spring/Summer issue of CH.A.D.D.ER

Library of Congress Cataloging-in-Publication Data
Success at last: helping students with attention deficit
  (hyperactivity) disorders achieve their potential / edited by
  Constance Weaver.
      p.   cm.
   Includes bibliographical references and index.
   ISBN 0–435–08808–4
      1. Attention-deficit-disordered children—Education—United
Stated. I. Weaver, Constance.
LC4713.4.S83
371.93—dc20
                                                                  93-30559
                                                                      CIP

Printed in the United States of America on acid-free paper
99 98 97 96 95 94 HP 7 6 5 4 3 2 1

Success at Last!

LIBRARY
ALMA COLLEGE
ALMA, MICHIGAN

ADHD makes every aspect of learning a challenge and makes getting into trouble easy. Difficulty in learning and ease in getting into trouble are a powerful combination of negativity. ADHD students, especially those who do not realize they are ADHD-positive, may never accomplish more than a sliver of their potential—unless they have help.

—John Weaver

Contents

Acknowledgments

Thanks to all the wonderful people at Heinemann who contributed to the production of this book. Particular thanks goes to Philippa Stratton, without whose encouragement this book would not have come into being.

Introduction

This book began at Pizza Hut, where my then teenage son John and I have had several memorable conversations. We were discussing his Attention Deficit Hyperactivity Disorder when John suddenly suggested, "Why don't you write a book about ADD?"

At first I thought the idea ridiculous, for I am neither a psychologist nor a psychiatrist. Eventually, though, I realized that I did know enough about educating students with an Attention Deficit Hyperactivity Disorder to at least write an article or two and to edit a book. The project was launched when I gave a talk on understanding and educating students with ADHD at the second international Whole Language Umbrella conference in 1990. With my handouts I included a call for papers that has resulted in the chapters comprising this book. These chapters are written from a rich variety of perspectives: that of parents; classroom teachers; teacher educators and researchers; special needs teachers in school or clinical settings; curriculum specialists, supervisors, and administrators; and, often, from more than one of these perspectives.

Though most of the chapters deal explicitly with Attention Deficit Hyperactivity Disorder and with students having such a disorder, many of the observations and suggestions apply also to those who have an Attention Deficit Disorder but not hyperactivity.

In varying degrees, each chapter reflects the system-theory conceptualization of ADHD that I articulate in my introductory chapter. That is, the articles reflect a conviction that ADHD is not a disorder located solely within the individual, but rather a set of dysfunctional relationships between an individual with certain neurological predispositions and an environment that generates certain expectations and demands, and elicits predictable reactions. Therefore, the authors suggest not so much how to directly change the individual diagnosed with an Attention Deficit (Hyperactivity) Disorder, but rather how to change our expectations, demands, and interactions within the classroom environment.

Most chapters also reflect a whole language perspective toward educating students with an Attention Deficit (Hyperactivity) Disorder, as I briefly sketch in the introductory chapter and describe more fully in the concluding chapter. In general most of the chapters demonstrate that while behavioral approaches may control behavior and lead to greater academic performance in the short run, approaches that respect the learner as a self-determining individual achieve significantly greater success in generating changed behavioral patterns in the long run.

Several common observations and recommendations emerge from combining system-theory and a whole language perspective toward educating students with AD(H)D. These include the following:

- Medication may help the individual.
- Teachers need to provide structure and to help learners with AD(H)D organize and carry out their work, even in whole language classrooms.

- Learners with AD(H)D find it especially beneficial to be able to choose activities and learning experiences in which they are interested and can more readily become absorbed.
- Learning is best facilitated when students' strengths are emphasized and their difficulties ignored or bypassed, and when teachers understand that taking risks is necessary for growth and therefore encourage and respond positively to learners' risk-taking.
- Students need time to gain self-confidence and to change, in both the academic and the social aspects of classroom life. It will usually take months of consistently acting upon whole language principles for teachers to see significant change, but the effort is worthwhile. The resulting change can be relatively permanent if new patterns of engaging in academic work and the social life of the classroom continue to be nurtured.

The benefits of a system-theory perspective combined with whole language learning and teaching are explained and illustrated throughout the book, culminating in several chapters that describe and document children's growth in whole language classrooms over an entire school year.

A 1991 memorandum from the U.S. Department of Education (see Appendix A) has clarified the right of AD(H)D students to special educational services, either under section 504 of the Rehabilitation Act of 1973 or under the "other health impaired" category of the Education of the Handicapped Act (now the Individuals with Disabilities Education Act), whichever is appropriate. However, one can infer from most of the chapters in this volume a skills-oriented resource room will be much less effective than a whole language classroom or resource room in helping AD(H)D students become literate and independent learners.

Regarding terminology, a word of explanation is in order. Some authors have used the term *Attention Deficit Disorder*, or ADD, to refer to students with or without accompanying hyperactivity, while other authors have used the term *Attention Deficit (Hyperactivity) Disorder*, or AD(H)D, to refer to either or potentially both. Still other authors have carefully differentiated between the two by using *Attention Deficit Disorder*, or ADD to describe the condition without hyperactivity, and *Attention Deficit Hyperactivity Disorder*, or ADHD, to describe the condition when basic attentional difficulties are accompanied by impulsivity and hyperactivity.

1

Understanding and Educating Students with Attention Deficit Hyperactivity Disorders: Toward a System-Theory and Whole Language Perspective

Constance Weaver

In effect, ADHD is not so much a disorder (located within the individual) as a set of dysfunctional relationships between an individual with certain predispositions and an environment that generates certain expectations, demands, and reactions.

Though the article begins somewhat technically for the sake of those acquainted with, or interested in, controversies in understanding Attention Deficit Hyperactivity Disorder, the thesis of this introductory article is rather straightforward: that ADHD can best be conceptualized as resulting from *both* the individual's neurological functioning and various environmental factors, and therefore, it is best dealt with by attending both to the individual and to external factors, not to one alone. This is the "system" perspective mentioned in the title of the article and reflected in the quote above.

Considering, then, that ADHD may be best described not in terms of the individual alone, but in terms of less-than-optimal transactions with others (the "environment"), what logically follows is that in teaching students who have an Attention Deficit Hyperactivity Disorder we should modify our expectations, demands, and reactions in relation to those who may have biochemically predisposed difficulties in focusing and maintaining attention and in controlling impulses. Setting the stage for other articles in this book, this introduction then suggests that whole language classrooms are best for students with ADHD because whole language principles lead to education that meets the most critical needs of these students. Whole language teachers are responsive to students' interests, needs, personalities, and difficulties.

In addition to discussing controversies regarding the nature and origins of ADHD, the article includes information on what characterizes ADHD. It describes basic whole language principles and briefly explains why and how acting upon these principles enables teachers to help students with ADHD succeed in school and with their peers. The article also suggests how the school might support students with ADHD and their teachers. The article has previously appeared in the May 1992 issue of the *American Journal of Speech-Language Pathology: A Journal of Critical Practice*.

Connie Weaver is a professor of English at Western Michigan University, where she teaches courses in the reading and writing processes, applied linguistics, and whole language education. Recent publications include *Reading Process and Practice: From Socio-Psycholinguistics to Whole Language* (second edition, 1994), *Theme Exploration: A Voyage of Discovery* (1993, written with Joel Chaston and Scott Peterson), *Supporting Whole Language* (1992, coedited with Linda Henke), *Understanding Whole Language* (1990), plus two articles and a concept paper on understanding and educating students with an Attention Deficit Hyperactivity Disorder, the latter published by the National Council of Teachers of English (1991), from which this article evolved. Connie's professional interest in ADHD stems from her son's being diagnosed at the age of sixteen as having an Attention Deficit Hyperactivity Disorder. (See Chapter 3 by John Weaver in this book.)

In the 1970s, various critics suggested that there was no such disorder as "hyperactivity." It was a mythical construct devised by parents and especially teachers who just could not or would not cope with the individual needs of the rambunctious and bored child. Hyperactivity and learning disabilities, it was argued, were concepts instigated by middle-class parents desperate for some acceptable explanation as to why their children were not succeeding in school (Schrag & Divoky, 1975; for more recent criticisms of hyperactivity, see Schachar, 1986, and Kohn, 1989; for related criticisms of learning disabilities, see Carrier, 1983, and Sleeter, 1986). In societal terms, such labeling revealed normality to be defined in terms of conformity (Hobbs, 1975). So-called hyperactive children, then, were simply those who failed in certain ways to conform to the expectations of society.

Recently there has been intensified support for the idea that "learning disabilities" may be more a social construct than a biological and neurological phenomenon. For example, Gerald Coles has mounted a detailed argument against the accepted "reductionist and determinist neurological thesis" accounting for learning disabilities (1987, p. 134), positing instead a theory of interactivity that places primary responsibility for alleged learning disabilities upon the various forces within education and society (Coles, 1987; see responses in the May 1989 issue of the *Journal of Learning Disabilities*). Bartoli and Botel (1988) have argued persuasively for what they call an ecological systems approach to understanding and alleviating reading/learning difficulties.

In addition, ethnographers like Denny Taylor have provided persuasive and shocking evidence of the harm done to children by an educational and psychological establishment determined to locate the cause of school difficulties in the learner rather than in the educational approach or the diagnostic procedures and practices of special education (1990). Taylor's case study of Patrick—a child whose accomplishments as a reader and writer were overlooked and even denied by school personnel because he did not score well on decontextualized tests—exemplifies what Coles argues so persuasively: that if "the structural forces and relationships in the interactivity that produces educational failure are not addressed, challenged, and changed, the educational 'poor' will be with us forever" (Coles, 1987, p. 212).

With such impetus comes increasing recognition that we need to examine how the environment contributes to the genesis, diagnosis, maintenance, and treatment of alleged learning disabilities and conditions like attention deficit hyperactivity disorder, or ADHD (the current label for what used to be called *hyperactivity, minimal brain disorder, minimal brain dysfunction,* and so forth). More generally, such arguments and anecdotal evidence indicate all too clearly that professionals dealing with the psychological health and educational success of children need to reconsider the mechanistic, linear thinking that leads to seeing the locus of learning difficulties as solely within the child (Heshusius, 1989). We need to reject the educational models that reflect a mechanistic paradigm: the medical model, the psychological process model, the behaviorist model, and the cognitive/learning strategies model (Poplin, 1988a).

At least in the case of ADHD, however, it would be inappropriate to replace a simplistic neurological deficit model with an equally simplistic environmental model, locating the child's difficulties entirely within the environment and therefore seeking remedies that address external factors only. What offers considerable promise for understanding ADHD and how to educate students with ADHD more effectively is a system-theory approach, drawing upon the kind of thinking espoused by Ludwig von Bertalanffy in his general system theory (1968) and further refined and modified by Gregory Bateson (1972) and others. This version of system theory rejects simplistic cause-effect reasoning and linear explanations, seeing causation as multidimensional and multidirectional. System theory both contributes to and supports a transactional, constructivist, holistic paradigm of human learning (Weaver, 1985; Poplin, 1988b; Heshusius, 1989; Weaver, 1993); an ecological perspective of learning disabilities (Bartoli & Botel, 1988); and a whole language philosophy of education (Goodman, 1986; Weaver, 1990; Edelsky, Altwerger, & Flores, 1991; and the November 1989 issue of *The Elementary School Journal*). Each of these stances views the individual as part of larger systems that intersect and interact with one another and with the individual, all simultaneously shaping and being shaped by each other.

Within this broad framework, the thesis of this chapter is twofold: (1) that ADHD is best understood from a system-theory perspective, and (2) that educating ADHD students should likewise be approached from this perspective, within which whole language education offers particular promise (see also Weaver, 1991 & 1993).

Understanding ADHD: A System View

Increasingly, clinicians and researchers have come to the conclusion that ADHD is characterized by problems in restraining impulses as well as in focusing and maintaining attention, though the official diagnostic criteria from the American Psychiatric Association's *Diagnostic and Statistical Manual,* version III-R, are currently not divided into categories. Their diagnostic criteria (1987) are as follows:

- fidgets
- difficulty remaining seated
- easily distracted
- difficulty waiting turn
- blurts out answers

- difficulty following instructions
- difficulty sustaining attention
- shifts from one uncompleted task to another
- difficulty playing quietly
- talks excessively
- interrupts others
- doesn't seem to listen
- loses things needed for tasks
- engages in physically dangerous activities

The hyperactivity involved in ADHD is related to, and may in fact stem from, the difficulty in restraining impulses (for example, Barkley, 1990). It seems likely that the American Psychiatric Association's forthcoming *Diagnostic and Statistical Manual*, version IV, will list the defining characteristics under two relatively separate behavioral dimensions: inattention-disorganization, and impulsivity-hyperactivity (e.g. Lahey & Carlson, 1991; see also Fowler et al., 1992). It is increasingly recognized that these patterns may be exhibited by adolescents and adults as well as by children (Weiss & Hechtman, 1986; Wender, 1987; Kane et al., 1990). Some of the characteristics being considered for the official American Psychiatric Association definition of ADHD in adults are the following (Kane et al. in Barkley, 1990):

Inattention
- trouble directing and sustaining attention (conversations, lectures, reading instructions, driving)
- difficulty completing projects, lacks stick-to-it-tiveness
- easily overwhelmed by tasks of daily living (managing money, paying bills, applying for college, etc.)
- trouble maintaining an organized living/work place
- inconsistent work performance
- lacks attention to detail

Impulsivity/Hyperactivity
- makes decisions impulsively and doesn't anticipate consequences
- difficulty delaying gratification; seeks out stimulation
- restless, fidgety
- makes statements or comments without considering their impact
- impatient, easily frustrated
- traffic violations (speeding, running stop signs)

Unlike learning disabilities, ADHD is commonly "diagnosed" not by standardized tests but on the basis of difficulty in coping with the demands of everyday life. Indeed, ADHD seems not to be a learning disability or difference per se (for example, Silver, 1990), nor even simply a special handicapping condition with respect to education. Often, the difficulties and dysfunctional behaviors associated with ADHD are not confined to the classroom or the school; instead, they occur across all aspects of individuals' lives, contributing to poor relationships with parents, siblings, peers, spouses and children, employers and coworkers, and the community. It is for this reason that assessment of possible ADHD involves observations by parents, teachers, and others who observe the person in naturalistic settings (e.g. Barkley, 1991).

What seems most noticeable to those who live, work, attend school, or engage in leisure activities with individuals who have ADHD is that they seem virtually unable to use what they know about the social inappropriateness or probable consequences of their actions to resist impulses—impulses to do anything except boring schoolwork, to engage in disruptive or hurtful or destructive behavior, to break rules and laws, and even to ignore their own determination to behave more appropriately and acceptably. They seem to be at the mercy of their emotions and impulses, which in turn are often reactions to the environment. In short, individuals with ADHD seem to have a biological predisposition to act in ways that society considers dysfunctional and/or inappropriate.

ADHD should be understood, then, not simply as a neurological condition, but as a social construct. *In effect, ADHD is not so much a disorder (located within the individual) as a set of dysfunctional relationships between an individual with certain predispositions and an environment that generates certain expectations, demands, and reactions.*

This is part of what it means to take a system view of ADHD. A system view rejects the simplistic notion that alternatives are necessarily mutually exclusive—in this case, that ADHD resides solely within the individual, or that ADHD behaviors are caused solely by the environment. Instead, a system view sees alternative explanations as more often complementary, leading to a fuller understanding of phenomena all too often viewed simplistically. A system view of ADHD requires at least the following:

1. It means recognizing that while ADHD may have origins in the individual's neurological functioning, in the individual's biology and physiology, it needs also to be understood in sociological terms, as difficulty in responding to certain kinds of expectations and external demands. In other words, it means conceptualizing ADHD in terms of both the individual and the environment.
2. It means recognizing that even the biological and physiological aspects of ADHD may stem from environmental rather than genetic causes, though heredity does often seem to be a factor.
3. It means not just "treating" or attempting to change the behavior of the individual, but changing expectations and demands and ways of interacting with the child, adolescent, or adult who exhibits ADHD behaviors.
4. In schools, it means attempting to meet the needs of students rather than trying to fit students into a rigid system, yet also accepting the possibility that some students may function better, socially as well as academically, with appropriate medication.

Figure 1–1 offers a visual representation of this system view of ADHD and the complex interrelationships that both give rise to ADHD behaviors and alleviate them. A system view of ADHD includes both a medical and a sociological perspective, as indicated also in the recent work of some psychologists focusing on ADHD (Anastopoulos, DuPaul, & Barkley, 1991; Barkley, 1990;

Robin, 1990; Robin and Foster, 1989; E. Taylor, 1986; implicit also in Gordon, 1991). Most of these psychologists emphasize the family as a system affecting and being affected by ADHD. The present article goes beyond the family, emphasizing the school and the classroom as systems that can either exacerbate or alleviate ADHD behaviors.

A Medical Perspective

It is largely because the traditional medical model of ADHD is a deficit model that the aforementioned social/educational critics and many educators have rejected the construct of ADHD. Nevertheless, there is growing evidence that intractable impulsivity, hyperactivity, and inattentiveness may be traced to roots in variant neurological structure and/or functioning.

FIGURE 1–1. *A both/and systems-theory model of the genesis and alleviation of ADHD behaviors.*

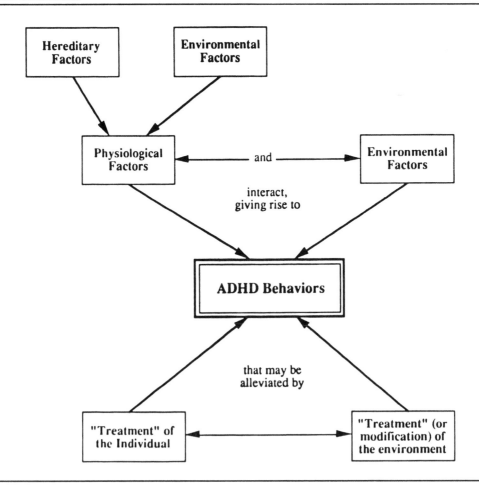

Some recent studies suggest differences in size or functioning of different aspects of the central nervous system (Hynd et al., 1991; Klorman, 1991). Blood flow studies and recent studies using such high-tech procedures as Brain Electronic Activity Mapping (BEAM), Magnetic Resonance Imaging (MRI), and Positron Emission Tomography (PET) increasingly link ADHD to underfunctioning of certain neural pathways within the central nervous system (Barkley, 1990, p. 29; Shelton & Barkley, 1990, p. 211). Other lines of research suggest that what causes this "underfunctioning" may be an insufficiency of certain brain chemicals, most notably certain neurotransmitters such as dopamine and norepinephrine (Zametkin & Rapoport, 1987). Other research suggests that individuals with ADHD may have impairment in the brain areas believed to regulate inhibition and motivation—the frontal-limbic system, particularly the striatum (Fowler et al., 1992, citing an interview with psychologist Russell Barkley). A recent and widely publicized study by Zametkin and his colleagues at the National Institute of Mental Health used PET scans to confirm earlier findings of reduced glucose metabolism in the brains of adults with ADHD, compared with other adults—particularly in the premotor cortex and the superior prefrontal cortex (Zametkin et al., 1990). See Figure 1–2.

Although there is no clear-cut evidence as to exactly which aspects of brain structure or functioning are implicated in ADHD, researchers seem to be converging on evidence that ADHD behaviors involve a bio/physiological condition, with heredity often a factor in a child's development of ADHD. Other causes may include brain damage, pregnancy conditions (such as maternal

FIGURE 1–2. *PET scan images: The image on the left is the normal control, while the one on the right is the ADHD adult. The left side of each image represents the right side of the brain. In the original color images, white, red, and orange indicate areas of relatively high glucose metabolism, whereas blue, green, and purple indicate areas of lower glucose metabolism.*

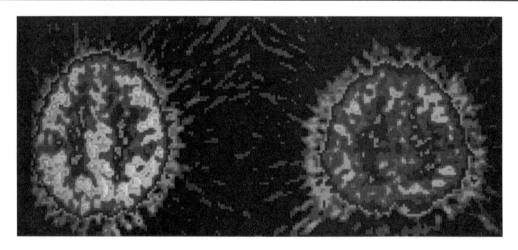

consumption of alcohol), birth complications, toxins (especially lead), infections, and diet. Although sensational claims have been made about food additives or sugar causing hyperactive behavior (especially Feingold, 1975), a sizable body of research has failed to confirm these as common causes of ADHD (see discussions in Barkley, 1990, pp. 95–100; Gordon, 1991, pp. 69–72). Nevertheless, research on prenatal factors and on other factors such as lead supports the conclusion that environment as well as heredity may contribute to the particular neurological functioning that seems to be a significant component of ADHD.

Overall, there is growing evidence of a neurological component contributing to the behaviors characterized as ADHD. In other words, ADHD does seem to exist in part biochemically—even though ADHD is constantly being defined and redefined by the experts; even though researchers do not completely understand its causes or the mechanisms by which it operates; and even though there is significant disagreement as well as a significant degree of consensus within the field (Shaywitz & Shaywitz, 1991).

From a system perspective, however, it is more appropriate to conceptualize ADHD in terms of *differences* in neurological functioning, rather than deficits—and of *quantitative* rather than qualitative differences (Shelton & Barkley, 1990, p. 214). These quantitative differences give rise to behaviors along a continuum, from what is socially desirable and functional for the individual to what is socially intolerable and self-defeating. Viewed this way, a medical perspective makes an essential contribution to a broader system view of ADHD (and of dyslexia and learning disabilities as well; see, for example, Chapter 11 of Weaver, 1994).

A Sociological Perspective

Research suggests, then, that environmental factors may play a role in the genesis of ADHD, as well as in its definition and diagnosis. Social and situational factors may also play a role in its maintenance and treatment. Regarding the initiation and maintenance of ADHD behaviors, people and situations can make it either *harder* for individuals with ADHD to restrain impulsive and hyperactive behavior and to pay attention and concentrate, or *easier* for them to exercise self-control and maintain attention. The following excerpt from a session with a therapist shows how a parent might inadvertently contribute to a child or adolescent's predisposition to ADHD behavior. The therapist's comments begin to clarify how, in system theory, ADHD is viewed as an interaction between the characteristics of the individual and the demands, expectations, initiations, and responses from the external environment. In this case the mother quickly exacerbates the teenager's predisposition:

THERAPIST: So what are the major problems at home?
MRS. COHEN: Matthew's bad temper. He gets really angry for no good reason. Then he curses, yells, and is totally out of control.
MATTHEW: You're full of it, Mom! I don't do that! You're just a nag!
THERAPIST: Wait a minute, Matt. I know you feel strongly about this, but I have to check out something with your mother first. Give me a play-by-play description of a recent temper outburst.

MRS. COHEN: I said, "Don't you have homework?" He said, "No," and I said, "Come on, your teacher says she always gives homework. Tell us the truth." And . . .

MATTHEW: See, there she goes bugging me and thinking I'm always lying.

THERAPIST: Matthew, I know you feel strongly. And I can see how when your mom puts you on the spot about homework, you come out slugging.

MRS. COHEN: Doc, you got it. He actually ended up pushing and hitting me last night.

THERAPIST: So, when you say that Matt loses his temper easily, you are talking about something between you and Matt, not just Matt. You ask nicely first. He doesn't answer. So you turn the screws a bit and press him, suggesting he is lying or holding back on you. He clobbers you back. We are looking at a sequence of communication between the two of you, not just one person losing his temper, right?

MRS. COHEN: I guess so, but it's his ADHD that makes him do it, not my question.

MATTHEW: There she goes again, with that ADHD shit! Next she's going to tell you about Ritalin, "the miracle drug."

THERAPIST: Matt, sounds like you get pretty mad and sarcastic when your mom blames your ADHD for everything. Mrs. Cohen, a person with ADHD is like a tightly stretched guitar string. The string can break if you pluck it too hard, but it must be plucked to break. Matt may be more likely to explode because of his biology, but it still takes your statement to set him off. And with the guitar, if you pluck the string just right, you can make beautiful music. You and Matt have the potential to get along with more harmony, even if his ADHD makes him like the tight string. This is a two-person problem. We need to change how you two communicate, not just Matt and not just Mom (Robin, 1990, pp. 471–72).

Here the therapist reframes the problem: ADHD does not merely reside within the individual. Rather, it arises as the individual transacts with the external environment. The individual has the *potential* for certain behaviors that characterize ADHD, but the extent to which and the ways in which these are manifested depend somewhat, and sometimes a lot, upon the external environment.

Situational demands can have a profound effect upon ADHD behaviors. For example, research clearly demonstrates that children with ADHD have great difficulty attending to tasks that they find boring, such as completing dittos and worksheets. They find it much easier to attend to tasks they find stimulating and meaningful. While some critics and even clinicians have assumed that such situational variation might automatically rule out a diagnosis of ADHD, other researchers have suggested that variation across situations might actually be a defining characteristic of ADHD (Barkley, 1990, p. 49). In other words, it may be primarily individuals with ADHD who find it virtually impossible to complete boring tasks, yet somehow (or sometimes) possible to complete what genuinely interests them.

What emerges from research and experience is a picture of ADHD as a "system" involving both intrinsic characteristics and environmental influences.

Within the life of an individual who is biologically/physiologically predisposed to certain kinds of behaviors, various forces intersect and interact: parents, teachers, and peers, for example; or home, school, neighborhood, and community. These participate in creating what is *perceived* as ADHD. It is a *both / and* phenomenon: both bio/physiological and sociological, involving the individual in transactions with others in society.

Educating Students with ADHD: Addressing the Individual Within the System

If indeed ADHD is both a bio/physiological and a sociological phenomenon, it seems only logical that alleviating ADHD behaviors may be accomplished by addressing either the individual or the environment, but preferably both.

Unfortunately, the most certain statement that can be made about alleviation of ADHD behaviors is that *nothing* consistently or typically produces long-term effects—an observation consistent with the hypothesis of a neurological factor.

Conventionally, there have been three basic approaches to trying to change the individual: a cognitive approach, which attempts to help individuals with ADHD develop self-control of their behavior; a behavioral approach, which relies on eternal control; and medication, which assumes a biochemical effect. Other approaches have had limited or dubious success, at best (Barkley, 1990; Goldstein & Ingersoll, 1992). Both cognitive and behavioral approaches seem to have limited effects, seldom generalizing or transferring to times or situations other than when the training programs are in effect (Abikoff, 1991; Gordon, Thomason, Cooper, & Ivers, 1991; Pfiffner & Barkley, 1990, pp. 538–39). To date, even the chemical treatments for ADHD, such as Ritalin, work only for a few hours at a time, and unevenly at that. Nevertheless, between 70 and 80 percent of children with ADHD do appear to exhibit a positive response to central nervous system stimulants (Ritalin, Cylert, or, less often, Dexadrine), an improvement significantly greater than that perceived with placebos (DuPaul & Barkley, 1990; also Baren, 1989; Gordon, 1991). These medications typically reduce impulsive and hyperactive behavior and increase attentive behavior during the hours for which each dose is effective (Mandelkorn, 1993).

In school situations, behavioral approaches may temporarily produce positive effects. However, behavioral approaches concentrate primarily upon managing students' behavior in traditional classrooms, without regard for the appropriateness of such classrooms (e.g. Parker, 1992). Traditional classrooms demand of students with ADHD everything they are not good at: sitting still and not talking, concentrating on dittos and other skills work that they find boring, and not speaking or acting impulsively. In other words, traditional classrooms exacerbate ADHD behaviors and thus intensify others' perception of the student as having ADHD. In the short run, behaviorists' procedures for carefully monitoring time and attention to seatwork tasks may control ADHD behaviors, producing temporary, localized compliance. But, in the long run, the inappropriate behavioral and curricular expectations may, in fact, engender resistance to this dehumanizing kind of schooling—in the form of behavior that is even more inattentive, disruptive, or harmful (Heshusius, 1989; Bartoli & Botel 1988, p. 219). Such intensified ADHD behavior further contributes to "blaming the victim" for behaviors that are more complex in origin.

Because the demands of the traditional classroom are so difficult for students with ADHD to meet, and because the appropriateness of these behavioral and curricular expectations is so rarely questioned, perhaps it is not surprising that most of the professional literature on the schooling of students with ADHD focuses almost exclusively on managing their behavior. This in turn leads many educators to conclude, erroneously, that students with ADHD can (at best) be only managed, not educated. Such a conclusion is a pervasive but inaccurate and unproductive consequence of locating the difficulty solely within the individual, rather than within the system.

What may hold the greatest promise is treating the individual with medication if that proves beneficial, while also changing traditional expectations and practices so as to maximize the student's success, both academic and social (e.g. Adams & Curtin, 1992; Whalen & Henker, 1991). What students with ADHD need is what students with learning disabilities—and indeed, *all* students—need: not a fragmented, skills-oriented curriculum, but a curriculum that keeps language and learning whole and meaningful, that offers students choice and ownership of learning, and that supports learners in taking more responsibility for their own learning and their behavior.

Whole Language: Modifying Educational Expectations and Practices

This is precisely the kind of education offered in good whole language classrooms. Whole language teachers do not merely settle for managing students in the classroom and assigning seatwork (dittos, worksheets, workbook activities) on isolated skills. Nor do whole language teachers settle merely for managing the behavior of students with ADHD, though an intelligent approach to helping children learn to self-manage their behavior may be part of the educational agenda (Collis & Dalton, 1990). Beyond that, whole language teachers are genuinely concerned about offering *all* children a challenging education (Goodman, 1986; Weaver, 1990; Edelsky, Altwerger, & Flores, 1991).

In practice, this means that students with ADHD are offered the meaningful learning experiences that make it somewhat easier for them to focus attention and to concentrate. Like other students, those with ADHD find it easier to attend to tasks that excite their curiosity and interest, that challenge them, and that they perceive as worthwhile (Barkley, 1990, p. 49). As psychologist Michael Gordon writes, "Down with education by ditto" (Gordon, 1991, p. 133), and, by implication, up with education that is thought-provoking, creative, and, above all, meaningful.

Many of the teacher and school strategies mentioned in the remainder of this article reflect the concept of scaffolding (Ninio & Bruner, 1978; Bruner, 1983, 1986; Gray, 1987); that is, others provide supports whereby individuals with ADHD can do collaboratively what they cannot yet do independently (see Vygotsky's "zone of proximal development," 1986).

The Potential of Whole Language Classrooms

Following are some characteristics of whole language classrooms and whole language teaching that make such education more promising than traditional education for students with ADHD.

1. Whole language teachers are particularly sensitive to the interests, abilities and needs of their students, both collectively and individually. They shape the curriculum with and in response to students, instead of expecting the students to cope with a prepackaged curriculum. Concurrently, they attempt to meet the needs of individual students. Of course, this is particularly important for children and youth with ADHD.
2. Whole language teachers emphasize all students' *strengths*. They find ways of using students' strengths to alleviate, compensate for, or avoid accentuating students' weaknesses.
3. Furthermore, whole language teachers often try to alleviate students' difficulties by working around their weaknesses—for example, by encouraging students with ADHD to compose on computers rather than to write laboriously by hand. These interrelated aspects of whole language teaching are particularly important for boosting self-esteem and self-confidence.
4. Whole language teachers avoid worksheets, workbooks, and isolated skills work—a particular boon for students with ADHD, who find it extraordinarily difficult to concentrate on such work.
5. Whole language teachers provide many opportunities for students to choose learning experiences that are meaningful to them: to decide what books to read, what to research and investigate, what to write and how to write it, for example. Students with ADHD often find it easier to concentrate on tasks they find interesting and meaningful.
6. Whole language teachers encourage students to think creatively as well as critically, and to engage in learning experiences that foster independence of thought and expression. This is especially important for many students with ADHD, who may often be among the most creative and divergent thinkers in the class.
7. Whole language teachers allow and even encourage a significant degree of mobility in the classroom, as students locate resources, confer with peers, and move from one learning center or area to another. They also tend to be tolerant of individual students' needs to fiddle with something, to move their feet, or to sit or lie in unconventional positions as they work. Recognizing that ADHD students may have strong needs to engage in activities involving the hands or body, whole language teachers may be especially likely to provide for these needs through various curricular activities:

hands-on math and science, creative drama, even music and dance, along with art.

8. Whole language teachers organize for collaborative learning: students work together on projects, share what they are reading and writing, help each other solve problems, work together to determine classroom procedures and resolve difficulties, and so forth. Discussion and conversation are valued aspects of whole language classrooms, another advantage for students with ADHD. As students work collaboratively, whole language teachers can help students with ADHD develop self-control and social skills, while helping other students come to understand and accept the problems of ADHD students and begin to respond to them more positively—even to help them control their attention and their impulses.

9. Whole language teachers minimize the use of formal tests, but when they must administer such tests, they attempt to adjust to the needs of individual students. Some students with ADHD work impulsively; they may need help in slowing down, in thinking about their answers, and in checking them. Other students with ADHD need extra time (even on standardized, timed tests), because their difficulty in concentrating slows them down. Whole language teachers seek ways to meet these needs. Furthermore, they typically minimize the use of test scores in evaluating students. This is particularly important for students with ADHD because they are rarely able to demonstrate their strengths on formal tests—standardized or otherwise.

10. Whole language teachers tend to communicate frequently with parents, encouraging them to share their understanding of their child, to work together for the child's success, and even to participate actively in facilitating classroom learning experiences. Though whole language teachers resist labeling students and therefore may be initially skeptical that a diagnosis of ADHD might be valid or that medication may be valuable, they are typically willing to listen to parents, to read what parents recommend, and to try other ways of helping their children. Such close collaboration with parents can have particular benefits for students with ADHD.

The success of whole language teachers in educating special needs students is described and documented in *Topics in Learning & Learning Disabilities,* January 1982; Rhodes & Dudley-Marling, 1988; Dudley-Marling, 1990; Stires, 1991; and Five, 1992. See also *Topics in Language Disorders* May 1991. Subsequent articles in this book provide some of the best evidence of how students with ADHD succeed in whole language classrooms.

Structure in Whole Language Classrooms

Of course, the traditional wisdom about students with ADHD needing structure in the classroom is more right than wrong: it is just that they do not need all the kinds of structure required in classrooms that emphasize education by ditto.

Good whole language classrooms have far more structure than initially meets the eye. In fact, experienced whole language teachers have come to realize that it is predictable structure and clear and consistent expectations that enable children to function flexibly in the classroom and to take increased responsibility for their own learning.

Like other teachers, however, the most effective whole language teachers realize that students with ADHD may need additional help in carrying out even the interesting, meaningful activities that the students are often eager to initiate, but not so able to complete—particularly if such activities and projects must be sustained over a considerable period of time and pursued outside of school. Among the kinds of structure that teachers can provide are the following:

1. To help students with ADHD grasp instructions, teachers can: (a) establish eye contact with the students before giving instructions or before repeating instructions for the benefit of these students; (b) write instructions on the chalkboard and make sure that the students have copied them correctly; (c) write down instructions for the students; (d) check to be sure the students understand instructions before beginning a task; (e) issue a complex set of instructions one step at a time. Such assistance may be needed even in whole language classrooms, where instructions often amount to suggestions and advice for accomplishing learners' own purposes.

2. Keep homework for students with ADHD to a minimum: by providing for work to be completed during class, for example, and even by assigning them less homework than other students. Having worked extensively with schools to help students with ADHD, psychologist Michael Gordon suggests no more than thirty to forty-five minutes of homework for elementary grade children with ADHD, and no more than an hour or so for the older students (Gordon, 1991, p. 132). Although students with ADHD are able to sustain attention longer to tasks they find meaningful, even whole language teachers may need to make concessions about how much they expect these students to accomplish outside of school.

3. To make sure students with ADHD are organized to do whatever out-of-school work *is* required, make sure that these students have such expectations and assignments written down, that they understand their assignments, and that they leave school with whatever materials they need to do their work. Teachers may see that such students have an assignment notebook, check the students' progress daily, and work with students and their parents to see that work is accomplished. Students with ADHD often need such support even when the homework involves a project in which they are highly interested.

4. Collaborate with students to develop an organizational plan for completing major projects, then develop a series of intermediate "due dates" and an assignment calendar. Subsequently, teachers may help students monitor their completion of each step of the work, or teachers may encourage and help the students' peers to do so.

5. Work with students and parents to establish a way to support the students in doing out-of-school work. For example, all parties may agree to establish

a "note-home" program, wherein the teacher reports on work assigned and/or certain agreed-upon concerns, especially on work completed or not completed and turned in. Even high school students with ADHD may need this kind of monitoring system daily (Pfiffner & Barkley, 1990; Copeland & Love, 1990).

For more suggestions regarding structure and other ways of helping students with ADHD in the classroom, one can consult Parker's *The ADD Hyperactivity Handbook for Schools* (1992) and the *CH.A.D.D. Educators Manual* (Fowler et al., 1992), published by CH.A.D.D. (Children and Adults with Attention Deficit Disorders), a national support organization for information on Attention Deficit Disorders. However, the suggestions in these resources do not necessarily reflect a system perspective of ADHD or a whole language philosophy of education.

Whole language teachers are usually quite willing to implement such procedures as needed for individual students, once they have become aware of the need. They are eager to find ways of enabling students with ADHD to succeed in school, regardless of the students' problems with impulsivity, hyperactivity, and inattention. And whole language teachers define success as actually learning, not merely responding to demands to behave. Fortunately, students' engagement in tasks they find meaningful tends also to alleviate some of the behavior problems.

In addition, however, whole language teachers may directly help students with ADHD learn to take more responsibility for their classroom behavior as well as for their learning.

A Whole Language Approach to Behavior Problems

The story of how a sixth grade teacher named Steve dealt with a problem situation illustrates how teachers can lead students with ADHD and others with behavior problems toward taking increasing responsibility for their actions. The anecdote is from Mark Collis and Joan Dalton's *Becoming Responsible Learners* (1990).

In this situation Tanya and Troy, both known for temper outbursts, were each struggling to gain possession of the video's remote control. Steve told them to put the control down, and Troy did let go, but Tanya then lifted it above her head and hurled it against the wall, yelling defiantly. The following excerpts from Collis and Dalton (1990) focus just on how Steve dealt with the problem of the broken video control:

"I'm too angry to talk now," says Steve, "sit here until we all calm down enough to talk sensibly about this."

(Five minutes later he returns to Tanya, reminding her that he will be contacting her parents about the incident because one of their class rules is that parents will be called when equipment is broken. Soon after initiating this discussion, Steve encourages Tanya to admit that she broke the remote control.)

"What can we do about the remote control?" Steve asks.

"I could fix it," Tanya offers.

"That's one idea, can you think of another?" prompts Steve.

"I could pay for a new one, or take it home for Mum or Dad to fix," the ideas come more quickly.

"Have you any more ideas, Tanya?" Steve adds after a little pause.

"No," replies Tanya.

"So we have three ideas. You could fix it yourself. You could pay for a new one or you could ask your parents to help you fix or replace it," Steve summarizes.

"Which of those ideas do you think you'll be able to do?"

"Well, I don't think I could fix it myself," Tanya says looking at the pieces scattered across the floor. "And I haven't got enough money to buy another one." Tanya pauses and looks down at her toes avoiding any eye contact with Steve.

"So which idea will work for you," prompts Steve.

"I could ask Mum and Dad to help me fix it or get another one I suppose," she answers reluctantly.

"So asking Mum and Dad to help you fix it or replace it will best solve our problem of the broken remote?" Steve queries.

"Yeah," Tanya replies a little more confidently.

"Well you talk to your Mum and Dad tonight and we'll get together tomorrow and see how you went. Remember I'll be talking to them this afternoon so they'll be expecting you to talk about what happened today pretty soon after you get home, right?" Steve adds smiling.

Tanya looks up and smiles faintly. "Right," she affirms (Collis & Dalton, 1990, pp. 31–33).

In this incident, Steve demonstrates "shared ownership" and responsibility, encouraging Tanya herself to consider ways of making amends for the damage she has done. This is but one example from *Becoming Responsible Learners* of how teachers can help students take more responsibility for their learning *and* their behavior (Collis & Dalton, 1990).

Collis and Dalton present at the outset what they consider to be three major classroom leadership styles: teacher ownership and control, shared ownership and control, and child ownership and control. They recommend and demonstrate shared responsibility, with gradual release of responsibility to the children, yet continued flexibility in responding to changing situations. See Figure 1–3 for the application of this model to the control of behavior.

Though such an approach will not *necessarily* be more effective than psychologists' cognitive behavior training in producing long-lasting effects, it has the decided advantage of being longer-term (the entire school year) and of occurring in a naturalistic setting. Furthermore, the teacher can always retreat to a greater degree of shared control for a time, later relinquish some control again, and repeat this pattern as necessary.

Some students with ADHD may never be completely able to avoid incidents in which strong emotion leads them to be impulsively hurtful or destructive, but they *can* learn more effective ways of dealing with the problems that their actions cause.

Additional Educational Services: The Larger System

For both students with ADHD and their classroom teachers to survive, they may need additional help from the school. In particular, the classroom teacher may need help assisting students with time-consuming organizational tasks (e.g. Pfiffner & Barkley, 1990; Gordon, 1991).

Public Law 94–142, guaranteeing special educational services, does not specifically mention an attention deficit *alone* as a condition qualifying children for those services. However, the Office for Civil Rights within the United States Department of Education has ruled that ADHD students are guaranteed special educational services by Section 504 of the Rehabilitation Act of 1973, if their condition substantially limits their ability to learn or to benefit from the regular educational program (Gordon, 1991; Copeland & Love, 1990). During 1991, additional guidelines were issued by the Department of Education to guarantee students the right to special educational services solely on the basis of an Attention Deficit Disorder (with or without hyperactivity), either under Section 504 or under the "other health impaired" category of the Education of the Handicapped Act (now the Individuals with Disabilities Education Act). A verbatim transcript of these guidelines is included at the end of this book, as Appendix A. For related information, see also Fowler et al., 1992.

FIGURE 1–3. *Different styles of classroom leadership, with respect to behavior (Collis & Dalton, 1990, p. 33).*

Teacher Ownership	*Shared Ownership*	*Child Ownership*
• strong teacher control	• shared control	• strong child control
• "I decide what you will do"	• "let's decide together"	• "you decide what you will do"
	• the teacher invites:	
• external control based on authority	—negotiation/input —responsibility —co-operation	• internal control based on self-direction/ discipline
• teacher is responsible for behavior	• for behaving appropriately, children are learning both independence and interdependence	• "I'm responsible for how I behave"
• children are dependent on the teacher		• children are independent of teacher
	• "I am responsible for my behavior and I care about the behavior of others"	

Here are some ways the school might support students with ADHD and their teachers:

1. Provide an appropriate chunk of time at the end of the school day for the students to meet one-on-one with the resource room teacher or someone else appropriate. The support person can then go over the tasks and assignments the students had difficulty focusing on during class, and make sure that the students are all set to do assigned homework. Such an academic support person could also help the students plan for completing larger projects and monitor the students' progress, relieving the classroom teacher of this sort of task.
2. Provide at the end of the school day someone to make sure that the students have their "note-home" form appropriately completed and signed by the teacher(s).
3. Provide an after-school supervised study hall for students with ADHD and others needing such structure to complete their homework before leaving the school grounds.
4. Provide a classroom aide whenever there are three or more students with ADHD in a class, with the aide's first priority being to work with these students.
5. Provide other pull-out or pull-in programs, as needed.

Many of these services could be performed by an aide rather than by a fully credentialed teacher. Indeed, significant help might be provided by administrative staff, a guidance counselor, a parent volunteer, an older student, or even a peer "buddy." Cost would be minimal, perhaps even nil, but such additional help might make the difference between school failure and school success for many students with ADHD. The importance of these kinds of assistance can scarcely be emphasized enough. If such support were more readily available, placement in a special education class would rarely be needed.

A word of caution is in order, though. Recognition of ADHD as entitling a student to special educational services can, unfortunately, result in such students receiving the same skills-oriented education that has often characterized special education pull-out programs. Special services do not *guarantee* that students with ADHD will receive appropriate understanding or educational support.

What holds significantly more promise for students with ADHD is a system approach, both to defining ADHD and to dealing with it. On the one hand, a system perspective encourages us to view ADHD as a socially dysfunctional cluster of behaviors caused or exacerbated by the environment's interacting with an individual who has a biological predisposition toward these behaviors. ADHD represents a set of less-than-optimal *relationships* between the individual and the environment. We can improve these relationships, then, not only by changing the individuals with ADHD but also by changing the environment: by modifying how we interact with the students as well as what we expect or demand of them. That is, we can take the productive *both/and* stance and approach that logically follow from system theory.

Acknowledgments

This article has been revised only slightly from an article by the same title that appeared in the May 1993 issue of the *American Journal of Speech-Language Pathology, 2,* 79–89. Both these articles draw significantly upon my concept paper published by the National Council of Teachers of English: *Alternatives in understanding and educating attention deficit students: Towards a systems-theory, whole language perspective* (Concept Paper No. 3, 1991). I wish to thank Michael Spooner and the editorial board of the NCTE for their conviction that this paper deserved wide circulation. I also wish to thank Curt Dudley-Marling of York University for critiquing an earlier version of the concept paper, Carole Edelsky of Arizona State University for repeatedly insisting on the validity of the social criticisms of the concept of ADHD, and my colleague Nickola Nelson for inviting me to submit the article to *AJSLP.*

References

Abikoff, H. (1991). Cognitive training in ADHD children: Less to it than meets the eye. *Journal of Learning Disabilities, 24,* 205–209.

Adams, P., & Curtin, C. (1992). The proactive teacher and the student with an attention deficit: A partnership for success. *Challenge, 6*(4), 1–5. (*Challenge* is a newsletter of the Attention Deficit Disorder Association.)

American Psychiatric Association. (1987). *Diagnostic and statistical manual of mental disorders* (3rd ed., rev.). Washington, DC: American Psychiatric Association.

Anastopoulos, A. D., DuPaul, G. J., & Barkley, R. A. (1991). Stimulant medication and parent training therapies for Attention Deficit-Hyperactivity Disorder. *Journal of Learning Disabilities, 24,* 210–218.

Baren, M. (1989, January). The case for Ritalin: A fresh look at the controversy. *Contemporary Pediatrics, 6,* 16–28.

Barkley, R. A. (1990). *Attention Deficit Hyperactivity Disorder: A handbook for diagnosis and treatment.* New York: Guilford Press.

Barkley, R.A. (1991). *Attention-Deficit Hyperactivity Disorder: A clinical workbook.* New York: Guilford Press.

Bartoli, J., & Botel, M. (1988). *Reading / learning disability: An ecological approach.* New York: Teachers College Press.

Bateson, G. (1972). *Steps to an ecology of mind.* New York: Ballantine Books.

Bruner, J. (1983). *Child's talk: Learning to use language.* Oxford: Oxford University Press.

Bruner, J. (1986). *Actual minds, possible worlds.* Cambridge: Harvard University Press.

Carrier, J. G. (1983). Explaining educability: An investigation of political support for the Children with Learning Disabilities Act of 1969. *British Journal of Sociology of Education, 4*(2), 125–140.

Coles, G. (1987). *The learning mystique: A critical look at "learning disabilities."* New York: Fawcett Columbine.

Collis, M., & Dalton, J. (1990). *Becoming responsible learners: Strategies for positive classroom management.* Portsmouth, NH: Heinemann.

Copeland, E. D., & Love, V. L. (1990). *Attention without tension: A teacher's handbook on attention deficit disorders (ADHD and ADD).* Atlanta, GA: 3 C's of Childhood, Inc.

Dudley-Marling, C. (1990). *When school is a struggle.* Richmond Hill, Ontario: Scholastic-TAB.

DuPaul, G. J., & Barkley, R. A. (1990). Medication therapy. In R. A. Barkley, *Attention Deficit Hyperactivity Disorder: A handbook for diagnosis and treatment* (pp. 573–612). New York: Guilford Press.

Edelsky, C., Altwerger, B., & Flores, B. (1991). *Whole language: What's the difference?* Portsmouth, NH: Heinemann.

Feingold, B. (1975). *Why your child is hyperactive.* New York: Random House.

Five, C. L. (1992). *Special voices.* Portsmouth, NH: Heinemann.

Fowler, M., Barkley, R. A., Reeve, R., & Zentall, S. (1992). *CH.A.D.D. educator's manual: An in-depth look at Attention Deficit Disorders from an educational perspective.* Plantation, FL: CH.A.D.D. (Children and Adults with Attention Deficit Disorders, a national support organization for information on Attention Deficit Disorders). Distributed by Caset Associates Ltd., Fairfax, VA.

Goldstein, S., & Ingersoll, B. (1992). Controversial treatments for children with Attention Deficit Hyperactivity Disorder. *CH.A.D.D.ER, 6*(2), 19–22.

Goodman, Kenneth S. (1986). *What's whole in whole language?* Richmond Hill, Ontario: Scholastic.

Gordon, M. (1991). *ADHD / Hyperactivity: A consumer's guide for parents and teachers.* DeWitt, NY: GSI Publications.

Gordon, M., Thomason, D., Cooper, S., & Ivers, C. L. (1991). Nonmedical treatment of ADHD/hyperactivity: The attention training system. *Journal of School Psychology, 29,* 151–159.

Gray, B. (1987). How natural is "natural" language teaching—employing wholistic methodology in the classroom. *Australian Journal of Early Childhood, 12*(4), 3–19.

Heshusius, L. (1989). The Newtonian mechanistic paradigm, special education, and contours of alternatives: An overview. *Journal of Learning Disabilities, 22,* 403–415.

Hobbs, N. (1975). The futures of children: Categories, labels, and their consequences. San Francisco: Jossey-Bass.

Hynd, G. W., Semrud-Clikeman, M., Lorys, A. R., Novey, E. S., Eliopulos, D., & Lyytinen, H. (1991). Corpus callosum morphology in Attention Deficit-Hyperactivity Disorder: Morphometric analysis of MRI. *Journal of Learning Disabilities, 24,* 141–146.

Kane, R., Mikalac, C., Benjamin, S., & Barkley, R. (1990). Assessment and treatment of adults with ADHD. In R. A. Barkley, *Attention Deficit Hyperactivity Disorder: A handbook for diagnosis and treatment* (pp. 613–654). New York: Guilford Press.

Klorman, Rafael. (1991). Cognitive event-related potentials in Attention Deficit Disorder. *Journal of Learning Disabilities, 24,* 130–140.

Kohn, A. (1989, November). Suffer the restless children. *Atlantic Monthly,* pp. 90–100.

Lahey, B. B., & Carlson, C. L. (1991). Validity of the diagnostic category of Attention Deficit Disorder without hyperactivity: A review of the literature. *Journal of Learning Disabilities, 24,* 110–120.

Mandelkorn, T. D. (1993). Thoughts on the medical treatment of ADHD: A physician's perspective. *The CH.A.D.D.ER Box, 6*(3), 1, 7–9. Published by CH.A.D.D. (Children and Adults with Attention Deficit Disorders, a national support organization for information on attention deficit disorders).

Ninio, A., & Bruner, J. (1978). The achievement and antecedents of labeling. *Journal of Child Language, 5,* 1–15.

Parker, H. C. (1992). *The ADD hyperactivity handbook for schools.* Plantation, FL: Impact Publications.

Pfiffner, L. J., & Barkley, R. A. (1990). Educational placement and classroom management. In R. A. Barkley, *Attention Deficit Hyperactivity Disorder: A handbook for diagnosis and treatment* (pp. 498–539). New York: Guilford Press.

Poplin, M. A. (1988a). The reductionist fallacy in learning disabilities: Replicating the past by reducing the present. *Journal of Learning Disabilities, 21,* 389–400.

Poplin, M. A. (1988b). Holistic/constructivist principles of the teaching/learning process: Implications for the field of learning disabilities. *Journal of Learning Disabilities, 21,* 401–416.

Rhodes, L. K., & Dudley-Marling, C. (1988). *Readers and writers with a difference: A holistic approach to teaching learning disabled and remedial students.* Portsmouth, NH: Heinemann.

Robin, A. L. (1990). Training families with ADHD adolescents. In R. A. Barkley, *Attention Deficit Hyperactivity Disorder: A handbook for diagnosis and treatment,* 462–497. New York: Guilford Press.

Robin, A. L., & Foster, S. L. (1989). *Negotiating parent-adolescent conflict: A behavioral family systems approach.* New York: Guilford Press.

Schachar, R. J. (1986). Hyperkinetic syndrome: Historical development of the concept. In E. Taylor (Ed.), *The overactive child* (pp. 19–40). Philadelphia: J. B. Lippincott.

Schrag, P., & Divoky, D. (1975). *The myth of the hyperactive child: And other means of child control.* New York: Pantheon.

Shaywitz, S. E., & Shaywitz, B. A. (1991). Introduction to the special series on Attention Deficit Disorder. *Journal of Learning Disabilities, 24,* 68–71.

Shelton, T. & Barkley, R. A. (1990). Clinical, developmental, and biopsychosocial considerations. In R. A. Barkley, *Attention Deficit Hyperactivity Disorder: A handbook for diagnosis and treatment* (209–231). New York: Guilford Press.

Silver, L. B. (1990). Attention deficit-hyperactivity disorder: Is it a learning disability or a related disorder? *Journal of Learning Disabilities, 23,* 394–397.

Sleeter, C. E. (1986). Learning disabilities: The social construction of a special education category. *Exceptional Children, 53,* 46–54.

Stires, S. (Ed.). (1991). *With Promise: Redefining reading and writing needs for special students.* Portsmouth, NH: Heinemann.

Taylor, D. (1990). *Learning denied.* Portsmouth, NH: Heinemann.

Taylor, E. A. (Ed.). (1986). *The overactive child.* Philadelphia: Lippincott.

Von Bertalanffy, L. (1968). General system theory. New York: George Braziller.

Vygotsky, L. S. (1986). *Thought and language* (A. Kozulin, Trans.). Cambridge: MIT Press.

Weaver, C. (1985). Parallels between new paradigms in science and in reading and literary theories: An essay review. *Research in the Teaching of English, 19,* 298–316.

Weaver, C. (1988). *Reading process and practice: From socio-psycholinguistics to whole language.* Portsmouth, NH: Heinemann.

Weaver, C. (1990). *Understanding whole language: From principles to practice.* Portsmouth, NH: Heinemann.

Weaver, C. (1991). *Alternatives in understanding and educating attention deficit students: Toward a systems-theory, whole language perspective.* Concept Paper No. 3. Urbana, IL: National Council of Teachers of English.

Weaver, C. (1993). Understanding and educating students with Attention Deficit Hyperactive Disorder: Toward a system theory and whole language perspective. *American Journal of Speech-Language Pathology, 2,* 79–89.

Weaver, C. (1994). *Reading process and practice: From socio-psycholinguistics to whole language* (2nd ed.). Portsmouth, NH: Heinemann.

Weaver, C., & Henke, L. (Eds.). (1992). *Supporting whole language: Stories of teacher and institutional change.* Portsmouth, NH: Heinemann.

Weaver, C., Chaston, J., & Peterson, S. (1993). *Theme exploration: A voyage of discovery.* Richmond Hill, Ontario: Scholastic; Portsmouth, NH: Heinemann.

Weiss, G., & Hechtman, L. T. (1986). *Hyperactive children grown up: Empirical findings and theoretical considerations.* New York: Guilford Press.

Wender, P. H. (1987). *The hyperactive child, adolescent, and adult.* New York: Oxford University Press.

Whalen, C. K., & Henker, B. (1991). Social impact of stimulant treatment for hyperactive children. *Journal of Learning Disabilities, 24,* 231–241.

Zametkin, A. J., & Rapoport, J. L. (1987). Neuro-biology of Attention Deficit Disorder with Hyperactivity: Where have we come in 50 years? *Journal of the American Academy of Child and Adolescent Psychiatry, 26,* 676–686.

Zametkin, A. J., Nordahl, T. E., Gross, M., King, A. C., Semple, W. E., Rumsey, J., Hamburger, S., & Cohen, R. M. (1990). Cerebral glucose metabolism in adults with hyperactivity of childhood onset. *The New England Journal of Medicine, 323,* 1361–1366.

2

Straight from the Source: ADHD from the Perspective of Young Adults Recently Diagnosed

Virginia S. Little, with Marnelle Best, Terri Redd, and John Weaver

This article began when Connie Weaver, the editor of this book, assembled three young adults in their early to mid twenties—Marnelle, Terri, and John—to discuss with each other and with her what it feels like to have an Attention Deficit Hyperactivity Disorder, how ADHD can affect one's ability to do schoolwork and to succeed in school, and how their personal and academic lives are different now that they have been diagnosed as having ADHD and are taking Ritalin. Over pizza one evening in June of 1992, these three young adults shared their feelings, experiences, and reactions (with their discussion occasionally punctuated by questions or responses from Connie). Their comments dealt mainly with their initial diagnoses, reactions to medication (specifically Ritalin), factors making it difficult for them to succeed in school, learning style needs, individual coping strategies, and helpful suggestions for teaching ADHD students effectively.

Connie had prepared some questions about ADHD and school to guide the discussion, but the actual conversation was so free-flowing that it seemed best not to publish the transcript nearly verbatim (as originally intended), but to reorganize it for greater clarity. That's where Virginia Little came into the picture. First a graduate student and then a colleague of Connie's, she had also taught many students with ADHD characteristics at an alternative high school and at a junior college. Therefore, Virginia (Ginny) was eager to combine information from the transcripts, research, and experience into an article that would further help others understand ADHD. Her intent actually resulted in two articles: a chapter she has written later in this book, and this one, which is mainly an edited version of the transcript from the discussion among Marnie, Terri, and John.

Virginia S. Little (Ginny) is currently a teacher educator at the University of San Diego and is engaged in doctoral work through the school for Transformative Learning at the California Institute of Integral Studies at San Francisco. She received her Master's degree as a reading specialist in 1979 from the University of Arizona, where her mentors included Ken and Yetta Goodman and Rob Tierney, noted whole language and psycholinguistic theorists. Ranging from elementary to university levels, her teaching experiences have spanned the country from California to Michigan as well as overseas, to include an international school setting. She has been a welcomed lecturer on working with "at-risk" and "nontraditional" student populations. Believing strongly in a whole language philosophy of education that fosters the empowerment of the learner, Virginia herself is an enthusiastic and dedicated learner.

Marnelle Best (Marnie) was diagnosed as having ADHD at the age of twenty-three, after learning about it in Connie's Grammar for Teachers class, in which Terri was also enrolled. Because of the stresses of ADHD without needed medication, Marnie withdrew from that class but returned a year later to complete the work, joining a subsequent offering of the same course in which Virginia Little was then enrolled. Now twenty-six, Marnie is a new wife and mother living in Germany, where her husband is stationed in the armed forces. Having completed the last class for her bachelor's degree by going to Rome to take a course on Expatriate Writers, Marnie is currently working for the Child Development Center on base. She says she loves working with the children because the ADD in her is allowed to come out and play. When she returns to the United States, she plans to obtain a certificate to teach.

Terri Redd was twenty-one when she was diagnosed as having ADHD, after being tested for the learning disability of dyslexia. Enrolled in undergraduate courses at Western Michigan University, Terri was not living up to her full academic potential. After the diagnosis Terri made the dean's list and graduated from WMU in 1991. She is currently a teacher in the Portage, Michigan, public schools and is working on her master's degree in counseling psychology.

John Weaver was diagnosed as having ADHD at the age of sixteen, when hospitalized after a suicide attempt that resulted, to a significant degree, from his inability to live up to his potential in school. John completed his senior year (with mostly A's and two honor certificates) at an alternative high school, which accommodated his learning needs better than the regular high school had done. After briefly attending a junior college, John found his niche in a technical school. In the fall of 1992 he graduated with highest honors from ITT Technical Institute in Indianapolis, having earned a Bachelor of Applied Science in electronics engineering technology. John is currently looking for a job in his field.

I remember each fall of my teaching career agonizing over what content I would teach and how to accommodate the various learning styles, interests, and individuality of my students. This became an even more challenging process when considering students who had been labeled by other educational and social systems as "at-risk" due to nonconforming social behaviors and/or a history of unsuccessful academic endeavors. Being an inquisitive person and an educator continually seeking new approaches, I came to realize the benefits of asking my students during the first few class sessions and intermittently throughout the semester, a range of questions about their attitudes, goals, learning styles, and difficulties. This provided me with invaluable information to help facilitate the process of knowing how and what to explore within the class, and most importantly, how to motivate the students to pursue their own learning interests. A key component of this idea is to listen to what the students are actually saying, withholding judgment and/or categorization, and attending to their own understanding and perceptions of their strengths, needs, and hopes as learners and human beings. Great insights are gained through sincere inquiry and shared information; in essence, through collaboration between a teacher and/or researcher and the students themselves.

Only recently familiarizing myself with characteristics of ADHD through reading research (Hallowell & Ratey, 1993; Fowler et al., 1992; Robin, 1992; Weaver, 1991; Weiss & Hechtman, 1986), I realized that it delineated not only the behaviors of my students, but the behavior of my brother as well. My brother Mark, never having learned to cope with difficulties that may have been largely attributable to ADHD, died at the age of twenty-six. This personal loss, as well as the desire to facilitate my students' learning, fueled my enthusiasm to explore the self-evaluations of the three young adults interviewed in the session with Connie. The transcript of the tape provided me with a clear description of ADHD characteristics, effects upon school performance, coping strategies, and suggestions for fostering more effective teaching and learning. A concluding commentary compares the discussion (reordered and revised from a transcript of their conversation over pizza) to current research.

Meet John, Marnie, and Terri, three adults recently diagnosed with ADHD

Connie: Can you describe what it's like to have ADHD?

TERRI: It's like watching TV, and you can be watching Channel 3 or Channel 8 or Channel 12. It's like watching all three channels at the same time. You know, you pick up a little bit of every channel.
MARNIE: Right, but they are all on at the same time.
JOHN: I remember at times I used to put the radio onto the station I like, watch TV, and read a book at the same time. I remember I tried it at least once or twice and I liked doing it. And I could tell you a little bit about everything that went on, but I'm curious about my concentration; it doesn't show that my concentration was good but it jumped from radio to TV to book, to radio to TV to book. I couldn't concentrate on one. . . . I needed something to shift me.

Connie: Do you remember in class, Terri, when you were trying to explain this to classmates? The way I remember it, it was something like "Here when I was trying to listen to Connie, I'd be just as likely to hear the people going up and down the hall, or classmates tapping their pencils."

MARNIE: She could count or tell you how many people went by.
TERRI: It is helpful for teachers to know that an ADHDer could even be participating in a conversation and have totally no recollection of it. It was weird because I was sitting in my psychologist's office, the very first time I visited her, and her desk was sitting here, with kind of a bay window on her right side, and the highway outside that goes right on Stadium out towards 131. While she's talking I guess I was looking to the right and she asked, "Can you tell me how many cars went by?" I couldn't tell her the color of the cars like some people do, but oh yeah, there have been eight cars that went by, and like a lot of people she says, "Who could do that? That just amazes me!" And then she said, "What did we talk about? What have I been asking you?" and I just sat there blank. I couldn't tell her what we'd been talking about, even though we had been carrying on a normal conversation. But I *could* tell her all the activity that had been happening around her office. And then she said, "Is there anything that's been bothering you?" It's like talking to someone and they have this little fuzzball on their shirt and you cannot concentrate. You want to pick off the fuzzball and your mind is constantly on that fuzzball. . . . You are carrying on a conversation, but in your mind you are thinking about what is bothering you also. Contrary to what other people think, you always believe that you are kind of different. I always believed that I was never stupid, and it kept me going. After I found out I had ADHD (I always thought I had dyslexia; I went out to Michigan State to get help with reading, but they never

told me I had ADHD) and when I found out I had ADHD I was like, right, and then it sank in and they were like "Well, when your Mom asks you to go upstairs and get something, can you do it?" I'm like "Yeah, I can go upstairs." My Mom goes "Yeah, but you don't come down with the thing I asked you to get." And then they discovered that I would open the door and see all these little things and then think about "Oh, I need a pencil, and that's a cute pencil," and I grab the pencil and maybe start coloring while my Mom's downstairs yelling, "Terri, where's the sewing kit?" or something like that. It's just gone and forgotten.

CONNIE: And the poor parents are like "Oh, my gosh!" "What's the matter with this kid?"

TERRI: I remember my Dad telling me I could not go on till I learned how to tell time. It was so funny when I went to the doctor and I took these tests and he reviewed it about a month later with me in his office. He told me I had no concept of time. I can tell you it's 2:00 and in an hour it will be 3:00, and I know how to read clocks and everything, and I can judge, let's say it's 5:00 now because the sun is going down and in the winter the sun goes down about 5:00, but I can't tell you if you walked out of the room and back in, how many minutes have gone by. I just don't know. It's because my mind has gone through so many things that, to me, it could be a whole day. That's how quick my mind moves.

JOHN: Everybody's minds move that quickly but not necessarily actually thinking about things, you know what I mean.

MARNIE: I read this article about ADHD people. It was about "blinks." Like you could be studying or something and then all of a sudden you'll find yourself not knowing how much time has gone by but you will have gone through five pages, or just stared at the pages in the book, and something you read caused you to think about something else. You are like lost, maybe like a blink where you have gotten off the track. It's so funny after I read that article, 'cause now I'll blink sometimes and then laugh at myself, knowing what I did just then. But then it's funny when people ask you what you are thinking about and you have to say "nothing" because if I told them what I was thinking about it would sound like, "Well, I started thinking about this, and then I thought about this, and that made me think about . . . and that's why I laughed because that was funny." And then you're not thinking one thought, you're thinking about ten million different thoughts. It will go quickly. In five minutes you will have thought about life from age three to the present.

TERRI: It is so weird. People always talk about me because someone will be talking and I will just laugh like, "I know." It will just come out of nowhere. It's like you have a total conversation in your head. It just goes back to the same thing: you're listening to that person and still communicating with them, but you're having a whole other conversation. It's amazing. I always think of people who have ADHD as the most intelligent people on earth. They understand normal people and they can understand themselves too. Normal people can only understand themselves; they can't understand us.

MARNIE: It's funny to have a conversation with an ADHD person too because even if they don't know they are ADHD, you can tell they are once you know you are. I just know one of my girlfriends has it. She is just like me. We'll be talking about one thing and within our conversation we'll say something that will spark a tangent. We talk about 10 million different things in 10 minutes. Tape recording a conversation like that would be hilarious. But it's just how our minds work!

JOHN: That reminds me of Keith, same exact story. We usually get into a debate about something, which will lead into another debate, sort of related, then end up on religions that I know nothing about, then finish little bits and pieces of what we talked about before.

MARNIE: You almost have to write down your topics and say "OK, we're talking about this right now" and when you go off on a tangent then write down what that is because sometimes you'll forget what you have to go back to, and then you'll start another conversation and then remember it!

Connie: How has ADHD affected your school performance? Maybe you should write your own article in addition to what we do with this article.

TERRI: Writing an article. I've been trying to write one for so long. It's really hard to know where to begin.

MARNIE: Write it from the ADHD point of view and then everybody will understand.

TERRI: It's really hard to know, it's like I need to keep a journal for about a year and then start writing from my journal and start putting my thoughts together.

JOHN: One thing for me is I like using a computer. You probably can write it down quicker, whatever comes to mind. That's my idea.

TERRI: I think what baffles my mind is that I really do not, they really don't, know everything that goes on in my mind and it's hard for me to tell them that they don't understand me.

* * * *

MARNIE: So you don't think yours is hereditary?

TERRI: It probably is. I probably get it from my Dad. I am very much like my father and he will admit that, even though my Mom was the person who initially went to get me help. I came home the end of my junior year in college totally frustrated. I didn't know what to do anymore. I sat tons and tons of hours in the library. You get nowhere. You read, and while you read you go off on a tangent or start thinking about something else. You have to start over again. A never ending battle.

MARNIE: You are happy that you finish a chapter and so glad you did. Then the teacher starts asking you questions and you don't know what's going on, and then they don't think you read the chapter.

TERRI: Or like you know it one day and the next you don't know it. And then there's the teacher saying "You just knew this!"

CONNIE: I had this happen to me during my master's orals. It finally got so bad I had to say "I haven't read it" because it got so embarrassing to say "I read it, but I can't remember it!"

MARNIE: See, I think I got it from both my parents and that's why I'm a double whammy. And I have it terribly bad. When I first told them I wanted to get tested for ADHD, my mother said, "Please, this is a bunch of bologna." But I expected that of my mother. But my father said, "Well, I've always had the suspicion that I had it." But I see evidence of both of them having it. And now, since I've been diagnosed, my mother has had my brother diagnosed. And he has it. Now she's more understanding and she's been more involved because my brother has it even worse than I do. He's twenty-five. I was at least able to get through and make some success of myself. Somehow. But my brother is just all over the place. My mom accepts it more now.

TERRI: See, I think children who have parents who know they have ADHD are so much more understanding. Like Laurie, my psychologist, right before she had her heart attack, started this support group. It was the most unbelievable experience I've had in my life. A group of people who are like you, someone to talk to you, saying "I do the same thing!"

MARNIE: It feels good.

TERRI: Yeah, it does. To know you're not the only person in the world that has this problem. I think I had to be mad at someone—school system, school teachers, somebody. I look back and think I was never a behavior problem in class. I wasn't terrible, you know, a bad student. I did fairly well, especially if you asked me to memorize something. Memorization was never a problem with me. That's how I learned. If I couldn't memorize it, I couldn't learn it. I would learn it for a short period of time, and then forget it. If Christmas didn't come around every single year I wouldn't know when it was.

CONNIE: (to John) You were always that way too.

JOHN: I never cared about dates or special events, probably for that reason. Mother's Day, Father's Day, Thanksgiving . . . All these things I have to look on the calendar for. Who knows when they come around?

CONNIE: Well, they're not all that consistent. I wouldn't be surprised if to this day you could not tell the months in order starting with the first month of the year. Could you tell the months in order?

JOHN: Certainly! But I couldn't tell when the special days are and so forth. I couldn't tell you what months they are. I always had problems knowing what number the month was.

MARNIE: I still have to say January, February, March, April . . . O.K., it's four. I still have to count. And the alphabet, too. I don't know what letter comes next unless I go a,b,c,d,e,f,g,h,i,j. O.K. j.

JOHN: Or which month has thirty or thirty-one days? I never knew that. They used to teach you a rhyme for that.

TERRI: I learned that in third grade. I argued about learning this poem because I just did not want to learn a poem about the months and days. But Sister Juanita, my principal then, told me to learn it and I will always remember. And to this day every time I see her I remind her that I learned this poem and I will always remember that.

CONNIE: Do you remember, John, how you learned your address?

JOHN: Someone got a stick and beat me over the head?

CONNIE: The teacher was probably ready to. I think it was first grade, but it might have been kindergarten. They wanted you to learn your address, so the teacher wrote it out—6912—and then the road and all that. You kids were supposed to write your address ten times to learn it. But what did you do? You went 6666666666, so of course you learned absolutely nothing.

JOHN: I did that with other things too! If I was going to make a long row of things, might as well do everything in repetition...6's all the way down, etcetera.

MARNIE: I do that! But I hated it when they had you write sentences.

JOHN: Yeah, it's easier to write one word.

MARNIE: You don't learn things when you write sentences.

TERRI: You don't. I'm the type of person who has to know "why" everything had to be. If you couldn't tell me why, then I couldn't learn it. I had to start with "why?"

CONNIE: I think that this is a very important point to make, that a lot of ADHD people when they do these things are not necessarily going to remember them, or are certainly not going to remember the minute details. Which is one reason why social studies is such a bummer when it's taught as names, dates, and places, rather than *why*.

JOHN: I'm curious about something else. We were talking about the need to know "why." I know for me, when I'm taught a concept, I would still like to know the absolute reason for it. If someone can give me a pretty good answer: (1) It usually sticks in my mind, and (2) You can figure out other things from there that fit into the same category. I think my mom will remember there came a point in my life when I didn't want to accept demands from parents and authority without knowing why. I told my mom, even if it's just because you want it done, tell me that. Don't just say, "Go do it," and keep repeating that. Just tell me why and I'll do it. For teachers, rather than just presenting the material and thinking the kid is just going to memorize it, I think it would be good to know the background, or what causes something to happen, and how that affects things which are similar. If you tell me the reasoning I get a picture in my mind.

TERRI: And that makes more sense. That's just like a three-year-old stage where everything is just "Why, why, why?" We are always in that stage. I still have to know why. I hate it when people just say one sentence and just leave it at that.

CONNIE: Marnie, I love the way you are asking these questions about the articles you are reading in our Grammar for Teachers class. If only more people would start asking "why" or whether this is true, or "I need to rethink what they have always told me." All too many students are indoctrinated into the memorizing, and as you know, I question my students into thinking about that and "Why?" and "Does that really make sense?"

TERRI: Math was the hardest subject for me because I always had to know why something happened. I could never forget third grade. My mom taught second grade and she had some third and fourth grade books around, teacher's editions. I was flunking out of math; it was just a subject I could not learn. I think it's because they don't tell you why; it's just you get the answer. And if you get the answer, it's just correct. I got stuck on the "why" part instead of learning how to do it repetitively.

JOHN: It's easier knowing "why."

CONNIE: Considering that this book is going to be read mostly by elementary teachers, it will help them to know what kind of problems are only going to get worse as you guys get older and the demands on you become more severe.

Connie: It would be useful to know such things as: What can you do relatively easily? What does an ADHD kid have great difficulty doing? What is an unreasonable kind of task?

TERRI: You know in school you always talk about being flexible. You have to give a student with ADHD time to adjust to a change. You can't just say we're not going to gym today, and expect them to do that right away. They will be totally lost.

MARNIE: I think teachers should be more aware of ADHD and look for it. They might have kids who *obviously* have ADHD, but they may have kids who are doing well in the class and still have ADHD. I was very smart in elementary school, but I had ADHD. In third grade I had a teacher who said I was "too social." I mean, I guess it would be hard to tell, if to her you are doing well and maybe I just seemed very social.

CONNIE: Well, I suppose the three of you have in common that you all aren't behavior problems, so that your hyperactivity wasn't causing that much of a problem in the class, and you all are very bright. Even without being all together, you do well.

MARNIE: We are lucky because there are ADHD people with all different levels. You can have ADHD with a high intelligence or with an average intelligence. The ones with an average intelligence do worse. Because we have a high intelligence we were able to make it through and do well. But once we got into college it was like, "Whoa!" With an average intelligence it would be even harder to make it through.

TERRI: I think if teachers were taught to look more at learning styles, not just for people with ADHD, but for everyone . . . like I'm a visual person, not a verbal person. If you talk to me all the other things are going to distract me, but if I can get it visually, then it will key me into something.

CONNIE: Right. Speaking of visual, my hunch is that a lot of ADHD kids would be helped with having directions written. I see that with John. I've given this whole set of directions I want John to do and he reacts like, "Are you speaking to *me?*"

TERRI: I think a lot of ADHDers need BOTH visual and verbal. I will read directions and not know what to do until they're explained to me. I remember a teacher in second grade who gave a different direction than what the paper had on it and I read the paper direction and got it wrong. Verbally she said it, and verbally I didn't get it.

CONNIE: So the directions were not followable. John, I remember some of those phonics worksheets in the first grade. If you followed the directions you would have gotten the wrong answers.

JOHN: Like earlier, I should repeat something. I was trying to concentrate on something, or reading something, and probably listening to you too, and didn't get either of them. I couldn't tell which was more important.

CONNIE: Don't you think sometimes the ADHD person doesn't think he/she is being addressed? And by then the directions have already been given?

JOHN: For me it's like, "I'm concentrating on something else. I'd rather finish this than listen." So I look up, you think you have my attention, and I'm still trying to finish something else.

CONNIE: I know! I find myself doing this lately!

MARNIE: I think you need to say it *and* write it down. It depends on the time. I could be both auditory and visual. If I'm listening to somebody in class I can remember that I need to put all my concentration into listening. If I can't remember, I want to go somewhere for reference. I want somewhere to go where I can read. That's where I had problems with this last class. There wasn't a textbook, so you had to get all your information from the lecture; it was impossible. I even asked the instructor if there was somewhere I could go to get this info. and he said, "No." That was a problem. When I was working on my incomplete, even on a one-to-one basis, I still had several "blinks." It was better, however, on a one-to-one basis, a lot better than in a classroom.

CONNIE: If you have that ability to work one-on-one. That is the main reason why, before the development of the kinds of diagnostic tests you two had, almost exclusively the parent and teacher ratings were used to diagnose. In a one-on-one setting with a therapist, lots of kids could concentrate for short periods of time, but they couldn't concentrate at home or at school, where there were more distractions! So doctors and clinicians found they couldn't rely on their own observations to diagnose ADHD; they had to draw on parents' and teachers' observations.

JOHN: I usually find that after an hour of really intense study, a five-minute break is needed. One thing I can't stand lately is we've had these work sessions in classes at ITT, and kids will be talking about what they did Friday night and the teachers don't do anything to stop it. So I just grab my coat and books and just leave. I usually tell the teachers, although they know by now, I'm just going down to the break room or to find a separate room. One psychiatrist who diagnosed me with having ADHD wrote out a little something for me. It gives a little personal history and the fact that I am a student with ADHD and what types of things this might mean and what types of setting would be better structured for me. So I usually show it to the teachers and have them put it in my school file. Although someone cleaned it out and no one has seen it since. One teacher even said, "Oh, I wouldn't think you'd want that in there!"

One other thing I pointed out to my mom: What if the person was being treated with medication? Do you think they could adapt? What if they were on Ritalin? Could they adapt a lot better to school and what their teachers expected?

Connie: What ways have you learned to cope with your difficulties and how has Ritalin affected your performance?

JOHN: But before we get to that I just want to say there are lots of people around me that are definite candidates for having ADHD. There aren't too many people, at least our age, who have been diagnosed with it. I hear lots of stories about little kids who have been put on Ritalin, whether they have

ADHD or not, just to keep them under control. I was told originally you don't find a lot of adults with it because they have learned to cope with it.

TERRI: And then it was thought when you get to adolescence that you grew out of it. That's not true though.

MARNIE: Or you learn to find ways to cope with it. My father has been teaching for twenty-eight years at the same place. He's like a workaholic. He comes home from a day at work and he'll clean up and totally zonk out on the couch. It drives my mother crazy.

JOHN: That sounds like my father, at home anyway. And me, at work. I remember the Rax restaurant, working there, trying not to bother the people around me. So I was just running everywhere. I just liked to rush around and get things done as fast as possible. In my mind, we were a "fast-food restaurant," let's do this *fast!* (Ha!) I ended up with drive-thru window, great, I'm fast and good with math. I liked being there.

TERRI: See, I used to take lots of math. And even in college I took lots of math. But now it's like you have such an exhausting day, and it's such a fast-paced day. When you go to sleep and wake up, it's a whole fast-race day again. Even if it's just a nap!

CONNIE: This instance about vegging out and napping reminds me: I read somewhere not long ago that brain research suggests ADHD people have a shortage of beta waves, which are the faster brain waves that we all use. And then I started thinking about John. I know you're tired partly because you're sleeping in the day instead of in the night. Well, maybe it's also because the brain is not producing enough beta waves.

MARNIE: When I got out of the army, I used to run every day. You feel so much better after you exercise. If you want to: take a nap, go out and walk, or something. A lot of times when I want to sleep it's not 'cause I'm tired, it's 'cause I'm bored.

CONNIE: The boredom issue is one worth exploring. Actually John hasn't told his story of how he got diagnosed. This psychiatrist, after talking with him, after having one meeting with him, asked me if I thought John might be hyperactive. And I said, "No, he can sit in front of the computer for hours!" He said, "Well, has it occurred to you that he might have an Attention Deficit Disorder?" Then I went into my other routine, how the second grade teacher suggested that. And I said that's why he hadn't been completing the worksheets is that he found them so boring. And the psychiatrist said, "Exactly. When I talked with John, everything to him was so 'boring.' Everything. I've found that with these ADHD adolescents, that seems to be a very common characteristic." He had not seen it in the professional literature. But that tendency to find everything boring, do you remember that, John?

JOHN: I don't remember the first time I talked to the doctor. I remember you telling me that. Mathematics. I used to be great at it; it got boring. Then you started seeing E's in algebra when I should have been able to ace it. Off the top of my head, I can't remember others . . . maybe a little bit in English. In some things, like math, which I should have been good at because things were so elementary to me, it got boring. The next thing I knew, concepts were passing me by; they got ahead of where I was at and I was like, "Oh well." Any subject I didn't particularly find interesting, for whatever reason, whether I thought the content was boring or it just wasn't being taught in a good manner, these classes just went downhill. Extra boring classes I just didn't put the effort into, or when I did I still failed. How many here were just horrible test takers?

MARNIE: I was terrible.

JOHN: I was, too. I don't know about you guys but I would get to the test and just freak out. Everything I knew was forgotten . . . for tests I would sweat even more than normal. These days I have calmed down a lot and I know that I know the material. I tell myself, "It's just a piece of paper. All I have to do is write down what I know." It may have taken me a year or more to get to that point, but I went from being scared, or telling myself I knew the material and getting in there and finding it was gone, to having confidence that, "Yeah, so what, there's a test on Friday? I am going to get an A!" A lot of reassuring myself has helped build my confidence. When your confidence is up for a test it helps. I just didn't have any back then.

CONNIE: Terri, do you remember what happened with the final exam in our class?

TERRI: It was Easter weekend and our paper was due that Monday, right? I went to Indianapolis and stayed up practically all night long and I got nowhere. I came to Connie and said, "You know, I've been writing and writing and writing" and it wasn't writer's block. . . . It was like your thoughts were in your head but you can't get it out on paper.

CONNIE: I didn't remember that. What I was remembering was that we had a test on parts of speech. First of all, I suggested that maybe since you were so easily distracted you would like to go to an empty classroom and take the test. You were still in that stage of half-accepting, half-denying your ADHD. So we compromised and you sat in the corner and then as people were turning in their papers and I was talking to more and more people, it got noisier and noisier, and relatively speaking, you bombed. Then you came into my office and I said, "Terri, let's talk about this." We talked about the circumstances; I think I said, "Let's just throw this thing out." Most teachers don't know that much about ADHD and I wouldn't either if it weren't for my experience with John. I had somebody last semester who turned in about three things late. They were brilliant. She's got a seven-year-old cousin diagnosed as having ADHD. He's talking about committing suicide at seven. This is in the Upper Peninsula where they don't have very adequate counseling help. Even the average psychologist doesn't necessarily know that much about ADHD. The more I worried about the cousin the more I thought, "Yeah, so-and-so, the college student, has it too." She couldn't focus on what she wanted to say. I know not all ADHD people are very right-brained, but I think she was, and I think a lot of people with ADHD are. John, do you have any idea why you were able to do so much better your high school senior year in the alternative school then you had done at Northern? I know it was probably easier, but were there some things about how it was structured, things that could be useful to somebody in terms of planning a successful program?

JOHN: Yes and no. As you know I was on Ritalin, so that helped. We were allowed to do all of our work in class. It was kind of structured as in you can't get up and wander around. You're there in class and also, if you have any questions or don't understand something, the teacher is always there. You're not given a reading assignment to take home and go "Hmmmm . . . it's over my head." Most of the teachers I think also realized that that's why a lot of the kids were there and had problems. That's why they took it slower. They spent the extra time necessary to go over things.

CONNIE: That reminds me, when I shared information with the principal on ADHD she said, "Gee, that sounds like the majority of the kids in the alternative school." I don't think she meant to deny John's problem or anything, but I think she really meant it, and that probably is one of the reasons why the majority of the students were there.

JOHN: The problem is most of the kids that were there hadn't been diagnosed. They had been there way beyond the normal high school years. We're talking the sixth high school year, even in such a "piece of cake" school as this was. I don't think I had many take-home assignments at all.

CONNIE: And I thought that was one of the reasons you succeeded.

JOHN: I also don't think I had as many classes.

CONNIE: They were two-hour classes. I just remembered that, and that's part of why they were able to give you the time to do homework.

TERRI: Did they deal with real-life situations, though? My boyfriend just did a paper on alternative vs. traditional or "normal" high school. Some of his juveniles do a lot better in there [the alternative school] because they relate to real world types of things, like they do math related to the real world instead of learning geometry.

CONNIE: I was just reading this week about an alternative program in Denver, Colorado. It sounds wonderful. The Denver Board of Education, with all of its great wisdom, wants to close the school because they aren't delivering the standard curriculum to the students. But these are people who dropped out. They weren't succeeding with the standard curriculum; that's why they're in the alternative school.

TERRI: What about an alternative school for kids that need something different but are still smart enough to make it through the regular high school?

CONNIE: The one in Denver was more on that order. It's not that the kids were stupid or anything, they just weren't able to put up with that boredom.

JOHN: A lot of people with ADHD, I suspect, are very creative.

CONNIE: That's another interesting thing. Looking back after John was diagnosed, I felt that most of his friends showed very similar patterns and in fact one had been diagnosed.

MARNIE: I think that people who have ADHD tend to draw to each other. We are so creative and so different. We can fit in the mainstream, like I can make myself normal, but I like myself best when I am totally off the wall. I wish that somebody would have seen this when I was in elementary because I did well for having ADHD. But if someone would have known, I could have been an honors graduate.

TERRI: They wanted to put me ahead to first grade while I was in kindergarten. I was already a year ahead and I was small to begin with. My mom was a teacher and she said that developmentally I was not ready. She said, "There's a time she can sit down and do the work, but then there's a time when she can't sit any longer." So, I don't know if my problems came in first grade when I was really bored, and so I tended to tune out. I think that's what a lot of people with ADHD do . . . they know it so they tune it out. But then they forget to tune back in at the right time.

CONNIE: Well you can see how John would typically fail tests of minute information in his literature classes, even if he read the book, which he didn't always do. Sometimes he read it, but found it boring. He just wasn't going to remember the details.

TERRI: I have never read a complete book before without being on Ritalin. I just kinda jumped and skipped around. I don't think I ever did it. I could never get through it. I couldn't concentrate long enough to see it through.

MARNIE: That's the only thing that I *could* do. I read a lot, especially in high school. All the time I had a book in my hand, not textbooks, but anything else, mostly the classics, I just love them. I think it's because I was able to totally abandon everything in my life and live in the book. ADHDers need an escape. I had books. Some use TV or now, video games. Some use music. It calms your mind. Settles it on one thing instead of twenty.

TERRI: You know, Ritalin amazes me because I know technically how it works, but for myself I have no idea how it works. I came home from college really frustrated and I'm crying and I don't know what to do. It's more to me than just saying, "I give up!" I had people that were there to take it out on, so I got mad at them, took it out on them. My mom asked me something about my reading, or was it my dyslexia or something of that sort. They had just seen *60 Minutes* and Cher was on there with dyslexia, and she had something like those colored things that you put your papers in and slide them down to make them look big; they're like those, but they're yellow and blue and green, and they help you kind of stay focused. I do know that white just kind of throws me off. When I was little my mom and dad used to say that I read upside down. I used to lay my body on the floor, with my back on the floor, put my feet up against the chair, and read looking up. My dad asked me why I did that and I said, "So the words don't move around." But that's about as far as we took it. When I read like on a bright paper, when I'm not on Ritalin, they kinda move all over the place and I really don't know where to begin so I end up skipping lines and nothing makes sense so I go back.

CONNIE: You know, about three years ago I was at a National Reading Styles Conference and I was a speaker. I was given a roommate who was a person trained in doing preliminary assessment for what they call "Irlen Lenses," named after this woman, I think her name is Helen Irlen, who discovered that a lot of people have some of these kinds of problems that are strange to the rest of us. And of course because you don't know that these visual problems don't happen to everybody else, you don't seek help. That's a good deal of the problem right there. You don't know that this just isn't normal, the words dancing off the page and the page suddenly turning white, or whatever. They found a lot of people can be helped with colored lenses. Whatever treatments work for them individually! Also, as you said, Terri, just colored sheets of transparent plastic help some people a lot—different colors, whatever works for the individual. You just put the colored plastic over whatever you're reading.

TERRI: My grandfather used to wear green glasses. And you know, because it's your grandfather, you don't think about it. But when I started looking back over my life and some of the things that happened, I kinda go "Hmmm." He always said he wore them because the light bothered him.

CONNIE: Well, I found when my roommate experimented with me a little bit with sheets of plastic, I could read better with a shade of green. And these slightly pinkish lenses are better than no tint at all. Blue is good, too, but green is even better, which kind of surprises me. And yet I don't have any *serious* problem with white pages or anything like that.

JOHN: You always did like green.

CONNIE: Yeah, but I don't think it's just a matter of liking it—green.

JOHN: I remember someone telling me that when doing outlining in books for studying, you should outline in the color you like. I never really did like looking at this bright yellow outline on this already kind of glaring white paper.

TERRI: I always outline because I like the way it looks when I turn the page.

MARNIE: It looks pretty—I like that too. I have finally read a whole textbook. I'm just so excited about this. It's so nice to look through the whole textbook and see outlining on every page and know that I did it. I wasn't even on Ritalin when I read it!

TERRI: I sat down and I was all alone the very first time I took Ritalin. I sat in my apartment in college and it was just like me running this race and someone holding you and going in slow motion. Where before when I wasn't on Ritalin, it was like me running a fast-paced race and not getting anywhere. It's like a treadmill and while you're doing things it's like you're going fast as can be but you're not getting anywhere. And when you get on Ritalin it's just like slow-motion. It's like you have all this time, you can do everything. I took a math test about a month after I got on Ritalin and I got my test back and I got like in the 90s somewhere. I was amazed! I knew I studied for the test, but usually when I studied I would make really stupid mistakes and now, I was just going, "I can't believe I did this! You mean I got this right!?" It just amazed me. I think that's why I went back to school, because I like it now. It's like I can succeed now.

MARNIE: My first semester I got tested and I went into the army and then I came back and went on Ritalin. Last fall was my first semester on Ritalin. I had a full course schedule, but like a dummy, I stopped taking my medication. I thought I didn't need it, so I just stopped taking it within the last month. I had been doing really well up to that point and then all of a sudden about three weeks later I found myself going crazy. I called up Laurie, crying, "Laurie, something is wrong! I don't know what's wrong. I'm going crazy!" She said, "Calm down. Have you been taking your medication?" "Well, um, not really," I said. She said, "Marnie, you have to take your medication." Well, she ended up calling this one professor of mine and he gave me an incomplete. I ended up getting a 3.65 and I've never done that well in college. ADDers need support for many things: staying on Ritalin, making schedules, sticking to schedules, planning ahead, etcetera. They need to realize that they *are* different and need special attention and it's not a "bad" thing.

CONNIE (TO TERRI): It was like night and day between when you first enrolled in that Grammar for Teachers class and now. I see a big difference between then and now, just in your conversations. And the same with Marnie. All I have to do is look at Marnie and there is a more focused person.

MARNIE: When I got in contact with you I was on Ritalin. I was more focused and other people noticed it, too. Like my parents noticed it and my boss at my job noticed it.

TERRI: See, my mom and dad can't pick up when I'm on and when I'm off. I think that's real strange. Actually it's not strange because they still think of me as the person that I was when I left when I was eighteen years old and that's how I will always be to them and that's the most frustrating part. I've grown so much!

CONNIE: Don't feel too bad. I don't want to tell you how old I will be on Saturday but suffice it to say it's a lot older than you. My mother just informed me at breakfast today when I was ordering that I needed to tell the waitress how I wanted my eggs cooked. I just stared at her. I don't think she even got the point.

JOHN: Since those first grades in college have you guys seen your grades come up even more as your expectations got higher?

TERRI: I was only in two semesters while I was on Ritalin but I live by it. I absolutely live by it. My boyfriend can tell when I need to take it, when I'm off and when I'm on. He works with kids, some of who are ADHD, and he has a good concept of it. He will tell me, "It's time to take it." One time I remember we had a midterm exam and this was when I was taking six classes. I opened up my calendar when she gave us a choice of two dates. I saw in my calendar that this and this and this date was packed. There wasn't any way I could fit another midterm in there. I just said it couldn't work for me that day. Of course the rest of the class was choosing that day. I was on Ritalin and didn't lose it the way I would normally if I wasn't on Ritalin. But instead of explaining it to everyone I kind of closed it off. I told the instructor, "Listen, I have ADHD and am trying to cope with it, and I'm looking at my calendar and it won't work." She said, "Terri, you know what will happen if you start reading a chapter today, and take a break tomorrow, and read one the next day. By the time next week comes you'll be all set." I thought, "It might work for you but it will not work for me." She just made it seem so easy. To a normal person it was very easy. That's how they solve their problems.

MARNIE: If someone said that to me I would have been saying, "Oh please. That's inconceivable."

TERRI: I think they plan everything out and then expect it to be this way. They see everyone else do it with ease and we are looking at ourselves saying, "I don't really know what I'm supposed to be doing." We need so much more direction when everything isn't normal in the daily routine.

CONNIE: OK, let's pick up on that other issue, too: the suggestion that you read one chapter a day and one the next. When John was in school up through about the eighth grade, he would let me give him that kind of help. So when he had a major project due, let's say quite a few book reports due that year, he got A+'s on all of them. Till your classmates started complaining about the +'s, then the teacher gave you just A's. Do you remember how you got those A+ papers, John? We would take a calendar and say, "If it's due this day, the final draft needs to be typed at least the day before. And in order to get the final draft typed the day before, when do we need to go over it to make the final revisions? And in order to make final revisions, when do we need to have our first or second draft?" We would work our way back to when you needed to go to the library and get the book. I also had to keep after you on this. I think most parents of these ADHD kids don't know this is a way to succeed, to help to get things done.

JOHN: At the time I hadn't been diagnosed with ADHD either. I just had a nice mom who was a teacher. But I still would hate that. I might get that far written on paper these days but I still wouldn't follow it. I might wait till the last day. I might wait till the last day to get the book and find out it's already gone. I did that in the past. I still love to wait till the last minute, it seems. But I can still get some good grades, like on the play I wrote.

CONNIE: You have also found that you have a lot more self-discipline than you used to have. You get things done on time.

MARNIE: But if you can't do it by yourself, it doesn't work. I could sit down and write a schedule, but I wouldn't follow it without being on Ritalin. Long-term projects are almost impossible for an ADHDer not on Ritalin. I have some correspondence courses right now that I know are not going to get done. I wish somebody would help me sit down and make out a schedule and then make me do it. It's really hard to study right now because I am not on Ritalin to study because I'm pregnant. But there is nobody to help me do this. I think if they would sit down with people who have ADHD and help them make schedules it would be easier. School is easier in elementary and junior high because you know when things are due—usually the next day. In college it's not due for two or three weeks.

CONNIE: It's the difficulty of focusing, to make yourself sit down and do something. It's really easy for the factors to compound with each other.

MARNIE: Well, it's easy for people to say, "All you need to do is sit down and do it." Well that's what's difficult! I can't even sit down and do it. I can't even make a schedule because there's too much that needs to be done and I can't look at all that stuff and put it down on a schedule.

TERRI: Yeah, I would get too involved in making the schedule itself, instead of filling it out. I would worry more about the lines and where they were. It would have to be artistic. I think it goes back to opening the drawer and not knowing what you are looking for.

MARNIE: I would do the same thing. I like how things look and like them to look pretty and neat. I understand totally.

CONNIE: I don't know if you know this, John, they started a program with Portage middle schools, to try and teach some of these students with ADHD.

MARNIE: What kind of program is it?

CONNIE: Well, note-taking is part of it, and planning is part of it, scheduling.

TERRI: I think it's for first year students. Like how to prepare for your classes.

"Well, you need a certain kind of notebook, and find *your* way of doing it and do it well. Like outlining, maybe you would like to outline differently to help you remember it." It didn't really help, but it helped you create your own way. It was better than nothing.

MARNIE: I know how to study. You should read the material before you go to class. Then after class you read over your notes and read the material again. I know how to do that, but I have never done that in my life. Knowing HOW to do something and DOING it are totally separate for ADHDers. I don't know if it's that I won't do it or I can't do it. And then there's taking notes. . . . I never know what to write down. I can't write as fast as the professor talks.

TERRI: I took a tape recorder to every single class I went to. What I didn't get down I would look over and write the number down from the recorder so I could listen to it later.

MARNIE: That's a good idea!

JOHN: I'd like to have a camera. We get so many diagrams, and so many professors use the whole board and write down things, then erase while you are trying to write down everything they say and trying to draw the diagram. I write large, sloppy, and fast. I am the only one who could read it later. I find lately that with a lot of the stuff, with all the concepts, it's more important for me to just listen to what he says. My roommate tries to write everything down and he writes small and neat. He doesn't get it all down, and he doesn't pay attention, so he hasn't heard the concept either, the explanation. The other thing, also, is knowing what is important to the teacher, which usually takes a while to figure out. At the beginning you probably have to write everything down, then as time goes by you learn what's most important to your teacher and write only that down.

TERRI: It's a wonder anyone ever makes it through college! You have so many teachers.

Connie: Yes, I know. Well, we've covered a lot of territory here. Thanks for sharing your experiences and feelings, to help teachers and parents better understand ADHD and how to support those who have the various difficulties associated with it.

Later Marnie wrote the following about the differences between high school, college, and her life today—and the role of Ritalin.

High School, College, and Today, by Marnie Best

I always knew that something made me different from the rest of the kids. I was always more sensitive, more "social" (as my third grade teacher put it), more eager and more talkative than the other children. I enjoyed having this peppy personality, and, to be honest, most of my teachers enjoyed teaching me. My life was definitely not ruined by having an Attention Deficit Disorder (ADD); to a point, it was enhanced. I was outgoing, creative, and got along well with others.

It was a rare occasion when I didn't appear on the honor roll, and I was always involved in extracurricular activities: I was in band, theater, cheerleading, yearbook, and the student council. I led the typical American girl lifestyle. No obvious signs of ADD were apparent.

It wasn't until I started college that the signs and problems of ADD popped up. All of a sudden, I had found a new freedom that I hadn't known existed—that of nonstructure. No longer did school run from 8:00 to 3:00, but rather, maybe 11:00 to 11:50, 2:00 to 3:30, or 6:00 to 9:00. And maybe one class was on Monday, none on Tuesday, three on Wednesday, and two on Thursday and Friday. My mind went beserk! For twelve years I had been on a strict school schedule that directed my exact movements. I would get up, go to school, go to practice, do my homework, go to bed—the same thing day to day from September to June, then break for July and August and start over again.

When I got to college, my schedule abruptly changed. It now was drastically different. My new schedule fluctuated so much that I had a thousand different things to do in a number of different orders. For example, the schedule consisted of sleep, party, eat, join a sorority; don't forget about this class; remember that in three weeks, four days, and two hours you have a paper due; and keep an eye out for that guy you're in love with because he's hanging around what's her name again.

Within this drastic schedule switch lay the key problem to my ADD. A normal, non-ADD mind would be able to make structure out of chaos. A normal mind would think: "I must sleep from 11:00 to 7:00 or 8:00, go to the library and start researching my paper, go to class, have lunch, go to class, have sorority meeting, do homework in library with boyfriend, and make a list of things to finish before the party this weekend." Very sensible schedule—looks like everything will work out fine.

Fade to ADDer. An ADD mind is not so cut and dried. An ADD mind would be thinking, "Go to party that you heard whats-her-name talking about to make sure your boyfriend is acting right; get to sleep about 2:00 A.M.; wake up around noon; missed eleven o'clock class and too exhausted to go to class at one o'clock; drag yourself out of bed for the sorority meeting; look at your syllabus and notice you still have three weeks until your paper is due so you have plenty of time to put it off; call a friend from the classes you missed to see if she went; get her notes and assignment; notice the assignment isn't due until after the weekend so call boyfriend and tell him you'll make him dinner at his apartment; pack your overnight bag; leave your books and take off. Not a very sensible schedule but very realistic. Believe me, I know. I lived it for nearly four years.

When I was twenty-three years old, tired of partying, tired of my sorority, tired of worrying about immature college guys and, most of all, tired of still being in college, I started to realize that something had to be done. Luckily, as fate had it, I happened to be enrolled in a class being taught by Dr. Connie Weaver. Since Connie was so involved in ADD, we often discussed the disorder in class. I knew that ADD had to be my problem—I just KNEW.

Connie referred me to a clinic, where I was diagnosed with ADD. The doctor said that it was amazing that I had gotten this far in school. I told him I just wanted to finish.

The clinic put me on the drug Ritalin, which is commonly used for people with ADD. The results were amazing. I went from a semester from Hell, in which I go a whopping 0.50 GPA, to a semester with a 3.61 GPA. My boss noticed the change, my parents noticed; but most of all, I noticed. For the first time in my life I was able to do my own prioritizing and my own scheduling. But, more importantly, I was able to stick to it! It confirmed in my head that I wasn't dumb, lazy, or even crazy—I just wasn't able to function as normal students did without being on Ritalin.

I finally graduated from college with a 2.65 GPA. It wasn't the greatest GPA, but having my degree was all that mattered after five years of serious struggle.

I am now married and have a beautiful baby boy. My life is great and I am happy. Of course there are ups and downs, but the pressures of school are gone. I have not continued on Ritalin because once again I have a reliable, structured life that I live by. But if I were to go back to school one day, I would definitely run to the nearest pharmacy with a prescription for Ritalin in hand.

Conclusions

Through careful reading and evaluation of the preceding discussion in comparison to current research on ADHD, several generalizations and conclusions may be drawn about implications for students, parents, and educators. All three students in the interview described difficulties in both school and outside environments commonly attributable to ADHD, including these core symptoms of ADHD in adults (Robin, 1992).

Inattention—poor persistence of effort
- failure to mobilize effort toward completion of tasks
- rapid loss of interest in ongoing tasks
- active search for something else to do when bored
- symptoms most common with low-interest, repetitious activities, for example, paperwork

Poor work performance
- not completing paperwork
- becoming easily bored by tedious material
- poor organization and planning
- procrastination until deadlines are imminent
- inability to work well independently
- not listening carefully to directions
- poor self-discipline in general

Emotional impairments: What is the inner pain associated with being an ADHD adult?
- Most ADHD adults are excruciatingly aware of their inadequacies but feel helpless to do anything about them.
- Grief. Sense of loss from inability to live up to potential. Don't work through grief because loss isn't clearly recognized if ADHD has not been diagnosed.

- Low self-esteem. Past of endless failure, projects unfinished, constantly at odds with others. ADHD adults begin to think of themselves as bad characters, inadequate, aimless, lazy.
- Hypersensitivity, emotional flooding. ADHD adults are thin-skinned. Their porous system absorbs everything, particularly criticism. They overreact. But if you take into account their inability to filter things out, causing them to become emotionally flooded, seeming overreactions make sense.

Several .suggestions were made by the ADHD adults in this interview for helping students, teachers, and parents cope with an individual's inattention difficulties.

1. ADHD students typically find regular school assignments "boring" and typically respond better to assignments that are relevant to their lives and interests—a practice consistent with a whole language philosophy of education. Knowing "why" something is to be learned and how it may relate to the particular individual is important to many students but is most particularly needed for the ADHD student to perform or complete given tasks.

2. Teacher and parents can help facilitate completion of longer goal-oriented tasks by helping them plan ahead and carefully schedule shorter increments. Just "telling" them isn't enough; individualized help, support, and monitoring of progress over time are essential.

3. ADHD students are not "dumb" or "bad" but need greater stimuli and challenge to enhance concentration. Varying activities and allowing ADHD students to choose activities that correspond with personal interests may greatly help to offset distractibility and inability to complete "assigned" coursework. This is again compatible with whole language learning concepts.

4. Tape-recording lectures for later listening, as suggested by Terri, seems an appropriate strategy for the ADHD student, whose mind may tend to wander during lectures and/or class discussions. Also highly valuable for the student with ADHD is instruction in study skills, including (1) note-taking, specifically what to take notes on and how to write down important points according to the particular teacher's objectives, and (2) test-taking skills, including relaxation techniques. In addition, self-esteem workshops may be a veritable prerequisite to academic success for students with ADHD.

5. Accounting for the particular learning styles of individual students may help them focus. It is apparent that for the ADHD student both visual and then auditory explanations for assignment directions help clarify desired expectations.

6. ADHD students seem better able to concentrate in a quiet and secluded environment for certain kinds of tasks such as test-taking. Teachers may want to provide an area in the back of the room or even in the hallway, where the student can retreat when normal classroom noise may overwhelmingly interfere with concentration. Similarly, the student needs a quiet place to study in the home environment.

7. Altering schedules and routines is especially disruptive and disorienting for the ADHD student; sometimes, however, making purposeful changes to accommodate their special needs may be vital. Discussing these kinds of adjustments prior to enactment will help the student understand purpose and allay anxiety about scheduling variation.

8. Parents may find it helpful to inform teachers of a student's ADHD diagnosis and/or provide them with clear explanations of what this involves for the individual student. Relaying pertinent information helps everyone involved to know how to react appropriately to, and cope with, the difficulties the ADHD individual may encounter. It is essential to understand and educate everyone involved: students, teachers, and parents alike.

9. It may be helpful to establish ADHD support groups. Teachers may want to participate in seminars to extend their knowledge of ADHD and how they can work effectively with these students. Parents may find it helpful to listen to other students relay similar difficulties being encountered by their own children, and ADHD students may find comfort in knowing they are not alone in their learning differences. Similarly, all three ADHD adults in this interview stated that having the understanding of parents and teachers was instrumental in their becoming more adept at handling their own difficulties.

10. Ritalin has proven highly effective for treatment of ADHD symptoms and in controlling distractibility tendencies, unlike other methods that have not been scientifically justified, such as diet control, vitamin supplements, or biofeedback (Goldstein & Ingersoll, 1992). Ritalin has been documented to aid not only concentration and focus but also appropriate behavior control, thereby enhancing academic success and improving interpersonal relationships. In individual cases, other psychostimulants (Cylert, Dexadrine) have proved more effective than Ritalin. Alternatively, certain antidepressants have been shown to help some ADHD people as well.

There is still much needed research to be done concerning the causes and related symptoms of the ADHD individual, but it is already clear that we do need to establish alternative methods of education for these individuals. Later chapters in this book demonstrate that whole language teaching practices may accommodate the varying needs of the ADHD student. Essentially, what we must remember is that we must find appropriate and supportive ways of enabling all our students to achieve their individual potentials and continue to encourage them to do so by being informed and professional educators dedicated to fostering the growth of the learners within our classrooms, and dedicated to our own learning as well.

References

Fowler, M., Barkley, R. A., Reeve, R., & Zentall, S. (1992). *CH.A.D.D. educator's manual: An in-depth look at Attention Deficit Disorders from an educational perspective.* Plantation, FL: CH.A.D.D. (Children and Adults with Attention Deficit Disorders, a national support organization for information on Attention Deficit Disorders.) Distributed by Caset Associations Ltd., Fairfax, VA.

Goldstein, S., & Ingersoll, B. (1992). Controversial treatments for children with Attention Deficit Hyperactivity Disorder. *CH.A.D.D.ER Box, 6*(2), 19–22.

Hallowell, E., & Ratey, J. (1993). 50 tips on the management of Adult Attention Deficit Disorder. *CH.A.D.D.ER Box, 6,* 1–8.

Robin, A. (1992). *ADHD in adulthood: A clinical perspective.* Madison, WI: Videotape Companion Manual.

Weaver, C. (1991). *Alternatives in understanding and educating attention-deficit students: Toward a systems-theory, whole language perspective.* Concept Paper No. 3. Urbana, Il: National Council of Teachers of English.

Weiss, G., & Hechtman, L. (1986). *Hyperactive children grown up: Empirical findings and theoretical considerations.* New York: Guilford Press.

3

What I've Learned as an ADHDer About the Problems and Needs of Students with ADHD

John Weaver

> *ADHD makes every aspect of learning a challenge and makes getting into trouble easy. Trouble in learning and ease in getting into trouble is a powerful combination of negativity. ADHD students, especially those who do not realize they are ADHD-positive, may never accomplish more than a sliver of their potential—unless they have help.*

This chapter began as John's written responses to some questions regarding his learning experiences in school and college, and how these might have been affected by his Attention Deficit Hyperactivity Disorder.

John indicates that he probably had few learning strengths before being diagnosed and treated for ADHD.

Explaining at the outset some of the ADHD-related difficulties and problems he encountered in school, John demonstrates how assignments that allowed for creativity made it easier to overcome or circumvent some of those problems. Continuing to draw upon his personal experiences, he discusses effective classroom environments, study skills and structures, and organizing for academic success; the philosophy underlying many of these recommendations is consistent with that of whole language. The chapter suggests many ways in which teachers can help ADHD students and is illustrated with anecdotes from John's own school experiences.

John Weaver was diagnosed as having ADHD at the age of sixteen, when hospitalized after a suicide attempt that resulted, in part, from his inability to live up to his potential in school. John completed his senior year (with mostly A's and two honor certificates) at an alternative high school, which accommodated his learning needs better than the regular high school had done. After briefly attending a junior college, John found his niche in a technical school. In the fall of 1992 he graduated with highest honors from ITT Technical Institute in Indianapolis, having earned a Bachelor of Applied Science degree in electronics engineering technology. John is currently looking for a job in his field.

Throughout my schooling my ADHD-related problems included, among others, boredom, loss of attention, loss of concentration, weak memory abilities, poor organizational skills, and impulsivity. These and other social factors resulted in low self-esteem.

Why do I think that a majority of these problems are ADHD-related? Partly because I've recognized myself in published descriptions of ADHD, but also because of my own experiences. Since taking Ritalin, I have seen major improvements in overcoming these problems. Take the medication away and the problems increase. I think that these problems of mine fit the bill for ADHD, and I think that Ritalin helps me to overcome them.

In school, teachers have done many things that have helped me deal with my ADHD-related problems. Before being diagnosed, however, I received little help, truly not enough for me to achieve success. After being diagnosed, I knew more about my problems and was able to tell others, such as teachers, what I needed to help me succeed academically. Based upon my personal experience and some reading about ADHD, this chapter describes some of what I've learned about ADHD students' needs and how teachers can help. I've drawn particularly from my high school and college experiences, because those are the years I remember best.

One of the things that greatly helped me was having assignments that encouraged creativity, or at least allowed for it.

The Creative Path to Academic Achievements

Before being diagnosed, one of the few strengths I found was in creativity. When teachers allowed and encouraged me to use my imagination, I found creative ways to get assignments done. Examples of this include a sixth grade oral report and a short paper assignment in my sophomore or junior year of high school.

I never liked oral reports/tests. Low self-esteem (among other things) affected my oral presentations at the early stage of elementary schooling. Once, during sixth grade, I had to do an oral book report. I read a book from the "Three Investigators" series—a mystery about a ghost haunting a house. I loved the book. I hated having to do the oral book report. I couldn't figure out how I could get in front of the class and give a report. I knew that I would panic. I knew that if I stood before the class to give my report I would forget everything that I had prepared. Due to low self-esteem (and my as-yet-undiagnosed ADHD), all I would be able to think about was what nasty things the other kids were thinking about me. My mother, my lifetime teacher, saved me. She helped me combat my problems in a creative manner. I gave my report under the guise of a ghost. For a costume, my mother allowed me to mutilate a bed sheet. My report was made into a commercial—a person in a ghost outfit trying to entice readers into buying a marvelous book. This creativity acted as a shield and allowed me to get past my fears (who could see my face to make fun of me?). It allowed me to experience the part, such as an actor playing a role, and I enjoyed myself. This increased my self-confidence, which helped me get through the report. I received an A.

What happened when the assignments didn't allow for creativity? In high school I had to give a few oral reports (tests) for my French class. During those years I froze up on regular paper and pencil tests; oral reports/tests were even worse. My low self-esteem and my fear of public speaking prohibited me from being successful with oral reports. In front of a class, I was paralyzed—it took me one minute just to get from one word to the next. I was a stammering idiot.

I often failed oral reports. I could not think of creative solutions to combat my problems.

Could creativity have helped? Yes. Could the teacher have done something more to help me with my situation? Yes.

A situation such as this needs understanding *first.* If I had been an A student, except for failing oral reports, my teacher might have realized that there had been a specific problem and she might have tried to help me overcome it. As it was, I was a poor student—for the various classes I had, my average grades were C's and D's. Sometimes it is easy for teachers to label students such as myself as lazy or "bad" students—students who just don't put effort into their schoolwork. If my teacher (and I) had known that many of my problems were ADHD-related, she might have been willing to offer me help. For teachers, the first part to understanding is to realize that having low grades doesn't necessarily mean that the person in question is a "bad" student, much less unintelligent.

Creativity could have helped, too. If the teacher had agreed to a private performance, perhaps I could have done a report with one other person helping me. . . . maybe even in costume. I can see it now . . . a friend and I dressed as a couple of famous French people. It could have been staged as a two-person play, with an audience of one. That, I might have been able to handle. Creativity could have made me feel more at ease while facing my fears.

I am not sure I will ever get over my phobia of public speaking. With creativity, though, I just might have a chance. Creativity can help students not only to complete but also to do well, assignments that they might otherwise consider impossible.

One reason creative assignments and projects are so important for ADHD students is that they (we) find it next to impossible to do whatever seems boring. Short papers are another example of possible boredom. The assignment: Read the chapter and then write a two- to five-page report explaining what you have read. In my sophomore or junior year of high school, my class was assigned to write about the story of Huck Finn. My friends Keith, Rod, Todd, and I didn't want to write yet another boring report on a century-old text. The four of us approached our teacher about an alternative assignment. We obtained permission for each of us to write a short story, with our main character exemplifying the values and personality of Huck. Out of my three friends' work, I only remember Rod's. Rod set his story in the future, where Huck Finn was personified by a space explorer. My own story was set in the medieval times, the title being, "Ahnjo: Huck Finn in a Medieval World." I received an A for my story. Sure, it may not be the best short story in the world, but I was given an opportunity to try something new, to express myself, and to enjoy what I was doing.

If I had been forced to do the same assignment (report form) as the rest of the class, I don't think I would have put nearly as much work into the project because I would have been bored. When assigned to write a short-paper report, students are often supposed to read a story and then to tell what happened in the story. Teachers also ask that, when explaining what happened in a story, the student not simply repeat the story. I sometimes find this difficult to do. By using my imagination, I was able to create my own story—and with that story, I was able to show my teacher that I had understood the concepts and moral implications that the author of *The Adventures of Huckleberry Finn* had worked into his writing. I was encouraged to think and to create rather than just to report what someone else had said.

Classroom Environments that Promote Thinking and Learning, Doing Homework, and Studying

After being diagnosed and treated for ADHD, I realized that I needed more than just creativity to help me overcome my ADHD problems. I soon discovered that there are many things teachers can do (and did) to help me and other ADHD students with our difficulties. It was during my senior year of high school and my three years at ITT that I found the help I needed.

I started my senior year of high school at an alternative education school. There, I noticed several differences between the alternative education school and the rather typical city high school where I had previously been enrolled.

The class structures at the alternative education school established a better learning environment. Each class was comprised of ten to twenty students, a limited number compared to the twenty to thirty students found in a typical high school classroom. The classes were scheduled to resemble a typical college plan. From Monday to Thursday, students had two two-hour classes a day, with one set of classes being the same on Monday and Wednesday and another set of classes being the same on Tuesday and Thursday. A fifth class, a four-hour marathon, was held on Friday.

The two-hour classes were just what I needed to help me learn how to handle school. Previously, I had never learned study skills. I remember learning a great deal from my math course that year. At the beginning of each class, my mathematics teacher collected the previous homework assignment. Approximately an hour an a half of each class was used to review homework and learn new materials. The next half-hour was used by the students to start on their homework assignments. During this time we were free to ask our teacher for help, and she willingly answered our questions.

In the typical high school when a teacher gives a homework assignment, such as in mathematics, the students receive the assignment within the last five minutes of class. The students take the assignment home, complete it, and hand in the assignment the next day at school. Sometimes teachers will review the assignment and sometimes not. A day or so after handing in the assignment, the students receive their work back from the teacher. The homework pages are filled with red slashes and minus signs. Students who did not do well think, "Oh well, I did poorly on another assignment. I just hope the next one is better." In this manner, students get to see that they messed up—but they don't necessarily understand *why* they messed up and they haven't had the chance to see if they can do the problems correctly. There is a cliché stating that "practice makes perfect." In typical high schools, students can only practice making mistakes. . . .

At the alternative education school I was given the chance to make my

help ADHD students only when studying requires that they *think* and *learn* rather than memorize.

Exercising Patience and Understanding

When confronted with an ADHD student, teachers need to exercise patience and understanding more than usual. During my third year at ITT, I encountered a particular situation (certainly *not* the only one) that required my teacher's patience and understanding. Every day, about an hour into the class period, a particular car alarm was activated. The car alarm usually kept going for about thirty minutes before it was shut off. One day, just after the class had been handed a test, the car alarm started sounding. Most students did not find the alarm to be too disturbing. I, however, found the sound of the alarm to consume my every thought. I absolutely could not concentrate on the test. The repetitiveness of the alarm completely disrupted my ability to focus; you see, repetitive noises can be dreadfully disturbing for ADHD students.

I tried to work on the test, but I couldn't. I finally explained my problem to the teacher. The teacher agreed to let me move to a room that was farther from the sound of the alarm. In the alternate room, I could not hear the alarm and was therefore able to relax and focus on the test. My only concern was that the teacher might think I had cheated; you see, I knew that I had been able to answer each question correctly because I had studied, learned, and remembered the material. I am thankful that my teacher understood what I needed (a quiet room) and then provided me with what I needed to be able to show him what I had learned. (Yes, I *did* score a 4.0 on the test.)

Helping ADHD Students Organize Class Materials

Even little things such as what type of notebook to use can be problematic for ADHD students. Having many things to organize can be another problem. That is one reason why having only two classes a day worked well for me. ADHD students are typically very unorganized, even with only a few things to organize; certainly I am.

Can teachers help students to become more organized? Yes.

I like the idea of having one five-subject, two-hundred sheet, college-ruled, perforated notebook for each and every class. I always used an entire notebook for one class; I didn't bother putting five different class subjects in it. The perforated notebooks are great because students can do more than just write down their class notes in them; students can write down every assignment given and can also do their homework assignments in the notebook. Keeping the homework in the notebook is a good idea so that it does not get lost before the student's next class period!

If students do not have perforated notebooks, then I suggest that in addition to the regular notebook, they buy a wireless Neatbook (by Mead), or its equivalent. These Neatbooks have from 80 to 120 perforated pages—just the right amount for doing homework assignments for one class. I would write class notes, examples, and practice problems in the regular notebook. I would then do all my homework in the Neatbook.

I like to color-coordinate my notebooks—for math, perhaps a red notebook and red Neatbook, then, for English, a blue notebook and blue Neatbook. Although it may *seem* petty, the color coordination of notebooks can really help students. When using a notebook, dating pages can be just as useful. I like to write the date at the top of a page whenever I start a new day. It would be wise for students to write the date at the top of each page (front and back) the day they write down any information.

I strongly urge teachers to share with their students such techniques as those I have mentioned and to guide students in implementing them. This would be helpful for most students; it's crucial for students with ADHD.

Here I would like to emphasize an important condition for academic success. Being treated for ADHD (with Ritalin) is what has made the help from teachers work for me. Without the medication I probably wouldn't have had the motivation to let such things as daily quizzes and homework assignments work for me. Before being properly treated, I really didn't care about my success; perhaps this was because, in the past, I had had more failures than successes. Ritalin has helped me to do well and therefore gain the motivation to continue doing the best I can in school. The point here is that teachers may give all the help that they can to an ADHD student, but the student may still fail if he or she isn't being properly treated for ADHD. Proper treatment for ADHD may, among other things, include consulting a psychologist or psychiatrist *who is particularly knowledgeable about ADHD* and taking prescribed medication, things that a teacher cannot provide.

I hope that, throughout the preceding pages, I have given teachers a better understanding of what it means to have ADHD as a student. Teachers should now realize that those things they take for granted—small things, such as being able to take notes or being able to remember things, and larger things, such as being able to learn—can be major challenges for ADHD students, even those who are highly intelligent. I have presented information and strategies that I hope teachers will use to help ADHD students meet those challenges *and* be winners.

Ways That Teachers Can Help ADHD Students

I could go on and on about my life as an ADHD person, mentioning countless experiences. (I *would,* too, if someone weren't helping me to control my ADHD impulses.) However, I should probably deliver to you the meat and mead of this meal. Starting below, I offer suggestions as to how teachers can best help students who have Attention Deficit Hyperactivity Disorder. Some of these points have been made earlier, while others are new. All these ideas (suggestions) are likely to be helpful for all students; but they can be, and most often are, imperative for helping ADHD students, who typically have difficulty in restraining impulses and in focusing and maintaining attention.

Understanding and Interacting with ADHD Students

As a starting point, teachers need to learn more about ADHD and the various (numerous) problems it can cause. Becoming informed about ADHD is an important step for teachers who want to help *all* students succeed in their classrooms.

When faced with an individual ADHDer, learn about the ADHD-related problems that he or she is experiencing and how these affect the student. Discover how ADHD is affecting the student's ability to do the following: Hear the teacher, understand explanations and directions, concentrate, pay attention, get assignments done, organize, and study. Note that this is only a partial list of problems that might be experienced by an ADHD student. Another such problem would be having difficulty relating to and interacting with peers, as well as others in the school environment. Perhaps the best way to find out about these problems is to *ask the student.*

It is very important, too, to help see that the student's other teachers know that he or she has ADHD.

> Before starting my third year of classes at ITT Technical Institute (for which I had to move out of state), I asked a favor of my psychiatrist, whom I had been seeing since my suicide attempt: I requested that he write a "To Whom It May Concern" letter. This letter, which was directed toward educators, presented a brief summary of my suicide attempt, the diagnosis and ongoing treatment of my ADHD, the problems caused by ADHD, and my progress in dealing with these problems. The document went on to explain the types of environments and situations that I found to be most problematic and which environments/situations I would feel most comfortable in and would find better for learning. This letter explained for the teachers what my problems were and what the teachers could do to better assist me in school. Presenting this letter to each of my teachers helped me (and my teachers) greatly.

Encourage students (or their parents, if the student is under eighteen years of age) to get from their psychologist or psychiatrist a "To Whom It May Concern" or "Dear Educators" letter. Suggest to ADHD students that they show the letter to *each of their teachers.* The letter should explain for the teachers that the student has ADHD, what general problems the student is experiencing, and how teachers can help the student deal with these problems.

Teachers should understand that ADHD students may be quite intelligent, even though they have trouble learning. Such students may easily become frustrated. Continued frustration and failure can lead to low self-esteem, even depression and despair. Help ADHD students deal with their frustration; turn it into something positive, such as determination to do well.

Be aware that many ADHD people are very impulsive, although medication may curb their impulsivity.

For many ADHDers, impulsivity is one of the ADHD characteristics hardest to control. When an action or reaction occurs, the "normal" brain starts creating options and sending them to a buffer, where they can be carefully examined before a decision is made. The impulsive mind, though, responds to the first few options that enter the buffer. Usually the first or second option is executed immediately, even before other options can be created. This impulsive process is similar to the operation of the autonomic nervous system. That is to say, when a person is impulsive, the brain uses a near-unconscious operational mode, immediately acting upon the first thought or option, without any conscious decision making. When ADHD people consciously realize that they are being impulsive, it is too late—they have already been impulsive and have carried out the actions their brain demanded of them. Yes, impulsivity is one of the characteristics of ADHD that is hardest to control. Truly, how can anyone control actions that are said and done before conscious thinking can occur?

Understand that ADHD students do things that they don't mean to do. Sometimes, they impulsively do the first thing that goes through their "brain buffer," even before their brain can offer other options. Try to help students be less impulsive. Since impulsivity can, however, be very hard to control, be understanding when ADHD students are impulsive.

For me, ADHD made every aspect of school a challenge . . . *except* getting into trouble. Impulsivity (a definite ADHD characteristic) allowed me to become frighteningly angry in seconds, to say things I shouldn't, and generally to do stupid things without carefully thinking about them first.

I remember a particular ADHD-provoked incident that occurred during high school. The hallways were full of kids and my friend Paul and I were chatting. As the class bell rang, Paul and I started to go our separate ways. We continued talking, however, by raising our voices to a near yell. A gym teacher, who was acting as a hall monitor, told me to stop yelling and get to class. Well, I still had plenty of time to get to class. I also figured that it was my prerogative if I wanted to keep talking to my friend. The other kids in the hallway were so noisy that it seemed as if a score of people were yelling. I did not understand why it was wrong for my friend and me to be yelling, but the teacher was insistent that I should stop. I finally screamed, "Shut the f*** up, you b****," finished my conversation with Paul, and casually walked away. Well, someone from the principal's office came and got me out of my next class. The principal made me sit outside his office for three hours before he invited me in to talk (listen). I think I got detention for a week. Impulsivity had found yet another way to get me into trouble.

Be patient with ADHD students; that is, be patient with both their learning difficulties and their impulsive behavior. Such students usually mean well, so continually putting them down, making them feel guilty, and punishing them will do a lot of harm and virtually no good.

Be patient when ADHD students ask questions. ADHD students are typically very curious and have a deep desire to understand what they are being taught (as well as understanding the rest of the world around them). Such students continually ask a myriad of questions. To others, these questions sometimes seem insignificant and unworthy of answers. However, ADHD students wouldn't ask questions unless they really wanted or needed to understand something.

Be environment-aware. Be able to recognize when others in the class are being too noisy for the ADHD student to concentrate. For example: Be able to recognize what noises, such as repetitive pencil tapping, might make it difficult for the ADHD student to focus on the work at hand. Keep the class quiet enough to minimize distractions for ADHD students. It is imperative that teachers try to prevent situations that breed a loss of attention, a loss of concentration, impulsivity, boredom, or low self-esteem.

As paradoxical as this sounds, noisy, isolated, unpredictable, predictable, and cluttered environments can all create problems for the ADHD student. I believe that a happy medium needs to be sought. In this section, however, let me discuss some of the ADHD-related problems with each of these situations.

Noisy environments: It is too hard for me to concentrate and read well under these conditions. I find it very hard to go from one word to the next when trying to read. This makes it very difficult to put all the words together to make a sentence and even harder to gain the meaning of the sentence.

Isolation: Being in total isolation can cause an ADHD person distractions, just as if the person were in a noisy room. An ADHD person is always taking in sensory information; if there isn't any outside input, it is like starving the brain: the ADHD person's brain may keep searching for noises and distractions because it can't find any obvious ones. This leads to not concentrating on the work to be done. Sometimes I need a *slight* distraction (or light background noise), just so that my brain can block it out. This forces my brain to pay attention to the work I need to get done. Note, however, that if the distraction is more than the brain can block out, the ADHD person will not be able to concentrate on the work at hand.

Unpredictable environments: Not the best, depending upon how severe the randomness is. Too much unpredictability can cause a loss of attention, a loss of concentration, a loss of organization, and overall confusion.

Predictable environments: Nice for a while. But I cannot stand the repetitiveness of the same teacher, same class, same hours, same teaching periods, same study periods, every day, every week, every month for long without going insane. If everyday procedures are too predictable, the ADHD student may quickly become bored. This leads to such things as not paying attention in class and not getting assignments done.

Cluttered environments: This can lead to loss of organization and, therefore, to unfinished study/homework goals. Cluttered environments can also cause a loss of attention or concentration: "Oh! Wow! I just found my remote control car (under my notebook). Let's go play!"

Give ADHD students time to learn and to understand while they are in the classroom. Allow them to complete part (or all) of their assignments during the class period. This will be very beneficial to the students *if* teachers take this opportunity to check each student's work to see that it is being done correctly. If the work is incorrect, help the student to understand what is wrong and why the work is incorrect. Be sure to praise students for work done correctly.

Encourage students, especially ADHD students, to ask questions—to ask "why." ADHD students want to understand. Asking "why" (and receiving a good answer) enables them to understand more precisely why things happen and how concepts fit together. Some teachers think that it does not matter if a student understands why he or she made a mistake; these teachers think that students need only to know how to do things correctly. I, however, believe that learning why mistakes were made increases a student's knowledge of how to do things correctly.

Spend extra time answering students' questions. Use the time before, during, and after class to respond to their questions. At the average high school, classes last about an hour, with only five minutes between class periods. If a teacher uses *all* the class time to present new material, students will still have many unanswered questions when the class ends. With only five minutes between classes, students do not have time to stay after class and ask questions (and teachers don't have time to stay and answer them).

In this situation, having more time between classes would be very helpful. Teachers, please think about this. If having more time between classes seems both useful and reasonable, then perhaps you could approach your superiors (Board of Education?) with a proposal. Perhaps you could propose that there should be ten-minute breaks between hour-long classes. Even five extra minutes would enable students to ask questions and to receive answers, giving them an understanding of the material before going to their next class.

Helping Students Organize and Structure Their Work

ADHD persons typically lack good organizational skills, mostly because of their inability to stay focused on any one task. Teachers can (should) help ADHD students—and indeed ALL students—to structure their academic lives. Caution is advised, however, because many ADHD people may resent having structure forced (and enforced) upon them. In other words, many ADHD people may resent being forced to do things, rather than being allowed to do them on their own terms.

Some forms of structure, such as using daily quizzes to encourage students to study, are subtle enough (and not applied to only ADHD students) so that ADHD students are not likely to be resentful. When contemplating extra structure solely for an ADHD student, teachers should discuss their thoughts with the individual. If one form of structure does not work, talk with the student and come to an agreement about using a different method.

Remember that since ADHD students know (hopefully!) what their problems are, they may be able to help determine what organizational structure might be beneficial. Between the teacher and the student, two-way communication is a must.

Help ADHD students organize to get homework done. Make sure that ADHD students have written down what their assignments are. Also make sure that they have written down the correct directions for doing the assignments and that they understand these. Make sure that the ADHD students have organized notebooks—this might include color coordination.

ADHD students commonly have trouble hearing, remembering, and following directions.

In my case, if the class was noisy and the teacher did not quiet the class down to a volume level of *zero*, then I may not have even realized (because of not focusing attention and hearing) that the teacher had given an assignment or directions on how to do the assignment. If I was paying attention and was listening to the teacher give directions, I still might miss a word or two, perhaps even a sentence. If I missed some of the directions and did not ask the teacher to repeat them, then I would have to rely on my peers to relay the directions properly (a gamble). The next problem would be to write down the directions so I could read them later. I tended to tell myself that I didn't need to write down directions, that I could remember what the teacher had said. Big mistake. One of my prevalent ADHD symptoms is poor memory! I definitely did not remember directions well.

Can I make myself sit down and do my homework? In high school this was especially hard for me. Even now it can be difficult. One problem was to remember that I had an assignment and take home my book. (Oh, got to remember to take the directions home too!) This all assumes that I want to do the work enough to take the books home. A lot of times I might get the books home (decided that it would be a good idea to do the work, maybe), but after I was home, I would never take the books out of my bookbag. Too boring. Didn't understand what was going on. Couldn't do the work. Had other things to do. I could (can) find a hundred different activities to do, instead of doing my homework. These were some of the problems I had.

Teach good learning strategies and study methods.

No matter what the testing method, the three main ADHD-related problems that I had with *every* test were *studying* the material, *learning* the material, and then *remembering* what I had studied. Without studying, learning, and remembering, every test was a failure.

During my third year at ITT Technical Institute, I finally developed a method of learning math that worked for me. First, I like to read the description of the formula and how to perform the correlate procedures. I pay careful attention to examples, practicing each one on a separate piece of paper. Before I start solving a new math problem, I write the laws and regulations fitting that particular type of problem. This ensures that they are in hand and also helps imprint them into my memory so that I can recall them during a test. I write out each problem the long way; that is, no shortcuts such as dropping parentheses or doing more than one basic math operation at a time. Yes, this takes too darn long (at least at first). But eventually I become proficient at writing things out the long way so that during a test I can (most likely) write out each problem the long way, every single line of it, and still complete the test without being the last one in the room.

With the help of Ritalin, I was able to change my study methods and habits for the better. I was able to create learning patterns and use them on a continual basis. This helped me to achieve a 3.9 GPA upon graduation from ITT.

Promote good study habits. When an ADHD student is interested in the subject being taught, using daily quizzes might be a good way to encourage the student to study each night.

Teach good test-taking skills. One very important skill is for the student to be able to relax. Without being relaxed, the student may not be able to effectively use any test-taking skills. (See Little p. 109.)

Help ADHD students to plan for the completion of long-term assignments. Help the students to break down assignments into manageable tasks. Help them set due dates for the individual parts (tasks) of assignments; and check periodically to see how they are progressing.

> Long-term projects: It is hard to remember to do each separate part of an assignment each week or month. It is also sometimes hard to determine how much time will be needed to complete the entire project and its separate parts.
>
> I tend to put off both long-term and short-term projects until I barely have time to complete them. In order to complete the assignments I end up staying up all night and put off everything else that I should be doing. A definite lack of organization and lack of ability to stick to an organized schedule are two major ADHD-related problems that I have. I, like many other ADHDers, procrastinate. Getting things done on time must be one of my biggest weaknesses.

Making Learning Come Alive

No matter how greatly ADHD students' structural abilities improve, the st dents will probably still have trouble in classes that they consider boring. For such classes, a different approach may be needed. The anecdote below describes the assertive approach of one teacher to combat boredom in his class.

> The year was nineteen hundred and eighty-seven, the bicentennial celebration of the signing of the Constitution of the United States of America. The city of Portage was constructing a lengthy extension to a comparatively short road called Harvard Street. Mr. Provancher, a social studies teacher, recognized this combination of events as an opportunity to involve his government class students in a project that promised to be fun, exciting, and quite memorable, while at the same time teaching his students important job-related and governmental process skills. Mr. Provancher discussed with his students the idea of persuading the city of Portage to rename the street Constitution Boulevard. One of the more interesting ways that Mr. Provancher generated enthusiasm for the project was by suggesting to a particular student that he could one day tell his children of his accomplishment: He could say, "Look, I was here. I did something. I helped name that street," ultimately giving him a sense of pride and immortality.
>
> After convincing the majority of his students that the project was worthwhile, Mr. Provancher and his class began researching, eliciting signatures on a petition, and convincing the city council to change the name of the street. The students' research had many purposes, including (but not limited to) finding out if any other street in the city of Portage was already named Constitution Boulevard, determining if there were post office box addresses on Harvard Street, and discovering how to change the addresses that were already listed as Harvard Street to addresses on Constitution Boulevard. When their research indicated that the city council should not find any faults with the proposal, the students solicited area residents to sign a petition. After gathering support, the students went before the city council with their proposal. Having no objections to the proposal, the city council took down the Harvard Street signs and replaced them with signs that read Constitution Boulevard.

The example of the bicentennial celebration illustrates, I think, several principles of effective teaching, all of which seem especially important for students who have particular difficulty focusing and maintaining attention.

The following are five important teaching maxims that this example reflects:

Don't let things (your class!) get dull (boring).
Know and use alternative teaching methods.
Promote imagination and creativity.
Create excitement.
Promote desire and interest.

Being Flexible and Creative in Finding Ways to Help

Offer incentives for learning. Extra credit can be a good incentive for most students. Again, a word of caution: Extra credit assignments may not be effective for ADHD students when used in classes that they find boring.

> Extra credit assignments helped me at ITT. My Pascal teacher expected us to document every computer program that we wrote; that is, to provide detailed notes within the program, explaining both the functions of individual commands and the usage of grouped commands. Since he gave extra credit to those students that went beyond what was expected, I continually documented my programs more extensively than was required. A menu program that I wrote was ten pages long when printed out. After I spent approximately sixteen hours documenting the program, it was over forty pages long. I received forty-four points more than the one hundred possible points for doing just what was required. With the use of extra credit, my teacher encouraged me to do more, to learn more.

Talk to ADHD students individually. Discover what would interest them and then offer that type of extra credit to the entire class. This gives ADHD students a possible edge (toward defeating the problem of boredom) while maintaining fairness for the entire class.

Give ADHD students extra help in learning and extra time for taking tests. Talk with them to find out what they need. In order to provide additional help, one of my teachers set up and attended hour-long study/help periods before and after school. Let students know that you are willing to do whatever it takes to help them learn and do well in school.

Because ADHD students find it difficult to concentrate, answering even simple test questions may require more time than other students need. Allowing ADHD students extra time to complete a test gives them a fair chance to demonstrate their learning and understanding.

Have more than one perspective. Some students learn better with visual stimuli, whereas others may do better with auditory stimuli. Some students will understand certain concepts readily; others may show only blank stares. When explaining things to students, be sure that you can give many different examples if needed. Make sure that you can explain things from a "different angle." No two students are exactly alike.

Know when to bend the rules. This can mean altering something as sacred as due dates so as to give a student just a bit more time, or it could be as insignificant as allowing the entire class a five-minute break (against school policy) during the middle of a two-hour class (this helps to relieve "brain jam") and letting the students bring the drinks (pop, not alcohol) back to the class (this allows you to get back on track quickly). There are too many situations to list here. But teachers can promote learning just by using their heads (and hearts) to decide when they can justifiably bend the rules.

Take the initiative; don't wait until the end of the semester/quarter to realize that a student has failed and that you could have done something more to prevent that from happening. Take the initiative to ask students how they are doing. Ask them what they are having difficulties with and what you can do to help.

Students, especially ADHD students, may give up if they are having a lot of trouble. They may not ask you for help. Perhaps they don't think you could or would help them. Let students know that ideas such as these are wrong. Make a *(the)* difference.

Teachers, be creative, imaginative, exciting, fun, friendly, caring, and under-standing.

Without teachers, there would be no students, no learning. Thank you, teachers, for giving of yourselves to educate children and for giving us a future worth looking forward to. Also, thank you for taking the time to learn about ADHD and how you can help ADHD students to be successful, to achieve things that, before, they only dreamt about.

Appendix: Suggestions for Teachers of ADHD Students

1. As a starting point, learn more about ADHD and the various (numerous) problems it can cause.
2. When faced with an individual ADHDer, learn about the ADHD-related problems that he or she is experiencing and how these affect the student.
3. Help see that the student's other teachers know that he or she has ADHD.
4. Understand that ADHD students may be quite intelligent, even though they have trouble learning.
5. Be aware that many ADHD people are very impulsive, although medication may curb their impulsivity.
6. Be patient with ADHD students; that is, be patient with both their learning difficulties and their impulsive behavior.
7. Recognize when others in the class are being too noisy for the ADHD student to concentrate.
8. Prevent situations that breed a loss of attention, a loss of concentration, impulsivity, boredom, or low self-esteem.
9. Give ADHD students time to learn and to understand while they are in the classroom.
10. Encourage students, especially ADHD students, to ask questions—to ask "why."
11. Spend extra time answering students' questions.

12. Help ADHD students organize to get homework done.
13. Teach good learning strategies and study methods.
14. Promote good study habits.
15. Teach good test-taking skills.
16. Help ADHD students to plan for the completion of long-term assignments.
17. Don't let your class get dull or boring.
18. Know and use alternative teaching methods.
19. Promote imagination and creativity.
20. Create excitement.
21. Promote desire and interest.
22. Offer incentives for learning.
23. Give ADHD students extra help in learning and extra time for taking tests.
24. Have more than one perspective.
25. Know when to bend the rules.
26. Take the initiative; don't wait until the end of the semester/quarter to realize that a student has failed and that you could have done something more to prevent that from happening.
27. Be creative, imaginative, exciting, fun, friendly, caring, and understanding.

4

Understanding and Appreciating the ADHD Child in the Classroom

Randy Lee Comfort

In this article Randy Comfort points out that most ADHD youngsters can become energetic, creative, productive, and successful adults—if only they can survive the "place called school." Describing both the ADHD student's strengths and typical weaknesses, she also emphasizes the fears and anxieties that often develop as a result of negative school experiences. The article mainly emphasizes the positive: how teachers and others can work more effectively with such children, bringing out their potential and helping them deal with and overcome what is difficult for them. By providing a supportive environment and maintaining reasonable expectations, we can help ADHD children succeed in school. As the author writes: "It is not fair to them to have to wait for adulthood to have their hour of glory."

Randy Lee Comfort is a graduate of Smith College and has a master's degree in social work and a doctorate in educational psychology. She is the director of The Learning Place, an assessment and remediation center in Denver, Colorado. Randy Comfort is the author of *The Unconventional Child* (self-published, 1980) and of *Teaching the Unconventional Child* (Libraries Unlimited, 1992) as well as coauthor (with Constance D. Williams) of *The Child Care Catalog* (Libraries Unlimited, 1985). She has published numerous articles in professional journals and regularly presents her work at national conferences dealing with learning disabilities, education, social work, and child welfare.

Although many parents and teachers traditionally have viewed an ADHD label as negative, and the connotations associated with being hyperactive usually have evoked frowns and worries, most people actually value high energy, creativity, spontaneity, and humor: the characteristics frequently displayed by children and adults with an attention deficit disorder. ADHD children may have trouble learning because of their attention deficit (it is hard to learn when paying attention is not something you do very well) or because they have a specific learning dysfunction besides the attention difficulties. (Learning problems can be the result of specific visual, perceptual, motor, or auditory weaknesses, or combinations of several of these dysfluencies. Soft-sign neurological vulnerabilities may be the issue when children perform inconsistently in the same subject area, or erratically across the board, so that one subject area is substantially weaker than others.) Most children with learning difficulties and most children with attention deficits are likely to be very fine, capable, wonderful adults once they have managed to make it through "a place called school" (Goodlad, 1984). Many ADHD individuals are creative, interesting, productive, enthusiastic, and able adults, who are as successful as they are precisely because of their energy, their quickness, their ability to move through a situation without becoming bogged down by details, and because of their incredible stamina.

For the most part, these energetic, fast-paced adults have not "outgrown" their attention deficit; nor have they "channeled their energy" or "managed their behaviors." Rather, they have, in the adult world, been given the freedom to choose their own direction and to use their unique style to their distinct advantage. These individuals are, in fact, often those we all envy because they "do" so much and have so many interests and ideas. It is curious that we should value the same traits in adults that we disdain in children. The truth is, the individual has probably not changed much at all; only the social perception and expectations have changed. Adults are not required to sit in a classroom all day attending to tasks that draw out all their weaknesses. Instead, they lead multifarious lives that allow them to be busy and active and that permit them to be involved in numerous projects and activities simultaneously. They usually do not do just one thing at a time, and they are more successful as a result. There are also some drawbacks: attention deficit and/or hyperactive adults continue to be hard to live with because often they are not focused, relaxed, or calm individuals. Not being well organized, they find it hard to maintain a schedule. Consistency and predictability are not strong traits for ADHD individuals any time in their lives, but emotionally they can feel better when they are older because they are not constantly being told to sit down or slow down or pay attention to this particular work sheet, and so forth.

As youngsters, ADHD children are typically impulsive, active, bursting with energy and ideas, and, thus, difficult to handle in one's classroom or home. Since they cannot choose their own activities and design their own schedules (or lack of schedules), and since they are required to go along with the group, to comply, to compromise, to fit in, they are frequently thwarted by those in charge of their various environmental settings. This is less true for adults, who have more opportunities to manage their own lives. ADHD adults have more leeway available in their choices of activities, work, lifestyle, and peers than do ADHD children, who are obliged to go to school and attend to specific subjects at certain times. The fourth grader cannot readily say to the teacher that the spelling test is not on the child's personal agenda for the day, and that the child will choose to go to the playground instead, thank you. Adults, however, *can* choose jobs more likely to meet their individual needs and style. It is unlikely that an adult who is enormously gregarious, energetic, creative, and fast-thinking would select the want-ad job requesting a gentle, quiet companion for an older woman who enjoys knitting and chats in the garden.

In my own practice, I focus on giving children choices because I think that they need to learn how to make and use them. I also try to build in the break periods that ADHD children need because I hope to show them how taking a planned time-off enables them to work better. ADHD children are so often random about their play and their activities that I try to help them to think about how to select what they want to do and when:

> Jared is a wiry, active, first grader who comes to my office once a week for reading tutoring. I have many interesting varieties of timers in my office—all of which get used during the busy hour session that Jared spends with me. As a warm-up, we

start with the five-minute egg-timer, and do a brief activity; then Jared is allowed to choose what it is he will play with later on during his free time. Next we move to a ten-minute timer, and do some seatwork, after which he is given a chance to run down the hall for a drink of water. As such, we proceed, using increasingly long periods of work time, followed by a break in which Jared does something of his own choosing.

Children who have learning difficulties without an attention deficit need break periods, too, but not nearly as often as children like Jared do. For me, and for many students, these constant interruptions interfere with the flow of what is being taught or learned, but students like Jared can concentrate better when they are provided with stretches between innings. It is important for the teacher or parent to structure these breaks, however, because it is not helpful to the child if they occur randomly or inconsistently.

The young child in school may recognize that large classes and busy environments are overstimulating and distracting for him or her, but there is nothing the child can do to avoid or compensate for this in the school setting. Ignoring distractions—something the child is incapable of doing—is what is repeatedly required of him or her. On the other hand, adults who know that large crowds, busy places, and highly stimulating environments are incompatible with their personal style can look for a job situation that is equally intellectual and challenging, but one in which the setting provides fewer distractions and less environmental stress.

If we keep the above facts in mind, we may think differently about how and why we need to alter our approaches to teaching and working with children with an attention deficit and/or a hyperactivity disorder. It also is important to remember that children generally like to please others and usually want to participate in ways that are engaging to their peers. They know that it is not in their best interest to be disruptive, alienated, and negative in class or at home. Becoming the class clown sometimes earns secondary rewards, so this behavior does get reinforced, but in my experience children would rather not assume contrived roles if they see viable alternatives. As teachers and as meaningful adults, we must think about how we might provide ADHD youngsters with a "growth producing environment" (Greenspan, 1988) rather than with an environment that perpetuates self-defeating behaviors.

Just as many children with specific dysfunctions appear to be "hyperactive" because their learning difficulties inhibit them from sustained attention, many youngsters with attentional problems have trouble learning because they cannot attend to a task or an explanation long enough to understand it, practice it, and master it. All these children need more than the usual amount of sensitivity, individual instruction, and follow-up than do most students. All students benefit from individual direction and personal attention; all value choice. What the ADHD child needs is not qualitatively different from what other students require; they just may need more of it, or more monitoring and structuring of their work and their behavior. Consistency and predictability are important ingredients in child-rearing at home and at school, whether for an especially active, impulsive youngster or for a quiet, diligent child. The qualities needed by teachers to work effectively with ADHD students are thus the same as those needed by all adults working with children, although it may be that the ADHD child requires more input more often than do most of his or her peers. The input may need to be more guided and structured, since ADHD children have trouble focusing their attention by themselves. ADHD children also require an enormous amount of flexibility and understanding from the adults in charge of them.

Like other students with learning difficulties—or hidden handicaps—children with an attention deficit can be hard to recognize as youngsters who need special attention because they often look and act "so normal." Even their impulsivity and their hyperactivity are relatively normal-looking behaviors. These children are not unusual or odd behaviorally; rather, they are just in high gear, doing more of what every child does. They may be louder and busier than most children, but what they do or say is generally not bizarre or strange. It is their "normalcy," then, that becomes their own worst enemy; they look and talk like most children, but they are, nevertheless, unable to control their attentional capacity. Trying very hard may work for a short time, but that becomes another detriment because success increases the likelihood of the teacher or parent saying: "He can do it when he tries," or "He is capable of doing the work; he is just lazy." While this may be relatively true at times, the "trying" comes with a very high price tag. In other words, trying is very tiring, and it can only be a short-term effort because the cost of attending is so exhausting that the ADHD individual cannot maintain that level of effort for very long. Despite their high energy level, intense attention depletes their productivity and further inhibits their success. Interestingly, while some children may fall asleep or wear out at this point, many others become even more wound up. In an effort to stay awake, they become even more scattered and impulsive, even more active and disruptive.

> Kathy is an eight-year-old who is like many ADHD children in that she becomes exhausted when doing academic work but can play with her toys on her own for a relatively long time. Reading and writing or math tasks require a specific kind of focused attention, but in her own play, she can quickly change subjects or items or conversations, and the play goes on. Kathy likes to play with dolls, but if one listens to the content of the doll conversation, one observes frequent idea shifts and topic adjustments. She brings out many toys in a few minutes and shows little cohesion or congruity in using them.

It is important, too, not to overlook the attention deficit child who is not hyperactive physically and thus does not stand out or make trouble in the classroom. Some children with an attention deficit do not have hyperactive behaviors or enormous physical energy accompanying their attention difficulties. This is the youngster who may appear to be a daydreamer or the one who is called nonfocused. "Doesn't stay on task" is a frequent description of this student. Quiet children who have an attention deficit disorder usually do not acquire help and remediation as early as do their more disruptive and energetic cohorts. They may lose more ground in school because they are overlooked longer. Emotionally, they suffer just as much because they become anxious about not being able to do their work and about the comments loaded upon them by teachers and parents who insist that they could do better if they tried harder. Figure 4–1 suggests some of the negative emotions that attention deficit students often experience in the place called school.

In looking at a setting or classroom that facilitates good learning for the unconventional student—particularly for the child who struggles with distractibility and impulsivity—one might want to keep in mind the following considerations. Just as we do not expect the blind student to be able to see, we should not expect the ADHD child to sit still for long periods, to work attentively for more than a few minutes, to ignore visual or auditory distractions in or outside of the classroom, or to remain engaged with a project for extended class sessions. Certainly the long-range goal is to help such students lengthen their span of attention and decrease their distractibility, but the means to these goals may be circuitous. It takes time and practice and a variety of approaches to help children move along the road. Keeping work expectations in small packages and managing behaviors one at a time are strategies that usually do help. Altering our own expectations for the children can facilitate their ability to succeed and can improve their self-esteem through achievement.

One way of helping a child to achieve is by asking the child to become involved in setting achievement goals and by jointly planning the means of reaching those goals. Too often, we forget to talk to children about what they want and need; we forget to include them in their own growing up and learning process. Asking a child what kind of help is needed or listening to a student talk about when he or she wants to work on something independently might give teachers and parents clues as to the child's particular learning style. Children probably work more successfully when they feel that the project is in their control—which does not preclude their asking for help or supervision, and which still allows the teacher or parent to have some guidelines or rules that must be followed.

> Brad is a seven-year-old who is very bright and humorous. This youngster never sits down for more than forty-five seconds at a time. Since his teacher is always annoyed with his persistent activity and lack of focus, Brad set a goal of trying to

FIGURE 4–1. *How ADHD Children Might Feel in School.*

Worried that they will not be able to follow the instructions

Scared about not being able to get all of their work finished

Embarrassed that their work does not look as nice or is "not as good" as most other students' work

Concerned that they could not or did not write the ideas in their head

Frustrated that they are not able to control their behaviors and their moods

Afraid that teachers and students will be annoyed with them

Anxious about losing track, daydreaming, checking out, and needing to move around stay in his seat longer. He and I have decided together to work on "task-completion."

"Brad," I say, as he bounces in the door and skyrockets toward the toy shelf, "remember the agreement that we talked about last week? Do you remember that we decided that you would come in and sit down at the desk for ten minutes of work, and that after every ten minutes you could get up and play for five minutes?"

"Oh! Yeah! I do!" Brad exclaims, jet-propelling himself toward the desk.

I have work laid out on the desk, but Brad has pencil in hand and is attacking the paper in front of him almost before I can catch my breath. Purposely, I have not written out any directions, and it is not clear what one is supposed to do, so when Brad starts to write out "answers," I know that he is just acting impulsively.

"Wait a minute, Brad," I say. "We need to talk for a minute about what you are going to do here."

"I know how to do these problems; they're easy," he remarks.

"Those aren't problems, Brad; they are answers. I want you to make up the problems that go with these answers."

With Brad momentarily taken aback, I have an opportunity to discuss with him the importance of waiting a few minutes to listen to a teacher so that he can understand all the directions. Asking Brad to write the problems for me makes this work more interesting to him. I ask him to make up a test that would be a good one for other kids in his class to take the next day. At the end of the ten minutes, Brad is not finished working out his problems, but I tell him that ten minutes have passed and ask if he would like to take his five-minute break. He chooses to forgo the break and keeps on working. In this way Brad has had a chance to monitor his own schedule, and he can feel more in control of his actions. He has also managed to stay in his seat longer and to complete a task, but much of that had to do with the very high interest level of the task. All school work does not present this same challenge.

Children with ADHD should be given work that necessitates their taking time to think and to problem-solve rather than allowing them to supply ready answers impulsively. Since these are speedy students (ones who do very well on beat-the-clock tests on math facts or spelling words), they need more opportunities to reflect and to sort through various possibilities of answers. It is good to ask them to explain why they chose the response they did, even if it is a correct answer. One also might inquire as to why they chose to discard some other response. They should learn that the teacher will not accept "because," "I don't know," "I just did," or "I just guessed" as satisfactory replies.

As discussed above, teachers will do well to anticipate that any extended effort by an ADHD child is going to be compensated by fatigue, which usually takes the form of hyperactivity and restlessness, not of sleep or drowsiness. It is a very good idea to plan a major break after intense reading, writing, or math periods. For the ADHD student, a break usually means doing something physical. While some students may enjoy reading a book, listening to music, or lying down daydreaming, the ADHD child will probably do better if given a chance to go out to the playground, to run some in-school errands, to make some noise, and to do something not requiring cooperation or interaction. Solitary play, free choice, and physical activity facilitate regrouping for this student. Without this kind of "relaxation" period, the ADHD student will probably be unable to carry on effectively. Although many teachers are reluctant to allow certain children to have special compensation time, it is well worth their while to do so in the case of ADHD children. The resulting havoc in the classroom if this type of student is *not* allowed to unwind is not worth the price. In fact, everyone, all students and the teacher, will benefit from giving high maintenance children a chance to reduce their energy level.

Once again, it is important that the adult not assume what will work for the child as a means of energy reduction. The teacher should ask how the student would like to use a ten-minute break time. "Do you want to go outside for a few minutes, or would you like to sit in the classroom and draw?" might be one way of presenting a choice. Alternatively, the teacher could say to the entire class that they would be having a short break, and that children could choose from three or four activities during that time. The activities offered must, in fact, comprise a wide variety so that there is opportunity to rest quietly or to play actively, to be alone or to be in a group, to be with the teacher or to be away from the teacher. Intuitively, children seem to have some sense of what they need to make themselves feel good. It is critical that the school day incorporate some time periods in which they have a chance to experiment with choosing activities that work (or don't) for them. In this way they learn how to become better problem solvers and better thinkers. Since the adult world does allow for more choice vocationally and avocationally, children need opportunities to make choices, trying out and practicing their skills, their likes and dislikes, in various situations.

A paradoxical, dichotomous situation that presents itself in working with ADHD children (as the reader will have noted by now) is that, on the one hand, ADHD children need structure and routine; but on the other hand, they need to be given a fair amount of independence and choice. Flexibility really becomes the key word in working with and in teaching ADHD children, maybe all children. Children with an attention deficit become anxious quickly if they do not know the routine and if consistency is not available; their anxiety then increases their activity level and decreases their attentional abilities. Even so, when they find a person or a schedule too rigid, they become scared and recalcitrant in that situation as well. What most ADHD youngsters are lacking is a good internal regulatory system, which means that they cannot always control or monitor their thoughts and their actions in the way they would like. Usually, they can tell you what it is they are supposed to be doing; they can recite the classroom or school rules. They know these things intellectually, but they can't make their bodies work in a way so as to carry out what they understand they should be doing. If they receive a new instruction while they are feeling "stuck" about where they already are, they will likely miss the new incoming information. This puts them doubly behind. They can't do what they thought they were supposed to be doing; now someone is saying something new, and they know they have no chance of doing that at all. Often, they may not even "hear" what is being said to them if they are still concentrating on something else.

Teachers who are aware of this kind of dilemma can set up a system of reciprocal cue-giving with the child. The teacher needs to work *with* the student during these difficult times. It is usually best to have a moment of one-on-one, or at least a soft hand on the shoulder, in order to calm the child down and facilitate a process of regrouping. A "let's take it slowly" approach is an effective one. Asking the child what he or she needs at the time can be beneficial, too. Maybe a walk around the classroom or a drink of water can help the child to reorient to what is going on in the room. Even a prediction or a promise of what can happen next might be helpful: "Let's do just three more lines here on this page, and then you may go outside for a few minutes."

Some things that we know are hard for ADHD students include important skills such as reflecting, planning, self-monitoring, filtering out distractions, controlling one's moods, and limiting one's activity level. Impulsivity is a major nemesis for those with ADHD, and teachers of these students are constantly battling against the child's inability to refrain from acting on his or her impulses. Anything that involves a series of directions or steps, extensive details, or orderliness is likely to be met with failure. Some of the difficulties ADHD children experience in school are listed in Figure 4–2.

Appreciating the fact that ADHD children rarely are misbehaving on purpose enables teachers to work more carefully and specifically with these students. As mentioned earlier, it is a good idea to break work and learning into small pieces, one step at a time with a "rest" or "time out" in between. This is not at all meant to imply that one should teach isolated skills all day long. Rather, a child might be presented with a theme or unit, or even a story, as a large picture, but that overall picture plan will have components that need to be looked at separately. One could use the example of an auto mechanic who does not just fix the whole car with a wave of a magic wand. The mechanic must deal with each piece of the car's inner parts individually to be sure that each one functions. Similarly, one must learn how to present ideas in an appropriate order, to spell words, to punctuate, and to write or type in order to complete a piece of writing that can easily be read, understood, and appreciated. Since ADHD children have a tendency to be big-picture people, it is

---

FIGURE 4–2. *What Children with ADHD May Have Trouble Doing.*

Choosing the right piece of information on which to concentrate

Staying focused on the right information for the right amount of time

Filtering out distractions

Coping with details or a series of instructions

Planning and monitoring work and behavior

Not talking or acting impulsively

---

important to spend some time helping them learn how to focus on details and on smaller units. ADHD children usually are impatient about details or "insignificant" facts, but they then make many errors in school and in life because they did not pay attention to all the directions or the parts of the instructions. (For young children, Simon Says is a very good game for practicing listening skills. "Find the things that are wrong in this picture" is another good way of practicing detail-focusing. Older children might be given a paragraph containing one misspelled word or one grammatical error to find and correct. Looking at paintings and being asked to locate one small detail in the picture is good practice, too.)

In addition to praising and encouraging a child's strengths, helping each individual child to recognize weaknesses is, I think, an important component to understanding his or her whole self. No one does everything well, so it is just as helpful to know what causes us trouble as it is to know what we accomplish easily. An ADHD child should have a chance to work on impulsivity, tuning out, getting restless, or whatever trait(s) gets in the way on a consistent basis. Children need to be helped to practice doing or not doing the difficult things. One child may need to practice sitting just a little longer before getting up (like Brad, in the example above), while another youngster may need to work on writing one more sentence, doing one extra math problem, or proofreading.

Sitting near the teacher or a designated partner is another useful strategy for the ADHD child. A cue system can be established so that the teacher will touch the child's shoulder or desk when the student has tuned out. A sensitive buddy or partner can be helpful in this way, too, so that the student doesn't feel singled out by the teacher. The buddy might be particularly helpful during a study hall or homework period. Parents or siblings can be beneficial during homework time too; they can help to monitor on-task work times and to alternate these with short periods for a break from studies.

Most ADHD children, especially those who do not have complicating learning dysfunctions, can and should be placed in regular classrooms if the school does not have an open classroom or pod system that is overly distracting, and if the classroom size is not too large. A whole language approach to learning is expedient for these students. It encourages a significant amount of choice and helps them to integrate their learning and to make sense of the various pieces of information they amass. Keeping things together is not an asset of ADHD individuals; therefore an integrated approach to learning is very valuable. It doesn't feel as though you have to remember so many parts if science is not separate from history or spelling. Cohesive learning takes place when subject matter is interrelated. A whole language approach is beneficial for these students in facilitating their efforts to bring meaning to a world that otherwise often seems fragmented and at odds for them. ADHD students have an opportunity to contribute more to a whole language classroom environment than they may feel able to do in more traditional settings, where they may not "know the answer" or be able to come up with the specific bit of information required. Collaborative and cooperative learning are common in whole language classrooms, and this emphasis, too, is valuable for ADHD students, who can profit by having another student or two around to help them with their work and their behavior. Also, they have an opportunity to work on one piece of a project that will fit into a final whole rather than having to do the entire project on their own. Figure 4–3 summarizes some of the practical ways in which teachers and others can help children with ADHD.

Even more important than the structure or the curriculum of the classroom, however, are the understanding, sensitivity, and training of the teacher. It is critical that the teacher appreciate that a child's alleged IQ, cognitive ability, or label of ADHD or learning disabled are not the measures by which the student should be taught or judged. ADHD children *can* learn what other bright students learn, but *how* they go about learning it is different. Some children with attention deficit disorders acquire information or knowledge quickly, but they have no patience for practicing or demonstrating what they are learning. Other children with ADHD cannot learn by reading or listening alone; they depend highly on the use of tangible manipulatives and they need to be intensively involved in their learning process. None of them can be expected to sit for extended periods of time without losing the train of thought—the teacher's or their own. Most of them come with high anxiety levels because they have learned quickly that they "forget" or "don't know" or "didn't pay attention to" whatever it is they were expected to have learned.

Ideally, teachers will receive some training specifically concerning attention deficit disorders and the various manifestations of this disorder. It is also useful for teachers to be taught techniques that have proven to be successful

FIGURE 4–3. *How Teachers and Others Can Help Children with ADHD.*

Write directions down as well as give them orally

Ask the child to repeat the instructions back to the person giving them

Use pictures and manipulatives in teaching and explaining

Have a personal code system between the teacher or parent and the child for monitoring in-class or social behaviors

Play games and do exercises that practice desired behaviors

Provide structure and planned programs that help children to organize and to monitor their behaviors

Establish schedules that build in frequent and physically active breaks

Offer choice, and allow for flexibility within the structure

Prepare the child for what will happen next

Understand and tolerate mistakes and use them for learning

Teach goal setting; plan for, and monitor, realistic steps toward goal achievement

Be careful not to overstimulate or to overexhaust

Limit possibilities of distraction and diversion

in working with ADHD students and to have a back-up person or supervisor to whom they can go for both suggestions and support. Working closely with parents will be beneficial for teachers, parents, and the student because all these people need someone with whom to go the extra mile. The energy and creativity of ADHD students should be utilized and valued rather than squelched! The energy is there, and denying it can only bring on frustration and emotional disruption. In any event, it can be exciting to meet the challenge of a child's enthusiasm and energy. Doing so brings satisfying results to all concerned.

There is great promise lurking in those with attention deficits because often these students see and hear things that others do not. They have ideas and thoughts that do not occur to other students. They may have uncanny abilities to remember details of events or pictures or tales—details that they can transform into marvelous inventions and stories. Many ADHD children are wonderful athletes with outstanding physical endurance, and most youngsters with attentional disorders have the potential for developing into highly energetic and successful adults who contribute creatively and productively to their communities.

If twelve, sixteen, or eighteen years of school are what lie between the emerging child and the emerging adult, this significant amount of time must be mostly positive and productive; but ADHD students are at risk for spending school year after school year in the bleak shadows of failure and frustration. While it is true that many ADHD children are more taxing for parents and teachers than are the quieter, more focused students, it is also true that the rewards sometimes feel richer and the challenge can be more invigorating. Even when this is not the case, however, all children have the right to learn and to spend their school day in an environment that feels emotionally safe as well as educationally stimulating. As we come to appreciate the individual styles and needs of children with an attention deficit, we typically become better teachers and role models for these clever and intriguing youngsters. It is not fair to them to have to wait for adulthood to have their hour of glory. Childhood and the social and academic life of school must belong to all students, not just to those who fit the norm or the statistical average. A lovely Chinese proverb says that small children should be handled like small fish: gently. Teachers would do well to offer this kindness to each little fish in the school!

References

Brobeck, J. K. (1990). Teachers do make a difference. *Journal of Learning Disabilities, 23,* (1), 11–12.

Clark, B. (1986). *Optimizing learning: The integrative education model in the classroom.* Columbus, OH: Merrill Publishing.

Comfort, R. (1992). *Teaching the unconventional child.* Denver, CO: Libraries Unlimited.

Cruickshank, W., Bentzen, F., Ratzeburg, F., & Tannhauser, M. (1961). *A teaching method for brain-injured and hyperactive children.* Syracuse, NY: Syracuse University Press.

Goodlad, J. (1984). *A place called school: Prospects for the future.* New York: McGraw Hill.

Greenspan, S. (1988). Fostering emotional and social development in infants with disabilities. *Zero to three, No. 1, (September).*

Levine, M. (1986). *Attention Deficit Disorders: The diverse effect of weak control systems in childhood.* Cambridge, MA: Educators Publishing Service.

Lewis, R. (1983). Teaching special students in the mainstream. Columbus, OH: Charles Merrill.

Stafford, P. (1987). *Integrated teaching in early childhood.* New York: Harper & Row.

Thomas, A., & Chess, S. (1977). *Temperament and development.* New York: Brunner/Mazel.

Vail, P. (1987). *Smart kids with school problems.* New York: Dutton.

Wender, P. (1987). *The hyperactive child, adolescent, and adult.* New York: Oxford University Press.

5

Adapting the Whole Language Classroom to ADD/ADHD Emergent Readers

Cinda Kochen

In many respects Cinda's article reflects the "traditional," behavioristic, skills-oriented view of education and of the difficulties experienced by the AD(H)D student. Drawing upon some of the professional literature that describes AD(H)D in medical terms, she writes, for example, of difficulties with such skills as short-term memory and visual memory—isolated skills that have frequently been tested by school psychologists. She writes, too, of "past maladaptive habits," another term reflective of the medical and behavioral models that emphasize what AD(H)D students do wrong and cannot do, locating the AD(H)D students' difficulties solely within the individuals themselves.

This fundamental orientation to a medical model and to behavioral psychology together reflect the traditional view of AD(H)D students that most other authors in this volume explicitly or implicitly reject. By providing a sharp contrast, Cinda's article helps us understand the perspective that these other teachers, teacher educators, parents, and AD(H)D students themselves decry as less effective and less appropriate for AD(H)D students than teaching that reflects a transactional, constructivist, and social view of learning.

And yet this is not the whole story. Cinda's article also indicates some acquaintance with whole language learning and teaching that reflects the emerging paradigm. Furthermore, I would urge other readers oriented to this new paradigm not to let the traditional terminology or perspective overshadow the other contributions that this article makes to the volume. For example, Cinda indicates the frequent value of medication for AD(H)D students, something those who eschew a medical model are likely to forget or to reject with insufficient knowledge of its possible benefits. In addition, understanding what is particularly difficult for most AD(H)D students should help even whole language teachers more readily accept these students, avoid accentuating their difficulties, and work around and/or deal more effectively with what is difficult for them—while recognizing, building upon, emphasizing, and celebrating their strengths. In fact, readers of subsequent articles may be surprised to find some of Cinda's suggestions actualized in classrooms that are conceptualized and described in radically different terms and from a different perspective.

Cinda Kochen received her Ph.D. in reading from the University of Colorado and also holds degrees in special education, elementary education, and learning disabilities. She has taught at all levels, from preschool through graduate school. An educator and parent of three children, Cinda has also developed educational programs for learning disabled and emotionally disturbed students.

As coauthor of *The Baby Swim Book: A TLC Approach for Teaching Your Child to Swim,* Cinda helped develop a swimming method for babies and toddlers that incorporated child development practices uniquely suited to various personality types. In 1985 she was named Colorado Young Mother of the Year.

> John had not much affection for his mother and sisters, and an antipathy to me. He bullied and punished me; not two or three times in the week, nor once or twice in the day, but continually. . . . There were moments when I was bewildered by the terror he inspired.

Jane Eyre angrily related these words in Charlotte Brontë's novel of nineteenth-century England (Brontë, 1847, p. 9).

She could just as easily have been describing an ADHD child living today. The ADHD child's constant movement, distractibility, drive to satisfy self-centered impulses, and lack of social skills can be bewildering and terrifying. The difference between then and now is that such children today, with caring and informed teachers and parents, have a chance of being understood rather than being blamed for their disruptiveness. As for John Reed's fate in the 1800s,

> He could not do worse: he ruined his health and his estate amongst the worst men and the worst women. He got into debt and into jail: his mother helped him out twice but as soon as he was free he returned to his old companions and his old habits. His head was not strong. . . . How he died, God knows (they say he killed himself). (Brontë, 1847, p. 198).

The prospects of a happy life for ADD/ADHD children were grim in past years. The prospects are still grim when such children find themselves in a classroom where lessons are not adapted to their unique needs. Indeed, it was not until the late 1980s, when medical research cut through the confusion surrounding hyperactivity and distractibility, that the physiological basis for and the psychological and behavioral manifestations of ADD/ADHD began to be understood.

This understanding is crucial to whole language teachers, since uncontrolled ADD/ADHD children can disrupt classroom procedures and negatively affect other children's learning. Moreover, the benefits of the whole language curriculum may pass by ADD/ADHD children unless modifications are made. These modifications fall into 3 categories: one, reduction of the children's hyperactivity and distractibility; two, modification of typical ADD/ADHD behaviors; three, adaptation of the whole language curriculum, especially at the emergent level. Attention Deficit Disorder without the hyperactivity component (ADD) and Attention Deficit Hyperactivity Disorder (ADHD) affect 3 to 5 percent of all schoolchildren (Braswell, Bloomquist, & Pederson, 1991, p. 6). In other words, each classroom of twenty-five children has a good chance of containing one such child.

Reduction of Hyperactivity and Distractibility

To modify the behavior of most ADD/ADHD children, it is helpful to first alter the physiological basis for their behavior. Attempts to change hyperactivity and distractibility with behavior modification training alone have been relatively ineffective. Try as they might to sit still, attend to directions, and to finish an assignment, unmedicated ADD/ADHD children frequently find that their physiology overrules their good intentions. Their resulting frustration, as well as that of parents, teachers, and peers, can quickly regress into the expectation of failure and emotional disturbance.

To make ADHD students' physiological functioning more compatible with learning situations, methylphenidate, a medication marketed under the name of Ritalin, is often used to stimulate the sluggish functioning of a particular area of the brain associated with attention. Medication has been shown in numerous empirical studies to be effective in reducing impulsivity and distractibility; however, its benefits to academic learning are general and not specific (Balthazor, Wagner, & Pelham, 1991, pp. 35–52). Medication merely improves the ability to cooperate and to respond to suggestions made by parents and teachers. It enables the children to attend to a situation long enough to understand what is expected of them and to carry out that expectation before being distracted.

For most unmedicated ADD/ADHD children the time used to process a situation is often too fast for thoughtful consideration of the appropriate response. In contrast, their actual motor response is slower than that of their peers. The double-bind result of this lack of time spent processing response alternatives, combined with a slow motor reaction, is often incorrect answers (Klorman, Brumaghim, Fitzpatrick, & Borgstedt, 1991, pp. 263–83). Medication appears to lengthen response processing time, improves vigilance in selecting appropriate answers, and leads to more accurate reactions (deSonneville, Njiokiktjien, & Hilhorst, 1991, pp. 285–95). The children are able to attend longer to oral directions and to process these directions more efficiently (Keith & Engineer, 1991, pp. 630–36). Although the improvement these children make cannot automatically be generalized to classroom learning, it does indicate that medication can be beneficial.

While Ritalin has been shown to be extremely helpful, it will not cure the problems of ADD/ADHD children; it only alleviates them temporarily. It does not have an appreciable effect on short-term memory nor on visual memory (deSonneville, Njiokiktjien, & Hilhorst, 1991, pp. 285–95). Moreover, Ritalin has little direct effect on social behavior. Since social behavior largely consists of learned habits, those antisocial habits must be unlearned; new, appropriate habits must take their place. Medication is merely a helpful tool that enables ADD/ADHD children to be receptive to learning new habits.

Modification of ADD/ADHD Behavior

While medication prepares the fertile ground necessary for growth and change in the children's behavior, past maladaptive habits remain part of their response repertoire. Like weeds, these habits are tenaciously rooted in the ADD/ADHD students' approach to learning. They are still their modus operandi. These old responses must be uprooted and replaced by new, effective learning habits that bring the children rewarding results.

Common maladaptive responses that often persist include impulsiveness, expectation of failure, obliviousness to authority figures, avoidance of social situations, search for positive reinforcement outside the classroom lesson, and search for negative attention within the classroom. In addition, despite the fact that medication reduces distractibility, ADD/ADHD students may still experience lapses in attention. They also may continue to exhibit temporal confusion, as shown by their inability to budget time and their lack of awareness of what they should be doing at any given moment.

Trying to replace these unproductive responses is discouraging, but success is possible in almost every situation. Whole language teachers, in particular, have the advantage of an approach that meshes easily with ADD/ADHD learners' needs. Modifications of their classroom approach and curriculum should come easily. The difficulty of implementing a plan to meet these children's needs comes not from the "what" that has to be done, but in the relentless persistence needed to carry out that "what." The course will be uphill, but with determination the crest of that hill can be reached. The course also will be easier if there is a plan that includes not only objectives to reduce maladaptive responses but also ways to replace them with appropriate behaviors.

Impulsiveness

Specific behaviors into which impulsiveness can be broken down include jumping to conclusions, failure to take time to evaluate all alternatives, and lack of a repertoire of rehearsal strategies to work through a plan of action logically. Essentially, the response of jumping to conclusions needs to be reduced; it needs to be replaced with time to process possible answers and a plan for how that processing should proceed.

For whole language teachers, this means checking in with ADD/ADHD students shortly after students begin working and before they have a chance to jump to a conclusion and get off track. Students then can be steered in the right direction by asking for their plan in accomplishing their personal objective that day. What will they do first? How will they do it? What tools, books, or information do they need? Where can they find those tools? Where is a good place to carry out their goals?

After getting the ADD/ADHD students started, teachers should monitor their progress from a distance, ready to intervene immediately whenever the students become distracted from their plan. Even if all is going well and the students are constructively occupied, teachers should stop by every five minutes to reinforce and encourage the students. They should give positive reinforcement, either tangible or social, whenever the students stick to their plan. Praise also should be given to students who patiently try to do a thorough job rather than simply finish the work to hand in quickly with little effort invested in doing their best.

Expectation of Failure

Another important set of objectives for changing ADD/ADHD children's behavior addresses their expectation of failure. By the time these children reach school age, many have become entrapped in the vicious cycle of failing and, therefore, expecting to fail. Their failure does not result from lack of learning ability but rather from their short attention span. Distractibility leads to noncompletion of an activity. This, in turn, usually leads to frustration and negative reinforcement. The next time they are directed to a constructive activity they avoid it because they expect frustration and failure again.

Even when teachers adapt activities so that children are assured of success, it's only the teachers who are aware of that assuredness; thus, it is not surprising that most children continue to avoid trying. Until they experience repeated successes, they will direct their intellect into task avoidance rather than into task completion. If those repeated successes do not come early in the children's education, that expectation may evolve into learned helplessness. Because they do not know how to make their environment work for them, they will avoid challenges and will wait for teachers, parents, or peers to rescue them.

To reverse this expectation for failure, teachers must replace it with expectations for success. In the whole language classroom, most students expect success. They have been allowed to choose the materials they like and to explore them at their own level. Self-motivation and persistence are usually inherent in the learning process, and students are involved, happy, and successful. For most ADD/ADHD students, however, the process breaks down because self-motivation is usually not strong enough to build the persistence needed to finish what they set out to do. Distractibility overpowers self-motivation, and the students once again experience failure.

Whole language teachers are accustomed to their students' self-motivation and their consequent pride in their achievements. In dealing with ADD/ADHD students, however, teachers must point out all the little achievements that lead up to a successful learning session. Teachers must arrange those first challenges so that the children feel success immediately and frequently. Neither should it be taken for granted that most ADD/ADHD students know success when they see it. They often are oblivious to success and their role in achieving that success. During their initial experiences with success in the classroom, they rely on teachers to make that connection for them.

Obliviousness to Authority Figures

Most ADD/ADHD children are attracted to whatever meets their immediate needs and satisfies their curiosity. This approach to learning is very compatible with the whole language approach, since it emphasizes child-centered rather than teacher-centered motivation. Problems begin to occur, though, when ADD/ADHD students' natural interpretation of child-centeredness leads to the exclusion of teachers. In reality, these students need more teacher input to stay on task and need more positive reinforcement than do most other students. But teachers must be careful only to encourage the students and not to complete the task for them, for the latter leads to learned helplessness.

Teachers can effectively alter their ADD/ADHD children's perceptions and get them to view adult assistance as valuable in satisfying their curiosity and meeting their goals. Teachers must be careful, though, to build their role as a catalyst to the learning process rather than as a crutch. If teachers provide a structure that students can use to achieve their own goals, the students will begin to see the value of their teachers and be more willing to approach them for help. Initially, the teachers may be seen merely as a tool to help the ADD/ADHD children achieve their own objectives. Later, a bond may begin to form between teacher and child, opening the door to interpersonal reinforcement.

Avoidance of Social Situations

Failure to initiate satisfying social interactions is as debilitating to most ADD/ADHD children as is failure to complete classroom activities. The intense distractibility inherent in their moment-to-moment existence prevents them from maintaining a social interaction long enough for a satisfactory relationship to get started. They do not have the patience to wait their turn or to listen to another person's opinions. Their typical lack of eye contact builds an unseen wall around them that few peers or even adults try to penetrate. Those peers who do initiate a social interaction are often overwhelmed by the whirlwind of impulsive physical activity that surrounds the ADD/ADHD children's drive to satisfy their need for stimulation.

Facilitating positive social interactions with peers and reducing alienation comprise, perhaps, the most difficult set of objectives for teachers to enact. They must change not only the behavior of the ADD/ADHD children but also the behavior of their peers. Once again, the whole language classroom is conducive to effecting these changes, as learning is often cooperative and accomplished in pairs or small groups. The drawback of the whole language classroom is that the antisocial nature of ADD/ADHD children can be embarrassingly apparent when their peer interactions become contentious.

The objectives in improving the sociability of these children can be broken into four categories: reducing maladaptive social behaviors in the ADD/ADHD children, increasing appropriate social behaviors in the ADD/ADHD children, reducing avoidance of ADD/ADHD children by their peers, and increasing initiation of social interactions by their peers. The teachers' role in carrying out these objectives is like that of a symphony conductor—they must coax a discordant group of individuals to subordinate their personal needs in order to coordinate a much more rewarding interpersonal achievement.

Although it may seem superficial, one effective route to increasing social interactions is to use primary rewards such as stickers, food, toys, or privileges earned by getting points for engaging in key behaviors. Key behaviors found in satisfying social relationships include eye contact, sharing materials, listening, and taking turns. By first using primary rewards to reinforce the key behaviors, teachers allow enough time for secondary, interpersonal rewards to incubate, until they are capable by themselves of motivating ADD/ADHD children to seek out social interaction.

Teachers often avoid primary reinforcers in favor of the self-satisfaction that comes from within the children. However, effective socializing often requires ADD/ADHD students to refrain from acting on their impulses, which they cannot easily do. Therefore, their attempts to socialize are often rejected and socialization becomes more frustrating than satisfying. Just as infants are concerned only with having their immediate needs met and must go through a lengthy process of maturation before the desire to please others becomes a source of pleasure, so ADD/ADHD children must be given time to learn to restrain their impulsivity. Primary reinforcers may actually help speed this learning process. For some ADD/ADHD children, if teachers wait for sociability to arise spontaneously without the advantage of primary reinforcers, they may find that it is slow to develop a foothold.

The Search for Positive Reinforcement Outside the Classroom Lesson

Often the distractibility of ADD/ADHD is thought of as being stimulated by objects and events outside the individual. In the past some teachers were encouraged to remove stimulation from the environment to the extent that they were not to wear make-up or jewelry or to decorate the classroom. In actuality, distractibility is stimulated as much from within the children themselves as it is from their surroundings. Even if they were placed in an empty, soundproof room, they would still experience frequent attention shifts. Consequently, when we describe most ADD/ADHD students as searching for positive reinforcement outside classroom activities, it is important to note that the impetus for that search comes from forces within the students.

This distinction helps explain why descriptions of ADD/ADHD students may portray them as being distracted by everything around them; but, when they are interested in an activity, nothing can pull them away from it. For whole language teachers this state of affairs should be a relief. After all, children who are curious and interested in everything are eager learners. The glitch that ADD/ADHD adds to this process is that their curiosity seems to be more for activities other than those common to the traditional classroom. Controlling this glitch requires teachers to direct the children's natural curiosity away from extraneous events and to create exciting learning opportunities within the classroom.

Essentially, teachers must draw attention to elements within the classroom that are exciting to the children and make those activities more exciting than other elements in the classroom surroundings. First, the children's attention must be directed toward the person giving instructions. Teachers must make themselves interesting by using eye contact, gestures, and a fascinating voice. As a last resort, teachers may have to gently position some of the childrens' bodies so that eye contact can occur.

Second, the directions must be given in clear, short sentences that are sequentially arranged. Two directions at a time are about the limit that most ADD/ADHD children can hold in their memory. If more directions are required, it is best to wait to deliver them after the first two directions are satisfactorily completed.

Third, the children must switch their attention from the instruction giver to the actual activity itself. Stickers, brightly colored placemats with no pictures, or felt-tip markers help define the limits of an activity and draw the students' eyes into the lesson. Fourth, locate the activity so that the children's backs are toward the center of the classroom and their faces are directed toward the task at hand. No more than one or two peers should be working at the same center.

Fifth, set up a cooperative learning situation in which the cooperation involves students reinforcing each other for accomplishments. For example, points could be given to a group for each child who contributes. When a predetermined number of points have been accumulated, the children in that group earn the privilege of baking cookies for the whole classroom.

Sixth, noncompletion of tasks must not be an option; however, this should be liberally defined so that if an activity is too difficult, the teacher can alter it to fit the children's capabilities. Moreover, during the initial stages of this behavior modification, it is as much the teacher's responsibility to assure task completion as it is the children's. That responsibility may take the form of verbal or physical encouragement, such as a compliment or a pat on the back. In addition, the teacher or other children may become the child's partner to provide support. Completing the task may also involve substituting easier-to-use tools such as a felt-tip marker instead of a pencil. Another way to assure task completion is to reduce the demands of an activity, perhaps by providing letters to trace or peers to read the first sentence while the ADD/ADHD children finish the paragraph.

Seventh, most ADD/ADHD students must be made aware that they have successfully accomplished an activity. For them, task completion is not always obvious. After finishing one activity, they may rush into another activity so quickly that the fact they have completed a task does not have time to register. Often losing awareness of the beginning and end of an activity, they miss the value of staying with a project and of taking pride in it. To them, life might seem like flashes of action with little purpose except immediate gratification. By leading them to an awareness of the temporal, sequential nature of completing an activity, teachers open the door for these students to the awareness and satisfaction that comes from a job well done.

Alleviating Impulsivity and Negative Attention Within the Classroom

"Why do these kids always get in trouble?" Such a question is often one of the first indications that children might have ADHD. On the other hand, getting in trouble may signify emotional or social problems independent of ADD/ADHD. For children who frequently get in trouble, all these possible scenarios must be considered. Because only a physician or psychiatrist can officially diagnose ADD/ADHD, teachers would be wise to consult their school's staffing team for the best approach in working with children who seem capable of attracting only negative attention.

Many ADD/ADHD students have spent so much time in their own world that they do not know how to enter the world of their peers and teachers. Unlike a neighbor politely knocking at a friend's door, ADD/ADHD students often know only how to break down the door. Being at the mercy of their impulses, they have a poorly developed awareness of others' feelings and do not have the patience to allow others a chance to express their ideas. Sharing the teacher's attention with twenty-five classmates is not part of their repertoire of responses.

Once again, the whole language classroom comes to the rescue. In traditional classrooms, where the teachers tend to be the sole source of attention and rewards, teachers do not have enough time in their day to give every student a needed dose of attention and still have time left to fulfill the ADD/ADHD students' daily requirement. In whole language classrooms, where teachers share with their students the power to reward and give attention, appropriate attention becomes available from many sources. In such classrooms it is much easier for ADD/ADHD students to obtain the attention they crave.

To assure that the process works well, however, does require planning by the teachers. Peers of many ADD/ADHD students do not automatically know the role they should play in giving healthy attention. On the contrary, the behavior they have witnessed conditions them to ignore, argue with, or fight their troublesome peers. Their teachers must bring them into the process (without singling out any other student by name) by positively reinforcing them for giving appropriate attention to other students. For example, peers can be given privileges or a pat on the back for telling other children what they like about their work or for inviting them to participate in their group. More mature peers may require only verbal acknowledgment of the encouragement they have given to others.

Peers also must be taught to ignore the negative effects of ADD/ADHD children's impulsivity. If students have tantrums, their peers must be taught to walk away or to look in another direction. It's also helpful to role play with them how to handle aggressive outbursts. They should be taught not to give any attention except that which is positive. If their positive attempts are rejected, they must leave the area to prevent becoming part of the ADD/ADHD students' audience.

In showing peers how to handle students who inadvertently generate negative attention by acting inappropriately, teachers should keep the instruction public rather than secretive. If such plans are hidden, students observe that being manipulative is a legitimate way of dealing with others. On the other hand, discussing the plan publicly, from the perspective that friends work together to help one another, enables students, including those with ADD/ADHD, to realize that the class is like a family. Members support one another because they care.

Adaptation of the Whole Language Curriculum to Emergent Readers

A concept vital to whole language teaching is the importance of conveying the value and joy of language and learning to our students. This is especially true with emergent readers and writers who have not yet begun attending to the details of individual words. From the whole language perspective, the meaning and purpose of language suffer when too much emphasis is placed on individual words and the letters of which they are composed. At the emergent stage, it is more important to impart the idea that reading is useful, predictable, meaningful, enjoyable, and accessible to everyone.

To accomplish this, we read with the children, play with the sounds of language, predict what language comes next, and engage in many other activities. Because of their distractibility and overall approach to learning, many ADD/ADHD students do not benefit as much from these activities as they could. If care is not taken, they will tune out and begin an avoidance of reading that can result in later reading delay. With simple adjustments in whole language practices, teachers can prevent such results.

The first adjustment deals with the predictability of language. For most children, predictability is a natural extension of their experiences with life. Children go to bed every night and get up every morning; they get thirsty, so they get a drink; they get sick, so they go to the doctor. If an unexpected event occurs, many children delight in being surprised and work extra hard in predicting what might come after the surprise. The language they use to describe these experiences is predictable, too. The same vocabulary and even the same phrases are used day after day.

But to many ADD/ADHD children, life is not predictable. They have spent most of their life jumping from one activity to another for no particular reason. To them life is a series of unrelated events tossed together in random order. They need help in discovering the patterns in their lives. Their daily classroom routine must be impressed on them by charts and frequent verbal reminders. Not only will they need extra help in discovering the clues that make reading predictable, but also they will need reassurance that their life, too, is predictable. One of the worst oversights many teachers make in working with ADD/ADHD students is assuming that predictability will come naturally to them.

A second adjustment teachers must make concerns story time. While most students love being read to, and, in turn, love telling stories to their peers while flipping through the pages of a book, many ADD/ADHD children may find such activities too slow-moving to hold their attention to the end of the book. Large-group reading situations are especially difficult.

There are four main reasons that group reading tends to turn off ADD/ADHD students. One, the teacher's attention is directed toward the book. Since the teacher's eye contact with the children is minimal, the ADD/ADHD students' attention begins to wander. Two, the visual presentation of the book is too far away to have a stimulating effect on these students, especially if the visual presentation also is being shared with twenty other classmates. For these students, sharing the teacher's presentation dilutes their share to the extent that they do not feel as if they own a part of the action. Consequently, their attention drifts off to action that is more personally connected to them.

Three, ADD/ADHD children's eyes, hands, and ears thrive on stimulation. Listening quietly while someone else reads a book to them leaves their eyes, hands, and ears available to the first more personal stimulus that comes their way. In a short time they become distracted as their eyes find something more exciting to watch, their hands find something to explore, and their ears tune out the teacher's voice so they can concentrate on the activity in which they are absorbed.

Four, to ADD/ADHD children, books often seem inanimate and impersonal. While most students discover multiple ways of relating to the story, ADD/ADHD children may not. It is difficult for them to connect to stories of the "there and then," as their attention is more often focused on the here and now.

For ADD/ADHD students to profit the most from story time, their teachers must find ways to connect them personally to the story and to make this relatively passive activity as active and stimulating as possible. The students' attention must become so absorbed in the book that all their visual, auditory, and kinetic energy is bound up in following the story. At the beginning of the story, the teacher must hook into the children's attention by establishing strong eye contact with them. Throughout the story, that eye contact will have to be frequently reestablished. Teachers also can hook students' eye contact into the story itself by pointing out details in the picture. Next, teachers can supply verbal sound effects in addition to reading the printed word. This helps keep the students verbally attentive. It is also helpful to use vivid facial expressions and physical gestures. If teachers bring elements from the art of storytelling into their reading, they will be almost guaranteed to keep ADD/ADHD children involved with the story.

Another adjustment teachers must make deals with ADD/ADHD students' documented difficulties with the sounds of language (Daugherty & Quay, 1991, pp. 453–61). While most students catch onto rhyming almost subconsciously while singing nursery rhymes or making up their own silly endings to songs, children with attention problems find such tasks difficult. When asked to think of a word that will rhyme with previous ones in a poem, they often choose a word that neither rhymes nor fits the meaning of the passage. Alliteration is also difficult, and they may be unable to pick out common sounds among words.

Although rhyming and alliteration at the emergent level may seem more like entertainment, they may be serious skills. Students who have difficulty grasping these concepts will have trouble breaking the sound-symbol code and using the patterns of that code to streamline their acquisition of reading. To assist these students in developing their rhyming and alliteration abilities, teachers can read Dr. Seuss or similar books. [Besides containing rhyming, such books also have very entertaining cues in their pictures.] The nonsensical story lines contain the element of surprise that demands the listener pay attention.

During the reading of these rhyming books, teachers can read the first several pages as they are printed, so that students incorporate the pattern of thought and rhyming. For the rest of the book, however, the second of an easy-to-predict rhyming pair should be left out and the children allowed to blurt out the word. The terminology of "blurting out the word" is especially important in describing exactly what the children are to do. They shouldn't take time to think; rather, they should react so that the process becomes automatic and spontaneous. As the students become proficient at solving easily predicted rhyming words, more complex pairs could be chosen.

Incorporating the few suggestions described above concerning rhyming and story time will make teaching more pleasant for the instructors of ADD/ADHD students. It also will reduce the likelihood that ADD/ADHD students who are emergent readers will become reading disabled. Currently as many as 40 percent of children with ADD/ADHD go on to be diagnosed as having a learning disability (Braswell, Bloomquist, & Pederson, 1991, p. 12). Whole language teachers, armed with the suggestions presented in this paper, as well as formulating and implementing their own apperceptions, can help ADD/ADHD children become eager and competent learners.

References

Balthazor, M. J., Wagner, R. K., & Pelham, W. E. (1991). The specificity of the effects of stimulant medication on classroom learning-related measures of cognitive processing for attention deficit disordered children. *Journal of Abnormal Child Psychology, 19*(1), 35–52.

Braswell, L., Bloomquist, M., & Pederson, S. (1991). *ADHD: A guide to understanding and helping children with Attention Deficit Hyperactivity Disorder in school settings.* Minneapolis: University of Minnesota Professional Development.

Brontë, C. (1847, 1984). *Jane Eyre.* Pleasantville, NY: Readers Digest Association.

Daugherty, T. K., & Quay, H. C. (1991). Response, perseveration and delayed responding in childhood behavior disorders. *Journal of Child Psychology and Psychiatry, 32*(3), 453–461.

deSonneville, L. M., Njiokiktjien, C., & Hilhorst, R. C. (1991). Methylphenidate-induced changes in ADHD information processors. *Journal of Child Psychology and Psychiatry, 32*(2), 285–295.

Keith, R. W., & Engineer, P. (1991). Effects of methylphenidate on the auditory processing abilities of children with Attention Deficit-Hyperactivity Disorder. *Journal of Learning Disabilities, 24*(10), 630–636.

Klorman, R., Brumaghim, J. T., Fitzpatrick, P. A., & Borgstedt, A. D. (1991). Methylphenidate speeds evaluation processes of attention deficit disorder adolescents during a continuous performance test. *Journal of Abnormal Child Psychology, 19*(3), 263–283.

6

Teamwork, Structure, and Schoolwide Commitment: Mainstreaming an ADHD Student

Bobbi Fisher

This article describes the teamwork, structure, and schoolwide commitment that enabled Bobbi, a classroom teacher, to successfully mainstream an ADHD child into her classroom. When Brett joined her class, Bobbi, along with Brett's aide, developed three goals for him: to help him appear and act like the other children; to make him feel safe and loved for the time he was in school; and to help him learn. Throughout the year and a half that Bobbi was his teacher, the following question continued to arise in her mind: "Could I help Brett reach the goals we had set for him, and establish and maintain a community for the other children in the class?" In other words, "Could I do Brett and the class, too?"

Bobbi Fisher is a first grade teacher at the Josiah Haynes School in Sudbury, Massachusetts. She has given workshops on whole language to teachers throughout the country and has worked with Don Holdaway at the Lesley College January and Summer Institutes. She is one of the founders and a past president of the Whole Language Teachers Association. Selected by the Massachusetts Department of Education as a 1988–89 Lucretia Crocker Fellow, Bobbi spent the year sharing her classroom program, "Whole Language for All Kids," with teachers and administrators throughout the state.

Bobbi is a member of the National Council of Teachers of English Commission on Reading and is on the Editorial Review Board of *Language Arts* and *The Reading Teacher*. She has published articles in *Teaching K-8, Workshop 2,* and *The Colorado Communicator.* Her book *Joyful Learning: A Whole Language Kindergarten* was published by Heinemann in 1991.

The first day that Brett joined my kindergarten class he sat in a chair near the rug area while the rest of the children sat on the floor. We read *Greedy Cat.* Everyone but Brett, that is. His body was perfectly still. Only his wide eyes moved to absorb the illustrations in the book and to stare in wonderment at the group of emergent and beginning readers who all seemed to be "reading" together.

Finally, he spoke out, "How do they do it?" I stopped to ask what he meant. "How do they know what to say?" The children responded.

"We hear the story lots of times and then we know it."

"We look at the words."

"We move our lips and pretty soon we know what to say. Try it with us."

Brett didn't try it right away. He had so much to learn and get used to first. But six weeks later I noticed that although he was still sitting on the chair apart from the group, his lips were moving as the class read together. I knew then that this child, who had been diagnosed as having an Attention Deficit Hyperactivity Disorder (ADHD), was becoming a member of our classroom community.

This article describes my school's commitment to support me in creating a successful experience for Brett and the class for the half-year he was in my kindergarten and the following full year when he moved with me to first grade.

The suburban school in which I teach has about 400 children in grades K–4. The children are given a lot of responsibility, and expectations for them are high. For example, they are expected to walk to specialists, to the library and to lunch unattended by teachers, and to act appropriately on their own at school meetings and other functions. There is a relaxed yet orderly atmosphere in the school, both among the children and the staff, and there is a lot of learning and laughter throughout the day.

In January 1991 my principal informed me that a foster child was living in our district. Our school system had the responsibility to enroll him or to arrange and finance an out-of-district placement in a classroom for emotionally disturbed children. My principal asked me to read the Department of Social Services report before we discussed the possibilities of bringing this child into the school and, specifically, into my classroom community. He wanted the two of us to consider and understand the ramifications of this decision before meeting with our school system's special services team (director of pupil services, guidance counselor, special education teacher, speech and language therapist, and school nurse), as well as an outside educational advocate appointed by the DSS. The team would collectively make the decision as to the best school placement for this child. My principal made it clear that my commitment as the classroom teacher and the commitment of the school special services team were both essential to the success of having him in my class and in the school.

Reports indicated a difficult beginning for Brett. The youngest of five children, he had lived with his mother and siblings for the first year and a half of his life before the DSS obtained custody. Before being placed in his present foster home in November 1990, he had been asked to leave two foster homes and had been expelled from two nursery schools. In April 1990 he was hospitalized for psychiatric services and diagnosed as having an Attention Deficit Hyperactivity Disorder. Ritalin was prescribed.

Current educational practice advocates that children with special needs be mainstreamed into the regular classroom whenever possible, rather than be placed in a substantially separate classroom or assigned to a pull-out program for the major part of the school day. The law asks that children be educated in the least restrictive environment. Many educators and parents believe that the most normal environment best supports these children socially, emotionally, and intellectually. I fully support this thinking, with one caveat: the entire school support team, in addition to the classroom teacher, must be committed to ensuring the success of the individual child in the classroom and school community.

As I read the reports my principal had given me, two conflicting thoughts emerged. One concerned the needs of this young boy, who required a normal, positive, supportive environment after five years of reported abuse and uncontrollable behavior. The other concerned my needs as a classroom teacher. Would I be taking on more than I could handle? Would Brett take too much time away from the rest of the children? Would he destroy the classroom community we had developed? I finally summed up all these questions in one: "Could I teach both Brett and the class?" This question continued to arise when his needs became overwhelming.

My classroom is what one would call a whole language classroom, and I felt that its philosophy and structure would offer the kind of positive environment in which Brett could learn and gain confidence. My responses to individual children and group situations are guided by seven beliefs about how young children learn—beliefs I have developed from whole language theory and personal experience working with children. They are as follows: children learn naturally; children know a lot about literacy before kindergarten; all children can learn; children learn best when learning is kept whole, meaningful, and functional; children learn best when they make their own choices; children learn best as a community of learners in a noncompetitive environment; and children learn best by talking and doing in a social context.

The day is organized around a natural learning classroom model (Holdaway, 1986), which includes Demonstration, Participation, Practice or Role-playing, and Performance. At the beginning of the day the class gathers for shared reading (Demonstration and Participation) in the reading area, which is filled with big books, trade books, and charts with poems and songs. During Choice Time (Practice or Role-playing) the children choose to work at the reading, writing, math, art, science, and dramatic play areas. At the end of the day we gather again to share (Performance) what we have done.

I went back and forth in my mind, wanting to include Brett, yet afraid that I couldn't be successful. But when I reread the reports, I focused on the positive things that he was able to do correctly, not simply the negative things he had done in the past. From all accounts he was very bright and without obvious learning disabilities. He had been on Ritalin for about nine months, during which time his uncontrollable behavior had subsided and his sensitive, caring, inquisitive nature had surfaced.

I went into the meeting with my principal, wanting Brett to come to our school if we felt that the school could include him. Since the philosophy of our school is that all kids can learn and our mission is to give each child the most positive, supportive learning experience we can, I knew I could count on receiving the administrative support I would need. The team members discussed Brett from their perspective, agreeing that he should come and that their roles for the time being would be supportive rather than active. They were ready to step in at any time, but we would start by including Brett in the class with the least obvious extra support.

The director of pupil services and special education for the town supported the team's decision to mainstream Brett and agreed to include a full-time aide for the remainder of the year. The special needs educator was responsible for writing and monitoring a diagnostic educational plan. Since she had worked in my classroom and was familiar with my philosophy and organization, she was able to write a plan that was compatible with my goals for the class and for Brett. The speech and language therapist was willing to consult with me and to work with Brett in the classroom rather than to take him out. The school guidance counselor was prepared to work individually with Brett, meeting with me as necessary, and the school nurse would bring him his medication and tend to his health needs.

The educational advocate appointed by DSS was the only team member not directly connected with the schools. His role (in locis parentis) was to assure that Brett received the educational support he needed. At this first meeting he expressed concern that our conversation was focusing on possible problems that might arise, rather than what Brett could do successfully. He wanted Brett to come to school with a "clean slate" and thought our prior knowledge might make it difficult for him to be successful. The team pointed out that although the school was committed to success, we had to be realistic about what could happen. Our prior knowledge was that before being hospitalized, Brett had been asked to leave the two preschools he had attended; we didn't want that to happen again.

It was agreed that Brett would start coming for an hour a day for the first two weeks, then two hours, and then for the full session of two and a half hours. The special educator, the speech therapist, and the guidance counselor volunteered to take turns being in the classroom with him until an aide was hired. His foster mother was willing to transport him during this transitional period.

On that first day, the guidance counselor and I met Brett in the lobby. He stared ahead and tentatively took my hand as we joined the rest of the kindergartners down the hall. During those transitional weeks, Brett was very quiet and outwardly calm. He listened attentively in the group, and although he needed specific suggestions about where to go during choice time, he would then sit and concentrate for a long time. Was this the active, out-of-control child that I had read about? Those reports had been written before Brett had started taking Ritalin, and it appears that the Ritalin had made a significant, positive difference in his behavior.

An aide, who had been an art therapist in a school for emotionally disturbed teenagers for several years, was hired. I had had the opportunity to interview her first, and we both felt that we could work together. Immediately Liz and I began to establish our goals for Brett and our roles in the classroom. We knew that it would take time to finalize these goals and roles and that we would be continually talking about and processing what was happening. The positive relationship we developed was a great relief to me because the question "Can I do Brett and the class?" was continually on my mind. Liz's presence helped me feel positive about the answer.

We developed three related goals: to help Brett appear and act like the other children; to make him feel safe and loved for the time he was in school; and to help him learn. Although we initially decided to concentrate on the first two goals, we began to notice that as Brett's intense interest in learning was being fulfilled, he began to act more like the other members of the class and to feel safe and loved. Clearly, the three goals were interdependent, but it took a while for us to feel that Brett was making progress toward any of them.

We agreed that during this initial phase my role would be to keep the class going and to work with Brett when his behavior was appropriate. Liz's role would be to help him understand his feelings, control his impulsive behavior, and learn the classroom routines and expectations.

As Brett became used to the class, he became more active and determined to do what he wanted. For example, one day I asked him to finish his drawing and help clean up. He turned to me and said, "No, you aren't my boss. I hate you." The other children were stunned that any child would speak to me in that way. After I told him that we don't talk to each other like that in this class, Liz spent time alone with him, discussing appropriate and inappropriate behavior. She helped him write an apology to me, which gave me the opportunity to talk with him as I do from time to time with the other children in the class. I thanked him for the note and told him that it made me feel happy with him. Talking about ways to make friends, I told him that I would help him play with Randy at the block area the next day.

Another time, when asked to do something, Brett ran up in the loft, picked up a chair, and threatened to throw it. Again, Liz removed him from the situation and talked with him about it. Throughout the day she was available to listen to his questions, discuss his feelings, and explain what was happening in the class.

The last half-hour of kindergarten continued to be a difficult time for Brett. The school nurse brought his medication at eleven o'clock as he came in from recess, and it took about fifteen minutes to become effective. Excited from the physical activity of outside play, he could not sit still or be quiet while I read to the class at the rug area. Consequently, for the remainder of the year, Liz continued to work individually with him at that time. She gave him something to eat and either read or drew with him. As they talked, she tried to answer his questions and to interpret what was happening in the classroom. Her support turned a potentially disruptive time for Brett and the class into a productive time for all, while helping Brett to work toward the goals we had set. Without Liz's intervention I could not have "done" Brett and the class during this period.

Liz continued to help Brett to understand his feelings and to learn classroom routines and expectations; and, as the year went on, he demonstrated fewer impulsive behaviors throughout the day. Liz was needed less to help him control his behavior. He started sitting with the rest of the children on the rug during group time, and I was more frequently able to respond to him as a regular member of the class.

Later in the year there were many days, especially during choice time, when Brett spent concentrated amounts of time drawing pictures or looking at books. His drawings were extremely imaginative and contained lots of details from movies or TV shows he had seen or from his family experiences. He loved to talk with his classmates as he drew. Some days he would spend the hour looking at books. Often requesting one of us to read to him, he would ask question after question as he turned the pages.

I read with him, conferenced with him about his drawings, included him in math games, and called on him during shared reading. He took his turn as leader for the day, and with intense seriousness led the class down the hall.

The children picked him for a partner, pulled him in the wagon, and laughed with him as they shared a snack at the snack table. Whenever possible, Liz stepped into the background and I stepped forward. Brett began to bond with me, and I began to bond with him. Meanwhile, my question remained: "Can I do Brett and the class?" Now the answer was, "Yes, sometimes." I still needed Liz, and so did Brett.

When I realized that I would be teaching first grade the next fall, I requested that Brett be placed in my class. I felt that having the same teacher would benefit him, and I knew that he and I would continue to have the support of the school staff when needed. Liz would be hired as his full-time aide for the first six weeks of school and would stay on as my classroom assistant for three hours a day, four days a week. This initial support would enable me to establish the procedures and community for my new class and would give Brett assistance as he made new friends and became used to being in school all day. First grade, though a new beginning for Brett, would be comfortable for him. He had spent a morning helping me in the classroom the week before school started, and he knew Liz and me and six of the children from his kindergarten class.

During the year he was consistently able to follow the regular procedures for most of the morning, freeing Liz to work with other children. He received his medication at eleven o'clock, right before recess; and by the time he got back to the classroom a half-hour later, it had taken effect. He was then able to focus on math and to be settled for the music or art specialist.

Afternoon, however, was much harder for Brett to adjust to, and it remained the most difficult time for him throughout the year. Lunch recess ended at 1:35, twenty-five minutes before he received his two o'clock medication, and he was much more active prior to the afternoon medication than before his morning dose. In the beginning he often returned from lunch shouting, running around the room to get his books for silent reading, tapping during group time, compulsively interrupting a story by asking questions, and reacting to an accidental bump with another child by shouting, "They're trying to hurt me on purpose."

Again my main question kept coming up: "Can I do Brett and the class?" My answer was, "Yes, until lunch. No, not in the afternoon, at least not in a way that would fit our goals." I knew I could still call on the school support team, which had been meeting monthly to review Brett's progress. In November, after Liz stopped being in the class full time, we discussed several options to help Brett during the difficult afternoon time. We considered the possibility of adjusting his medication, and his foster mother and psychiatrist were willing to consider changes if a better solution wasn't found. My principal offered to find a volunteer to work with him outside the classroom at the library or in the computer room. The third grade teacher across the hall volunteered to take Brett in his room, and the school nurse said that Brett could spend time in her office.

After reviewing our goals for Brett, we felt that they could best be achieved if he could stay in the classroom. Offering him an alternative setting would set him apart from his peers and indicate that we didn't think he could manage.

Also, the afternoon was devoted to reading, and I didn't want him to miss it. In spite of his active behavior, he always participated during shared reading, became engaged in books during sustained silent reading, loved sharing books with friends during peer sharing time, and enjoyed the story I read to the class at the end of the day. And, he was learning to read.

For the remainder of the year Brett spent most of the afternoon in the classroom, slowly learning to adapt and to control himself. Occasionally, when I felt that he was disturbing the group or when he decided he needed to be in a less stimulating environment, he went to the nurse and read, drew, or talked with her. He always came back more settled and ready to be a member of the classroom community.

Throughout the year Brett continued to enjoy looking at books and hearing stories. He was engaged during group time, and when we read with him, he often selected some of the little books and used his finger to point word for word. We kept following his lead as he developed as a beginning reader. He loved drawing and began to add letters to his pictures. First they were just random letters, but soon he started using his "ear spelling" and invented spelling in his writing. Conventional words, such as *the* and *like,* and standard spelling patterns such as *ing* appeared in his work.

One day, in invented spelling, he wrote in his journal, "Thank you, Mrs. Fisher, for the backpack." I was elated. I could read what he wrote and shared his success with everyone on the team.

As I look back on the year and a half that Brett has been in our school and reflect on the progress he has made, I can attribute his success to teamwork, structure, and schoolwide commitment. A dedicated and committed team, which worked steadily to support both Brett and me, was put in place early. Liz, his most powerful and faithful advocate, read with him every day, sat by him to explain directions he didn't understand, talked with him about his feelings, took him places on Saturdays, and made last-minute telephone calls to sign him up for the town soccer program. My principal, the special educator, the guidance counselor, the speech and language therapist, the school nurse, and the director of pupil services were always available to listen to my concerns, support alternative procedures, talk with Brett, celebrate his successes, and enable him to work toward the goals we had set for him. With appropriate role models he steadily learned to behave like the other children. A predictable daily routine and consistent adult expectations helped him to feel safe and loved, and a classroom committed to learning enabled him to learn. Mainstreaming under these supportive conditions can be successful for all.

References

Cowley, J. (1988). *Greedy cat*. Katonah, NY: Richard C. Owen.

Fisher, B. (1991). *Joyful learning: A whole language kindergarten*. Portsmouth, NH: Heinemann.

Holdaway, D. (1986). The structure of natural learning as a basis for literacy instruction. In M. Sampson (Ed.), *The pursuit of literacy: Early reading and writing,* pp. 56–72. Dubuque, IA: Kendall/Hunt.

7

Attention Deficit Hyperactivity Disorder: One Mother's Perspective

Diane Audsley

Writing from the perspectives of both parent and teacher, Diane Audsley narrates the struggles and successes of raising a child with Attention Deficit Hyperactivity Disorder. She chronicles her son's life from infancy through the elementary school years while describing how ADHD affected her son and her family. Diane focuses on practical solutions and modifications in educational programs for children with Attention Deficit Hyperactivity Disorder in a public school setting.

Diane Audsley first became aware of Attention Deficit Hyperactivity Disorder in 1978, when she was working with a child in her second grade classroom who had been diagnosed with the disorder. Since 1986, when her own son was diagnosed with ADHD, she has studied much of the available literature on the subject and has been active in the local parent support group for parents of children with ADHD (CH.A.D.D.). In addition, Diane is currently working toward a doctorate in reading instruction at the University of Missouri. She has made presentations at numerous conferences throughout the United States. President of her local TAWL group (Teachers Applying Whole Language), Diane is currently a second grade teacher at Fairview Elementary School in Columbia, Missouri.

"BACK TO SCHOOL." That phrase used to bring to mind idyllic visions of children walking to their first day of school wearing bright new clothes and shiny new shoes all displayed against a vibrant background of autumn leaves swirling through the air. As a teacher I couldn't wait to meet my new students. The anticipation of what we would accomplish and learn together during the year was exhilarating.

I have a different perspective now. My son has ADHD. Instead of wondering if he will like his teacher, I worry about whether or not she will understand him. Rather than wonder who his new friends will be, I worry that his peers will not accept him. Instead of wondering what new concepts and ideas he will learn in class, I worry about whether or not he will be able to maintain concentration long enough to get the general idea of class discussions.

My husband and I first noticed differences between Nathan and other children when he was just an infant. He cried constantly, but I just assumed that I had a colicky baby. I noticed some improvement when he was able to move for himself, spending hours bellyflopping across our living room carpet like a seal. As long as he was moving, he was content. He also loved to jump. When someone picked Nathan up and held him under his arms, his knees immediately began bobbing up and down. My arms would tire long before his knees would.

One of our first contacts with school was when Nathan's preschool teacher called to inform us that Nathan had been in a fight. His teacher had walked into the boys' bathroom to find Nathan and several other boys flailing their arms at each other while rolling around on the floor. At the end of the year, his teacher was concerned that Nathan might not be ready for kindergarten, since he continued having trouble sitting still and paying attention for even short periods of time.

In kindergarten it was more of the same. On one occasion he was sent to the principal's office for "kicking" his teacher. I later found out that it was not malicious kicking. He was swinging his feet and kept knocking the teacher with his foot. Although he stopped when asked, soon he was at it again. Nathan's kindergarten teacher reported that he had difficulty staying on task and completing work. I was beginning to dread parent-teacher conferences.

At home in our neighborhood, Nathan was involved in numerous small accidents. He fell off his bike when he didn't notice loose gravel and lost two permanent front teeth. Nathan swung a wooden baseball bat, not realizing that there was a little girl behind him, and hit her squarely in the head. While walking out of a movie theater, he was hit in the side of his head with a glass door because he wasn't looking ahead. He was almost never aware of safety concerns.

Nathan was irritable most of the time and he became frustrated quickly. He was not able to change activities easily. It was difficult to wake him in the morning, but just as difficult to get him to sleep at night. It was a fight to get him in to the tub to take a bath, but just as hard to persuade him to get out of the bathtub. He didn't usually want to go on outings, but once we were there he didn't want to leave.

Nathan was a challenge every day. My husband and I were becoming so frustrated that we decided to take Nathan to see a child psychologist. After several sessions the psychologist determined that there was no psychosis, but that our son did have a classic case of ADHD. He recommended that we try Ritalin. Our pediatrician concurred with the psychologist, and Ritalin was prescribed for Nathan.

The Ritalin did help somewhat. Nathan's activity level decreased, and he was able to pay attention for longer periods of time. We had also been modifying our family life gradually, almost without realizing it, for some time, as Nathan always felt better when he knew exactly what to expect. Because disruptions to his schedule, even minor ones, could become disasters, our schedule at home became more and more consistent. I woke Nathan at the same time every morning. We decided the night before what he would wear to school, so it was already laid out for him in the morning. Instead of asking him what he wanted for breakfast, I gave him a choice between two or three options. Limitless choice was too mind-boggling for him, yet no choice at all was irritating. After school we also followed a routine. Play or TV was permitted until dinner at six o'clock, then homework until it was complete, followed by play if there was time, a bath, and then bedtime. Every day followed the pattern as much as possible. During homework time I would have to sit right at the table with him to help keep him on task.

Summers were less rigid, but summer held its own set of problems. Nathan expressed an interest in playing T-ball one summer. Since my husband and I were eager to get Nathan involved in normal activities with other children, we signed him up immediately. Our T-ball experience was disappointing, to say the least. When Nathan was in the outfield, he totally lost concentration on the game. Balls would drop to the ground all around him while he stared off into space, examined some insect crawling by, or engaged in some other activity completely unrelated to T-ball. His teammates began to get angry with him, and Nathan lost self-esteem.

Nathan's second grade year was his worst of all. He had an inexperienced teacher who, try as she might, had no idea how to handle him. He was falling farther and farther behind in his school work, but more upsetting than that was his getting a reputation at school for being a troublemaker. He was not socially accepted by his peers and had no close friends at school. At this point we also started noticing that Nathan was exhibiting "tics." He continuously popped his eyes, cracked just about every joint in his body, and made a coughing noise that sounded like a bark.

Beginning to feel overwhelmed again, my husband and I decided to take Nathan to see a child psychiatrist. The psychiatrist explained that Ritalin can cause tics in some children, so he changed Nathan's medication from a stimulant to an antidepressant. He also recommended that Nathan begin psychotherapy in an effort to raise his self-esteem and to help him deal with his frustrations.

During this time Nathan was also tested at school to determine if there were any handicapping conditions that might be slowing his academic progress. His I.Q. tested within the average range, as did his academic skill. He did experience some difficulty with pragmatic language and some speech patterns, and writing skills were also a mild concern. The psychometrist and other test givers all noted his lack of attention, his inability to stay on task, his low frustration level, and his constant need to be in motion. The label that the diagnostic team recommended for Nathan was Behavior Disordered. I was quite upset. As a teacher I knew what that label could do to a child in a school setting. I was not prepared to permit that to happen to my son. I informed the diagnostic team that my husband and I would decline special education services for Nathan if the only way to get them was to accept that label. In the end, the assistant director for special education interceded on Nathan's behalf. She suggested that Nathan be diagnosed as health impaired. This label has allowed Nathan to receive the services of the speech therapist, the learning disabilities resource teacher, and the counselor, without the stigma of being considered a problem child.

In third grade Nathan's life made a turn for the better. He had a wonderful classroom teacher who was very even-tempered, consistent, and gentle. She worked very closely with the school counselor to design a behavior modification program that helped Nathan take more responsibility for his school work, finish work on time, and become more socially acceptable to his peers. Meeting each week, Nathan, the counselor, and his classroom teacher decided on an area of Nathan's work habits that needed improvement. For instance, one week the area chosen was writing his homework assignments down on an assignment sheet. This may seem like a small task, but it was difficult for Nathan to remember his homework assignments. And unless we knew what the assignments were, we couldn't help him complete his work at home. At first he was to remember to write his assignments down two to three nights a week, gradually increasing to four or five nights a week. If he met his goal for the week, he was allowed to choose a friend from his class to play a computer game for ten minutes in the counselor's office. This approach not only helped Nathan become more organized and enabled him to finish his assignments but also enhanced his standing with his peers. Children in his class were more open to Nathan's friendship because they knew he might choose them to get out of class and play a game. Granted, this is a bit manipulative, but it has been highly successful, and I believe children like Nathan can benefit from a little manipulation in their favor now and then.

In addition to having help from the counselor, Nathan's classroom teacher was also working very closely with the speech/language therapist. Nathan was not as able as other children to pick up on social subtleties. He was unsure as to how to go about initiating and ending conversations, how to ask to join in play with other children, how to disagree with peers or adults without sounding angry or disrespectful, how to accept compliments gracefully, and how to manage his voice tone and volume. His speech therapist placed Nathan in a small group of children and they practiced these areas of concern together. She also taught Nathan ways to control anger and frustration by counting or quietly removing himself from certain situations.

At this point in Nathan's life he was seeing his psychiatrist every other week, his school counselor once a week, the speech/language specialist twice a week, and the learning disabilities resource teacher three times a week. He also continued to take the antidepressant medication on a daily basis, and we attempted to maintain as consistent a lifestyle as possible at home.

His fourth grade year was even better than his third. We chose a classroom teacher for Nathan who was known for her even, consistent structure. All the programs initiated for Nathan in third grade remained in place in fourth grade. His grades were above average to excellent, and he started receiving invitations to birthday parties and to other children's homes for play or sleepovers. We encouraged these relationships at home by inviting other children over to our house and making sure that the activities we offered were both highly motivational and something at which Nathan had expertise (such as a "hot" new video game or a complicated LEGO set).

It has taken our family many years to learn how to cope with Attention Deficit Hyperactivity Disorder, and we experience new challenges every day. Nathan has recently completed the fifth grade and has continued to improve. We have found some strategies to be consistently helpful each year in dealing with ADHD in a public school setting.

We have found throughout the years that without a doubt, the most important variable in determining success has been the classroom teacher. It is her attitude in dealing with Nathan and toward parents who need to be extremely involved in their child's education that has made the difference between a successful school year and a disaster. Some of Nathan's teachers believed education to be totally the child's responsibility. He was expected to remember assignments and to have all supplies needed to complete assignments. Needless to say, this attitude was completely disastrous for Nathan, particularly in his early years. When he has had teachers who believed that a child's education was a collaborative effort involving the child, the teacher, and the parents, Nathan has experienced the greatest success.

Daily assignment sheets that were sent home—listing not only what still needed to be done but also what Nathan had been able to accomplish on his own—were the most helpful. Those sheets not only let us see exactly what homework was expected to be completed but also gave us all a sense of achievement concerning what he had been able to complete without help.

Some teachers have been very helpful in breaking down long, involved projects into smaller increments and then helping Nathan to monitor his progress toward the final goal. It has been particularly helpful to have at the beginning of an extended project an overview of the entire project so that we could be preparing Nathan for what lay ahead and, in addition, to have the project broken down into smaller components with specific due dates. In that way he knew how much needed to be completed each day.

Nathan was also much more successful when he was given a choice about his learning. He particularly enjoyed literature study groups because he was allowed to choose which book he wanted to read from a small group of choices. He was usually very motivated to read the book because he felt that he himself had made the decision to read. The literature groups had some social bonuses, too. They gave him something in common to converse about with other children in a fairly structured situation. Knowing what to expect and what was expected of him in this situation, Nathan consequently was able to perform in a socially acceptable manner. One teacher also encouraged Nathan to respond to the literature artistically, which happens to be an area in which he excels. Nathan enjoyed this aspect of literature study, and it allowed his peers to see Nathan in a positive light.

Nathan also performed much better when he was given a choice concerning what to write. There were occasions when Nathan was asked to complete assignments like, "Pretend you are a piece of chalk in the chalk ledge. Write what you see." This type of assignment completely baffled him. He couldn't draw on personal experience, and that made it extremely difficult for him to organize in his mind. On the other hand, when he was given a choice about what to write, it was much easier for him to organize his thoughts. The key to success with writing assignments is interest. For instance, when Nathan's fifth grade class was studying the Civil War, he was required to write a report. One of Nathan's interests is weapons, so he researched and wrote a report on weapons of the Civil War. He was interested in the topic, and it met the criteria for the report.

The use of a computer on which to compose also helped. We purchased one for our home, and he was allowed to use one at school. The computer was helpful not only because it eliminated the time spent agonizing over handwriting and spelling but also because when the piece was complete, it looked good. This gave Nathan a sense of pride in his accomplishment.

Nathan experienced the most success in classrooms that were structured and predictable. By structured I don't mean highly traditional, where everyone sits in rows without moving or speaking until the teacher calls on the students to do or say something. By structured I mean that every child knows the routine and feels safe in the knowledge that he/she knows what to expect from each situation. There may actually be considerable movement in these classrooms as children get supplies and/or reference materials needed for the projects in which they are engaged. They may be scattered around the room, conferring with the teacher or other students. The noise levels in these rooms is usually a bit higher than in traditional classrooms, but the freedom to expend energy by moving around in the classroom, in addition to the security of routine and the higher level of motivation usually present in these classrooms, will often compensate for the distraction of the noise. In these classrooms Nathan was not expected to remain totally silent, which was impossible for him anyway. Children with ADHD who are lucky enough to be in this type of classroom tend to find themselves more socially accepted because they don't stand out so negatively with their inability to keep quiet and still.

As a teacher, having a child with ADHD has made me much more compassionate toward children in general and those experiencing problems specifically. I understand the struggles they go through to function the way that most children do without thinking. I can also empathize with parents more easily. I understand the pain of watching a child struggle with what comes so easily to other children.

I firmly believe that to help a child with ADHD function in a school setting, there must be a coordinated effort involving everyone working with the child. ADHD cannot be handled only by teachers, or only by parents, or only by medical personnel. It takes a joint effort involving everyone caring for an ADHD child to ensure that the child receives the best educational experience possible.

8

Coming of Age: Working with Older ADHD Student Populations

Virginia S. Little

Particularly if they have been undiagnosed and have never received understanding, support, or medication that might help them deal with the problems associated with ADHD, older students have typically developed low self-esteem, as well as (mal)adaptive behaviors reflecting their rejection of the school and social systems that have treated them as lazy, as incompetent, and even as failures. Working with such students thus presents special challenges. Drawing from the research on adult ADHD but especially upon her own experience teaching in an alternative high school and in a junior college, Virginia Little describes teaching practices that work especially well with these older students. She focuses upon helping them develop self-esteem and self-worth as well as social, organizational, and academic skills. Obviously, all are interrelated.

Virginia S. Little (Ginny) is currently a teacher educator at the University of San Diego and is engaged in doctoral work through the California Institute of Integral Studies at San Francisco. After she received her degree from the University of Arizona with a strong background in whole language principles of education and in psycholinguistic theory, she received commendation for her work with Juvenile Court students in Tucson, Arizona. Virginia taught for an affluent private high school in Lake Tahoe, Nevada, where the student population was largely affected by substance abuse and prior academic failure; and she received an excellence in education award for her work in an alternative high school in Michigan, where students were placed on the basis of poor attendance, behavior, or achievement in the regular school framework. More recently she has been involved in a community college program for the nontraditional student. She has been a welcomed guest speaker on the topic of "at-risk" populations, and continues to broaden her understanding of the special considerations and problems these students exhibit.

During the last fifteen years a majority of my teaching experiences have involved students exhibiting characteristics of ADHD. Academic and personal pressures for these individuals increase as they enter high school and college. Working with these students at the alternative high school and in a community college program for the "at-risk" student has shown me how to help empower these students to manage their lives and to succeed in their academic pursuits.

I have only recently familiarized myself with symptoms, characteristics, suggested treatments, positive school settings, and approaches for the ADHD individual through such resources as Hallowell & Ratey, 1993; Fowler et. al., 1992; Goldstein & Ingersoll, 1992; Weiss & Hechtman, 1986. That is unfortunate, as these readings and research would have certainly broadened my understanding of many of my students and aided my ability to work effectively with them. My heart was broken more than once as I watched students' lives crumble: some died; others will spend their lives in jail; some continue to live in destitution and/or despair, feeling powerless to change who they are. Fortunately, because of my educational background supporting a whole language philosophy and perhaps also largely because of my intuition, I was effective in guiding some of these students to success. I still hear from, and mentor, many students from as long ago as fifteen years. One is an elementary teacher herself; many are married with successful careers and happy lives. Some of what we did in the alternative school and at the community college was highly effective in helping these people to guide their lives onto a more positive track. Those ideas I am pleased to share with you. They are consistent with current research surrounding ADHD, and through experience I know they work.

Structuring and the Effects on Inattentiveness

The alternative high school where I taught for five years provides students with several key components that foster success for the ADHD students in particular. The school day is scheduled from 7:30 to 1:30 in the afternoon (shortened because of limited passing time between classes) with a half-hour lunch block and an integrated curriculum. This shortened school day is beneficial in that it addresses the difficulties ADHD students have in sustaining concentration. In addition, academic classes are interspersed with "option" classes; in these, the students are involved in physical and/or creative activities that enhance their ability to then focus on intermittent academic subjects. Also scheduled into the day are several "breaks," when students are allowed fifteen minutes to move around, to socialize, to smoke with parental permission, or to counsel with an advisor or teacher. As ADHD students typically have difficulty sitting still, the structure of the school day as well as classroom organization can greatly affect their ability to "stay on task."

Within the classroom I had various learning centers: a computer area, where students could do preprogrammed lessons or write and compose; a reading area with comfortable chairs, lamps, a variety of adolescent novels, and high-interest magazines; a study area, where students could complete assigned work with help from me or from the teacher's aide; and an instructional area for teaching students in a group setting. In one class period students might typically move to three of the four areas, depending on motivation and/or sustained interest. We would meet as a group at the beginning of class and discuss potential objectives for the class period. Each student had an individualized folder for recording each day's goals and accomplishments and for my comments, encouraging remarks, and suggestions for further exploration or inquiry by the student. ADHD students have difficulty monitoring and scheduling, so accounting for daily, even hourly, progress was one way to help them accomplish their goals.

Students often began and completed homework within the classroom framework, where they could receive immediate feedback. When they did take work home, this generally reflected their own interest or desire to continue or extend a project or assignment begun in the classroom. Reviews for tests or long-term project scheduling were coordinated between the teacher and students. Tasks were divided into small segments and then carefully monitored to assure concentration and completion, easing the typical burden of responsibility on the student. Notes home to the parents often accompanied longer assignments, along with the student's overall plan for completion. Checklists were provided for the parent to complete, stating how much time was spent on homework, where the student chose to study, and what the student was able to accomplish. There was also space for additional comments and questions. All this was helpful in eliciting parental involvement in the habits and progress of their children and in encouraging communication between home and school.

ADHD students seem to do better with consistent routines, an offer of choice in participation of activities, and careful monitoring of their work with immediate positive feedback. Organizing the classroom with predictable frameworks, along with overall school structuring, helps to compensate for impulsivity and hyperactivity demands. This organization can greatly improve the ADHD students' chances of academic and personal success.

Motivational Factors

Regular kinds of school-related tasks are often considered "boring" by the ADHD student, especially if the material is not made relevant to their personal lives and interests. Allowing students choices within the framework of teacher-guided objectives may help curtail this common response. The importance of self-selection is well defined by Lester Laminack in his reflections on his own son's early literacy development.

> Now if you liked piano lessons and wanted to learn, you probably didn't mind the thirty-minute practice sessions. You may even have spent more time than that, because you liked them so much. But forced practice and contrived activity places control in the hands of someone else. Then the motivation that fuels the act is no longer a self-sustaining internal fire that drives the individual to work through approximations to control. Instead, the flame is external. And when that's so, human beings tend to run to avoid being burned. (Laminack, 1991, p. 39)

In allowing students to make choices and determine directions for their own learning, we empower them to control their own lives and educational paths while simultaneously "fueling" interest. Students may also want to be involved with more than one project at a time, given their tendency to have short attention spans and high levels of distractibility that lead them to seek more exciting, or simply different, options from the task at hand. Allowing flexibility, while simultaneously encouraging eventual completion of tasks begun, promotes a sense of accomplishment. A student may, for example, begin writing a story on the computer, become "bored" after fifteen minutes, and then elect to draw an illustration to accompany the text once completed. In the midst of drawing, the student may then decide that he/she would like to visit the reading section to look at other illustrators' drawings or to read a magazine before returning to the original work on the computer. Each digression is recorded in a portfolio folder with space for the student's comments about what has been done and/or completed. Ongoing, sometimes daily, conferences between the teacher and the student establish positive interactions geared towards fostering productive behavior, teaching students to become more responsible for their own learning, and facilitating personal growth. The student can readily observe tendencies toward progress or regression when recorded on paper.

I also found that the students' motivation to do their best was increased when I demonstrated that I valued their work and efforts—by displaying examples around the room, the hallways, the principal's office, and the school entryway; by publishing collective writings in a weekly paper; and by simple praise.

Some of these kids have never experienced school-related success, and while initially they may act as if they don't care, their first sheepish grin over their accomplishments belies their facades and eventually grows into boasting. Students with a history of not doing well adopt an attitude of "who cares?" as a defense mechanism. If they don't try, they aren't vulnerable to failure. The risk can be too much if they do not receive encouragement and support to begin and to finish what they start. All students want to do well and are capable of doing so. But before we ask them to believe in themselves, they first need evidence of our own belief and trust in them as learners.

One aspect of ADHD that I wish I had been more aware of is the neurological factors that affect motivation, as described below:

> "Knowing what to do is a strategy problem. Doing what you know is a motivational problem." . . . There is a neurological basis for the motivational difficulties in children with ADD. The frontal-limbic system, particularly the striatum, is believed to regulate inhibition and motivation. Recent brain-based studies on people with ADD indicate impairment in these areas. (Barkley, cited in Fowler et al., 1992, p. 14)

I can remember being frustrated at times with students who, it seemed, *chose* not to do as well as I thought they could, erroneously believing it was a matter of *choice,* which is incorrect. It is a product of their neurobiology. Knowing this previously would have helped ease my frustration with their seeming lack of effort. Even so, I believe that continued visual, verbal, and written encouragement for what they *did* accomplish—focusing on their strengths rather than on their faults—was a powerful motivating incentive that helped counter any regressions. This is supported by Weaver's description of ADHD as a system involving both individual characteristics and environmental influences:

> In effect, ADHD is a disorder defined by the expectations of society—an *interpretation* of behaviors that may have a bio/physical basis, but that are certainly exacerbated by *some* kinds of environmental conditions and alleviated by others. (Weaver, 1991, p. 20)

In other words, positive interaction with the students provides stimulus and impetus for them to do well. Establishing an environment sensitive to their needs will help students feel more "in control" of their own actions and/or reactions. Although the motivation comes from within the individual, it can be positively or negatively affected by external interactions that must be carefully considered by the educators and/or parents involved. ADHD students need our support.

Behavior and Classroom Interactions

Connie Weaver suggests earlier in this book that, unfortunately, the professional literature on the schooling of ADHD students focuses almost exclusively on managing their behavior, using principles from behavioral psychology. Rarely do the professionals in this field consider alternative ways of *educating* such students. But whole language teaching can alleviate the behavior problems. Furthermore, the environment of whole language classrooms and whole language teachers' expectations for students make these teachers less likely to perceive some of the typical ADHD behaviors as seriously troublesome.

The alternative school where I instructed indeed focuses on behavior modification techniques to control disciplinary problems instead of seeking ways to provide a more adaptive environment. All the teachers were required to attend a seminar and to implement Lee Canter's Assertive Discipline techniques. This involves writing the students' names on the board for disruptive or inappropriate classroom behavior and subsequently placing checks next to their name for continued noncompliance. Punitive consequences are attached to each check, culminating in the removal of the student from the classroom.

I chose not to use this method, as many students become "check masters." Knowing that their behavior was certain at times to be viewed as "deviant" and feeling unable to curtail such responses, they often might elect to misbehave to accomplish what the guidelines were meant to avoid: removal from the classroom. Especially when faced with a task that did not interest them or was too easy or too difficult, or when confronted by a teacher or other students, they would escape the situational demands by disrupting, withdrawing, and/or becoming aggressive.

I had very few behavioral referrals from my class, largely, I believe, because the students were engaged in what they were doing. The classroom atmosphere was relaxed; students often worked cooperatively, sharing their ideas and strengths. Conversation between students was encouraged, rather than discouraged (as it would be in the traditional classroom setting), thus saving the teacher from numerous repetitions of "PLEASE be quiet!" Respecting others' rights to learn, students would not interrupt a classmate who seemed engaged and did not want to be disturbed; however, they would commonly share their ideas and develop projects with willing partners. Mobility within the classroom and even self-selected "time-outs" were accepted practices. Students know their own thresholds of interest and frustration much better than we sometimes do, and I encouraged my students to become responsible for monitoring their own progressions and digressions.

Positive notes home were a common practice, with each student receiving at least one per month. Many of these students or their parents had never received communication about what could or should be praised; rather, they had typically been inundated by notes stating such things as "Johnny is a consistent behavior problem at school." I imagine that this kind of information comes as no surprise to these parents, and it is also not surprising that often no suggestions are offered for improving the situation. Perhaps we should all recall our grandmothers' advice: "If you don't have something good to say, don't say anything at all." Focusing on positives rather than negatives produces more positive results.

Related to this was an invention of mine called the "Communications Board," a bulletin board designed for sending and receiving notes from students to other students and for establishing an open format for me to write encouraging words to students I saw struggling or to whom I might just want to say, "Hi! Just wondering how you're doing?" Among the most popular activities in school, writing notes to other students holds intrinsically powerful motivation; it is also a constant source of aggrievance for teachers, and needlessly so. Some of the best ideas come from viewing a situation through new eyes. The kids are strongly motivated to engage in the activity; it has personal connection. All that's needed is to find ways to channel the action in a more positive direction. Note writing is authentic communication and develops desired skills, so why not encourage rather than discourage it? Seems easy enough.

In essence, behavior in the classroom will reflect the students' level of comfort and confidence in pursuing their interrelated personal and academic interests and abilities. They will elect positive over negative interactions and are generally eager to please someone who provides support and encouragement. Negative behaviors should be discouraged through individual conferencing and counseling without ridicule, and through assuring the student that, while the behavior may have been unacceptable, the student is valued and respected. As human beings with inherent needs for security and approval, we all share the desire to be heralded for who we are and what we do well. So often, teachers forget this.

Raising Self-Esteem

Raising self-esteem is the single most important component of any instructional framework. If each of us possessed the self-confidence to actively pursue our desired goals and dreams, if we truly believed in ourselves enough to become our own ultimate "best," *imagine* what a world it would be! Now think about how difficult it must be for an ADHD student to cope with an ever-diminishing level of self-esteem: consistent failure becomes a self-fulfilling prophecy. On the other hand, once the cycle is broken and students learn that they can succeed, the effect is much like that of water bursting forth through a dam—powerful, and ever more powerful as it gains momentum. Once students learn to believe in themselves, progress becomes rapid and sustained. How is this accomplished?

Journal writing provides a strong communicative link between a teacher and the students. Kids will write things they haven't the courage to say. And they will tell you *everything* if they trust in your confidentiality. Often I was able to circumvent potentially troublesome situations with students by knowing ahead of time what was causing difficulties prior to an incident. Some of these students lived severely traumatic lives, reflective of the violence in today's society and of the breakdown of the family structure. They want to be safe, and they will entrust their hopes, feelings, and fears to an open ear. Students in my class were informed whenever intervention or sharing of their entries with "authorities" was deemed necessary. They did not object.

In addition, journal writing provided a creative outlet for expression of their inner thoughts. Many of their entries were poignantly written. I published the collective writings in magazine format to be distributed throughout the school and community. These writings also empowered the students to see their own thought processes more clearly and to examine their growth. I would often hear students when rereading previous entries exclaim, "I can't believe I was so upset by that!" or "Geez, that's a pretty good poem I wrote." Once on paper, their attitudes and emotions seemed to be more manageable, and they could compare their current feelings with those of the past, while mind-mapping a direction for their future. Journal writing provided a nonthreatening means of honest communication both with the teacher and within the individual. In our classroom, journal writing was interactive: my written as well as verbal comments and questions about the entries served to raise the students' sense of self-worth by demonstrating sincere concern for, and involvement in, their lives and in their progress toward becoming a happier, more fulfilled individual.

Enhanced self-esteem is also one of the positive consequences of something previously mentioned: establishing with the student short-term, attainable goals that ensure success. I used to tell my students, "Take a bunch of little baby steps—step, step, step. Don't sweat the big stuff; concentrate on *right now*." This is especially helpful for the ADHD individual who has difficulty focusing on the task at hand. Sustained concentration without distraction can be fostered by starting with short time periods, during which the students can more readily sustain attention. The student initially selects a length of time for which concentrated activity will be attempted, allotting five-minute breaks between timed sessions. When the students find their minds wandering, they are encouraged to make a list of what they were thinking about. Later they address those distractions and try to resolve issues that are interfering with concentration. Gradually, the time lengths increase as the individuals learn to sustain focused attention and to choose topics and projects that hold their interest. I always provided choices of activities I knew were manageable, interesting, and challenging. Tasks that are "too easy" or "too hard" defeat purpose and decrease motivation. I find that as students experience the exhilaration of completing a "job well done" they seek more and greater challenges. They replace their typical attitude of "I can't" or "I don't want to" with a belief in "I can!"—a school motto I coined in 1982.

In the alternative school, karate also served to raise self-esteem. Sixty students, many of whom exhibited ADHD and ADHD-related characteristics such as aggressive behavior, inattentiveness, distractibility, and low self-esteem, selected karate as their optional activity. This class had several advantageous effects. First, the students were encouraged to believe themselves an elite group, especially if they made it to their first belt (though some did not). Physical exercises were rigorous and discipline tightly controlled. Initiates were directed to carry themselves with pride. Anyone involved in violent confrontation in or out of school was dismissed from karate class. The only justifiable explanation for fighting was "life endangerment." The lesson taught was that retreat is an acceptable defense, for, if you know who you are, you don't have to prove it to anyone.

Many of these students had previously reacted impulsively to situations common to adolescents such as name calling, rumor spreading, and gang challenges. They learned to regard themselves as "above" that level of interaction. The physical rigor of the program developed fitness and an accompanying sense of self-worth from having accomplished something difficult. Ceremonies accompanied belt awards and were conducted in the presence of the rest of the student body. Trophies won in interstate tournament competition were proudly displayed in the case in the school's entryway.

Inherent in the art of karate is self-discipline, self-control, and an ability to center one's focus. These are useful survival tools, for the ADHD individual in particular. Meditation techniques (e.g. Samples, 1987) were taught to enhance the ability to limit outside distractions and to calm the spirit. Positive self-talk fostered a strengthened sense of self. Hallowell and Ratey stated in the January 1993 edition of the newsletter from CH.A.D.D. (Children and Adults with Attention Deficit Disorders):

> Exercise is positively one of the best treatments for ADD. It helps work off excess energy and aggression in a positive way, it allows for noise-reduction within the mind, it stimulates the hormonal and neurochemical system in a most therapeutic way, and it soothes and calms the body. (Hallowell & Ratey, 1993, p. 7)

The students enrolled in my karate class consistently made honor roll regardless of former erratic academic performance. Behavioral referrals throughout the school declined significantly among the "karate kids." All staff members were notified as to who was enrolled in the class and some consistently used the karate terminology to remind students of their dedication to the art. Expected to demonstrate a high standard of conduct, they readily complied.

In addition to this daily elective program in karate, one of the most powerful components of the alternative school program was the outdoor adventure seminars. In the fall of each year the students attend a day long field trip to a local center designed to link participants (ranging from corporate businesses to local school-age students) to themselves, nature, and each other. Setting goals, problem-solving, working cooperatively, sustaining attention and encouraging success were all inherent within the framework established between the center and the staff prior to the experience. Activities range from group obstacle tasks such as a "trust fall," to rope courses set fifty feet up in the pine trees, to repelling a sixty-foot wall. Rain and cold do not delay the adventure. One of my best experiences was on such a day, when pelting cold rain without respite threatened to dampen spirits. The students and staff overcame not only adversity but the natural elements, through internal fires fanned by the community effort to persevere. Our cheers echoed loudly in the bus on the way home.

Kids, as well as adults, lose their sense of cool when fifty feet in the air. The toughest will be found hugging trees and swearing never to let go. Walk across a swaying rope bridge to the next platform? Unthinkable! Staff and peers encourage and chide until finally the person takes the risk and successfully meets the challenge. For everyone to succeed, for everyone to be safe, we all had to work together. Accomplishment and survival required trust and a transcendance above what was initially deemed impossible but then overcome. What prevailed for some for weeks, and among the students for as long as I knew them, was an indominable spirit. They had been able to reconnect with nature, their inner sources of strength, and their sense of community. They had learned to persevere. And they learned a little something about the essence of what is sacred.

Occasionally we would also implement a special week-long seminar at the center for a particular group of students having similar difficulties, though often very diverse in personality. These seminars were more intensive and evaluative in nature but geared toward similar goals—raising self-esteem, learning to problem-solve effectively, developing a sense of self within a community culture, and reconnecting with our first teacher, mother nature.

What is interesting is the effect that others' expectations for standards of behavior and performance have upon our students. It appears that if we believe they can do well and if we instill this belief in them, raising their individual self-esteem, there is generally a dramatic increase in the incidence of success. Ah, the power of positive thinking! What is frightening, however, is the impact on so many students surrounded by people and environments that are far less than supportive. No wonder so many kids are so masterful at negative attention-seeking strategies and that they so readily seem to "give up."

Carefully organizing school and class structures, providing continual and consistent monitoring of progress and positive feedback, compensating for needs of physical mobility and mental stimulation, and focusing particularly on raising self-esteem by empowering the individual: All contribute to creating a transactional educational environment that celebrates the joys of learning and growth. While these kinds of strategies are effective for all learners, they are essential for those with ADHD.

ADHD Adults in the Community College Setting

The Achievement Plus Program at Kalamazoo Valley Community College, designed and implemented by Dr. John Corbin (but as yet unpublished), served to address many similar facets of nontraditional students' needs in both their academic and personal lives. However, working with adults rather than teenagers introduces several new variables.

The Achievement Plus Program is a self-selected group of students who have acknowledged their lack of confidence in whether they will succeed in their academic pursuits by returning a postcard in the weeks prior to the beginning of class sessions. The program involves a closely knit staff, including counselors, educators, and administrators who provide ongoing support and services to the students in the program. During the first semester, students take needed remedial reading, writing, and math courses in addition to a personal development course. I was the instructor for both the reading and personal development courses. The students enrolled in the Achievement Plus Program included diverse populations with several multiethnic groups, recent high school graduates, an ex-convict and mental patient, a former prostitute, a fifty-five-year-old mother who had been a paper factory employee for twenty years, single working mothers, and several career oriented adult males. By the end of the semester a "family" had been created amongst these fundamentally different students. Most have continued their academic endeavors successfully; this is remarkable, since many had exhibited strong ADHD characteristics and variable success in past endeavors.

Although the reading course was previously skills-based and centered around textbook activities, I restructured my reading course to exemplify a whole language philosophy and instructional methodology. This helped to balance the variety of needs posed by such a diverse group of students. Each week, students wrote in their personal journals and summarized and reacted to professional readings. Students were required to read eight books from four different genres, including children's literature, classics, fiction of their own choice, and nonfiction books geared toward personal or professional development. Students were allowed choices within this framework and devised many creative ways to report on their readings, including collage representation of plot and theme, oral dramatization of book sections, and written and oral presentations to the class.

Several of these students with clear attributes of ADHD had never previously read an entire book. I brought in several books and talked about their content to generate interest, besides providing a bibliography with short summaries. This was for reference and motivational purposes only; students could select any books that stimulated personal interest and motivation to read. As students completed their "first-ever" books, excitement in the classroom generated sharing of new ideas and book titles. Students were becoming responsible for, and involved in, their own learning. Self-esteem grew. Previously viewing themselves as nonreaders, these people became literary club members. I will never forget the oral reading of a children's classic to the class by a tattooed, forty-four-year-old ex-convict. Everyone in the room was visibly moved.

As in the alternative high school program, students were allowed choice of activity, freedom of expression, and an environment that promoted and rewarded risk-taking, thereby encouraging students to explore their own emotions, interests, and academic pursuits. For some of these students this was the first time they could feel good about themselves and this in turn created a sense of security that urged them to become even greater risk-takers in their own endeavors.

The personal development class, which I nicknamed "Life 101," provided the students with an array of coping strategies both in and out of school. As adults, these individuals had concerns more far-reaching than those of the high school students. How to successfully manage work, school, relationships, and academic pursuits is therefore integral to the course.

As with my other courses, journals provided an ongoing means of assessment for each student. Weekly guest speakers, mostly on-campus staff and former A+ students, relayed their struggles in accomplishing personal and professional goals, establishing a noteworthy mentoring program. On the basis of in-class introductions, the students each selected a personal mentor to contact for support and advice. Students came to understand that they were not alone in their journeys toward self-reliance. It is a shared and continual process for us all. In addition, the students learned the value of networking: People are sometimes our best resources!

Off-campus retreats were an integral part of the program as well, providing time for the students to fraternize with their mentors in a more relaxed environment. Seminars were conducted on such things as entrepreneurs and their secrets of success, employability skills, group processing and group problem-solving tactics, and enhancing self-esteem. Many of these people had never been outside of their own familiar environments, and a weekend "away" from pressures and responsibilities to focus on themselves as individuals was an enriching experience.

Many of the course activities came from a resource text entitled *Becoming a Master Student* by David Ellis (1985). The chapters include test-taking skills, time and money management, note-taking, creativity development, memory, relationships, health, and others. With its variety of practical applications, this text is a valuable resource for students focusing on personal scheduling and management; it is especially pertinent to students with an Attention Deficit Hyperactivity Disorder. For example, one exercise requires the students to fill out a daily schedule, recording activities in half-hour increments. This helped many people to assess where they were spending most of their time and energy and to consider how they might better accomplish desired goals. Time in front of the TV, chatting on the telephone, or socializing became less of a priority when these individuals began pursuing more important goals.

The "Relationships" chapter explored ideas surrounding self-esteem and developing interpersonal communications. This is also very helpful for the ADHD individual, who often tends to blame others and not to look within to find the true source of the difficulty.

In coordination with the "Health" chapter, the Achievement Plus program paid for and required each student to receive a complete physical exam by on-campus resources. This provided both the students and the staff with pertinent health-related information that could affect their development and success as students. It would be beneficial for this evaluation to include an ADHD diagnostic for targeted individuals. Several of these students exemplified the behaviors and characteristics of ADHD in both their personal and academic lives. Medications such as Ritalin or Cyclert might well diminish some of the barriers interfering with their progress, such as distractibility, difficulty completing tasks, inattentiveness and the tendency to daydream, making and sticking to deadlines, and so on. As the program and staff continue to develop, hopefully so will the available resources.

The "Creativity" chapter included guided meditation and relaxation techniques very similar to the ones offered through the karate class in the high school; it also incorporated creative writing and thinking strategies. This offered the ADHD individuals new ways of viewing previous "problems" through an enlightened awareness of their thought processes and of how to direct their often highly creative energies.

The structure and content of these courses and this program did wonders for the students I encountered exhibiting the ADHD profile. They were given a support system and personal strategies to cope with previously debilitating circumstances and barriers to their own growth and development as students and as individual people.

Conclusions

I feel extremely fortunate to have worked both in the alternative high school and as a member of the A+ team at the community college. These experiences provided me with a window to the world of the ADHD and at-risk student, prompting me to consider ways that I might empower them to reach their higher aspirations. I am thankful that much of what I chose to do, in following a whole language philosophy of education, was appropriate in light of what I have now learned through my readings and research on ADHD. I continue to seek ways to improve myself as an educator. The rewards are great when students previously labeled as "failures" achieve monumental successes. Observing students' strengthening of heart and spirit as they overcame their fears and failures was heartening; it was, indeed, one of the most rewarding accomplishments of my teaching career. I will always remember these students and have learned invaluable lessons from them. I hope more people will become aware of the difficulties that ADHD students face in their academic pursuits and in their social interactions and will join in the effort to promote their growth as competent and highly valuable members of our society.

References

Ellis, D. (1985). *Becoming a master student.* Rapid City, SD: College Survival Inc.

Fowler, M., Barkley, R.A., Reeve, R., & Zentall, S. (1992). *CH.A.D.D. educator's manual: An in-depth look at attention deficit disorders from an educational perspective.* Plantation, FL: CH.A.D.D. Distributed by Caset Associations Ltd., Fairfax, VA.

Goldstein, S., & Ingersoll, B. (1992). Controversial treatments for children with Attention Deficit Hyperactivity Disorder. *CH.A.D.D.ER Box, 6*(2), 19–22.

Hallowell, E., & Ratey, J. (1993). 50 tips on the management of Adult Attention Deficit Disorder. *CH.A.D.D.ER Box, 6,* 1–8.

Laminack, L. L. (1991). *Learning with Zachary.* Richmond Hill, Ontario: Scholastic.

Samples, B. (1987). *Open mind/whole mind.* Rolling Hills Estates, CA: Jalmar Press.

Weaver, C. (1991). *Alternatives in understanding and educating attention-deficit students: Toward a systems-theory, whole language perspective.* Concept Paper No. 3. Urbana, IL: National Council of Teachers of English.

Weiss, G., & Hechtman, L. (1986). *Hyperactive children grown up: Empirical findings and theoretical considerations.* New York: Guilford Press.

9

Lessons from a Witch: Seeing Our Students and Ourselves Differently

William P. Bintz

I work from awkwardness. By that I mean I don't like to arrange things. If I stand in front of something, instead of arranging it, I arrange myself.

—*Diane Arbus*

In "Lessons from a Witch," William Bintz puts the needs of students with an Attention Deficit Disorder within a larger context: that of special needs students in particular, and simply of students in general. From a fictional witch, from an actual preservice teacher and her middle grade student, and from a high school student, William concludes: "When things aren't working out well in the classroom, don't focus on changing the nature of the learner; focus on changing the nature of the curriculum." This principle underlies the other chapters in this section and the next, as well as some of the previous chapters.

William P. Bintz is currently a doctoral candidate in the Language Education Department, School of Education, at Indiana University, Bloomington, Indiana. Previously, he has taught middle school and high school language arts in Chicago, Illinois, Aquadilla and San Juan, Puerto Rico, and Dhahran, Saudi Arabia. In 1988, he was a Visiting Lecturer in Language Education at the Armidale College of Advanced Education in Armidale, New South Wales, Australia. He has taught undergraduate and graduate courses in elementary and secondary reading methods classes at Indiana University. At present, he teaches secondary language arts methods classes at Western Kentucky University. His personal experience and professional interests include whole language, alternative education, constructivist inquiry, and collaborative research.

Winnie is a witch. And, like most witches, she loves black. Her house is black. She has black carpets, black chairs, and a black bed with black sheets and black blankets. Even her bath is black. Winnie also has a black cat, Wilbur, and that's where the trouble starts.

Sometimes, Winnie accidentally sits on Wilbur as he sleeps peacefully in a chair. Since both are black, it's hard for her to see where the chair stops and where Wilbur begins. At other times, she trips over Wilbur as he sits on the carpet in the hallway. Something has to be done.

One day, Winnie waves her magic wand and turns Wilbur into a bright green cat. Now, she can see him everywhere in the house. This works, of course, until Winnie puts Wilbur outside in the yard. There, he blends in perfectly with the tall green grass, making it impossible once again for Winnie to see where the grass ends, and where Wilbur begins.

The next day Winnie rushes out the back door, trips over Wilbur lying in the grass, turns three somersaults, and crashes into a rose bush. Winnie is furious. She takes her magic wand and waves it five times in the air. Suddenly, Wilbur has a red head, a yellow body, a pink tail, blue whiskers, and four purple legs. Now, Winnie can see him anywhere.

Winnie, of course, is relieved, but Wilbur is miserable. He's embarrassed by the way he now looks. He doesn't want to be seen by anybody, so he climbs the tallest tree to hide. After a while, Winnie can't stand to see him so sad. One day, she has an brilliant idea. She waves her magic wand in the air, yells ABRACADABRA!, and Wilbur is changed into a black cat again. He quickly scampers down the tree, glad to be himself again. But, Winnie isn't done yet.

She grabs her wand and waves it in the air again, and again, and again. Suddenly, instead of a black house she has a bright yellow house with a red roof and a red door. She also has white chairs decorated with red and white cushions. The carpet is green with pink roses, the bath is gleaming white, and the bed is blue with pink and white sheets and pink blankets. Winnie can now see Wilbur no matter where he is.

I introduce this chapter with a retelling of *Winnie the Witch* (Paul & Thomas, 1987) for three reasons. First, I want to use Winnie as a metaphor for describing some of my own recent experiences as a reading educator and reading researcher and for discussing how these experiences have helped me think differently about curriculum and curriculum development. Second, I want to use this story as an invitation for teachers, students, and parents to shift perspective, to change the "angle of vision" (Tchudi, 1992), so that we can begin to see differently those students who have problems with attention and impulsivity, as well as other "special needs" students, and to see ourselves differently as well. And, third, I want to use this story as a potential for generating some new conversations about how we can best promote learning, particularly among students labeled as having special needs.

Belief as Perspective

In a world of uncertainty, one thing is for sure: What teachers believe really matters. In particular, what teachers believe about literacy, literacy learning, curriculum, assessment, and schooling significantly influences how they create classroom conditions for learning. It's important, then, for teachers to identify and reflect on what really matters in their professional lives. More specifically, it's important for them to continually articulate what beliefs they currently hold, to interrogate to what extent these beliefs reflect the best we currently know about learning, and to ask themselves how to create classroom contexts that best support learning.

Therefore, I want to begin by asking, what do we currently believe about special education, including education for those with an alleged attention deficit disorder? And do these beliefs reflect recent advances in literacy and literacy learning?

Current Perspective

Salvage and Brazee (1991) contend that special education is rooted historically in a medical model of learning. This model assumes that the role of special education teachers, like physicians, is to "treat" students. In this context, treatment denotes a process whereby teachers diagnose student deficiencies, prescribe appropriate remedies, and accurately assess to what extent specific weaknesses have been corrected or "cured" over time; that is, to what extent students have learned whatever is supposed to be learned. Over the years this model has developed a number of labels for classifying students diagnosed as needing special treatment. These include labels such as attention deficit disorder, slow learners, learning disabled, culturally deprived, semilingual, limited–English speaking, special needs, and more recently, *"at risk."* Very often, specific "treatment" for these individuals comes in the form of individualized educational programs or "plans of action," designed to offer developmentally appropriate curricular experiences for individual students (Flores, Tefft-Cousin, & Diaz, 1991).

Traditionally, these beliefs have been widely recognized and accepted by the special education community. Recently, however, an increasing number of special education teachers and researchers have started to seriously challenge these beliefs. These educators demonstrate that current theoretical assumptions and instructional practices in special education are inadequate, given the best we know about literacy and literacy learning, and thus do little more than perpetuate a deleterious mythology about special needs students.

Flores, Tefft-Cousin, and Diaz (1991) claim that this mythology perpetuates several erroneous assumptions about special needs students. These are some of the assumptions: (1) special needs children have a language problem, their language and culture is deficient, they lack experiences, and these deficiencies cause them to have learning problems; (2) special needs children need to be separated from the regular class and need a structured program based on hierarchical notions of language development; (3) standardized tests can accurately identify and categorize special needs students with learning/language problems; and (4) special needs children have problems because their parents don't care, can't read, or don't work with them.

Viewing special needs students differently, these researchers propose instead a set of alternative assumptions: (1) special needs children are proficient language users and bring potentially significant curricular experiences into the classroom; (2) special needs children need opportunities to develop language and literacy; (3) special needs students can be successful in regular classroom programs; (4) the language and literacy development of special needs students can be effectively monitored by observing their language use in authentic settings across the curriculum; and (5) parents of special needs children are interested in the achievement and success of their children in the school setting and can be partners in the educational experience of their children (Flores, Tefft-Cousin, & Diaz, 1991).

To be sure, these new assumptions challenge traditional views of special education. More importantly, they challenge special education teachers to suspend their current beliefs in order to think differently about special needs students. In short, they challenge us to shift perspective.

Shifting Perspective

Like everything in life, all teaching and learning are grounded in perspective. As teachers and learners, the perspective we hold greatly influences the questions we ask, the observations we make, the conversations we understand, and the meanings we construct in everyday life. Historically, my own perspective on special education was firmly grounded in the medical model discussed earlier. For years I believed that to teach was to transmit information by diagnosing, categorizing, treating, and assessing student performance. And for years this belief went unexamined and unchallenged.

Recently, however, I've shifted my perspective on teaching and learning as a result of my experiences with three individuals: Jane, a high school junior; Sara, a preservice teacher; and Winnie, the fictional witch introduced earlier. These individuals have taught me many important lessons about teaching, learning, and living. Specifically, they have taught me not only to see my students and myself differently but also to think differently about curriculum and curriculum development. Let me briefly introduce each of them to you.

Sara

When I first met Sara, she was a senior at a major midwestern university, and a preservice teacher in the teacher education department. At the time she was completing her nine-week student teaching practicum at a local middle school, and I was her university supervisor. About midway through the practicum, I made one of my weekly visits to observe her teach. When I arrived at her room, the class had not started. Sara was up at the chalkboard writing down assignments for students to complete that day. As soon as she saw me, she stopped writing and walked back to where I was standing. She said, "Thank goodness, you're here. I have got to talk to you as soon as this class is over." I asked, "Is anything wrong?" She responded, "Yeah. . . ." but was interrupted by the bell signaling that class had begun.

When the class ended and the students left the room, Sara poured her heart out to me. She began by saying, "I am going crazy. I am just going nuts with this class, and, in particular, with one boy in this class. It's a pre-algebra class, and I can't get anything done. Now, on the whole, the class is really okay. But there's this one boy who is constantly disruptive. He won't sit still. He has no attention span at all and won't do anything I ask him to do. He constantly interrupts me, and, if he isn't bothering me, he is bothering others while they are trying to work. He is in constant motion. He moves from one desk to another, talking to people he has no business talking to. When I finally get him settled down, he asks me to repeat what we are doing in class that day. I feel frustrated because I really don't know what to do with him. I've tried all sorts of ways to make the material fun and enjoyable, but nothing seems to work. I am starting to feel guilty because as I am preparing to come to school in the morning, I'm finding myself secretly hoping he will be absent that day. I can't help it. When he's not there, everything is so much better. But I don't want to feel that way."

Now, since I did not actually know this student, I felt at a loss as to what specific advice to give Sara. I did say, however, that at this point it might be good for her to sit down with the student, share with him some of her frustration, and see what insights and possibilities that conversation might bring. She agreed to give it a try.

The next week I visited Sara again in her class. Unlike the previous week, she came up to me and excitedly said that she had some interesting news to share. Once again, after class we sat down and she reported on her conversation with this student. Apparently, when she shared her frustration with the student, he immediately responded by assuring her that she wasn't the problem in the class. Rather, the curriculum was the problem. He went on to explain that basically he was bored in her class, but not bored with her. While he never had taken pre-algebra before, he already knew the material that she was covering in class and could prove it to her if she wanted. He went on to explain that even if he didn't know the material, he could learn it in a much better and much faster way than how she was currently teaching it. Essentially, he felt that she was teaching everybody the same material in the same way. He was confident, however, that he could get a few of his friends in the class to prove to her that they could learn the material more effectively if she would allow them to. In the end, his argument was this: he was disruptive basically because he had to adapt to the curriculum instead of the curriculum adapting to him.

Jane

When I first met Jane, she was a sixteen year old junior at a medium-sized urban high school in a large midwestern city. At the time I was a member of a research team investigating the reading experiences of students from grades 6–12. This project called for individual members of the research team to interview a number of high school juniors at four different schools. The purpose of these interviews was to glean insights into the types of in-school and out-of-school reading experiences that students typically had in progressing from middle school to high school. Jane was one of forty-four high school students who participated in this project.

On the morning I was scheduled to interview Jane, I went through my normal routine. Stopping in the main office, I notified the secretary that I would be in the building that day. This morning, however, unlike the others, the principal came out of her office and asked to speak to me for a few minutes.

As I sat in her office, the principal stated that she felt it was necessary to talk to me before I interviewed Jane. Essentially, she wanted to provide me with some background information. During the fifteen minutes that we talked, the principal gave the following account of Jane.

Jane is a very intelligent person, with above-average standardized test scores. She is also an anomaly. In general, she dislikes school and attends erratically. She has been a discipline problem in class on countless occasions— disruptive, manipulative, uninterested in and even apathetic about school work. She often doesn't participate in class, refuses to do homework, and deliberately rejects her classes by engaging in such practices as handing in signed but incomplete tests and activity sheets as soon as they are given to her. At best, her grades are D+. She can't wait to graduate and leave school. In short, she has not had many positive experiences with school, despite her obvious potential.

Afterward, I thanked the principal for talking to me about Jane. I stayed in my chair, since I was scheduled to use her office to interview Jane ten minutes later. As the principal left, she turned and said, "Good luck."

Soon after, Jane entered and sat directly across from me. I briefly introduced myself, then talked about the nature of the research and the purpose for the interview. She nodded, saying, "Go for it." I did.

I started by simply asking, "Why don't you just talk a little bit about what school has been like for you since the sixth grade, and, in particular, talk about the kinds of reading experiences you have had since then?"

Without hesitation, Jane launched into a fairly detailed description of her educational and instructional history. At first, she talked about all the good experiences in elementary school, when she had enjoyed school. She liked her teachers, enjoyed learning, received good grades, and made good friends. In junior high school, however, Jane started to dislike school, and in the ninth grade rejected it outright. By the end of the interview, much of what Jane reported about her high school experiences confirmed what the principal had told me earlier.

After Jane finished her story, I asked if there was anything else that she wanted me to know, anything that she felt I needed to know but hadn't ask. She paused, then said, "Yeah, you really need to know one more thing. You need to know that everything I have said to you this morning, everything like how I don't come to school when I can get away with it, how I flunk all my classes, how I disrupt my classes, and how I refuse to do my assignments, well, you need to know that I do all those things deliberately. You see, all my teachers think I'm not a very good student. They complain that I won't read what they assign, or even be seen around school with any textbooks. Well, they're right. But they are wrong, too."

She continued. "You see, none of my teachers know this, or could possibly believe this, but I am a very good student. I am also a very good reader. In fact, I often feign sickness so that I can stay home and just read in my room all day. Reading is important to me. It has always been important to me. I like to read, and in actual fact, read a lot. But my teachers think I'm not a good reader because I won't read what they tell me to read. They don't understand that I won't read what they assign because it doesn't interest me. They also don't understand that I read a lot because I read things that I am interested in. In school, teachers don't make any room in the curriculum for my reading. They only make room for their own, you know, for reading they have to assign. So, you really need to know that I deliberately don't go to school, I deliberately don't do the reading assignments, and I deliberately don't take tests because that's my way of rejecting school reading. It's also my way of legitimating myself as a reader and my own reading interests. My teachers have no idea that's what I am doing."

Winnie the Witch

Since I've already introduced Winnie at the beginning of this chapter, I won't go into any more detail about her other than to say that in the story she learns a very important lesson from her cat, Wilbur. I believe that the story offers us all a lesson in the potential available when we shift perspective.

In this story it's clear that things just aren't working out very well for Winnie or for Wilbur. Winnie is frustrated because she can't seem to prevent sitting on or tripping over Wilbur throughout the day. And Wilbur is frustrated because, no matter where he is in the house, he can't seem to stay out of Winnie's way.

In the beginning, Winnie assumes that Wilbur is the problem. She believes that, if only she can change him, the problem will be solved. And, that's exactly what she does. She changes Wilbur from a black cat to a green cat to, finally, a multicolored cat. Not long after, however, Winnie learns that changing Wilbur doesn't solve the problem. In fact, if anything, it makes the problem worse.

In time, Winnie begins to think differently about the problem. In particular, she begins to think differently about the source of the problem. She begins to ask, if Wilbur isn't the problem, then what is? In the end, by asking a different question, Winnie is able to shift perspective and in the process learns a very important lesson: *If things aren't working out well, instead of changing the cat, change the conditions under which he lives.*

Now on the surface it might appear that these three individuals (Jane, Sara, Winnie) have very little in common. For starters, Jane and Sara are real people, whereas Winnie is a fictional character. But even if Winnie is excluded, Jane and Sara still appear to be very different individuals. For instance, Jane is an adolescent; Sara is an adult. Jane is a student; Sara is a teacher. Jane is a city girl; Sara is a country girl. Jane is unsuccessful in school; Sara is successful. Jane actively resists school-based learning; Sara actively promotes it. Jane is burnt-out on school; Sara is turned on. For Jane, school is meaningless and oppressive; for Sara, it is meaningful and liberating.

And yet, at a deeper level, while all three are very different individuals, I believe they all share a very similar experience. Each reports an experience where, in one way or another, "things were just not working out well." For Jane, going to school was not working out well because she had little or no voice in the curriculum. For Sara, attempting to teach a recalcitrant student was not working out well because he was not really cooperating with her in covering the curriculum. And, for Winnie, living with Wilbur was not working out well because he was always getting in the way and preventing her from getting on with her business.

But, more importantly, these individuals are connected in that they all not only came to shift perspective but also to share a common perspective, one that enabled them to think very differently about *why* "things were not working out well." In Jane's case, her teachers believed that she was the real problem. To them, Jane was not being a very good student, despite her obvious ability. And yet Jane came to believe that she wasn't the problem at all. Rather, she came to believe that the problem was rooted not in her, but in the imposition of a stultifying curriculum.

Obviously, Jane and her teachers have different notions of what the problem is, as well as what must be done to solve the problem. On the one hand, Jane's teachers believe that the situation is a student problem, and that one way to solve the problem is to change the student by "tightening up" on her; that is, to tightly prescribe and monitor a restricted set of curricular opportunities that give Jane no voice or choice in the matter. Jane, on the other hand, believes just the opposite. She believes that the situation is not a student problem but a curricular problem, and that the way to solve the problem is not to restrict or close down the curriculum, but rather to open it up.

Similarly, Sara in the beginning also believed that her student was the reason why things were not working out well in the classroom. Unlike Jane's teachers, Sara is a novice teacher with very little experience dealing with students who, like the one in her classroom, are rarely focused, often disruptive, and always difficult to manage. However, after having a conversation with this student, Sara, too, began to realize that the situation was not an instructional problem, as she originally thought, but rather a curricular problem. That is, she came to understand that the reason things were not working out well was not due so much to student weaknesses as to curricular deficiencies. Sara came to understand the problem differently. The problem evolved from being defined as what specific knowledge could she teach this student, to how could she find out what he perceives the difficulty to be, and how could she create a classroom context that would best resolve this difficulty.

Finally, in Winnie's case, when things were not working out well, she too believed, at least initially, that Wilbur was the problem. She tried to solve the problem by making him literally look different. But in the process, and despite her good intentions, Winnie succeeded in not only making Wilbur look different but also in making him feel different, making him feel excluded, isolated, and alienated. Fortunately, in the end Winnie, like Jane and Sara, was able to understand that, while superficially it seems more logical to change a "cat" (substitute "student") to fit the "environment" (substitute "curriculum"), ultimately it is wiser to change the environment to fit the cat.

In the final analysis, my experiences with Jane and Sara in conjunction with my reading of *Winnie the Witch* have all pushed me to think differently not only about special needs students, but also about curriculum and curriculum development. More than anything else, these three individuals have taught me a modified version of the lesson Winnie learned from her cat: *When things aren't working out well in the classroom, don't focus on changing the nature of the learner; focus on changing the nature of the curriculum.*

References

Flores, B., Cousin, P. T., & Diaz, E. (1991). Transforming deficit myths about learning, language, and culture. *Language Arts, 68* (September), 369–379.

Paul, K., & Thomas, V. (1987). *Winnie the witch.* New York: Kane/Miller.

Salvage, G. J., & Brazee, P. E. (1991). Risk taking, bit by bit. *Language Arts, 68* (September), 356–366.

Tchudi, S. (1992). *Travels across the curriculum.* New York: Scholastic.

10

Instructional Paradigms and the Attention Deficit Hyperactive Disorder Child

Barb Wallace and Shirley Crawford

Barb and Shirley begin their discussion by contrasting some key assumptions of traditional skills-oriented classrooms with those of whole language classrooms. The heart of this chapter is an interview with the mother of an attention deficit student, in which she documents and describes the differing impact of the two kinds of classrooms on her son Randy, now age eighteen. In the former kinds of classrooms, his self-esteem and self-confidence, social relationships, and learning all suffered. In the latter kinds of classrooms, he blossomed.

Barb Wallace has experience as a teacher, administrator, and education consultant. She works closely with teachers and administrators in developing and implementing curriculum, with particular emphasis on a holistic approach to language and learning. As a recognized leader in teaching and learning in Alberta, Canada, she makes presentations to parents and speaks at workshops and conferences. Barb has a number of publications to her credit. She is currently Supervisor of Curriculum for Foothills School Division #38, Alberta.

Shirley Crawford has many years' experience teaching in elementary and secondary schools across Alberta and has also taught reading and language arts courses at the University of Lethbridge. She provides professional development to teachers and guidance to parents through her workshops on language arts and responding to children with exceptional needs. Shirley also has several publications to her credit, including various school district curriculum and policy handbooks. She is currently a Program Specialist for Foothills School Division #38, Alberta.

The decisions we make in our everyday lives arise from a set of beliefs. For example, one might wear a seat belt as a safety measure or to abide by the law, depending upon one's belief system. Teaching is no different. Jaggar (1989, p. 19) quotes Helgeson, Blosser, & Howe (1978) from the Rand Corporation study: "'The teacher is key. What science (or math or social studies or language) education will be for any one (child) for any one year will depend on what the child's teacher believes, knows, and does—and doesn't believe, doesn't know, and doesn't do.' The quality of our own understandings about language, reading, writing, child growth and development, materials, and methods will to a large extent influence what is done in the classroom."

In the course of any one day we make numerous decisions about children and curriculum based on the beliefs we hold about learning. Based on theory and research, observation, practice, reflection, and social dialogue these beliefs can either aid or deter the progress of children. The Attention Deficit

Hyperactive Disorder (ADHD) child has not escaped unscathed and in most instances has shown adverse effects from traditional special education assumptions about teaching learning and appropriate classroom behavior. "By definition pedagogy is always concerned with the ability to distinguish between what is good and what is not good for children" (Van Manen, 1991, p. 10). Current pedagogical literature reflects research from various disciplines supporting some basic assumptions about learning. The following points made by Church (1992, pp. 10–16) are based on such findings.

- Children learn through active involvement in experiences that have real meaning for them.
- They draw upon their prior knowledge about the world and about language to develop new understandings.
- Children develop and use a broad range of strategies as they learn to solve problems.
- Children become increasingly more independent in their learning and thinking through experimentation and self-reflection.
- They learn best when their learning is integrated so that they make connections among the language processes and across subject disciplines.
- Children learn through social interactions.
- Collaboration with other children and adults enhances their learning.

While it is now recognized that the majority of children will master literacy in a developmental, constructionist manner, education of the ADHD child has traditionally been based on a reductionist point of view. Poplin (1988b) contends that the reductionist paradigm underpins all four models, the medical model, the psychological process model, the behavioral model, and the cognitive strategy model, which principally provide guidance to the field of learning disabilities. Subscribers to these models believe that identifying and establishing desired behaviors will produce efficient learners.

In the philosophy underlying reductionism, a diagnosis was made and a cure prescribed. Standardized tests were used to identify and categorize deficits. In some classrooms ADHD children and others at risk received prescribed structured programs based on hierarchical theories of skill development. It was expected that a "specialist" teacher would administer the correct dosage of the prescribed medication (chemical and/or educational) and in turn the child would be well. Taylor (1990) contends that "Identification and prescription results in labelling which often negates any possible positive effect from the extra assistance." Instead, it appears to decrease the child's self-esteem and to create a feeling of powerlessness. To compound the problem, these children usually find themselves separated from the "regular" classroom students; this deprives them of good models and limits their opportunities to extend their knowledge base. Segregation also conflicts with Vygotsky's (1978) assertion that individuals will understand and use a particular cognitive process if exposed to demonstrations by more proficient learners. Segregation of less proficient learners leads to modeling of peers who are also confused about the process. This tends to force the teacher to assume the role of sole transmitter of knowledge.

Teachers who subscribe to this model tend to have a very subject-oriented focus that often precludes flexibility. These teachers may see ADHD children as being very disruptive to their routines and academic progress. ("They never complete their work!" explained one teacher.) ADHD students require much time, patience, and understanding. The demand on teachers' time creates frustration and could lead to blaming the child for conflicts that result. Teachers sometimes blame a child's poor classroom performance on deficiencies in the child's cultural background, a neurological disorder, or upbringing at home. There is a neurological factor in appropriately diagnosed instances, but the environment (for example, classroom expectations) plays a critical role in the behavior exhibited. Teacher responses to the "deviant" behavior will cause other children to accept or reject the ADHD child. If in order to make academic progress, the ADHD child must adapt to and learn traditionally prescribed academic tasks, he is doomed to fail.

The paradigm shift now occurring in education suggests a brighter future for the ADHD child. The constructivist/holistic paradigm reflects what we know about how learning occurs. For example, it is recognized that the speech development for most children occurs without formal instruction. When children come to school, they are able to use the language in understandable ways. While unable to define verbs, adverbs, and conjunctions, they know where to use these. Poplin (1988a) says: "Constructivists posit that learning is a process whereby new meanings are created (constructed) *by the learner within the context of her or his current knowledge*" (p. 404). In a setting where learning is viewed in this way, the knowledgeable teacher begins by attempting to determine what the child already knows, for example, about print, text, language usage, reading strategies, and the conventions of language. Sarason (1991) states: "First you must understand and digest the fact that children, all children, come to school motivated to enlarge their worlds. You start with their worlds. . . . You look at them to determine how what they are, seek to know, and have experienced can be used as the fuel to fire the process for enlargement of interests, knowledge and skills."

Teachers must therefore be "kid watchers" who *really* know their students and place importance on each child's beliefs, attitudes, and concept of self as a learner. If children think they can, they will. In the words of Poplin (1988a) "To the constructivist, learning is not simply the taking in of new information as it exists externally (in adult minds, in the curriculum or text), it is the natural, continuous construction and reconstruction of new, richer, and more complex and connected meanings by the learner" (p. 404). Teachers who recognize this allow for flexibility in content, instructional strategies, and organization. They capitalize on the children's background knowledge, interests, and strengths in developing learning opportunities. This accommodates varying levels of ability and performance. Routines in these classrooms have built-in activity breaks, choices, flexible grouping, discussion, and reflection time. The highly active child is not seen as a problem in a classroom where children are actively engaged in learning. By modeling their acceptance of the ADHD child, teachers encourage other children to value the child as well. In these classrooms the ADHD child can function successfully and make lasting friendships. One parent concerned about her ADHD child commented, "We don't want sympathy that we have a child who is ADHD, or learning disabled; we need acceptance and understanding."

What follows is a conversation with the mother of an ADHD child, a teacher, who saw her child as a casualty in the educational system. Randy's success in constructivist/holistic classrooms—where teachers made decisions based on their understanding of Randy and how children learn—was in direct contrast to his experiences in classrooms operating on the reductionist philosophy. His lack of interest, little progress, and loss of self-confidence in the reductionist setting made the mother extremely frustrated. This led her to delve further into the professional literature, trying to assist her child and to relieve her own anxieties. She documents for us Randy's experiences in the two vastly different classroom settings. There were variations of the two paradigms, but for the purpose of this interview we asked her to contrast classrooms at the extreme ends of the continuum.

INTERVIEWERS: You mentioned that Randy had experienced two types of classrooms. Could you elaborate on that for us? What were the major differences?
MOTHER: For the purposes of this discussion I will refer to the two types of classrooms Randy encountered as classrooms A and B.

First, when discussing Randy's performance with teachers in classroom A, their questions, such as "What is his diagnosis?", "Is he on medication?", "What is his reading level?" and "Is he learning disabled?" dominated the discussion. Questions were always addressed to us, his parents. Yet, when we tried to explain some basic adaptations that would prevent difficulties for Randy, our suggestions were disregarded. It often left us with an uneasy feeling. We questioned whether parents' input into their children's educational program was valuable. Doesn't knowing what has worked in the past count?

Second, inflexible routines and prescribed programs were already established in these classrooms, and Randy had to adapt to them. His interests, background knowledge, and strengths were not a focus in programming for him. His comments about the settings focused on the trouble he got into; for example, he said: "——and I were always talking," "Mrs.——kept me in at recess to do my spelling sheets," "We hid in the corner and made plans." Other comments related to extrinsic motivators as he said, "I got lots of stickers," "I did the most sheets!" and "Mrs.——took us for lunch when we finished that workbook." He does not remember those years for the knowledge, skills, or attitudes developed.

In the other type of classroom (B) governed by the new paradigm, the most glaring difference appeared to be the acceptance and recognition by the teacher that children are proficient learners and that they bring a wealth of knowledge to the educational setting. Children with ADHD are no exceptions to this. Randy felt that his contributions regarding interests, background knowledge, and experiences were valued in such classrooms. These are the placements he reflects on fondly. When he speaks of the teachers in these settings, he says that he appreciated their "sense of humor," "knowing where I'm coming from," and "always [being] there for me." In such classrooms Randy was not segregated for instruction but had the support and modeling of "regular" students.

Our initial contact with classrooms such as B precipitated questions like these: "What are your favorite subjects?" "What do you do for fun?" "Do you like to read?" "Will you be walking to school or taking the bus?" and "Do you know where to get the bus?" These questions were all directed to Randy, assuming that he had ideas, feelings, and worries. The teacher's comment on the bus schedule set him at ease because he typically finds security in knowing the day's sequence of events. A much more student-focused approach was immediately evident in classroom B. We usually left those classrooms feeling confident that our child would receive the best possible education.

INTERVIEWERS: Earlier on, you mentioned that your suggestions were not always well received. Would you care to share some of those suggestions?

MOTHER: The suggestions were things as simple as his needing a lock with a key instead of a combination for his locker and the need for assistance with excessive copying. Handwriting seems to be a major problem with children like Randy. The other day another mother of an ADHD child commented that her child's greatest delight with his new class was the reduction in the amount of copying he had to do.

INTERVIEWERS: It is obvious that the one classroom caused you frustration as a parent, especially considering the amount of reading you have been doing about thoughtful education, child development, and whole language.

MOTHER: Yes, you're right. In classroom A the assumption was that there was a need for more direct instruction focusing on the separate parts, broken down into minute skills, in order to later understand the complexity of the whole. In addition, the program was based on a model in which the expert diagnosed and prescribed a remedial program to correct the problems. Thus, it was assumed that there was something wrong with Randy and also that the wrong could be corrected by some kind of intervention or strategy. The instruction that followed plugged Randy into the sequence where he was supposedly deficient and attempted to provide what was missing. It was a hierarchical model that ignored Randy's interests, personal knowledge, strengths, and learning styles. Instead, the focus on subskill mastery amounted to giving him more of what research shows that learners have difficulty doing—connecting the fragmented bits into a meaningful whole.

Some of his own frustrations were expressed in this kind of statement: "The worksheets were dumb. They were grade 1. They made me look like a dunce. The teacher says I can't spell, Mom, but I got a star in spelling yesterday!"

INTERVIEWERS: Did you see a difference in the work he was expected to do in the two types of classrooms?

MOTHER: Yes I did. In classroom A Randy did not progress—not, I feel, because he was unable to learn, but rather because he was never given the opportunity to really develop an understanding of topics. Content and a sequence of skills were prescribed by textbook and workbook writers without regard for creating a whole picture of Randy as an individual. For example, he became totally confused about numbers, and particularly money, because its use was never tied to his real world. He was accustomed to using money to buy things and could not relate this to the worksheets. Initially, he did not progress in language arts because the fragmented, isolated skills were not related to his understanding and enjoyment of the stories he had been writing and reading at home.

On the other hand, curriculum decisions in classroom B were based on the assumption that Randy, like his peers, did have some worthwhile knowledge. Learning was facilitated through the use of Randy's own experiences, enjoyable literature, reflections on ideas, and interests. These settings provided a wide variety of materials to read, discuss, and reflect upon. Randy was allowed choices in reading, in writing, and in research—topics, method of reporting, presenting, and discussing. Discussion was an important part of learning, and Randy's ideas were accepted and respected by his teachers and therefore by his peers. He was proud of his own work and loved to share, despite his difficulty with attention to task and handwriting.

INTERVIEWERS: How did these differences affect Randy?

MOTHER: In classroom A Randy had little input into the decision-making processes, which resulted in dependence on the decision makers. Randy's tendency to give up demonstrated that attitudes instilled by this approach did not encourage risk-taking, but instead limited or minimized his growth.

In classroom B there was a major focus on making decisions and taking risks. This enhanced Randy's feeling of self-worth and better prepared him to deal with real-life issues. The environment gave him confidence to share his ideas and opinions, even if they were not totally acceptable to his audience.

INTERVIEWERS: How do we reconcile the need to address prescribed curriculum expectations while meeting the needs of the ADHD child?

MOTHER: Topics that enhanced reading and writing skills for Randy included anything related to vehicles, skiing, his dog, and his family. His most glorious school day was one on which he presented a speech on "How to sell a car" to the school assembly of six hundred students. He just glowed with enthusiasm and had no difficulty attending to the task as he prepared, practiced, and presented the humorous oration. He had met many learning goals without having an imposed sequence of skills or topics. In preparing his speech for the school assembly, he had to consider who his audience was as he prepared for them. He had to make decisions about how best to present it so that his audience would become and remain interested. It was interesting to see the number of revisions he was willing to make. He added and deleted and made several word changes. He talked about the various advertising techniques he could and eventually did use. We were amazed at some of his explanations. They were certainly very logical and suited the topic. There was no question in our minds that the experience provided Randy with very worthwhile learning. Many curriculum objectives could and must have been met by that one assignment.

When asked about that particular assignment, Randy beamed with delight.

"Oh, yeah! That was a story that I made up. Well, it started off becoming, um, about this car salesman, about, in his teens and he meets this mystery girl that comes to buy a car and it turned out to be a mystery, a novel, and a love story all mixed into one."

INTERVIEWERS: What of evaluation? Was progress determined differently?

MOTHER: In classroom B the major focus in evaluation and reporting was on pointing out what Randy was able to do. His report cards included this kind of comment: "Randy is expressing his ideas orally and in writing. He is beginning to use capital letters and periods to indicate sentences. His narratives include

FIGURE 10–1. *Randy's journal writing.*

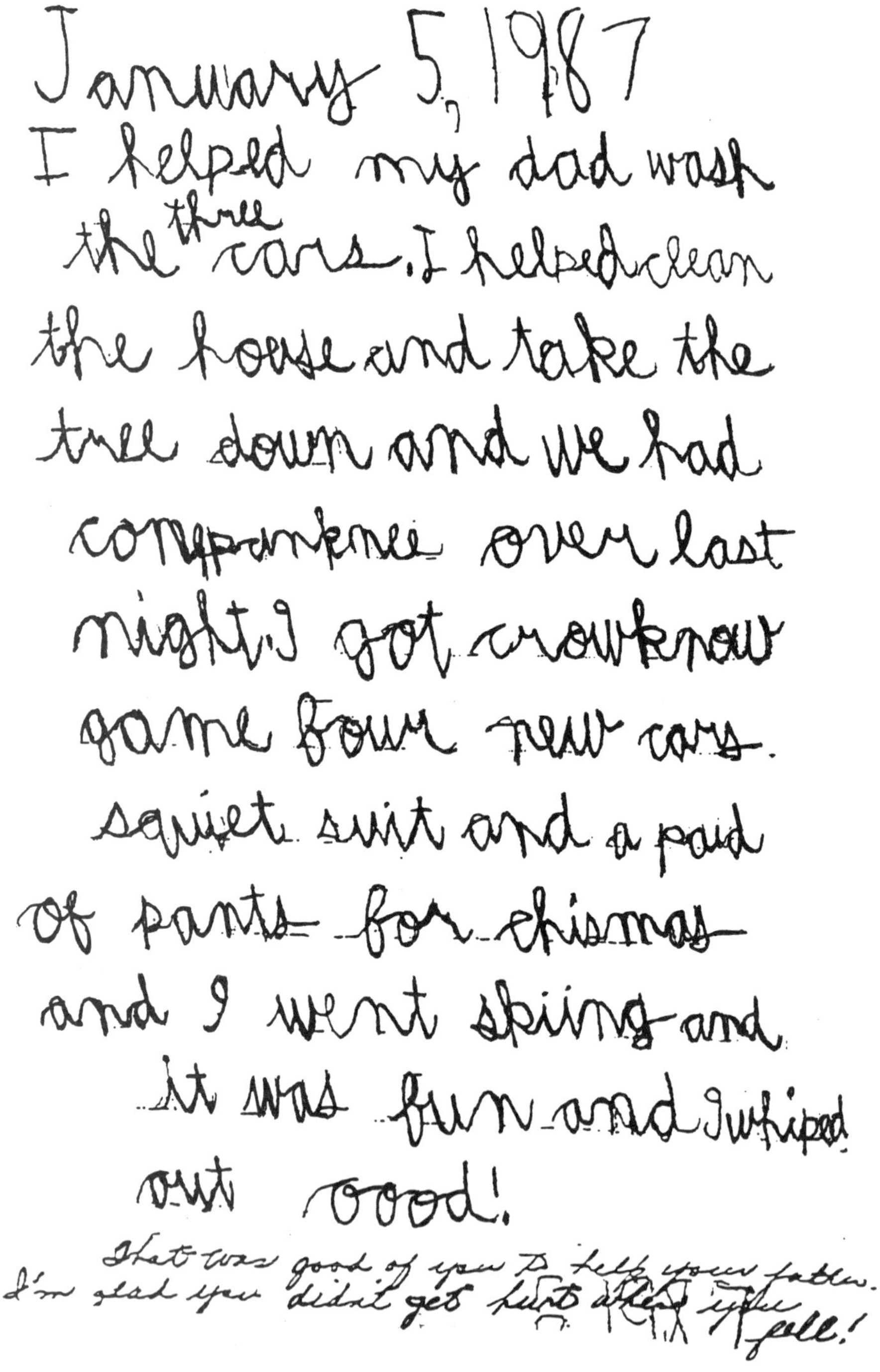

January 5, 1987
I helped my dad wash
the three cars. I helped clean
the house and take the
tree down and we had
compankinee over last
night. I got crowknow
game four new cars.
squiet suit and a paid
of pants for chismas
and I went skiing and
it was fun and I wiped
out oood!

That was good of you to help your father.
I'm glad you didn't get hurt when you fell!

beginnings, middles, and endings. His spelling attempts show a good understanding of beginning and ending consonant sounds." Further comments delineated focus for future lessons. For example: "Randy is working on increasing reading speed and fluency. He is starting to use very descriptive words as he writes. He is working at improving letter formations and increasing his writing speed."

In contrast, classroom A teachers pointed out what Randy was unable to do. For example: "Cursive letters are very large and incorrectly formed. Speed of writing is very slow and pencil grip is poor. Randy has a problem listening to a sequence of three directions to be performed physically over a period of ten to fifteen minutes. He has a problem sequencing simple paper and pencil tasks with three simple directives." Behavioral objectives played a central role in this reporting. Specific standardized scores were also important and were reported at least twice a year. Comments about future action focused on what the teacher would do rather than placing responsibility on Randy. For example: "Phonics through the spelling program will be modified so that Randy does half of each assignment area in the spelling program." (This disregarded the fact that Randy has a hearing loss that hinders sound discrimination.) "Regular class reading assignments will be modified through quantity of assignments."

INTERVIEWERS: Journals are used a lot in schools today. Were Randy's experiences with journals different in the contrasting classrooms?

MOTHER: In classroom B he did not realize that he was writing a journal (Figure 10–1) because it became a dialogue between him and the teacher. It was almost like a long story. When asked about that journal, Randy responded: "That was not a journal, it was our sharing book. Mr.————wanted to learn more about me. He told me about himself, too. Don't call that a journal. Journals are yucky!" The teacher responses here were different, too. For example: "That was good of you to help your father. I'm glad you didn't get hurt when you fell!", "Maybe someday you will play on a professional team. I really love hockey too!" and "Are you going to tell me about all the different makes of cars?"

INTERVIEWERS: What were Randy's feelings about journals in the other type of classroom?

MOTHER: When asked about journals in classroom A, he responded, "I hated journals! I just said the same old boring thing day after day." Comments in his journal reflected his lack of interest as well. (See Figure 10–2.) Comments focused on hating school and word-for-word repetition several days in a row. Typical teacher's responses include: "Tomorrow I would like to see you write at least one sentence, please!" and "Randy, try to start some of your sentences differently. You use 'I like' and 'I have' too much." It was not surprising that he felt negatively about these journals.

INTERVIEWERS: To change our focus for a moment, we would like to ask some questions that might assist others in understanding and working with the ADHD child. First, how are you able to tell if your child has an Attention Deficit Hyperactive Disorder?

MOTHER: It is not too difficult if the attention deficit is accompanied by hyperactivity because kids are constantly on the move. There is a disorder in which the child has an attention deficit without hyperactivity, and this is more difficult to pinpoint. Psychologists do have checklists to help with identification. Generally, when hyperactivity is present, I would look for the following traits:

1. Is the child constantly in motion and fidgeting?
2. Does the child have difficulty taking turns in games?
3. Is the child very egocentric?
4. Does the child often blurt out answers before questions are completed?
5. Does the child have difficulty sustaining attention and is he or she easily distracted?
6. Does the child complete tasks and/or play activities?
7. Does the child often lose and break things?
8. Does the child talk excessively and not listen to others?
9. Is the child aware of the possible consequences of engaging in dangerous activities?
10. Does the child often interrupt or intrude on others?

INTERVIEWERS: We know that this is frustrating for you; but, having heard the list of symptoms, we would like to know how and by whom Randy was identified as ADHD.

FIGURE 10–2. *Journal entry reflecting lack of interest.*

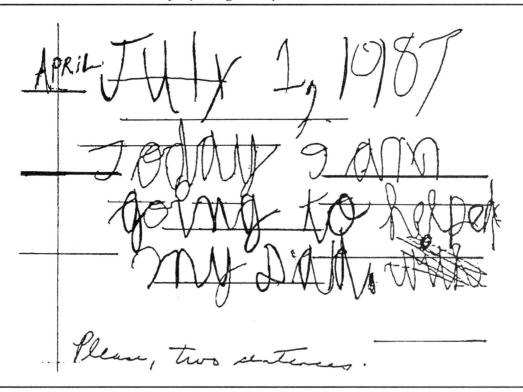

MOTHER: We knew that he was more active and distractible than his other siblings even before he went to school. With the help of family counseling we began to develop predictability in his life, reduced the amount of food colorings and sugar that he ingested, and provided attention for positive behaviors. We avoided taking him to places or events where there would be a lot of confusion or excitement because he could not handle unpredictability. He just went wild in those situations! Although his first few years of school were not easy for him, he was accommodated in meaningful learning situations. It was not until Randy went into an "A" type classroom in grade 3 that it was necessary to officially "diagnose" him. At that time the school personnel referred us to a pediatrician who labeled Randy as ADHD and prescribed Ritalin.

INTERVIEWERS: Did the Ritalin help? Was it necessary for Randy to remain on Ritalin?

MOTHER: Yes, Randy did sit down and do his worksheets in classroom A during the time he was on Ritalin. There was a significant positive difference in his attending behavior, and he got into fewer altercations at school. He had difficulty sleeping and his appetite declined, but we felt that it did enhance his self-confidence. When he moved on to a new classroom, there was a trial without Ritalin and he was able to function without it. The years on Ritalin did allow him to experience some success, and as a result he began to feel good about himself.

INTERVIEWERS: You have obviously had some very trying experiences with the education and raising of your son. What were your greatest frustrations as a mother?

MOTHER: The most frustrating experiences were always in convincing educators that we as parents had pretty good insight into Randy's needs. Children with attention problems need consistent routine. It's even more crucial for teachers to know what has worked for these children and to try to continue maintaining their success. Every fall we could be sure that Randy would have a hard time at school as he changed teachers and routines. He grew to hate school more each year. We feel his school life could have been much more successful if educators had listened to us a little more. We were labeled as interfering, coddling parents. It made us seethe as we saw our son, who loved reading and writing at home, become more and more alienated from school and finally drop out.

Another frustration that parents will encounter, as we did, is other professionals who make conflicting recommendations and create conflicting programs. For example, the contrasting paradigms found in schools also exist in the field of speech pathology. When the focus was on real, meaningful speech, he attended happily and progressed significantly. When the focus was on articulation of isolated sounds, he hated going and did not progress. His own comments about the latter type: "It's boring," "I've done all that before," and "I know it already."

INTERVIEWERS: Having spent eighteen years with Randy, an ADHD child, are there some suggestions that you would like to give to parents and teachers of ADHD children?

MOTHER: Suggestions for parents and teachers are generally the same as far as behavior is concerned. In order to apply "an ounce of prevention," here are some recommendations:

1. Involve the child in decision making.
2. Keep the child actively involved and ensure frequent activity breaks.
3. Outline upcoming activities and be sure that the child knows what is expected of him or her. Avoid changes of familiar routines without first warning the child.
4. When a new routine or situation is to be encountered, actually walk the child through the expected behavior or activity.
5. Provide positive feedback while describing the action or task that was performed well. Positive feedback is essential; ADHD children get so little of it!
6. Above all, show them that you care about them and that they are important people.
7. Share your experiences with other parents and teachers of ADHD children.
8. Whenever possible, avoid situations that are stressful and difficult for them.

Conclusion

In discussing Randy's progress we have chosen to address educational settings that exemplify contrasting paradigms. It was interesting to note the effect on Randy's learning as he alternated between classes where teachers presented skills in meaningful contexts and those where skills in isolation were the modus operandi. The interviews with Randy's mother and his own comments reflect the effect that these contrasting approaches to learning have on one impulsive, sometimes overactive, and distractible child. Observing Randy (through the eyes of his mother), as he struggled through school with varying degrees of success, made it clear to us that ADHD students in particular show greater happiness and more success in situations where practice centers on holistic theory, with a focus on meaningful, relevant content. He thrived in placements such as classroom B, where a teacher accommodated his uniqueness; on the other hand, he lost confidence when faced with accentuation of his differences and alleged deficits in situations such as classroom A.

These reflections and the experience of the authors yield some direction for educators in meeting the needs of highly challenging students such as Randy. In situations where Randy was expected, like everyone else, to behave appropriately—to be a reader, to be a writer, and to be a scientist—he would do just that. When Randy had the help of a scribe, xeroxed other student's notes, or used a computer to assist him with large amounts of writing, he responded by writing or dictating more of his ideas. When respect was shown for his ideas, he felt good about himself and incidentally found that other children treated him better. When activity and discussion prevailed in classrooms, Randy easily maintained his attention as the teacher valued and triggered his background knowledge before and during projects.

An inquiry approach for activating learning involved Randy in his search for meaning. It allowed him to feel more independent and to think through experiments on his own. He was better able to make connections with subject integration relevant to his interest and ability. A thematic approach allowed him to make connections with various concepts through discovering similarities and differences. The prevalence of collaboration with other students and his teacher acknowledged the strength of his prior knowledge, enhanced his communication skills, and ensured mastery of content. Randy's behavior showed positive effect when thoughtful teachers accentuated his strengths, minimized his disability, and modeled acceptance for his classmates. In Van Manen's words, "We can speak of pedagogical thoughtfulness as a form of knowledge; and yet pedagogical thoughtfulness is less a body of knowledge than a mindfulness orientated toward children" (Van Manen, 1991). Randy's genius at living up to the teacher expectations whatever they happened to be, good or bad, was amazing.

We may attribute the fact that Randy can read and write today to those few classrooms upon which he reflects fondly and where he experienced genuine success due to the pedagogical thoughtfulness of a few sensitive teachers. He can also be thankful that he had parents who did not give up on him or abandon his education.

> If a man does not
> keep pace
> with his companions,
> perhaps it is because
> he
> hears a different drummer.
>
> Let him step to the
> music which he hears,
> however measured or
> far away.
> —*Henry David Thoreau*

References

Anderson, A. B., & Stokes, S. J. (1984). Social and instructional information in the development and practice of literacy. In H. Goelman, A. Oberg, & F. Smith (Eds.), *Awakening to literacy,* (pp. 24–37). Portsmouth, NH: Heinemann.

Church, S., et al. (1992). *WAVES. Language across the curriculum primary handbook.* Toronto: Houghton Mifflin Canada.

Goodman, K. (1986). *What's whole in whole language?* Portsmouth, NH: Heinemann.

Goodman, Y. (1990). *How children construct literacy.* Newark, DE: International Reading Association.

Harste, J., Woodward, V., & Burke, C. (1984). *Language stories and literacy lessons.* Portsmouth, NH: Heinemann.

Helgeson, S., Blosser, P., & Howe, R. (1978). *The status of precollege science, mathematics, and social studies in U.S. high schools: An overview and summary of three studies,* Vol. 1. Washington, DC: Government Printing Office.

Hirsch, E.D., Jr. (1987). *Cultural literacy: What every American should know.* Boston: Houghton Mifflin.

Jaggar, A. M. (1989). Teacher as learner: Implications for staff development. In G. S. Pinnell & M. L. Matlin (Eds.), *Teachers and research: Language learning in the classroom* (pp. 66–80). Newark, DE: International Reading Association.

Lindfors, J. (1987). Children's language and learning 2nd ed. Englewood Cliffs, NJ: Prentice-Hall.

Newman, J. (1985). *Whole language: Theory in use.* Portsmouth, NH: Heinemann.

Poplin, M. S. (1988a). Holistic/constructivist principles of the teaching/learning process: Implications for the field of learning disabilities. *Journal of Learning Disabilities, 21,* 401–416.

———. (1988b). The reductionist fallacy in learning disabilities: Replicating the past by reducing the present. *Journal of Learning Disabilities, 21,* 389–400.

Sarason, S. B. (1991). *The predictable failure of educational reform: Can we change course before it's too late?* San Francisco: Jossey-Bass.

Smith, F. (1988). *Joining the literary club.* Portsmouth, NH: Heinemann.

Solway, D. (1989). *Education lost: Reflections on contemporary pedagogical practice.* Toronto: OISE Press.

Taylor, D. (1990). *Teaching without testing: Assessing the complexity of children's literacy learning. English Education, 22,* 4–74.

Van Manen, M. (1991). *The tact of teaching: The meaning of pedagogical thoughtfulness.* London: University of Western Ontario, Althouse Press.

Vygotsky, L. S. (1978). *Mind in society: The development of higher psychological processes.* Ed. M. Cole, V. John-Steiner, S. Scribner, & E. Souberman. Cambridge: Harvard University Press.

Weaver, C. (1990). *Understanding whole language: From principles to practice.* Portsmouth, NH: Heinemann.

Wells, G. (1986). *The meaning makers: Children learning language and using language to learn.* Portsmouth, NH: Heinemann.

11

Learners with a Difference: Helping Them Learn in a Whole Language Classroom

Linda Erdmann

Formerly a special needs teacher, Linda Erdmann describes how she has created in regular primary grade classrooms an environment that makes learning and social acceptance possible for *all* students, including those who have an Attention Deficit Disorder, with or without hyperactivity.

Explaining some of the difficulties that AD(H)D students have in traditional classrooms, Linda explains why she thinks that, in most cases, so-called disabilities belong not to the children but to the instructional program. In detail and with examples, she describes the principles undergirding whole language education that enable AD(H)D children, as well as others, to find greater success in whole language classrooms than in traditional classrooms. Finally, Linda shares strategies she has found successful with learners she humorously but appreciatively describes as having certain kinds of characteristics: Little Itches, the Firecracker, Mr. or Ms. Center Stage, the Three Sillies, Impulsive Izzie, the Picker of Rug-Fluff, the Whirling Dervish, and Slower than the Rest. Obviously, most of these characteristics are common among those diagnosed as having an Attention Deficit Disorder with hyperactivity.

Linda Erdmann currently teaches second grade at Harwich Elementary School in Harwich, Massachusetts. Her classroom provides an environment in which all children, including special needs children and "would-be" special needs children, learn and grow together without pull-out support services. During her thirty years in education, Linda has been a classroom teacher of grades K, 1, 2, and 6, a special needs resource room teacher, a special needs program coordinator, and a language arts coordinator. Recently she spent a year as a Lucretia Crocker Fellow, giving workshops and sharing with teachers throughout Massachusetts her program *A Community of Learners: Whole Language for All Kids*. Linda is a past president of the Whole Language Teachers Association and has presented at national conferences, including the International Reading Association and the Whole Language Umbrella.

Until six years ago I was a special needs teacher. My educational environment was a resource room. My children were first and second graders who were labeled learning disabled, mildly retarded, hyperactive, attention deficit disordered, visually-perceptually-motor handicapped, developmentally delayed. My room and others like it were overflowing with kids who were there because they were unable to learn the way they were being taught in the regular classroom. Troubled readers weren't learning from the basal reader, which exposed them to isolated phonics rules and then, right away, to the exceptions to the rules. They were unsuccessful with so-called linguistic-patterned "a pig can jig" kind of reading. They didn't read for pleasure or meaning. Instead of "real" literature, they read exercises intended to teach them "about" reading. Active children were expected to sit at their desks without talking and to complete page after page of workbooks and worksheets, while their teachers worked with a reading group at a table in the front of the room. Those children with an attention deficit or an attention deficit hyperactivity disorder were unable to sit for even short periods of time. They found it impossible to do the boring worksheets or to become interested in the boring stories. They became disruptive and accomplished little in environments that made it even harder for them to restrain their impulses and control their hyperactive behavior.

Having moved away from this skills-based instruction, I patterned my special needs resource room environment on the natural learning model (Holdaway, 1986, p. 62). The children were becoming readers and writers. Active children had opportunities to move. They were able to listen to exciting literature and respond in a variety of ways. They were able to lie on cushions on the floor to read, and to join in dramatizing bits of the stories as we read. There was joy and laughter, both in the teaching and in the children's learning in the resource room experience. But each day the children left the resource room to return to the skill and drill worksheets; to the need to sit still and quietly at desks in rows; to the expectation to "spit and sputter" read as they were encouraged to sound out the words; to the admonition "don't guess" as they tried to predict an unfamiliar word; to the reminder "don't keep going back" as they reread to pick up language and meaning cues. I encouraged classroom teachers to try shared reading and guided reading, to allow children to have time to actually read and write and to select some of their own books and writing topics. I didn't dare to suggest that they allow for some movement and make other modifications for ADD and ADHD children. The ADHD children were already too disruptive to quiet classrooms. At the time, there were no provisions for in-class support for the children and/or teachers; that is why these children were usually taught in the resource room for most of the academic part of the school day. I often wondered if teachers ever thought about why these children were frequently more successful in art, music, and gym.

My efforts to bring about change for these children were met with varying degrees of resistance. Some colleagues recognized the success and enthusiasm that their children were experiencing in the resource room as they read real literature and wrote for real reasons. These teachers were convinced, however, that what was happening could come about only in a special needs setting, with small groups of children.

So, day after day, the children returned to their *own* classrooms in which they held limited membership but wanted to be full members. Not only had they missed parts of what had happened in the regular classroom, but, moreover, they were not given credit for being members of the "literacy club" (Frank Smith, 1986, p. 37). These children needed to feel they belonged to a community of learners. The sense of "belonging" was clearly missing.

Try as I might, I could not create this community within the resource room environment. The children weren't with me long enough. Each child knew that the reason for his or her being there was an alleged academic, social-emotional, or behavioral deficit. Jimmy expressed it well: "I'm not even good enough for the low group." But I wanted to make literacy happen naturally for all kids. They would *all* learn to use reading, writing, listening, and speaking to discover and learn through language. The children would learn and grow together. Together. Belonging. Even those we've called learning disabled. Each of us is a "learner with a difference." I believed then, and still believe, that for most learners the disability belongs to education, not to the learner.

But I had some knots that had to be untangled. My confusion resulted from conflicts between my assumptions about learning and the expectations associated with my role as a special needs teacher. Should I continue to give the battery of psycho-educational tests, which ask children to read nonsense words, read words in isolation, and complete other tasks which haven't much to do with making meaning and would further convince children that they knew little? Should I continue to stigmatize them with a pathological diagnosis, remove them from their peers, and stamp them as being different from the rest? No. The special needs, in most instances, did not belong to the children but to the instructional program. I refer to these as *educational disabilities*.

Educational Disability

The instructional programs in our schools have created educational disabilities in children by

- teaching in ways they can't learn
- marching them through prescribed sets of curriculum objectives as though the sequence were sacred
- putting kids into ability groups—forcing those in low groups to see themselves as nonreaders and nonwriters
- denying kids access to real books until they can "read"
- putting five- and six-year-old children into a position to fail
- expecting kids to learn language from sitting all day without talking
- asking questions that call for only right/wrong answers
- reprimanding them for wrong answers so that they don't dare to respond again

Then . . .

- referring them to resource rooms
- subjecting them to testing that would further convince them they know little
- stigmatizing them with a pathological diagnosis

I needed to know whether I could, indeed, create the kind of learning community that I believed in. I needed to demonstrate, first to myself and then perhaps in a subtle way to others, that the natural learning model would work. I knew that I had to find a better way to reach these children. I needed a classroom.

A new principal listened to my plan. He listened to my beliefs that a whole language classroom can work for most kids. He listened when I explained that a whole learning curriculum is the most supportive curriculum and that a whole language classroom the most supportive classroom. He listened when I explained that children learn from each other, that they would learn to read and write as naturally as they had learned the tools of their spoken language. He listened when I asked to keep all kids in the classroom for the entire day. (I believe that, by sending kids out to first one specialist and then another, we are fragmenting the very children who have the greatest difficulty coping with fragmentation. Such fragmentation is particularly disruptive for ADD and ADHD children who have difficulty responding to one set of classroom routines, let alone several.) He listened when I said that children need strong role models and that placing in resource rooms the children who were hyperactive or impulsive and who had difficulty with attention was counterproductive. He listened, and he gave me the transfer from the special needs resource room to a first grade classroom.

During the three years I taught first grade, I became convinced that a whole language classroom works for all children, including ADD and ADHD students, and is essential for kids in danger of being severely mislabeled. Each year the percentage of learners with a difference was significantly higher in my room than in other classrooms. The first year, for example, nine of the nineteen children in my classroom had been identified as having special needs. Another five were considered "at risk." In my first grade classroom, there were no pull-out support services, and there were no "special needs" groups at a table in the back of the room. Because of what I've learned about kids and their learning, I asked the speech/language specialist and the motor development specialist to work within the room to support children on Individual Educational Plans (IEPs). While they were in my classroom, these colleagues supported the children in a natural way. Joining the child in the current setting, they worked with the group of children on whatever experience they were engaged in at the time.

In this setting, I watched Alex, an emergent reader, beam as I read Byrd Baylor's *The Other Way to Listen* (1978). Alex was the first to notice the poetic language. "That's poetry," he said. "Them sounds come from deep down inside." The expressions on the faces of the other children acknowledged that Alex had noticed something they hadn't. They learned about poetry from Alex. In reading, Alex was slower than the rest. His private kindergarten had recommended a substantially separate placement for him, but that would have meant he would spend much of his day out of the classroom. He would have missed the opportunity to grow from the rich literary experiences his classmates enjoyed. His classmates would have missed the opportunity to have their appreciation of Alex deepen because of his recognition of the beauty of language.

In this setting I watched Brian, labeled attention deficit disordered, hyperactive (ADHD) and learning disabled, learn to control his body so that everything close-by didn't go flying. I watched him learn to follow an organizational plan for keeping track of his materials, to focus his eyes and finger on the print, and to become a reader and writer.

In this setting I watched B. J., also labeled ADHD, learn to respect wait-time when requested to "think in your mind and put your finger on your shoulder when ready." He moved from refusing to write unless given the "book spelling" to writing a book in which he mentioned, "My Mom is speshul becuz she keps a ruf ovr my hed." He moved from having violent temper tantrums when he couldn't have his way to being able to take part in a student-directed play, working out snags and following through to production.

In this setting all the children learned and grew. Someone asked me once, at the close of a workshop I gave, whether the ADD and ADHD children become "normal." I'm not sure what "normal" means. These children gained self-control and self-esteem, some more than others. Most learned to recognize and celebrate their unique capabilities. The ADD/ADHD didn't vanish, but the children and I learned to work with their abilities. Did all the children master first grade curriculum? Some did. Some went far beyond what is considered to be first grade curriculum. Some did not. My view of learning is not bound by what is first grade stuff. Only in schools do we attempt to put knowledge of the world into little boxes, to label each box with a grade level, and, so, to limit some children's experiences and to condemn others to failure. Instead, we need to value each child's growth over time. I document the growth with the following: anecdotal records; running records and tapes of the children's reading; writing samples; drawings; and interviews with the children and their parents.

I taught first grade for three years, working to create a classroom that would reflect my whole language beliefs about children and learning. Following those three years, I received a Lucretia Crocker Fellowship from Massachusetts' Department of Education to share with teachers across the state of Massachusetts my program, *A Community of Learners: Whole Language for All Kids*. At present I teach second grade children. I'm still refining my practice, building on lessons learned during those years as a first grade teacher and working to make learning happen in my classroom for all children, including those who are differently abled. I'm still learning from colleagues who share their ideas and expertise.

When a child's father was dying of cancer, Debbie Darson, our school adjustment counselor, joined our class meeting to demonstrate ways to deal with death and dying. Debbie stops in to listen when I'm feeling at my wit's end and to offer, "Have you thought of. . . .?" Marvin Stout, our school psychologist, came in to observe Adam, who returned to school after vacation unable or unwilling to participate in any class experience, even saluting the flag. Marvin took Adam once a day to chat for a few minutes about how things were going. Marvin and I met briefly to plan for modifications to support Adam in the classroom. Christine Twombly and Christine Leofanti are colleagues who also teach second grade. At lunch each day we discuss ideas we've tried and books we've read. Kathy Johnson, who teaches next door, shares organizational hints, professional readings, and great children's books. These classroom teachers I'm learning from now are some of the ones who strongly resisted change, back in my days as a special educator.

The reason my whole language classroom works for all kids is not because of my special needs background. The program works because of the practice that evolved as I applied what I learned from educators like Don Holdaway (1979) and Brian Cambourne (1988) about the way children learn. I believe that children respond to high expectations, to immersion in an environment rich with the sights and sounds of literacy, to authentic demonstrations of skills and strategies being used efficiently, to opportunities to try out their new understandings away from the watchful eye of the observer, to responsive teaching that accepts successive approximations, and to the love, joy and laughter of the community in which they are full-fledged members.

Helping Learners with a Difference Learn in a Whole Language Classroom

I believe that **all children can learn** and flourish in a whole language classroom. Children can best learn from being together. Through being together, they learn the skills needed for growing together. By labeling children and removing them from the classroom or relegating them to a special needs table in the corner of the room, we have deprived the very children who most need to learn to work together of opportunities to do so, by isolating them.

The children in my first grade classroom were together all day. Some children came with labels that reflect a medical model: moderately retarded with fine and gross motor involvement, language disorders, speech production difficulties, attention deficit disorder, emotionally disturbed, visual-perceptual-motor deficits. I tried to make sure that these labels remained attached to the paper in someone's file and not to the children. I was firm in communicating my expectation to special needs staff that these children were expected to be in the classroom for all "academic and social development." Language support would also take place within the classroom in consultation with the speech/language specialist. The child who needed occupational therapy received help outside the classroom. This help was usually scheduled before the official start of the school day. We were together as a class the entire day, learning from the needs that grew out of being together.

Because I was committed to immersing the children in the environment the entire day, I needed to convince the specialists who were to service the children that their needs were being met. The specialists and I negotiated in order to arrive at the kind of data they would be willing to accept as evidence of growth. I showed them the kind of longitudinal records I would collect to document each child's development, and I invited them to monitor the children's growth by visiting the classroom to observe their performance. I knew that the kind of growth I expected in young learners would probably not be demonstrated on tests of isolated skills, nonsense words, and so forth. Trying to measure a year's growth with one standardized test is like trying to capture a trip around the world with one snapshot. Fortunately, these professionals agreed to leaving the children in the classroom setting as long as they were growing in the ways we agreed upon.

Throughout every moment of the day it was important to demonstrate to the children that I believed all children could learn and that I expected them to learn. Procedures for beginning each day were written on the board. During the first days of school these procedures were simple ones: "Move your attendance button [on a magnetic board] to indicate whether buying lunch, milk, or nothing. Put your things in the closet neatly. Read in your *I Can Read* book" (a collection of familiar songs, chants, and poems that grew weekly as we learned more selections). I read the procedures to the children those first days but soon expected them to learn to read and follow them with the help of a friend, if needed.

The expectation that all children can learn was soon internalized by the children. Denny entered our classroom in October from a self-contained special needs program. About a week after he joined us, I noticed that the children at his table were reading songs and chants from their *I Can Read* collections. I knelt by Denny's table and asked if he'd like to read one of the familiar chants to me. "I don't read, you know," Denny drawled in his slow, drawn-out speech. Brian, himself an early emergent reader, replied, "Sure you do. Everybody in this class is a reader and a writer!" With that comment Brian took Denny's finger, saying, "Here, we'll do it together." And together they did it, using their memory to support their use of text as they moved their fingers together across the page. Expectations. Brian expected that Denny was a reader. He expected to help someone who needed it. He expected the experience to be joyful. And it was. It was also a lesson to me to keep on expecting and to continue to act on my belief that all children can learn.

I believe that **children learn when comfortable and confident.** Don Holdaway taught me the importance of being the bonded adult whom children want to emulate. I know that the way I talk and interact becomes a part of me and determines how children view themselves. I need to help children know that I like them. There is no room for grumpy actions, sarcasm, belittling or uncaring comments, and put-downs. Some children are harder to bond with than others. It helps in particularly frustrating situations to remind myself that the child is using the best coping strategies available to him or her at the time and that it is our job as educators to help develop more effective strategies. Some days I have to work harder than other days to achieve these standards. But I know that, in order for children to engage with my demonstrations, they need to see me as someone they want to be like.

Helping ADHD children to feel comfortable and competent in my classroom means taking a close look at the materials I use and the way I arrange them. Yogurt cups, for example, do not work to hold paints because they are too tall and have too small a base. Using them is asking for accidents to happen and for the child responsible to feel embarrassed and humiliated. Instead, I use margarine tubs because they are much less likely to tip. Math materials are also arranged in sturdy containers, not filled to the brim, and enough space is allotted so that they don't have to be precariously stacked. Many ADHD children have difficulty moving their bodies through space in a controlled manner. A spill of hundreds of tens blocks and thousands of centimeter cubes can be disastrous.

Children need to know that they are trusted and respected and that their ideas are valued. I trust them to solve problems that arise. When there is friction, I ask, "What things are working well for us now? What things aren't working so well? How do you feel about what's happening? What can we do to make things better?" I list their responses, and we decide on a plan of action. "How can we help each other to carry out our plan?" is an important concluding step. Sometimes we use puppets to make talking about difficult issues easier. At other times role-playing is effective.

I demonstrate problem-solving strategies and trust the children to use them. "What could you do about it?" is a frequent comment when there isn't a chair at a place or no room in the circle for a latecomer. Or when the paint spills, I model the procedure that we use instead of tattling. A child who feels offended describes to the classmate what happened and how he or she felt about it. "I felt furious when you pushed me." Next, the child says what he or she wants to happen. "I don't want you to push me anymore." If necessary, the two can have a discussion. If the problem can't be solved at that level, the children add the item to the class-meeting agenda. During class meeting, classmates offer their ideas for a solution to the problem (Nelson, 1987).

The children know that they are trusted to help one another and to solve problems. They know that their ideas are valued when their classmates ask for help and listen to the suggestions. During a class meeting when we were discussing what things were working well and what things were not working so well for individuals, Alex said, "Journal writing and writing workshop aren't going good for me."

Rosie asked, "What isn't working about it for you?"

Alex replied, "I don't know my letters and sounds, and it takes me too long to look them up on the alphabet sheet [a sheet with letters and a picture associated with the letter sounds]. By the time I find them, I forget what I want to say."

Denny commented, "You could tell your story in pictures. That's what I do."

Rosie offered, "I can tell that you have a lot to say, Alex. I'll help you read the alphabet books during workshop time so you'll learn your letters real quick."

Ben contributed, "Just don't write so much. That way you won't need so many letters." (Authentic performance of trusted problem solvers.)

Feeling comfortable and confident in an environment means that we recognize and accept both likenesses and differences, strengths and weaknesses. The children and I celebrate ways we are alike and ways we are different. Favorite books that facilitate discussion, acceptance, and celebration are *Ira Sleeps Over; Leo, the Late Bloomer; When Will I Read?; Crow Boy;* and *Molly's Pilgrim.* I demonstrate my own strengths in reading, playing the piano, and drawing. I share the story of how I finally learned to swim at the age of twenty-five (in spite of years and years of lessons) when a perceptive swimming instructor taught me to relax and to trust the water to support my relaxed body. I demonstrate weaknesses by trying unsuccessfully to get the basketball into the hoop and by bringing my guitar to play for them. On several occasions the children have learned, as they had to hold the note until I found the new chord, that guitar playing is by no means a strength.

In order for children to be comfortable and confident the environment needs **to support risk-taking.** My guitar playing also models the willingness to take risks by "having a go" at something I can't do expertly. The children have accepted and rewarded my approximations, and we have discussed the importance of recognizing and acknowledging someone's best efforts.

Children learn in environments that value and accept approximations. Accepting approximations is especially important for learners who are struggling in one area or another, whether in social-emotional development or academic areas. As children are learning to build a community, their behaviors are frequently crude approximations of the expected actions. I find it necessary to be alert to these behaviors and to reinforce them so that the children get the feedback they need as they try to refine the behavior.

Lucas worked hard to learn social skills. He was a very large first grader. His gangly body towered over the other children as he moved awkwardly through space. He spoke rarely and when he did speak, he did not establish eye contact. He turned his part of a group circle into a corner as he pushed himself as far away as possible. I reinforced the times he joined hands to form the circle (before he edged himself away). I reinforced the times he sat close to another person during choice time, for, even though he wasn't ready to initiate conversation, Lucas had made an approximation of social interaction.

In the academic areas, most of the information I use in teaching comes from watching the kids' approximations. These approximations of the conventionally correct forms are cues that guide my responses. Combined with my knowledge of the child, child development, and the curriculum, these approximations help me to create just the right disequilibrium to nudge the child a step further. They inform me as to the strategies the child is using. These approximations are cause for celebration, as they grow closer and closer to the conventional behavior. Noticing and valuing approximations helps me to describe children in terms of what they **can** do.

As I use approximations in reading to guide my response, I also watch for these approximations to guide my response to children learning the social skills necessary for building the community. Matthew's slaps on the back may well indicate that he is ready to become a member of the group, rather than the antagonistic "new kid in the class." I need to check out my observation of Matthew's rather unskilled attempt. To do so, I find a moment to ask Matthew: "Matthew, I noticed that you gave Andrew a slap on the back. I wasn't sure what it meant. Were you trying to tell him something?" Together, or perhaps with another child, we might plan a next step.

Thinking of approximations as "rough drafts" of social behaviors has helped me guide the children in revising and refining these behaviors. As the children and I accept rough drafts in their written expression, we learn to accept and revise rough drafts in behavior when appropriate. Discussing behaviors as rough drafts helps me to guide the child's revision in ways that are nonjudgmental and nonpunitive.

Children learn from our responses. I have planned and worked hard on my own teacher language so that my responses demonstrate acceptance and not evaluation. During shared reading and during writing conferences, I use comments such as these: "Uh-huh." "I see what you mean." "Could be." "I hadn't thought about that." "That reminds me of the way Tana Hoban writes caption books for young children." I model describing helpful behavior. Instead of saying, "That's good!" I might comment, "I noticed that you moved the chair so that Lucas could get through." Frequently during the day, I comment on what someone has achieved through practice. "Lauren listened to that tape again and again. She even decided to stop the recorder at the end of each page so that she could practice that page. Now she's ready to share." I often ask children to describe their own process for learning something or for solving a problem.

I demonstrate that everyone's answer is valued. I try to use comments that acknowledge a response, or comments that will teach. The judgmental comments I previously made do not teach and may well serve to inhibit the children's responses. To meet one child's response with "Wow! That's great!" can be limiting to others ready to share ideas that to them might be less than great.

Although it seems almost impossible sometimes, I try hard to respond to ADD and ADHD children when their behavior is appropriate. I really believe in "catching them doing good," though crisis situations usually cannot be ignored. I've found it helpful to establish private signals with some students to let them know that they are on the right track or that they need to change current behavior. These signals, such as a "thumbs up" or another signal meaning "what do you think about what's going on now?" can be unobtrusive reminders.

Young children learn best in noncompetitive environments. In the classroom, collaboration is encouraged because we know that what we can do cooperatively today, we'll be able to do independently tomorrow. The children help each other work, play, and learn. Evidence of the first graders' collaboration was everywhere. Around the room were notices: "I cn hep you lern to reed *Midnight Farm*." "Who will help me lern to read *Charlotte's Web?*" Within an hour-long workshop period, various groups would read, cast, costume, and rehearse a play. Children would invite others to serve as guest illustrators for books they were publishing. They would work in groups to write poems based on the form of an original, write them on charts, and do the illustrations together. When the children learned that Matthew was getting into trouble on the playground during recess, they came up with a plan to present to Matthew. They arranged for Matthew to have two special friends during recess to help him find activities that would be fun and appropriate. Making a schedule, the kids assigned two kids per recess to play with Matthew (who had been slotted for a residential placement for emotionally disturbed children before he transferred to our school).

In the classroom there are no high, middle, and low groups. Neither are artificial attempts made to disguise the fact that some children are more competent in reading, just as others excel at drawing, building models, running, making friends, or solving problems.

There are times when I take groups to work on reading or spelling strategies, problem-solving, writing strategies, or guided reading. These groups are flexible, purposeful, and temporary. At other times I work with ADHD students and others on mime activities such as tossing and catching imaginary balls across the circle. The children can, upon signal, change the kind of ball from a Ping-Pong ball to a beach ball, for example. Other relaxation activities and drama warm-up experiences are good ways to help children learn how to focus, learn balance, and discover how to move their bodies through space with greater control. Providing these experiences in small groups ahead of time for ADD and ADHD children helps them to feel more competent when the total group participates in similar activities.

Children at all stages of reading competence are able to meet together for literature studies. Prior to meeting for discussion, the children read with partners, listen to tapes, or listen to another student read the book aloud. That way, children who may not have been able to read the text independently are able to make valuable contributions to the literature discussions.

The children support one another. Brian had struggled to learn to read all year. Just keeping his eyes on the page was a major challenge that he mastered. I was doing a running record as he read an unfamiliar selection, *Sing to the Moon* (Cowley, 1982). Several children noticed the difficulty of the passage and the way that Brian concentrated on the print and the pictures. A little later I saw a line of children standing, paper and pencil in hand, in front of a beaming Brian. When I asked what was up, the responses were, "We're getting his autograph." "Did you notice how he kept his eyes on the page?" "Did you notice how he figured out 'hot water bottle' from using the picture?" "He really kept his eyes on the words!"

Children learn in structured environments. Children need a structured environment in which to learn and to be creative, and they function best in a predictable environment. Whole language theory supports the development of independent, self-directed learners. My classroom structure provides the framework for children to develop self-control. Expectations and limits are clearly defined. The children and I participate together in setting them. They know what to do when, where to get materials, and where to return them. They know that I do not do for them what they can do for themselves. They know that I expect them to solve problems rather than to seek answers from me. As I respond to their questions with further questions that suggest alternatives, they begin to ask questions of themselves.

Our routines are so familiar that substitute teachers often comment, "Your children can run the classroom by themselves." When a visitor observed our writing workshop, Sadie, a special needs child, asked her to do a "pop-in writing conference." The visitor replied, "I'd love to do one, but I don't know what it is." "Well," said Sadie, pulling out a chair for the guest, "you just sit down here. I'll teach you how and then you can do one for me." That self-direction comes from structure. It reaches far deeper than the structure of chairs in rows and teacher in control at the front of the class.

The structure that develops independent, self-regulated learners does not just happen. Its creation is the result of frequent demonstrations and of class meetings to discuss what is and isn't working for the group and how to make things better. This structure is important for all children, but it is a critical classroom component for ADD and ADHD children.

Children are responsible. The children are responsible for developing acceptable standards for group living in our classroom. They are responsible for its atmosphere and conditions. These responsibilities do not develop overnight, but through hard work, approximations, and many revisions. The stage for the development of responsibility is a predictable environment, clearly communicated expectations, and class meetings to help work out the kinks.

Learners take responsibility for their own learning. Once Brian Cambourne (1988) helped me to understand this important principle, I knew that I did not need ability grouping, a hierarchy of skills, or a program to ensure that a child mastered one skill before exposing him or her to the next level of skill. Brian convinced me that the learner determines what parts of the many demonstrations to engage with and decides what he or she will take (if anything) from the experience. Children in the home are accustomed to assuming this responsibility as they make decisions each day about their own language learning, for example. No one has established an exact sequence of what word or what syntactic structure will be learned at the moment. The adults in the home continue to give whole, meaningful demonstrations and trust that the child will engage with, and learn, what is pertinent to his or her current needs. (Cambourne, 1988, pp. 61–63).

Alex convinced me that what I learned from Brian Cambourne really works in the classroom. In September, during shared reading of *The Hungry Giant,* we noticed the *ow* as the giant ran away from the bees, shouting, "Ow!!" (Cowley, 1984a). We made lists of words with the sound. In January, when we read *The Mitten* (Tresselt, 1964), we noticed another sound of *ow,* as in *snow.* Alex, a child labeled attention deficit disordered, hyperactive, and learning disabled, had participated in those shared reading times. But Alex didn't connect with the sound/symbol relationships of *ow.* In September, Alex was tuning in to the spaces between words. He was learning that words which look alike are usually the same word, that *STOP* on a traffic sign and *STOP* in a book are the same.

In May, when we read *The Sunflower That Went Flop* (Cowley, 1984b), I heard a joyous shout coming from Alex. "Oh, glory," he exclaimed. "There's that *ow!* Here it's /ow/ in *flower.* But look at it there! There it's /o/ in *grow.*" Alex had connected. I learned to relax, to continue to touch lightly on the skills, and to provide lots of demonstrations of the skills and strategies that readers and writers use to help them. I learned from Alex to trust children to take from the demonstrations what they need at the time.

Children learn when they make their own choices. A goal for my classroom is for my students to become self-motivated, self-directed, and self-regulated. Providing choices is an important step toward helping children become self-motivated and self-directed. We educators have limited children with special needs by making choices for them. In my classroom is a large collection of trade books for them to read. The books are in bins according to categories. Predictable books; books with lots of rhyme, rhythm, and repetition; books with minimal text and lots of supportive illustrations—all these are mixed in with more challenging books but are marked with a self-adhesive signal dot on the cover. The dots help emerging readers choose appropriate books. Other collections of readers such as *Literacy 2000* (Rigby), *Storybox* and

Sunshine Books (Wright Group) and *Bookshelf Books* (Scholastic) are in separate bins, clustered roughly by the amount of support provided by the text and illustrations. (I have learned, however, that motivation, repeated listening, and prior knowledge can support a child as he or she reads a self-selected book that I may have considered too difficult.)

The children sit in assigned seats at tables; however, for large parts of the day they choose their own seating arrangements. There are times when I assign learning partners, but for many experiences children choose their own partners. I have learned that in most cases they choose appropriately for the experience. Children who have difficulty reading, for example, choose competent readers for jobs calling for efficient reading. Capable readers often rush to choose children whose strength is in drawing when the experience involves drawing or painting.

Children choose their own writing topics during writing workshop. It is important to me that my children with special needs realize that their lives hold important stories for them to write about and share. Writing workshop was a favorite time for Mae Timmons, our speech/language specialist, to be in my first grade classroom. As she knelt beside the children, she engaged them in rich dialogue about their lives. She usually repeated their stories and ended with a question, "And what are you going to do now?" She made sure to spend time with children who were on IEPs (Individual Educational Plans) for language, as well as the general population in the classroom. As she observed the rich language exchanges going on within the classroom setting, she became convinced that fewer children needed to be on special needs plans for language. She became convinced that they just needed to be in classrooms where they could use the language they already had.

Children choose their own learning experiences during parts of the day. Their responses to books can be in the form of making puppets and putting on a puppet show, drama, posters, building dioramas, modeling with plasticine, writing letters to recommend the book to friends, book talk, and so on. Given choices, every child has a chance to be successful. Such opportunities are especially important to ADD and ADHD children, who have great difficulty completing worksheet after boring worksheet.

Who Are These Learners with a Difference?

In the preceding pages I've shared my beliefs and practices that have helped me to create a classroom that works for all children. For most children, these practices are sufficient; other children need more. I'd like to share strategies that help these children. To do so, I need to cluster the strategies according to the characteristics of the children, so that the readers will be able to match the strategies to the child. Some of the characteristics will be typical of ADD and ADHD children. I've chosen some humorous titles, not in any way to ridicule or to attach another label to the children, but so that the teachers who read this will recognize the kids I mean. We all have them!

Little Itches are just that. Their bodies wiggle, their hands are into everything, and they can be distracting to others. In interacting with them, I developed the following guidelines:

- Clearly and specifically communicate expectations for the particular experience.
- Pick up the pace of the demonstration. During shared reading, the Little Itches serve as my gauge to the timing, and as to whether I am back into the "transmission mode," determined to teach rather than to touch lightly—to just demonstrate what efficient readers do and move on.
- Issue invitations to the child to choose a seating location that will help him or her to meet expectations.
- Involve the child in the demonstration, giving him or her the pointer to point to the text, or a Post-It note frame or Stikki-Wikki to put around some part of the text or illustration.
- Establish a secret signal as a reminder to meet an agreed-upon expectation so that, in reminding, you don't have to disrupt the community spirit.

The Firecracker is prone to temper tantrums and easily explodes. I've found it helpful to:

- Try to anticipate the outburst and diffuse it by giving the child a job or responsibility. Often the signal of impending trouble is easily read from the child's body language or by redness that begins in the neck and creeps up to the face.
- Help the child to recognize the signals of an impending outburst, and establish a spot where he or she can *voluntarily* go to *cool down*.
- Enlist the support of the group in recognizing the signals and in helping the child. Often, role-playing or play with puppets (in which the puppet asks the child how friends can help) is an effective way of finding out ways to help. Sometimes children have been able to share during class meeting the things that may trigger the angry outburst.
- Read to the class Norma Simon's book, *I Was So Mad!*

Mr. or Ms. Center Stage needs to be in the spotlight continually. It has helped to:

- Involve the child in changing roles. Plan group activities with role assignments written on cards that children can hang around their necks. Occasionally, assign roles such as listener, recorder, encourager, and so forth.
- Group the child with verbal peers for an activity.
- Try "My Turn, Your Turn" activities in which the children pass an object such as a beanbag or an old tennis ball back and forth. Holding the object is a tactile reminder that it's your turn.
- Assign both leadership and supportive roles, keeping in mind that the goal is not to squelch leadership but to help the child develop appropriate leadership skills.
- Use feedback from class meeting. The children share their feelings and frustrations with the child, enlist the child's help in making a plan, and give feedback on how the plan is working.

The Three Sillies seem to locate each other visually, even when they aren't seated together, and engage in giggling, antics, and other behavior that is probably attention-getting but seems annoying and silly.

• Laugh with them at appropriate times.
• Avoid *buying into* their behavior by scolding.
• Ask, "What is the appropriate behavior right now?"
• Video-tape the group. Later, in private, play the tape for the children who were involved in the behavior. Ask them to identify behaviors that are working, not working. Ask them to set goals for behaviors that will work to help the group.
• Challenge them, again in private, to participate in a group activity that would take a great deal of self-control (such as passing a friendship hand-squeeze silently around the group). I've been amazed at how well children rise to the challenge. Then there's an opportunity for positive feedback.

Impulsive Izzie answers before you've finished asking the question, but there are ways to guide the child who leaps and then looks.

• Establish the routine of waiting ten–fifteen seconds or more after asking a question. Say to the children, "Think of your answer in your mind. Put your finger on your shoulder (or head) when your response is ready." This lets them know that I expect everyone to think and gives the child who is ready to blurt out the answer a signal to focus on.
• Use crafts and cooking experiences. These are highly motivating to help the child learn the cause-effect relationships associated with impulsivity. Modeling with clay, bread dough sculpting, and similar activities call for a certain amount of careful planning and following of procedures if the product is to be successful. In selecting the experience I need to have high expectations that will be within the reach of the children.
• Continually ask, "Can you think of another way . . . another?" I've found that these children are frequently among the most creative and divergent thinkers and can contribute additional responsive answers after the well seems dry.

The Picker of Rug-Fluff seems to be avoiding the demonstrations and to be more involved with the fluff than with shared reading or other demonstrations. I've observed this behavior in children who have had previous failure in experiences with letters, sounds, and symbols. They seem to avoid anything having to do with print. The following suggestions may help, as they have helped in my classroom.

• Involve the child in choosing an old-favorite selection.
• Let the child know that you will call on him/her next. The child usually tunes in, and this strategy results in success when I've framed the question to call for something that the child *can do*.
• Use Post-It tape to mask words for the children to predict as we read aloud (for example, "The frog ——— across the grass"). As we do this oral-cloze (using grammar and meaning to predict), the children become excitedly

engaged with the predictions. Sometimes I ask how they made their prediction. They respond by saying: "It sounded right." "It made sense." "It fit the pictures." If my goal is to help the child focus on graphophonemics (letter/sound relationships), I ask. "If the word is ———, what letter would you expect to see at the beginning? (or at the end?)" Invariably, the child is engaged as I slowly pull back the tape to reveal the masked word.

- Ask the child, "What do you notice?" about the text. Everyone can experience success at this nonthreatening request for a response.
- Make descriptive comments when the child notices print. "I noticed that you read with your finger and made a match between the word and what you said." "I noticed that you read 'lady' here. 'Woman' would have made sense. What helped you to decide?"
- Draw the child into the text by asking him or her to look for visual patterns, repetitions, and so on.
- Ask the child to be the one to hold the pointer.
- Trust in learners' responsibility to take from the demonstrations what they are ready to use at the time. (This is the hardest part for me to do. But I know that children are learning, even when it may not be my agenda!)

The Whirling Dervish, constantly in motion, may have difficulty maneuvering his or her body through space without upsetting materials, supplies, even the furniture in a crowded classroom. Here are helpful strategies.

- Meet the child at the door in the morning to help him or her get set up successfully for the day. Getting off to a good start is especially important. For these children, one thing seems to precipitate many more.
- Assigning a place for group lessons is helpful. A beanbag chair seems to have a calming effect. Sitting on the floor is usually impossible and a chair can too readily be transformed into a locomotive; moreover, the child in constant motion is likely to fall off a chair, when there is no table to help by providing an anchor. The other children know that this child needs the beanbag chair to help him or her attend. They know that special accommodations of extra time or materials are often provided because it's my job to make the best possible match between each child and the classroom environment.
- Set aside time to play "Statues," a game in which children assume various positions and hold them until a signal is given. Talk about how the bodies look and feel in the various positions. Encourage the child to recapture the "listener" position during part of a lesson.
- Teach about each person's space, and practice respecting that space during lively activities.
- Provide periods of movement that end with an agreed-upon signal and the words "See how fast I stop."
- Demonstrate taking a deep breath by inhaling silently and slowly, then silently releasing the breath between pursed lips. This helps to relax.
- Use guided visualization based on a calm, relaxed part of the book.
- Involve the children in quick pantomimes while reading a story. A favorite of my children is to turn themselves into Caroline being "a paragon of virtue" as we read *Boss for a Week* (Handy, 1982).

The child who is **Slower than the Rest** is the child who is struggling to learn to read. Here are some special pointers.

- Read, read, and read some more to the child. Enlist the help of other students, older students, and volunteers from the community.
- Make sure to include many caption books, predictable books, and books that are songs written down. Keep these books in a location so that the child can select from them.
- Provide a book box to store books the child has read. Provide opportunities for him or her to reread these many times. When the box is full, the child can choose which ones to remove in order to make room for new ones.
- Help those who read with the child to understand the reading process. I meet with volunteers and provide a booklet explaining the procedures for them to use while reading with the children. My colleague Kathy Johnson posts the procedures on the wall in front of the table where volunteers read with children.
- Look at the child's miscue. Relax and give the child a chance to self-correct. We want self-regulated readers who monitor their own reading. If the child doesn't self-correct and the miscue doesn't make sense, ask, "Does that make sense?" or "Does it sound right?" If the miscue makes sense, decide whether to draw attention to it. Consider waiting until the child has finished reading, in order not to interrupt the flow of reading. Say, "If that word (chicken) were 'hen,' what would you expect to see?"
- Notice and comment on all attempts at self-correction and use of strategies such as rereading, reading on, and the like.
- Use guided reading to build a bridge for the child who is ready to move toward reading unfamiliar material.
- Look at progress as development over time, not as getting the child ready for next year's teacher.

The framework and the strategies have helped me to create a classroom in which all children learn and flourish—a classroom that avoids creating special needs; a classroom in which children who have special needs can learn and be successful alongside their peers; a classroom in which children recognize that we all have a place in the choir and valuable contributions to make.

Even the most knowledgeable, competent, and caring teacher needs support in providing the most effective classroom program when there are several needy learners. That first year I was alone and, except for thirty to forty minutes of specialist time three days a week, depended exclusively on volunteers to be my other pair of hands. The next year I had a full-time teaching aide because I invited a child whose needs were so severe that he had been assigned a full-time aide to join our classroom. The aide came with the child. Teachers who are making their classrooms work for *all* children need administrative support to make sure that their classrooms are balanced, that they have books, manipulative materials, and plans in place for children who may need to be removed from the classroom for short periods of time. Teachers need in-class support from special needs personnel who are knowledgeable and competent in whole language learning or who are, at least, willing to learn. I fear that with the new emphasis on the "inclusion model" of special education, children will be left to fend for themselves in inappropriate programs. Moreover, teachers who are willing to create appropriate programs and who care deeply about learners with a difference may find themselves stretched beyond their limits.

Jared's end-of-the-year card reflected his recognition of the philosophy I hold for myself as a professional—the philosophy I model for the children in my classroom. Jared wrote on his card, "Your rily growing in teching."

Creating the classroom I've described isn't easy. Sometimes too many needy kids were placed in my room so that it began to resemble one large resource room. Sometimes, because of budget considerations, there wasn't enough support. Sometimes when I needed another pair of hands I used parent volunteers, volunteers from the retired community, and older students. There were times when, not having the answers, I needed to turn to colleagues but had only one or two who understood. That's changing now as the teachers in my school are becoming learners who are willing to have-a-go at making their classrooms work for all kids. Now we learn from one another as we read, attend conferences, take courses, and share. It's all about "rily growing in teching."

References

Professional Sources

Cambourne, B. (1988). *The whole story: Natural learning and the acquisition of literacy in the classroom.* Sydney: Ashton Scholastic.

Holdaway, D. (1979). *The foundations of literacy.* Auckland, NZ: Ashton Scholastic. Available in the U.S. from Heinemann.

Holdaway, D. (1986). The structure of natural learning as a basis for literacy instruction. In M. Sampson (Ed.), *The pursuit of literacy: Early reading and writing* (pp. 56–72). Dubuque, IA: Kendall/Hunt.

Nelson, J. (1987). *Positive discipline.* New York: Ballantine Books.

Smith, F. (1986). *Insult to intelligence: The bureaucratic invasion of our classrooms.* Portsmouth, NH: Heinemann.

Children's Literature

Baylor, B. (1978). *The other way to listen.* Illus. P. Parnall. New York: Macmillan.

Cohen, B. (1990). *Molly's pilgrim.* New York: Bantam.

Cohen, M. (1977). *When will I read?* New York: Dell.

Cowley, J. (1982). Meow. In *Sing to the Moon.* In *Storybox in the classroom,* stage 5. San Diego: Wright Group.

Cowley, J. (1984a). The hungry giant. In *Storybox in the classroom,* stage 1. San Diego: Wright Group.

Cowley, J. (1984b). *The sunflower that went flop.* San Diego: Wright Group.

Handy, L. (1982). *Boss for a week.* New York: Scholastic.

Kraus, R. (1971). *Leo the late bloomer.* New York: Crowell.

Lindbergh, R. (1987). *Midnight farm.* New York: Dial.

Simon, N. (1974). *I was so mad!* Toronto: General Publishers, Ltd.

Tresselt, A. (1964). *The mitten.* New York: Scholastic.

Weber, B. (1972). *Ira sleeps over.* Boston: Houghton Mifflin.

White, E. B. (1952). *Charlotte's web.* New York: Harper & Row.

Yashima, T. (1955). *Crow boy.* New York: Viking.

12

Growing Together: Whole Language Teaching Fosters Successful Learning for ADHD Children

Carole F. Stice and John E. Bertrand with Cherrie Farnette

This article draws upon a larger research study to focus on how Cherrie, a teacher at Westminster School in Nashville, came to understand that her ADHD and LD second graders needed to have more control over their own learning in order to become self-confident, successful learners in the classroom. The differences from October to April are highlighted by vignettes taken from observational notes, as well as by early and late writing samples from two ADHD children. We see Cherrie's growth, along with the children's, through the observations of Carole and John, two university researchers, and through Cherrie's own reflections. Even with someone who considered herself only an "emerging" whole language teacher, these ADHD children made tremendous gains.

Carole Stice is a professor of reading/language arts education and a research associate with the Center for Research in Basic Skills at Tennessee State University in Nashville, where she has taught graduate and undergraduate education courses for eighteen years. She has also taught elementary, junior high, and secondary reading. Carole has tutored nonliterate adults and worked with staff development at the district level in Georgia and Florida. She has also spent two years with the State Department of Education in Florida, working on their statewide Right to Read project. Since 1985 Carole has conducted three research projects on whole language and "high-risk" children and has authored several articles. She has a Ph.D. from Florida State University and is the mother of one daughter.

John Bertrand has worked as a research associate for the Center for Research in Basic Skills at Tennessee State University for the past five years. During that time he has authored several articles, many on whole language. His interests range from workplace literacy to school/community partnership programs to literature-based classrooms. A natural spinner of yarns and an oral storyteller, John enjoys telling stories and reading aloud to young children. He has taught elementary and junior high in Virginia and Tennessee. He received his Ph.D. from Ohio State University in 1987. During the year he spent involved in the research at Westminster School, he fell in love with the school and the children and joined the staff there as a fourth grade teacher in the fall of 1992. John is married and has one child.

Cherrie Farnette earned a master's degree in early childhood education at Peabody College with a Kennedy Foundation Grant. She has evaluated and trained Headstart teachers throughout the Southeast. She has taught fourth, fifth, and sixth grades in Birmingham, Michigan, and has worked as an ESL teacher, reading specialist, and supervisor of instruction in Laredo, Texas. Cherrie has also worked at Wayne State University in Detroit, teaching language arts methods courses, supervising student teachers, and coordinating special education student teaching while taking courses toward an advanced degree. She has coauthored several activity idea books for teachers, including *Special Kids' Stuff*. She taught for five years at the University School in Nashville before joining the faculty at Westminster as a second grade teacher. Cherrie is married and is the mother of two children.

The Invitation

Our involvement with the Westminster School began with what we thought was a typical request for a half day's in-service. The new director of this small private school invited us to provide some training for teachers interested in developing a literature-based, integrated curriculum. The teachers had decided to end their reliance on basal readers, workbooks, dittos, and skills lists. They wanted to explore a more holistic curriculum.

The Setting

Westminster School specializes in children with learning disabilities and attention deficit hyperactivity disorders (ADHD). The school has enjoyed an excellent local reputation since its inception in 1968. There are fifteen classrooms serving about 170 children in grades K–8. Each classroom has ten to twelve children with one teacher and an assistant. The school's library of some 2,600 titles is adequate for supporting forays into a wide variety of topics and genres. In addition, each classroom is supplied with at least a hundred trade books, which teachers supplement with books from nearby public libraries.

Each in-service was well attended, and the teachers were enthusiastic. Several professional books were purchased by the director and made available, and many individual, informal discussions of professional literature occurred throughout the year. The school's director was very supportive, encouraging teachers to explore new ways of teaching. We emphasized that changes as dramatic as the one these teachers were proposing would take time.

During the in-service sessions, we explored teachers' beliefs about teaching and learning, reading and writing. Together we examined the reading and writing processes and how these are presented in whole language classrooms. We explored the relationship between learning language and learning in general. The teachers examined several reasons why it was important to keep language whole, to focus on learners' strengths, and to help children make meaning for themselves.

We talked about the need to read aloud to children several times a day and about the place of reading and writing throughout the curriculum. The teachers engaged in literature study groups themselves and discussed the elements and procedures involved in thematic teaching. We explored the concepts of ownership and authenticity from a whole language perspective and encouraged the teachers to slowly incorporate what they felt comfortable trying.

The Teachers

All the teachers considered themselves beginners in whole language. Several graciously opened their classrooms and allowed us to observe any time of the day and to stay as long as we needed. They welcomed us into their classrooms as colearners.

We observed in four classrooms on a regular basis from August until Thanksgiving and again in the late spring. Each teacher's morning language arts block provided the setting for most of the observations. We took extensive field notes and collected samples of the children's writing throughout the year. We reviewed our notes and the children's writing for evidence of patterns that appeared to reflect what was occurring in these classes. We knew very early that we were witnessing not only teachers in transition but also changes in the learning and behavior of the children.

The Children

At the beginning of the school year, many children exhibited wide mood swings. Most showed great anxiety and were easily frustrated and upset. Several of the children had difficulty focusing their attention. They were alternately withdrawn, frightened, and angry. Many believed there was something wrong with them, especially regarding their own learning abilities.

The vignettes that follow represent the essence of the instructional emphasis, typical teacher-child transactions, and change across the year in one classroom. The excerpts from field notes and selected samples of children's writing are interspersed with the tentative conclusions we have drawn from them.

We entered Cherrie's classroom in early October and observed there two mornings a week until just before Thanksgiving. Her classroom is very small, measuring only 17 × 23 feet. Many books and children's writings are displayed. There are books on shelves, in baskets and tubs, and in closets. The books along the chalk tray and floor at the front of the room are all fairy tales. There is a unit underway on different versions of folk and fairy tales.

The children's desks are arranged in two configurations: a U-shape seats seven children, and a square accommodates the other five. There are nine boys and three girls in this room.

The girls, Evelyn, Emma, and Wendy, are quite different from each other. Evelyn is hyperactive and very bright. Emma is very quiet, exhibiting characteristics of an attention deficit; however, she always understands what is going on around her. Wendy appears to be under great stress. She is usually the first to cry whenever there is a problem.

The boys are Dylan, Garth, Chris, Charlie, Jonathan, Dan, William, Matt, and Tyrone. Of the boys, Dan is the most creative; Charlie is the most withdrawn and distracted. The rest of the boys appear to be easily frustrated and under considerable, self-imposed stress.

Three of the boys and one of the girls are on psychotropic medication. In addition, one boy takes medication daily for severe allergies. Five of the children are considered to have some degree of attention deficit and/or hyperactive disability in addition to their other learning disabilities, and they all had great difficulty attending to the tasks at hand when school started.

During one of our first conversations, the teacher wondered aloud how seven-year-olds can already be so totally devastated and feeling like such failures. She talked about Matt, whose parents told her that he cried every single night during first grade. They had to take turns helping him with his homework because he simply could not do it alone. The stress on the family was extreme, since there was a younger child who was already more advanced than Matt in both reading and writing. Matt's parents knew he was bright; they didn't understand what was happening to their child.

Three Days in the Life of This Classroom

After the morning roll, pledge, and class business, Cherrie conducts a morning math event she calls "magic number." This is usually followed by read-aloud and some type of art, silent reading, and a writing event.

October 16

I enter the classroom while they are still working on the morning magic number. Today's number is 40 because it's been forty days since school started. The teacher explains that they are running late, "And 40 is such an exciting number," she says. Some of the children echo agreement and they continue with their patterns. (Everyone appears to be attending to the teacher except Dan, who is coloring, and Tyrone, who is helping him select crayons. Of course, they may be attending, too.)

Teacher: Who has another pattern for 40? Dan, Christopher, and Matt are helping the teacher do the 8's.

Teacher: How many 8's do I need?

Teacher: People, you are so good. Number sentences are just words, like any word sentence. They say things. If you read them right, then you'll do them right.

Dylan gives $1 + 1 + 2$ ten times equals 40. William says $4 + 4 + 8, 4 + 4 + 8$, etc. Garth says, "It's going to work." The teacher says, "I don't think so." They continue until it is clear that the pattern breaks down after 32.

Teacher: "This is not a pattern. But it's good thinking, William. Maybe it would work if you started with 8. You'd have to try it and see."

William says, "I have a short one."

Teacher says, "OK, let's hear it."

William: "Forty-one minus one." The teacher accepts that and puts it on the board with the others. They continue working on math for a few more turns.

The children all appear to enjoy this math event and to feel comfortable with it. Cherrie then reads aloud at least once. Then she engages the children in some type of writing and art activity. Finally, they read silently. She says that she wants to encourage children's self-selections and expression of their own ideas. During this week she has read several versions of *The Three Little Pigs*. Writing ideas come from the reading.

Later That Same Morning

Cherrie leads a brief discussion about the differences in the versions of "The Three Little Pigs" stories they have read. They brainstorm a list of five or six major differences including different pictures, different wolf, different setting, different language patterns and word choices, and different authors and illustrators. The teacher writes these on the board. The children add that in one version the pigs got eaten. In one version the first two pigs ran to the next house, and they ate the wolf.

The children are to draw or write about a favorite character from the fairy tales or to make up a character of their own. They have the choice.

The teacher says, "OK! Let's see how independently you can work. Help is here if you need it."

Teacher: "Does it matter if you can't spell it?" Several of the children say, "No!"

Teacher: "Right, not this time. Use your own spelling in your head. We will help you spell it later."

The children are already started. Matt comes to the teacher. He shows her what he has written. She smiles. He returns to his seat and continues writing.

"Look," says Garth, "I wrote ———."

Teacher: "Yes. Give me more. Tell me more." Garth goes back to his desk and writes furiously.

In a few minutes Garth says, "That's it. I'm not writing any more." But he does.

Garth is an eight-year-old who is full of both creative and destructive energy. According to Cherrie, he registered at Westminster at the last minute with his parents who appeared as fearful and traumatized as he was. Garth had excelled in math in his last school but was afraid to write and could barely read. In September his behavior fluctuated from overactivity and enthusiasm to tantrums, withdrawal, and denial. He refused to perform until he felt secure. According to Cherrie, "he preferred to act out his frustrations and anger rather than let himself know how afraid he was that he has nothing to share."

Cherrie is beginning to know the children. She knows what they can do and what their strengths are. She is learning what they have difficulty with and what they need from her. Most of the children, she says, need great support and encouragement. Most need patience and time. All need an honest appraisal of their work. They all need to express themselves frequently in talking and in writing, as well as through art, music, and movement.

Same Day

Cherrie begins reading aloud with much expression *The True Story of the Three Little Pigs* by Scieszka. She pauses, inviting the children to insert text as prediction. They make comparisons with other stories, especially with wordings. For example, this wolf says "May I come in" instead of "Let me come in." William and Matt seem to be the best at remembering the exact words.

The teacher reads slowly and holds the book low so that the children can see while she reads. (I think they have missed the bunny ears, snouts, feet, and so on sticking out of the hamburger.) Christopher is concerned about the wolf's eyes.

The teacher stops occasionally and, with gesture and facial expression, invites the children to join in. When she reads "Dead as a door nail" the second time Garth chimes in, "Dead as a door knob."

William says, "I feel sorry for the wolf."

Teacher: "Oh, so do I. Poor old wolf. He was just defending his granny." Dylan interrupts and disagrees. The teacher lets him tell why. (I didn't catch what he said.) Then she finishes reading. Children notice that in the last picture the wolf has gotten old.

When she finishes reading, some of the children ask if they can act out the story. Cherrie thinks this is a wonderful idea and immediately proceeds to facilitate the activity. Some of the children go back to their seats. Others, those who really want to participate, remain on the floor at the front of the room.

After they cast the three pigs, the wolf, and the mother pig, the teacher begins to narrate the story for the "characters." (She has been teaching about characterization.) The three boys who are the three little pigs are rolling on the floor, snorting and oinking.

Teacher: "Once upon a time there was a mother pig and her three baby pigs. Their mother said. . . ." She turns to Emma, who is playing the mother pig, and Emma says, "Grow up."

The teacher says, "And what else does she say?" Emma says, "Be big." The teacher says, "Yes, and what else?" Emma says, "Go out in the world. You need to make your own houses." The teacher smiles.

She continues: "The first little pig was sort of lazy and he wasn't very smart either because he built his house of straw as fast as possible and then he went to sleep." (She has been getting some of this from William, who is the first little pig.)

Teacher: "Now the second little pig wasn't quite as lazy as his brother." She turns to Dylan, who is the second little pig, and asks why the second little pig built his house of twigs. Dylan says, "So he could go out to play." Teacher continues, "He built his house of twigs and then he went out to play. Now we have a lazy pig and a playful pig. The third little pig was the brains of the family."

Teacher: "Yes, he was a smart, hard working pig." Some of the children laugh.

Cherrie has followed the children's lead while keeping her own instructional focus. They are exploring story elements as well as oral and written language connections. This is accomplished in an atmosphere of cooperation and fun. Rather than dreading school and trying to avoid involvement, the children now look forward to each new day.

That Afternoon

The teacher says: "You know, all we have been doing is building up to where you are ready to write about your character. All the things you've been saying about your character, you can write."

Jon: "I don't want to say anything."

Teacher: "Oh, you've been telling me all about 'the ant who talks too much.'"

They discuss his ideas about his character, and Jon agrees he has come up with lots of ideas. He begins to write.

Everyone gets started writing. William says, "This is hard. How do you spell———?" The teacher says, "What do you do when you don't know how to spell something?" William turns back to his paper and tries to spell it himself.

Teacher: "William, who is your character?"

William: "A smart butterfly." Jon comes to his defense and says, "It's an imaginary butterfly." William nods in agreement.

Teacher: "Well, it's your story. OK, folks. Now you have some quiet time to finish your story. Think about your character—a day in the life of your character, perhaps."

When they finish, the teacher tells them she is going to read a new story. Someone sees the big book of *The Three Billy Goats Gruff.*

They are going to compare and contrast several story elements (for example, characters, setting, and events) across stories as well as across versions. Cherrie says she is going to use this story to ask if the children want to retell it from the troll's point of view.

Cherrie offers children creative activities and encourages them to try to do things on their own. She is interested in developing their confidence and independence. She wants them to see connections among books and between school and their personal lives. She believes that these children will write more if they write fantasy and let their already rich imaginations flow. And she is aware of the interest they exhibit whenever they share their own writing.

Same Afternoon

Teacher: "Bring your story if you want to share it and come up here and sit. You can read yours after we listen to the morning story."

Dylan says, "Mine needs work. I need more time before I share." Jon agrees. Evie and Dylan appear ready and eager to read their stories.

William: "I'm not reading mine first."

Teacher: "Why not?" William smiles and shrugs but appears really to want to read his work.

When the children are settled, the teacher begins reading *The Three Billy Goats Gruff.* As she reads, the children join in, reading along on the repetitious parts.

As soon as the story is over, Matt raises his hand to ask if he can read his story first. (Apparently he has just been waiting for the end of the book. There appears to be a great deal of energy in this class for reading and sharing their own writing, perhaps even more interest in that than in read-aloud.) He reads his story, and the teacher helps.

Then Jonathan shows her his story. "Can I read mine now?" he asks.

Teacher: "Oh well, since you're so excited. My goodness, it's already one and a half pages long." He smiles. He stands next to her, and she puts her arm around him. As Jon reads his story, the other children quiet down and listen.

Emerging whole language teachers frequently describe their struggle to let go of control and follow the children's lead. This struggle is not necessarily won or lost in a single event but is usually a continuous and uphill fight in which old habits and inclinations die hard. By the end of October, Cherrie is moving away from her good start with language and literature; she decides that the children really need more direct focus on sentence construction. Halloween themes provide the venue. For two weeks the children write sentences that explore such elements as what the main character is doing, what the main character is like, what happens to the main character. They resist this attention to form in favor of their own expression.

October 30

Teacher: "Today, we're going to read Halloween books." She shows the children the Halloween book that she is going to read. "Put your pencils down. We're going to do something really different. This I think you'll like, but you have to follow instructions—follow only the instructions."

The teacher draws a big circle on the chalkboard. "Estimate the size of your circle with your fist."

I hear someone guess, "We're drawing a spider." Charlie and Dan have the most trouble with their circles. Evie wants hers to be perfect. Dan nearly cries. "I don't understand!"

Teacher: "Just watch," and she does it with him until he gets it. He says, "Yep, it's a spider." (Neither Dan nor Charlie can readily transfer from the vertical plane of the chalkboard to the horizontal plane of the paper on their desks. They are both very frustrated and anxious.)

Garth says, "Maybe it's a donut with legs." Everyone laughs. Teacher says, "Make a writing line by folding your paper up to the bottom of your spider. Now write *spider* here." She shows them on the board. Chris is nearly always ahead of everyone else. "This is going to be the beginning of a sentence," he says. The teacher writes, *The spider is* ———.

Then she asks, "Now what is the spider doing?" As the children begin listing words, the teacher writes them. William says *jogging*. Teacher smiles and writes *jogging* on the board. Dan says *webbing*, Emma offers the word *climbing*, Garth says *falling*, and so on. Teacher says, "OK. Now what kind of spider do you have?"

The children begin to provide words again. Garth asks, "Can it be a color?" The teacher says that all the colors are telling what kind. Garth says *brown*. Jon says *brave*.

Teacher: "Good. The brave spider. . . ." Matt says *young*. Evie says *old*. Dan says *brown recluse*. (Dan nearly always gets the broad meaning but misses the specific pattern being explored.)

Then the teacher asks, "All these words do what for our spider?" Emma: "Tell what he does."

Teacher: "No." Dan says, "Describe the spider." (The child who really had the hardest time "doing" this activity understands it perfectly.)

Teacher: "Now we are going to look for words that tell what the spider is doing." On the board she puts, "The cool spider (that was Dylan's) is climbing up the mountain."

Jon: "I don't get. I just don't get it." (This is the closest to a frustrated outburst I've heard in some time.) The teacher calmly shows him.

Teacher: "That tells me where; now tell me how or when."

Dan: "The skinny spider is starving in the Sears Tower."

Teacher: "Boy, that gives me a whole lot of information for my imagination."

Matt: "The young spider is looking down at the girl spider."

Teacher: "Wonderful, Matt."

This instructional event was arbitrary. It related to the upcoming holiday but not to anything else, as far as the children could tell. The children were easily frustrated by it. They became excited again only when she let them write their own Halloween sentences. This represents much of the type of writing in which the children were engaged early in the school year. See Figure 12–1 for Matt's sample writing on October 30, 1991. Garth's sample for the same day is shown in Figure 12–2.

Cherrie was creating a classroom where everyone worked together to help each other in a highly literate, low-risk environment. She realized fairly early

FIGURE 12–1. *Matt's writing, October 30, 1991.*

that the children must make connections within and across texts. She encouraged them to compose both oral and written stories. She helped them explore the elements that make up good stories. Early on, she established her standards of achievement and the daily routine of the classroom. The children were able to stay engaged for longer and longer periods. However, Cherrie was still the primary decision maker; the locus of the curriculum resided with her. She had not yet begun to explore themes that the children requested, and a great deal of the instructional focus was still on words and sentence construction. While she was beginning to recognize the children's need to show greater ownership of their learning, she did not immediately see how to get there.

We ended this phase of our work in Cherrie's classroom just before Thanksgiving, leaving one or two professional resources with her that she asked to borrow. Because of other commitments at the university, we did not officially reenter the field until the following March. While we expected to see growth, we were not prepared for the magnitude of the changes we encountered. As Cherrie said, "These children have learned as much or more than any group of regular education children I ever taught." She was extremely proud of this class.

By March they were all working independently and confidently. "It's because of whole language," she told me. "In a whole language classroom I've learned to deal with the meaning of things from the children's perspective and for their lives. We don't *focus* on mechanics, such as where commas go and if they can do the workbooks or not. We don't focus on what they *can't* do well. School is fun and meaningful, and the kids really get interested and involved. For these kids, that's absolutely vital."

FIGURE 12–2. *Garth's writing, October 30, 1991.*

The big Cat is black.
The big fat cat is angry.

Over time, the children and the teacher had become a tight-knit community of learners. The evidence of how much they grew and what they learned is seen in their writing, their reading, and in what they say and do.

April 29

The children are finishing magic number for the morning. Today's number is 158. The teacher has just applauded a really good pattern offered by Garth. She tries to end the math session but Matt has *one more*. He offers $30 \times 5 + 8 = 158$. The teacher asks the other children to check. Now she asks for a short number combination and Matt gives $311 + 45$. The teacher looks puzzled, but the children at Matt's table catch on and say they know what he means. "He has it backwards. He means $113 + 45$." They laugh.

The class just won't let go of the math. Evie is doing $1 + 5 + 8 \times 11 + 4 = 158$. Checkers verify without the teacher asking. Matt says, "But I got 159 on the calculator." The teacher goes back to the chalkboard. "Why did we have to learn to do these in our heads before we used the calculator?" Someone answers, "So we'd know if they made sense or if our fingers made a mistake." Teacher: "That's right." Matt does it again and still gets 159. Evie gets up and goes to his seat. "Let me see your calculator," she says. She redoes it and shows him. He agrees. (It is her problem, after all.)

The children cooperate with one another. They are proud of themselves and of each other's work, but both the classroom and the learning process belong to the children. They are becoming independent learners. They are confident of their ability to know and to figure out.

During a week in late April, the children are developing a unit on hats and caps. They are reading both fiction and nonfiction and are writing stories and drawing pictures about hats. They are learning geography, history, sociology, math, and science during their unit on hats and caps.

Since today is Hat Day, the children are wearing their favorite hats. Cherrie continues focusing her instruction on what she believes the children need. Her standards are still high, but she has relinquished most of the control on content, working the teaching of reading, writing, and several subject areas into the children's interests. The children have chosen to write "hat" stories this week. Many of the children wanted to use dialogue in their stories, and today they are exploring quotation marks in books.

After Magic Number

The children are looking in the comics and in books at how quotation marks are used. They find periods, capital letters, quotation marks, and so on. The teacher says: "What might we say if we were in the comics and were talking? What might Chris say? What might Dylan say?" The children begin to suggest dialogue. Most of them relate to the hats everyone is wearing. These include a baseball cap, an Australian bush hat, Mickey Mouse ears, a golf cap, and a cowboy hat.

Dan says, "Charlie's golf cap makes him look like a New York detective." The teacher says, "What would a New York detective say?" Evie volunteers, "Go catch a crook and don't come back without him." The teacher writes that in a bubble on the board by a drawing of a cartoon character wearing a golf cap. The children all read it.

Then she puts on a striped hat and asks for a quote from a railroad engineer. They give her one. Then she puts on a glittery top hat and asks for a quote from a clown.

Charlie says, "I think that's a dancer."

The teacher says, "Yes, this could be a hat a dancer might wear. What might a clown or a dancer say?"

Charlie thinks. (Nearly a minute goes by.) Then he says, "I don't know." The others wait patiently. When the teacher finally asks someone else, she receives an answer; but Garth says, "Charlie will do one." (They do not make fun of him. They try to protect him.)

Teacher: "I'll come back to you in a minute, Charlie."

This class has become a family of learners in which everyone respects, protects, and supports everyone else. No one is made to feel inadequate. No one is made to feel impaired. Consequently, these children take risks with each other and have made remarkable progress.

Same Day

After reading a nonfiction book about hats, the teacher asks Tyrone for a quote from someone who is wearing a ski mask. He can't give one. She waits. Whole class is absolutely silent while Tyrone tries. He is visibly upset that he can't do it.

Dan says, "If someone can't think of one, just go on to the next page."

Then Tyrone says, "I've got one."

Teacher: "OK, Let's have it."

He says, "I've just had surgery, and I can't take this thing off till next year." The children laugh.

The teacher says, "That's a good one. It was worth waiting for. I like that one. Thank you." Then they all go on to the next picture. . . .

Later, as the children begin writing their hat stories, Cherrie shows me a place on the chalkboard where she has written "Editing and Proofing Guide." It contains all their own ideas, definitions, descriptions, and examples, dictated by the children the previous day. She tells me that the children are going to use this to proof their stories. She says that she is going to type it and turn it into a booklet for everyone to keep.

Editing and Proofing Guide

Periods: At the end of a telling sentence.

Exclamation points: At the end of an exciting sentence or short sentence. (Ex. Boo! Hi! Yea!)

Commas: Go in dates, in addresses, to separate thoughts, before someone talks.

Quotation marks: Around what someone says. (Jane said, "Hi!")

Upper Case letters: Go at the beginning of a sentence, when using I, in story titles, for days of the week, months, things said in excitement, names of states, countries, other titles.

Reversals: Such as b and d.

Spelling: Look it up. Ask someone. Skip it till later. Use another word.

Handwriting: Look at a good model.

Spacing: Make sure it's enough.

Teacher: "If you are through proofing, take out a book and read until we look at everyone's story."

Evie asks if she can tell her hat story. Teacher says, "Have you practiced it? Is it ready?" Evie says yes and the teacher says, "At the end of reading our hat stories today, you can tell your story."

Dylan brings his paper to the teacher. She says, "Oh! Wow, Dylan! [It's two pages long.] Let's check yours." He sits on her lap. Evie and Wendy are at the back table helping each other to proof. Garth, Matt, and Jonathan are on the floor proofing theirs. Emma and Tyrone are still writing and working on proofing. The teacher says to Dylan, "Read this page." He does. She says, "Great!"

Cherrie turns to me as Dylan revises something on his paper. "I can't believe their proof list. This is the first time we've formalized it. Before, we just sort of checked over our papers." She smiles, clearly pleased with what they know and can do with editing for mechanics. This has not dampened their enthusiasm for sharing their writing. If anything, they appear more eager and confident than ever. Cherrie is using the children's leads to encourage and support their taking risks with language and learning. She is always protective and accepting of what they do, finding some way to turn a negative perception into a positive one, if not a triumph.

After a Bathroom Break

The teacher calls everyone to the front of the room. "Is everyone ready to share?"

Evie is first. She says it was hard to write this story. The teacher asks why. Evie says, "Because I don't like to wear hats."

Teacher: "Oh!" She elaborates about how it's easier to write things you know and like. Then she says, "But look at what Evie wrote. She wrote a story about a little girl who didn't like to wear a hat. That was really a good way to approach it. Sometimes we can turn what we don't like into a good idea, as Evie did." Then they talk about putting their draft papers on the computer to proof them before or after they share them.

Teacher: "What is most important when we first start to write?" Nearly everyone answers in unison: "Getting our ideas on paper!"

Teacher: "That's right." She reminds them what a good audience is. They listen and they look and they don't write or draw or talk.

Garth is next. Evie asks, "I want to know how many pages."

Teacher: "I don't know, but you'd better settle back; it's long." The teacher says, "Wow, Garth! All because of the selling of a hat. Garth is a real novelist."

Dan says, "He's always writing stories about love—a subject he knows nothing about." Everyone laughs.

Matt reads next. He has a little difficulty reading. His story is about a magical top hat flying around the world and meeting other types of hats that people wear in different countries. The teacher asks Matt how he got his information. Matt says, "My daddy helped me. Every time I got to a new country we'd look up what kind of hat they wear."

Teacher: "Good research. What is research, Matt?"

Matt: "It's when you find out information you need or want to know."

Besides encouraging children's connections and extensions of their learning, Cherrie doesn't allow them to fail. The children have learned this attitude from her; they do not allow anyone to be feel like a failure or to be embarrassed. Therefore, this is a safe and supportive environment in which curiosity flourishes. The teacher said that she was afraid that for some of the children this would be the best school year they might ever have.

Same Day

When Evie reads, she doesn't want to show her pictures. Chris says, "She always says that, but her pictures are always good." Everyone agrees. Evie smiles.

Emma is next. She reads her own, but softly, covering her face with her paper. The teacher says, "We want to hear you" and moves the paper down. When Emma finishes, the teacher says, "Great job! I'm really proud of you. And the other one you did is just as good. You can share it later if you like." The children applaud as Emma sits down. She smiles. (This is one of the few times I've seen her smile.)

During this school year, the children came to love school and to love reading. Matt especially learned to love books and to really feel good about his own learning. He was curious about the world and enjoyed writing about the things he was learning. Garth continued to excel in math. He also learned to read very well. According to Cherrie, he came to love poetry and to enjoy telling "really long stories." See Figure 12–3 for Matt's second writing sample, dated April 29, 1992, and Figure 12–4 for Garth's second writing on the same day.

Creating a Community of Self-Confident and Successful Learners

Five of Cherrie's second graders had been identified as having ADHD, and all of the children were considered learning disabled. Yet by March, they were willingly and cheerfully reading good books, exploring math, writing, and learning to revise and edit their own work. And they were supporting one another. All this growth took place in an environment rich in literature and content. It was an atmosphere of trust, inquiry, and calm good humor.

FIGURE 12–3. *Matt's writing, April 29, 1992.*

Around the World hats

Once upon a time a boy was wearing a
hat. It was winby outside and all of the
Sudden the boys hat felt off. It fiov
from nashville toward the west. It went to
JApAN. the hats in JApAN are different
thay wear wise hats. from JApAN to INDiA
thay wear turbans from thar to AustRALiA
in AustRAiLA thay wear weird cowboy hats
frm thay to BRASi in BRASi thay wear
Loag straw hat from thay to EGYpT
in EGYpT thay wear FeS from thur to
Germany thay wear a hunters hat

and Back to Nashville

Gone were the frustration, angry outbursts, and inattention to instructional events that characterized this classroom in general—and Matt and Garth in particular—during the initial weeks of school. They had been replaced by enthusiastic interest in the topics at hand and eagerness to participate. Ideas and imaginations were rich. Learning and self-confidence were evident in everything that the children did and said.

In our final interview Cherrie said: "Teachers are guides. They must provide

FIGURE 12–4. *Garth's writing, April 29, 1992.*

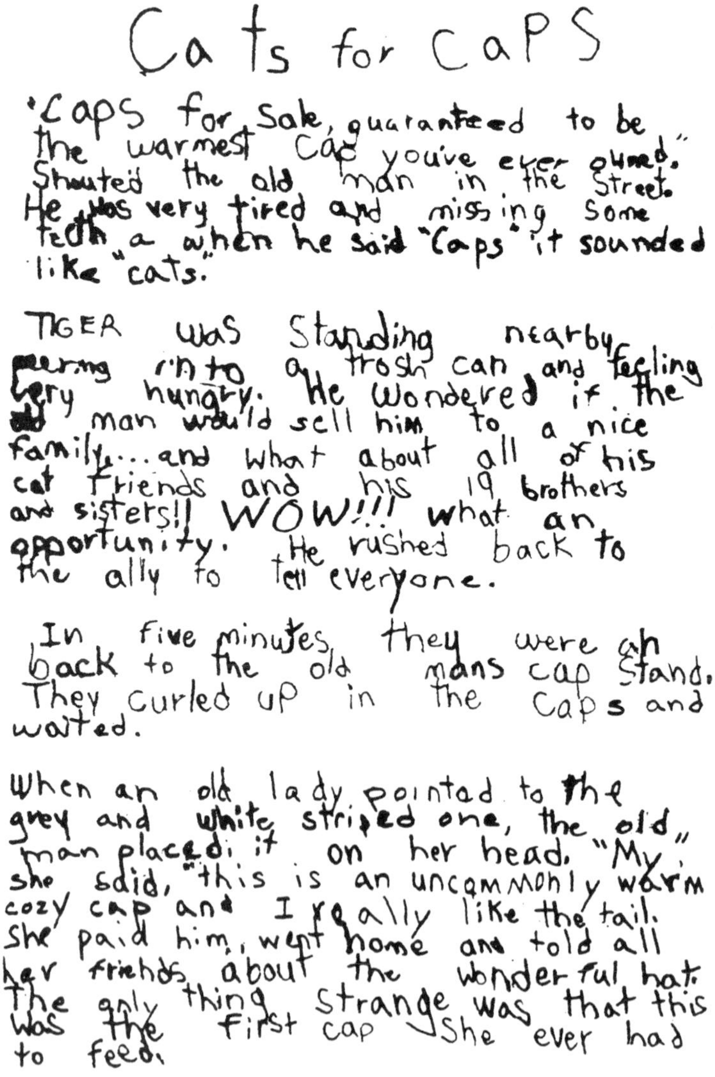

Cats for CaPS

"Caps for Sale, guaranteed to be the warmest cap you've ever owned." Shouted the old man in the Street. He was very tired and missing some teeth a when he said "Caps" it sounded like "cats."

TIGER was Standing nearby peering into a trash can and feeling very hungry. He Wondered if the old man would sell him to a nice family... and What about all of his cat friends and his 19 brothers and sisters!! WOW!!! what an opportunity. He rushed back to the ally to tell everyone.

In five minutes, they were all back to the old mans cap Stand. They curled up in the Caps and waited.

When an old lady pointad to the grey and white striped one, the old man placed it on her head. "My," she said, "this is an uncommonly warm cozy cap and I really like the tail. She paid him, went home and told all her friends about the wonderful hat. The only thing strange was that this was the first cap She ever had to feed.

children with opportunities and quality experiences. To me, the most important part of teaching is when the children feel successful with whatever they are doing."

She expressed her strong belief that children must be encouraged and supported to work independently as well as cooperatively. "The children made great strides this year. Next year I want more help with evaluation and self-assessment for the children. I also want to integrate more." She added: "I want to teach more from the children's interests and their lives. You know, I believe whole language is the best hope we have to keep from losing these children to their rage and frustration."

All children flourish in a positive and literate atmosphere in which they can safely risk their fragile egos. Reflective teachers view children as individuals whose lives inside and outside the classroom blend to enable them to become whole learners. In that way children gradually begin to lose their labels. Learning appears to be easy rather than difficult. When children are adequately supported in their learning and are treated as capable and trustworthy, they can overcome many of their problems and can function well both in and out of school.

Reference

Scieszka, J. (1989). *The true story of the 3 little pigs! by A. Wolf.* New York: Viking Kestrel.

13

Trading on the Strengths of ADHD Students Helps Other Students, Too!

Mary Lou Hess and Beverley Bailey

In Mary Lou's classroom and school, whole language learning and teaching have become an accepted part of classroom instruction. As a structure for learning, whole language provides the flexibility that challenges children with diverse backgrounds of knowledge and skill and with differing patterns of behavior—and does it in such a way that children are not identified, labeled, or otherwise constrained as learners.

This chapter describes Mary Lou's approach to meeting the needs of her ADHD students—and thereby to making learning more meaningful for *all* students. She describes the three boys in a recent class who demonstrated serious problems with attention and behavior, and she articulates the teaching style she has developed over the last several years and how it meets varied needs. Then Mary Lou turns to the heart of the chapter: a discussion of how she introduced a poetry unit designed to succeed with these boys in particular, then a math unit, and finally a science unit. Each of these units reflects key principles of whole language classrooms, including the most basic principle of meeting students where they are and drawing upon their strengths. The importance of students' taking significant ownership of their own learning is also discussed in a section on the boys and traditional instruction.

Mary Lou Hess is a fifth grade teacher at Chester School, East York Board of Education, in Toronto, Canada. A teacher for fifteen years, she has most recently been working on perfecting her abilities as a whole language teacher, with a particular focus on successful integration of all students in the classroom. She has prepared articles, papers, and workshops on the topic of whole language instruction. Currently, she is transferring her whole language philosophy to the teaching of math and science, as this chapter indicates. It is her particular concern to work for the validation of teachers' voices in the community and among other educational personnel.

Beverley Bailey has been a counselor and special education teacher. Currently, she is a teacher educator and doctoral candidate at the Ontario Institute for Studies in Education in Toronto, Canada, where she is conducting research with teachers on the process of mandated change. Her role in this chapter has been that of participant observer, discussant, and editor.

From the very first day of school, several of my fifth grade students, all boys, made their presence known. I could hardly ignore them as they talked out, squirmed in their seats, and wandered around the room, distracting the other students who were trying to make a good first impression. Throughout the year Peter, Chris, and Vito consistently required more teacher attention than any other students did. In fact, so much of my time was used in responding to negative behavior that it took deliberate work to see their strengths. Peter, for example, was a leader. Left unchecked, he could completely sabotage a lesson. Although Peter had never formally been diagnosed with ADHD, Peter's previous teachers agreed with me that he exhibited the standard behaviors of hyperactivity: he called out and fidgeted during instructional periods and wandered around the room during work periods, rarely concentrating on tasks for more than a few minutes.

You can imagine my surprise when Beverley, who was observing my class on a regular basis for purposes of this study, suggested that his actions were deliberate and controlled. She related an incident in which she saw him dance around at his seat and make funny faces while I had my back to the class. As soon as I turned around, he stopped. On another occasion she noticed Peter catch Chris's and Vito's attention and, when my back was turned, lead them in rocking back on their chairs, making faces, or throwing bits of erasers. Peter rarely got caught in these scenarios because he kept his eye on the teacher. When he did get caught, he denied his misbehavior with such vehemence that I began to doubt my own perceptions. In fact, his tears and temper tantrums almost convinced me that I was cruel and hard-hearted. Through collaboration with Beverley, I realized that Peter was not a standard ADHD student. He chose, in fact, to act hyperactive when it suited his needs.

In struggling to find Peter's strengths, I started to notice that his ability to express himself orally was a great asset in literature circles. He expressed opinions clearly and convincingly, supporting his ideas with references to the text. His advanced reading skills and well-developed oral ability meant that he was one of the few students in my fifth grade class who joined a group of predominantly sixth grade students for literature circles. Instead of being intimidated by the older students, he thrived on the opportunity to banter with them.

Peter's loving to be the center of attention added color to the class. At our Valentine's party, when all the students, particularly the boys, were too shy to dance, Peter took the floor and entertained the class with his impersonation of a rock singer. His only prop, a meter stick, became an imaginary guitar. As he shook and jived to the music, many of the other students joined in the fun. For the school musical, later in the year, Peter practiced with intense concentration on his part.

Peter's desire to be in charge was expressed in other positive ways as well. If one of the leaders in his French group was absent, he took over immediately, explaining instructions and finding the appropriate materials. He was the only one in the class who noticed a window that should have been closed to make the air-conditioning effective. He popped up and closed it before I even realized that there was a problem. His mother also benefited from his responsible behavior, such as the time he minded his baby sister so that she could enjoy the demonstrations at the Science Fair.

Chris's behavior was much more impulsive and spontaneous than Peter's. I had learned about Chris's immature and irresponsible behavior from his previous teacher and soon noticed that he was always ready to leap into situations that were distracting. He soon lost control and attracted the teacher's attention with his loud voice and boisterous manner. During work periods he rarely stayed at his desk for more than five minutes. I was most likely to find him getting a drink, going to the washroom, borrowing a book from a friend on the other side of the room, or sharpening a pencil. On the playground he often got into fist fights. During gym class he exploded when the calls were not in his favor and spent more time serving penalties than participating in the game.

During lessons Chris interrupted to share personal anecdotes. Their thin connection to the topic of instruction was frustrating for everyone. His incoherent, rambling rendition brought mutters to "shut up" from his peers. To gain peer approval he would resort to references to flatulence and was rewarded by the titter of self-conscious giggling. He infuriated the girls by calling them names or by starting rumors about their love life.

Chris was diagnosed as ADHD with a specific deficit in language. He became tongue-tied when excited. His written work was undeveloped and disorganized. In spite of these obstacles, Chris had an enthusiasm for learning that amazed me. Always willing to try anything, he volunteered for tasks that I initially thought were beyond his capability. In a recent study of short-story writing, Chris voluntarily finished writing his kidnapping story for homework. He proudly announced to me the next morning that he had written six pages at home. He was so keen to read his piece to the class that I had no choice but to hold group-share immediately after the morning announcements. As he read his piece he constantly glanced up from his paper to check his peers' response. His ingenuous smile indicated his satisfaction.

Chris's innocence and enthusiasm pushed me to question the validity of his results on standardized tests. During our study of native people Chris volunteered to read and report on one of several newspaper clippings I had found on the topic. My intention was to provide this resource as an enrichment activity for the more capable readers like Peter. I assumed that Chris was too naïve to know that the reading level was much too difficult for him. Though I wanted to encourage his interest, I was afraid that the advanced vocabulary would discourage him. After all, who was I to question the findings of the "experts," who rated him three grades behind his peers in reading? Chris persisted in waving his hand in the air and so, against my better judgment, I gave him a newspaper clipping.

The next morning Chris told me that he had had trouble with some of the words, and his mother *had* to help him. He explained that he still did not understand all of it. But he showed me his work, and I sensed his pride in having persisted with a difficult task. He had glued the article to a blank piece of paper and written, in his best handwriting, a few sentences explaining the article. I acknowledged his effort by helping him read it to the class. Instead of being discouraged, he was affirmed as a learner. I realized that it was very important to let Chris take on challenges in spite of the limitations that his test scores suggested. I could not let the results from tests which had been administered out of the context of the classroom determine what Chris was able to achieve when he was interested and supported by his family and the educational environment.

Vito, the third boy who exhibited attention deficit behavior, was less disruptive than Peter and Chris. He was small for his age, and his large brown eyes deceived one into believing his innocence when he pleaded his case in disputes with his peers. During partner activities he bickered about his share of the work, often changing his mind about what he was willing to do. Few students wished to work with Vito because he rarely did his share; thus, he required adult mediation during cooperative activities. Since Vito had little interest in writing, his written assignments were incomplete and undeveloped. His reading was slow and tedious; he preferred to "read" books like *Where's Waldo?* and *The Great Waldo Search.* Not surprisingly, he was labeled as ADHD with a specific deficit in language.

Vito marched to the beat of a different drummer. He was the last one to be ready at dismissal times, even resisting his peers' urging to hurry up so that the class could be dismissed. He lingered at the end of the day to play a few games on the computer. An organized desk was an impossibility for Vito; the contents spilled out whenever he searched for materials. Forgetting homework books was his trademark. Classroom routines were often neglected; and even at the end of the year, I had to remind him to keep his knapsack at the coatrack and not at his desk.

During instructional periods Vito's inattentiveness was not readily discernible. He doodled on his desk or played with things. Not until I asked him a fairly straightforward question, to which he had no response, did I realize that he had not been paying attention. Once I became aware of his habits, I had quite a collection of elastics, string, rulers, and action figures that I confiscated from him during lessons. Sometimes he did get caught up in a lesson but, ignoring class rules, would call out a response. More often, he whispered quietly to a buddy and missed important concepts.

At daily activity periods Vito's first choice was the construction center. Unlike Chris, who built only tanks and guns, Vito constructed elaborate machines and vehicles. Curious about how things worked, he took a motor out of his toy dinosaur at home. He brought it to school, rigged it up to a popsicle stick, and transformed it into a mini-propeller. Vito was also the one who found a snake and brought it to school. Much to the relief of some of the girls, he soon realized that he could not provide a suitable environment for the snake, so he released it.

Vito took great pleasure in working on art projects, working slowly and carefully on the most meticulous and exacting projects. The intricate folds of origami intrigued him; he never tired of this activity. He worked for hours at school and at home creating an exquisite mosaic design. Each section contained a different shape that he had painstakingly cut out and glued carefully in place. The concentration involved in cutting out the numerous hearts, triangles, squares, or circles was mind-boggling.

My teaching style has gradually changed over the years, enabling me to focus on the strengths of boys like Peter, Chris, and Vito rather than on their weaknesses. By the time they entered my class, I had come to feel that the labels they had been given unfairly limited my expectations of their achievement.

The Evolution of My Teaching Style

My style of teaching evolved as a response to the diversity of abilities, cultures, and interests of the students attending Chester School, a large, urban school. For example, one day at writing workshop time, Barinder, Barbara, and Gina were sprawled on the floor listening to Gina's narrative. Gina, who intends to be a writer when she grows up, had Barbara's full attention. Barinder, however, appeared uninterested and lethargic as she leaned back on the wall and stared at the ceiling. I wondered if she had been up late again watching rented Indian movies in her mother tongue. Or was she jealous of Gina, who had been in Canada for only one year and could already read and write English with ease? Then there were Mai of Cantonese background and Khaajal from India, who also seemed to be making little progress with written English. They worked hard in class, particularly Khaajal, who loved to write but whose invented spelling was indecipherable even to me, an experienced teacher of fifteen years. Many of my boys like Vincenzo, Serge, and Peng disliked writing but were curious and interested in their surroundings. When Vincenzo brought a spider in a bug jar to school, the interest in insects spread like wildfire among the boys. Soon there was a bug jar on almost every boy's desk. Serge, who reads with ease, became the class expert on spiders as a result of his extensive reading. These students were among the thirty in the class with Peter, Chris, and Vito; together they represented thirteen different cultural backgrounds and the full range of academic exceptionalities: gifted, learning disabled, language delayed, slow learner, and ADHD.

I have developed a particular teaching style in response to the varied needs of my students. My most successful lessons include activities that immediately engage and immerse the students in the topic. I try to keep the amount of time I talk to the whole class to a minimum for several reasons: the learning disabled students have difficulty processing oral instructions; in addition, the ADHD students have short attention spans; the slow learner can absorb only small amounts of information; the English-as-second-language students understand about half of what I say because of their limited vocabulary; and the gifted get bored quickly. The activities are an integral part of the lesson because they create interest and form a common base of experience from which we can share ideas, develop concepts, and enlarge vocabulary.

My teaching follows a predictable cycle that the students soon recognize and appreciate. I begin a unit of study by having the students work on whole class activities that develop skills and concepts appropriate to the topic. At this stage the students' time, materials, grouping, and pacing is also decided by me, the teacher. Over a period of a week or two, I gradually relinquish control to the point where the students collaborate with me about groupings, materials, activities, and pacing. The final stage of working on an individual or collaborative independent project completes the cycle. I feel strongly that students must be given the opportunity to work through their own meanings. The independent project enables students to take responsibility for their learning. This cannot be facilitated if I am at the front of the room orchestrating events. While students work intensively on independent projects, I am free to concentrate on specific needs with individuals and small groups. Students usually feel confident about working on their own because I have helped them develop the necessary skills and concepts to experience success. I am also available to support them when they make poor decisions.

Talk is an important characteristic of my teaching. Students in my class are supported in their learning by the many opportunities to talk. The self-esteem of learning disabled and ADHD students is raised because these learners often make their best contributions through oral expression. The English-as-a-second-language students benefit from hearing the language. All the students, in fact, revise and refine their work as a result of the increased communication. At whole class discussions, small group discussions, peer conferences, and individual conferences with the teacher, I demonstrate encouraging and challenging comments. I expect the students to talk during work periods (and have finally learned to relax with the increased noise level!). The students soon learn that if there are thirty students in a class, then there are twenty-nine other teachers in addition to me in the room. They also learn that their talk must be related to their work; I expect to hear them articulating their reasons and ideas. Through the many opportunities to express their ideas orally, they discover what they know and what they are still uncertain about. Peer response motivates the students to revise their work and keeps them interested.

I have learned that I have to give my students time if I want them to be responsible for their own learning: time to listen to each other, time to make mistakes, time to experiment and abandon, time to revise and revisit, time to refine, time to celebrate final products. I have to resist the pressure I have internalized to expect quick results that can be easily transferred to a mark on the student's achievement form. I have to trust that the students will eventually make meaning out of the experiences I have provided. I cannot succumb to mindless memorizing of facts to please a bureaucrat when such information makes no sense to the student. As I become increasingly able to give the students time, I also have time to be more responsive to my students. I have time to listen to, and understand, their reasoning and thus individualize my responses. Students also have more input. As they become more involved in the topic, they offer ideas and suggestions. Instead of squelching their enthusiasm because I have to rush to "cover" the curriculum, I take time to include and build on their input. The collaboration is empowering for the students and refuels my energy.

An integral aspect of my teaching is requiring all students to display their learning in a public way. Going public gives them a reason for revising and refining their work. In addition, they experience great satisfaction and pleasure in entertaining and informing their peers. Their self-esteem is enhanced when they sense that their learning has significance for others as well as themselves. They gain confidence in themselves as learners when they see that they can contribute positively to the academic life of the school.

My approach to the teaching of children includes teacher-directed activities, independent projects, many opportunities to talk, time to revise, and the public display of one's learning. This has proven to be an effective approach to my very challenging ADHD students.

The Boys and Poetry

I have observed over the years that the successful students in a traditional classroom are those who are able to sit still and work quietly at paper and pencil tasks. The boisterous, inquisitive children who need to talk, to be physically active, and to mess with materials are considered problems. These children are usually boys. These boys soon learn, through the labels the educational system gives them (learning disabled, ADHD, and so on), that they have little ability and hold little hope of achieving success at school. Knowing the school population, I expected to have once again this year several boys that exhibited ADHD behavior. I had found in the past that my heavy emphasis on quiet, individual reading and writing tasks at the beginning of the year often put me in conflict with this type of learner. It usually resulted in frustration for both me and my hyperactive students.

I decided to organize a language unit that would be specifically aimed at uncovering the strengths of the ADHD students and that would enable them to succeed. I knew that I would have to plan activities capitalizing on their energy. Selecting activities that focused on concrete, physical modes of expression was no easy task. My personal preferred mode of expression is writing, and my class is considered a model for teachers in my school district interested in the writing process. I would be risking a lot to change the focus of my program.

I decided to start my year with a study of poetry because it lent itself to oral expression. After all, most ADHD students loved to talk. I chose activities that focused on drama as a mode of expression. Maybe hyperactive boys would respond to a program that legitimized movement. I also felt that poetry would appeal to any reluctant readers I would likely have because it did not involve a huge investment of time. Fortunately, I had access to a varied and large poetry collection in the school library.

Since the introductory activities stressed the oral aspect of poetry, I selected poems with much repetition and a strong beat. We read them aloud in unison or in groups, shouting or whispering, rapidly or slowly. (Because I share an open area with another teacher, I had to coordinate my poetry classes with times when her class was not in the area.) We discussed which dramatic reading was most effective in conveying the mood of the poem. Already I was establishing my expectations for behavior; I would not accept silliness and nonsense.

I slowly gave the students more responsibility for the lesson. I gave out copies of poems and assigned verses to groups to perform. The cooperative nature of the task appealed to Peter and Chris. Picture Peter sitting on his desk top teaching one of the ESL students the words. Chris, at another group, is yelling out ideas about how he thinks the stanza should be read. Vito, though less enthusiastic, does manage to read along with his group as they practice.

The noise level is high, but everyone is on task. Five minutes later I call the class to order, and all the groups perform. We discuss the effective aspects of each mini-performance. We also make suggestions for improvement. Once again, the expectations are made explicit and clear. Peter, Chris, and Vito have no difficulty accepting the feedback because it is not directed at them individually but as a group. When Chris asks if they can perform their verse again, I know that I have hit on an approach that makes him feel competent. I also am able to show him that he has good ideas by building on his request and having the groups trade verses and develop a different interpretation.

To connect our study of poetry in school to their own lives, I give them a homework assignment. They are to remember a poem or riddle they learned when they were young or to ask a parent for a favorite riddle or proverb. All three boys did their homework; in fact, Chris shared a poem in his first language, Greek; and Vito shared a wisecrack in Italian. The students loved listening to the sound of these languages.

Once Peter, Chris, and Vito showed me that, besides enjoying the shared reading, they could remain on task and behave appropriately during these activities, I introduced to the whole class the idea of using gestures and actions to complement the meaning of a poem. Once again, we worked as a whole class on one poem, giving each student a line to say and dramatize. During the few minutes of practice time, I notice Chris happily refining his leap to go with the line "Pop over and see" (in "A Busy Day" by Michael Rosen). Peter is showing a buddy his motion for "Pop out for a walk." When the class is called to order, Peter and Chris are among the first to come to attention. They can hardly wait to show off their part. The students perform the poem, and we discuss revisions. Everyone remarks on Peter's excellent action and Chris's loud, clear voice. The positive remarks reward them for appropriate behavior and encourage the rest of the students to take greater risks. By this time in the unit the students have had many opportunities to talk. They are realizing that they can learn from each other, even from the "bad" students like Peter and Chris.

Peter, Chris, and Vito are reading a lot more than usual without even realizing it. During part of the language period, the students read poems of their own choosing. They are allowed to read in pairs or individually. I encourage them to read the poems aloud so that they can hear the rhythm and sounds of the words. Reading with a partner allows Chris and Vito to get help with their reading without losing face. I also start to share leadership with the students by inviting them to read aloud to the whole class at group-share some favorite poems they have discovered. This serves two purposes: it exposes the students to a variety of poems, and it gives the students an incentive to read.

Peter and Chris seize on this opportunity to gain attention. Peter signs up almost every day to read a poem. Chris's enthusiasm and need for attention lead him to volunteer to read the longest poem in the collection, *The Cremation of Sam McGee* by Robert Service. I was caught in a dilemma: I wanted to encourage his eagerness to read, but I knew he would lose the attention of his peers with his lack of fluency. I tried to negotiate with him to let me read every other page, but he was adamant. He wanted to read the whole thing by himself without any help from the teacher. I bargained with him: he could read the whole thing on one condition—that he read it fluently and with no mispronunciations. I offered him the assistance of my student teacher. Chris worked hard for two entire language periods learning to read this Canadian classic. The illustrations by Ted Harrison made the story come alive for him. Imagine the confirmation of him as a reader when he finally read it to the class! The emphasis on oral expression was working. These boys showed me that they could concentrate for extended periods of time.

At this point in the unit I assigned the students their independent poetry project: to memorize and present a favorite poem to the class. The students had received plenty of guidance through the introductory activities. Criteria for an effective dramatization had been developed as a class and made explicit. They had been immersed in the resources so that finding a favorite poem would not be a formidable task. The independent project gave them many choices: poem, length, partner, presentation. I knew that I was successful when none of the three boys came complaining to me about not finding a good poem. Their favorite phrase, "This is boring," did not pass their lips.

Peter and Chris teamed up with another boy. They cleverly divided the work to take advantage of each student's strengths. Their poem, by Michael Rosen, required a narrator who had the most lines. Peter, the most capable of the group, had no trouble memorizing this part. The other two boys did all the actions and said a few lines at the appropriate times. True to form, their dramatization involved lots of action: running behind the coatrack to signify a change in character and crawling under a desk to symbolize a cave with hidden treasure. Their actions were entirely appropriate, and their movements were carefully choreographed to allow for smooth transitions.

Vito had social problems. He changed his mind several times about which lines he would learn and nearly lost his partner. He had trouble memorizing his part and even forgot when to come in.

In keeping with my emphasis on process, self-evaluation, and peer evaluation, I videotaped their presentations at a mock dress rehearsal. Once the students got over their embarrassment of seeing themselves on TV, they got down to the serious business of critiquing their work. The video camera was an excellent tool. The students made their own decisions about what to improve. Peter, who had resisted my suggestion that he speak more slowly and loudly, understood that this was valid advice. Vito, who practically had his back to the audience and could not be heard, decided to change his position.

With the students given time to refine their performances, we made a final videotape that was shown to the parents on Open House night. I suddenly realized that all the students, and especially Peter and Chris, had developed such a fine performance that they should share their work with other classes. Accordingly, they performed for their first grade buddies. The applause brought smiles of pride from Peter and Chris. Vito, who did not want to be embarrassed in front of a live crowd, finally mastered his lines. He also became envious of his partner, who did such a fine job of hamming up his lines that he brought spontaneous laughter. At the last performance for a class of intimidating sixth grade students, Vito finally blossomed. Not wanting to be upstaged by his partner, he too hammed it up and received rewarding laughter. The aspect of performance seemed to be an important motivating factor for Vito.

The dramatization project was so successful that some of my students, including Peter, Chris, and Vito, asked if they could do another one. By this time we had spent three weeks in language with no writing, and I was getting twitchy. Wanting to encourage their enthusiasm and to support their positive attitude, I offered drama as a choice during activity period. For the first time Vito opted out of building with Legos. He joined with some other boys to work on "Jimmy Jet and His TV Set" by Shel Silverstein. To my surprise he took the initiative to spend an entire evening at home cutting and decorating a cardboard box to symbolize the TV. The details of his construction showed that he had read the poem carefully. There was a hole in the top for his head to fit through when he dramatized Jimmy Jet turning into a TV. Wires hung down from the bottom of the box to be symbolically "plugged in" at the appropriate lines. He had even brought in a cap fitted with tinfoil-covered wires to wear on his head to represent the antennas mentioned in the poem. He also recorded some sounds from a sitcom to enhance their performance. The class was impressed with the props and the entire performance. I was pleased that Vito's strengths had been tapped.

The students were given a second independent project: to make a picture book of one of their favorite poems. I felt that this would be a fairly painless transition to writing. As they copied their poem and decided how many lines should go on each page, they became aware of the influence of white space on the meaning of a poem. Peter, Chris, and Vito were also forced to pay close attention to spelling as they copied out the poem. This was an individual project that once again offered the students lots of choices: poem, length of poem, number of lines on each page, illustration. Chris divided his poem into twenty-four pages, one page per line. He did not fail to point out the fact to me and his peers that his was the "thickest" booklet in the class! I gave the students plenty of time and emphasized process. Each student had to do a mock book before going to a good copy. This project appealed to Vito, and he spent hours adding details to his illustrations. He produced such a fine book that his mother requested that it be laminated to preserve it. Some of the students, including Peter, donated their books to the library.

The final project in the poetry unit was writing a poem. I had already presented many different models of poems; now I asked the students to try experimenting with their own writing, using these models. Writing along with them, I shared my first drafts. After we had written many short entries, I asked the students to read through their writing notebooks, looking for one that they would like to develop, refine, edit, and publish. The extended time I had given them for experimentation meant that they had a bank of material from which to choose. They all wrote a final poem and displayed it in the class.

The illustration project overlapped with the writing project and provided a convenient outlet for Peter, Chris, and Vito, who could not concentrate on writing for more than twenty minutes. In spite of all the models of poetry they had been exposed to over the past four weeks, they still had great difficulty writing. Chris resorted to the worn-out line "Roses are red, Violets are blue. . . ." Fortunately, I was able to help him because he had had many positive experiences with poetry. I suggested that he look again at the poem he had illustrated and try to use it as a model for his own writing. This model helped him immensely, providing structure and form for his writing. (See Figure 13-1.) Here is the Michael Rosen poem he used as a model.

On the Beach
There's a man over there
and he's sitting in the sand.
He buried himself at tea-time,
now he's looking for his hand.

There's a boy over there
and he's sitting on the rock
Eating apple crumble
washing dirty socks.

There's a woman over there
and she's sitting in the sea.
I can see her
but she can't see me.

There's a girl over there
and she's sitting on a chair.
Standing just behind her
is a big grizzly bear.
—*Michael Rosen*

I gained some sense of the power of this approach when an experienced colleague who was working with my class during this unit remarked on its success. When I told him that I had deliberately planned this unit to meet the needs of my students who had a reputation for being disruptive, he expressed his surprise. He had not noticed that I had done anything special or different for these boys. In fact, he remarked that the capable and gifted students were equally challenged and excited by the dramatization project. He had spent time videotaping an excellent dramatization by three of my brightest girls who had voluntarily given up recesses and activity periods to work on an extra poem.

The Boys and Traditional Instruction

During music classes I sit at the back of the music room, pretending to read as the lesson is being taught. Inconspicuously, I observe Peter, Chris, and Vito. The children are seated in rows of chairs. The music teacher has an active program in which the children participate in rhythm clapping, singing, and playing the recorder. She has wisely separated the three boys: Peter sits in the back row, Chris in the front row, and Vito several seats over from Peter. Peter has the hood of his pullover up and is slouching down in his chair. Vito looks around the room and squirms in his chair. During the introductory echo clapping, Peter deliberately claps the rhythm faster than anyone else in the class. The teacher is frustrated but cannot pinpoint the culprit. The students are

Hess, Bailey

FIGURE 13–1. *Chris's poem.*

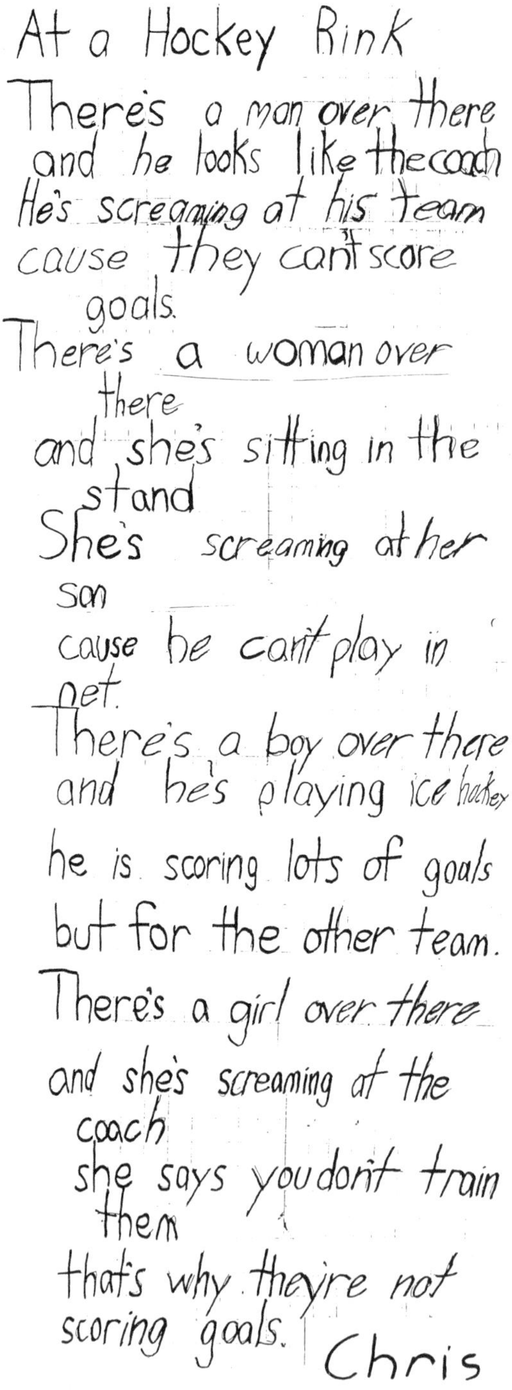

At a Hockey Rink
There's a man over there
and he looks like the coach
He's screaming at his team
cause they can't score
      goals.
There's a woman over
      there
and she's sitting in the
      stand
She's screaming at her
son
cause he can't play in
net.
There's a boy over there
and he's playing ice hockey

he is scoring lots of goals

but for the other team.

There's a girl over there

and she's screaming at the
      coach
she says you don't train
      them
that's why they're not
scoring goals.   Chris

then led in a series of breathing exercises. Chris laughs and talks out. Vito joins in with Chris's loud laughing and makes weird noises during the vocalizing exercises.

Peter has been trying to look compliant but is not following instructions. When the teacher moves to the piano, Peter seizes the opportunity to take control. He eyeballs the other two boys and leads them in rocking on the back legs of their chairs. Peter keeps his eye on the teacher, who is accompanying their singing. Whenever the teacher looks his way, he puts on his most innocent face. He changes the misbehavior to making noises under his armpit. Chris and Vito follow his lead. Unfortunately, they are so busy imitating Peter that they are caught by the teacher and reprimanded.

I am puzzled by the boys' negative response to the music lesson. I expect the high level of activity and participation to contain their hyperactivity. Why were they cooperative during my introductory poetry lessons but not during the music lessons? The teaching style in both cases appears the same. Both lessons incorporated student activity. The music teacher and I both stand at the front of the room and orchestrate everything: the activities, the student groupings, the pacing, and the timing.

Upon further reflection I realize that the goal of my teacher-directed lessons is very different from that of the music teacher's. From the very beginning of the poetry unit, Peter, Chris, and Vito know that they will eventually get to use the skills I teach them in an independent project. They know that there is a gradual progression in my teaching style, starting with complete control of the lesson by the teacher and working toward student-teacher collaboration. My teacher-directed lessons are only a beginning, not an end point as in music. I believe that the boys were willing to listen because they were looking forward to making some of their own decisions during the independent project stage. I was explicit with the goal of my lessons. They knew that my lessons were giving them direction for their own work and would enable them to experience success. All three boys thrived on peer response and were motivated by the opportunity to demonstrate their learning to their peers. They realized that they needed the skills I taught them in order to produce an effective project. The goal of my lessons influenced how the students listened.

The goal of the music lesson is very different. The teacher's style is constant from lesson to lesson. The students know that the teacher will always decide everything; they also know that there will never be an opportunity for peer response. They will never be encouraged to develop a rhythm to share with the class. They will have to continue to echo the teacher's. They will never be given percussion instruments to develop an accompaniment for the songs; the teacher will always accompany their singing on the piano. They will never get to decide how the songs will be sung: fast or slow, loud or soft; the teacher will continue to decide. They will never perform the songs for other students in the school; they will continue to do breathing exercises to improve their tone. The boys feel no responsibility to cooperate because they know that they will never get an opportunity to demonstrate their ability to use the skills. They know that, with the teacher deciding everything, they will never be expected to contribute or be challenged to defend their own ideas during the lesson.

The Boys and Math

I decided to plan a unit in math based on the same principles that I had used so successfully in the poetry unit. I taught a geometry unit on tessellations. A tessellation is a tiling, made up of the repeated use of polygons and other curved figures to completely fill a plane without gaps or overlapping, just like the tiles on a kitchen or bathroom floor. (See the sample of Peter's work in Figure 13–2.)

This unit would give students the opportunity to exercise their spatial sense within mathematics (Giganti & Cittadino, 1990). Like the poetry unit, the topic of tessellations drew not on the boys' deficits but on their strengths. Doing tessellations does not require ability with numerical calculations. Rather, tessellations depend on visual and spatial awareness, particular strengths of Chris and Vito. In fact, this topic was so new that the boys had no preconceived notion about their ability to succeed. All the students would have equal access and chance for success.

FIGURE 13–2. *Peter's tessellation.*

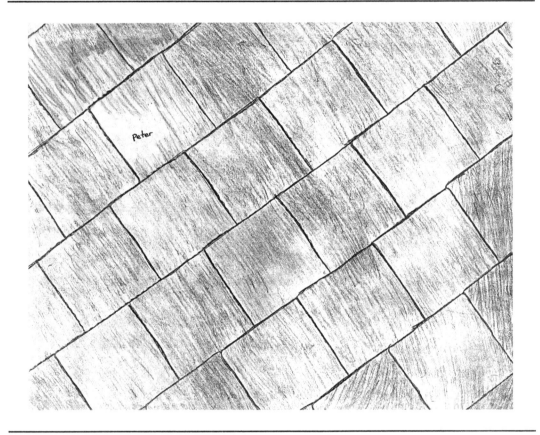

In the beginning I gave the students a variety of two-dimensional shapes to work with. As in the poetry unit, immersion in the materials from the very beginning caught their attention while developing appropriate concepts. We spent time talking about their discoveries. Instead of the teacher feeding them all the answers, they were challenged and guided to make their own conclusions. This was similar to the poetry activities in which the students were guided in whole-class activities to decide what characterized an effective performance.

The relevance of tessellations to the real world was also an important part of the unit. The students toured the school in small groups, making sketches of tiling patterns that they found. They looked for examples of tiling in magazines and made a collage. For homework the students made sketches of tessellations found in their driveways, bathrooms, and kitchens. Chris and Vito demonstrated to me the transfer of knowledge from the theoretical to the practical when they pointed out some tessellation patterns on the walls of the subway station during a class trip. What a pleasant change from the usual playfighting, yelling, and laughing while waiting for a train.

As with the poetry unit, the students were given lots of time to work through a variety of activities before they were expected to embark on a final independent project. The final project combined art and geometry as the students developed their own shape for tessellating and decorated it with details. By the time they started the independent project, not only did they have the necessary skills to produce a fine piece of work but they also knew, through experience with previous smaller tasks, what characterized an excellent product. They were as capable as I in evaluating their final product, as evidenced by their self-evaluations. Examples of tessellations by the artist Escher had fired their imagination. Vito, in particular, was engrossed in his art-geometry project for days. The detail in his patterns was mind-boggling. (See the sample of Vito's work in Figure 13–3.)

Peter, who has poor fine-motor skills, was also successful. The element of choice served him well. He did a very simple but effective design using bold colors. Going public with the final piece played an important part in motivating the boys to complete their independent projects with care. They knew that their work would be displayed in the main hallway of the school. Their hard work brought them much attention, as teachers and students throughout the school commented on the beautiful display.

The Boys and Science

The school's Science Fair was fast approaching, and I wanted once again to highlight these boys' strengths. They seemed to be motivated by the opportunity to perform for an audience. I knew they would be disruptive, bored, and unhappy doing the traditional science display, which often amounted to each student copying an experiment from a book in his neatest handwriting and beautifying it with elaborate lettering. I decided to have the students perform before an audience demonstrations that illustrated a scientific concept. I

FIGURE 13–3. *Vito's final tessellation project.*

thought that this would be a wonderful way to build on their learning and success from the poetry unit.

I found a variety of demonstrations that focused on one topic, the properties of air. The demonstrations had a strong performance element in that they were all discrepant events—things that behave at variance with what one would normally expect. I started the unit with one of these demonstrations. After filling a plastic bag with air, I inverted it over the mouth of an empty jar, sealed it with tape, and announced the challenge: Who think they can put the bag in the bottle without breaking the bag or the seal? Chris and Vito immediately volunteered. They were convinced that this was a "simple" task. Imagine their surprise when it was an impossibility. They were fascinated and totally engrossed by the demonstration.

The lesson continued as I gave the students time to talk and encouraged them to develop an explanation as to why the bag would not go in the bottle. They got the important message that science is not tricks and magic, there are reasons for certain happenings. They learned that in science I expected them to observe carefully and to think about why certain things happened. I believe that this is particularly important for these restless boys, who tend to go from one stimulating experience to another without reflection. The class discussion helped them to slow down and to be more thoughtful. Although Peter, Chris, and Vito held side conversations throughout the class discussion, their talk was on the topic as they shared theories with their friends. Through discussion I helped the students understand that both the bag and the bottle contain air and that air occupies space.

Keeping the didactic part of the lesson short, I got the students immediately immersed in the topic by providing them with bags, tape, and bottles so that they could do the demonstration on their own. As they reproduced the demonstration, I conferred with individual students, helping them understand and explain why they couldn't force the bag into the bottle. When Chris interrupted the class to announce proudly that he was able to put his bag in the bottle, I involved the class in a discussion on possible explanations for this. A classmate suggested that either he had not sealed his bag securely with tape to the mouth of the bottle or his bag had a hole in it. Chris carefully searched and discovered a pinhole in his bag.

All my introductory lessons demonstrated discrepant events about air and air pressure. Each lesson followed the same format: a challenge or hook, the demonstration, and discussion and explanation. The lessons usually lasted about twenty minutes and were totally teacher-directed. The boys contributed many appropriate comments and theories. They listened and watched carefully because the demonstrations were intrinsically interesting and because they knew that their turn would come. But, by the end of two weeks, they were anxious to get to work on their own. They were allowed to choose from any of the demonstrations I had already done or from a selection of demonstrations related to air that I had not performed. The students were responsible for collecting the materials, making the demonstration work, and writing and memorizing a script that included a hook, questions for the audience, and an explanation. My lessons had modeled all these aspects.

Peter, Chris, and Vito were excited about the opportunity to entertain and amaze other students in the school. I had told them that they would be performing for another class of fifth grade students and for their parents at the Science Fair night. Peter immediately joined a bright student who chose to perfect a demonstration that he had shared with the class during the introductory stage. Peter's buddy had wowed the class with his demonstration of putting a water-filled balloon in a bottle without breaking the balloon. I was initially surprised that Peter was willing to play second fiddle, but upon further reflection I realized that he felt prestige in being associated with the only demonstration in the class that was entirely researched by a student. Offering Peter the opportunity to choose his own partner greatly benefited him. He learned about air pressure from his friend. They worked cooperatively on the script and made wise decisions about what part each would take. Peter, who was less confident about the explanation, presented the challenge or hook at the beginning of the demonstration; his buddy handled the materials and gave the explanation. Both boys were motivated by the element of entertainment: they wanted their friends in the other fifth grade class to be impressed with their demonstration.

Chris had more difficulty getting started. He was so taken by the element of entertainment that he completely rejected all the choices I had offered as being too boring. He wanted to do something different, like Peter, but he did not have adequate background. He thought that it would be a great idea to fill a plastic bag with hot air and release it. He did not seem to realize that the audience would not find it very unusual to see the bag rise. For that reason, I rejected his idea. Although he was annoyed with me, it was important for him to understand a new concept well enough to be able to demonstrate and explain it. I sensed that he did not want to repeat one of the demonstrations I had done for the class, but his reading level was too low for him to imagine the potential in some of the other demonstrations of which I had made copies. Therefore I explained in detail two possible demonstrations and gave him a choice. A day later he and his buddy had collected all the materials and proudly showed me their demonstration. They worked out a script together and performed it to an appreciative audience. Chris's mischievous smile throughout the performance showed that he was getting the attention he craved.

Vito's initial response to the science assignment was frustrating. He decided to perform the demonstration that I had done with the bag and the bottle. I was pleased that he chose such a simple one and was sure that he would be successful. I provided the bottle, but he expected me to also find him a plastic bag with no holes. When I refused, he spent several days and miles of masking tape trying to seal up the bags he found lying on the floor after lunch. The day before he was to perform his demonstration for the class for suggestions and revisions, he was still searching for bags. His performance for the class was very rough because he had not written a script. His peers pointed out that his demonstration did not work (they could put the bag in the bottle) and that his explanation did not make sense. Vito just shrugged off their comments and did not seem to care that his demonstration was clearly inferior.

That same day the class watched the sixth grade students perform their demonstrations and picked up more ideas on how to involve the audience. Enthusiasm was high as the class worked hard that afternoon to refine their performance in preparation for the next day's presentation to the other class of fifth graders. Vito was the exception. He wrote a few lines of his script but spent most of the time wandering around the class watching the other students.

The next day Vito performed his demonstration along with everyone else in the class. When he challenged a fifth grader to put the bag in the bottle and the boy succeeded, Vito suddenly realized that his explanation was irrelevant and that the audience was not amused. As in the poetry performance, he was envious of his peers who were getting a positive response from the audience. That afternoon as the students were putting the final touches on their performance in preparation for the evening performance for the parents, Vito drew me aside. He asked me if I would listen to his explanation and see if it made sense. I conferred with him until he was able to articulate his reasoning clearly. He went away and wrote it down. Minutes later he returned, showing me his script and asking if it made sense. I was amazed at his change in attitude. That evening Vito came to school armed with ten bags. He was prepared. He selected a huge bread bag that ballooned over the top of the jar. Much to Vito's delight, no one was able to put it in the jar, not even his little sister who had come with the family for the show. Time and response had worked in Vito's favor.

Conclusion

As the year progressed and I created and invented as I went, I realized that indeed the successes I had had with my students in my language arts program were skills that I could use to advantage in math and in science. I felt that I had learned a universal truth—by changing my approach to teaching I could establish an environment that allowed my students to change their approach to learning. By surrendering so much of my power to the students, I had gained the power that comes from seeing my programs effectively do what I had planned them to do—provide a structure for student growth and learning. By focusing on the needs of my ADHD students, I had in fact developed a program that worked well for all my students.

It is easy with such an active approach to forget to ensure the skill development of the children. There are two ways that I do this, aside from an ongoing reference to skills. Sometimes I say that something is just not good enough and that more thought is needed. I am, of course, there to help with further revisions. Other times I am able to let the process in itself be the teacher—to allow students to come to the point where they realize that they need to know more before they can do what they know they are capable of. The tack that I take is context-specific and depends on the situation at the time. However, I do try to work from a basic concept that at all times a child's classroom activities should be meaningful, always resulting in a learning experience. How to make sure that the learning experience occurs becomes a matter of judgment in the situation.

With the best will in the world I have not succeeded in creating perfect students; I realize this forcibly in the last days of the school year. I will settle for knowing that my ADHD boys had a good year, one where they learned some positive and empowering things about themselves as learners. I have reason to hope that the skills they learned will remain with them as they continue through their school years.

I shall let Chris have the last word. On a field trip taken in the next-to-last week of school, he had a hard time with his behavior during an unstructured time. When he swung his pack around and caught another child on the face, I took him aside for a little "chat." I explained to the contrite child that he had to learn to think before he acted. "I do think," he said.

"Well, you have to show me by the way you act that you're thinking," I explained. He looked at me with his big brown eyes. "But, Mrs. Hess, I've been showing you all year!"

References

Giganti, P., Jr., & Cittadino, M. J. (1990). The art of tessellation. *Arithmetic Teacher, 37,* 6–16.

Handford, M. (1987). *Where's Waldo?* Toronto: Grolier Limited.

Handford, M. (1989). *The great Waldo search.* Toronto: Grolier Limited.

Rosen, M. (1986). On the beach. In *Smelly jelly smelly fish.* London: Walker Books.

Rosen, M. (1987). A busy day. In J. Booth, D. Booth, J. Phenix, & L. Swartz (Eds.), *Impressions,* Shared Reading Four. Toronto: Holt Rinehart and Winston of Canada.

Service, R. (1987). *The cremation of Sam McGee.* New York: Greenwillow.

Silverstein, S. (1974). Jimmy Jet and his TV set. In *Where the sidewalk ends* (pp. 28–29). New York: Harper & Row.

14

A Fifth Grader with ADHD Becomes a More Involved and Independent Learner

Cora Lee Five

This story of Mike spans the entire school year, showing how he gradually begins undertaking literacy and learning activities that formerly were difficult or impossible for him, begins taking more responsibility for his own learning, and finally—one magical day in February—becomes an active member of the class community.

In reading the story of Mike, we see that extensive one-on-one support for learning can also develop learned helplessness that must be overcome if special needs students are to become independent learners. We also are given evidence that isolated skills work might be more harmful than beneficial to learning, especially when the child is removed from authentic reading activities to do the skills work.

Though Cora emphasizes Mike's growth as a learner rather than her role as teacher, we also see clearly what characterizes this classroom in which an ADHD student and other special needs students could begin to act and perceive themselves as learners. One of the most important ingredients is time: time to develop new behaviors and expectations for themselves, with gradual release of adult support as they become more able to take charge of their own learning.

Cora Lee Five is a public school teacher in a fifth grade classroom. She is a teacher-researcher who has been studying children with special learning needs as well as new approaches to teaching and learning. Her book *Special Voices* (1992) tells the stories of how children with special needs flourished in her regular classroom community. She has conducted workshops for teachers, spoken at national conferences, and written articles and book chapters on her work. In 1990 Cora Five was given a Professional Best Leadership Award by *Learning Magazine*. She is a member of the Middle Childhood & Adolescence and Young Adulthood/English Language Arts Standards Committees of the National Board for Professional Teaching Standards and serves on the National Council of Teachers of English Committee to Evaluate Curriculum Guides.

A miracle occurred in my classroom one day during one week in the beginning of February. Mike, an ADHD child, became part of my fifth grade classroom community of learners after months of living on the fringe. I knew from years of experience that his entrance into the learning community had probably been happening gradually over time, but it seemed to occur suddenly that day in February in one long moment when everything else seemed suspended and I held my breath as he raised his hand and entered into a discussion we were having in history.

I was particularly interested in Mike because for many years I have been following the progress of children with special learning needs who were mainstreamed into the regular classroom. I have observed that in a positive, supportive environment they can become active members of the class. They do not have to learn in isolation, using materials that increase their sense of being "different." I was excited when I saw my class list. I looked forward to observing the progress of all my students, but I was especially eager to see how Mike, an ADHD boy, would develop in a supportive classroom environment.

Mike's Background

Mike was the youngest of the four boys in his family. He, like one of his older brothers, was a late talker and had trouble pronouncing certain words. His mother noticed this and, as a result of her experiences with her older son, put Mike in a pre-kindergarten program in a special school for children with speech and language problems. It was here that the director of special education for my district and my school's psychologist observed Mike and recommended a learning disabled classification for his speech (articulation) and language problems. They suggested that Mike attend the special Board of Cooperative Educational Services communication class that was held in another school in the district for kindergarten, first, and second grade. He was in small classes of seven or eight children for these grades.

Mike's kindergarten experience was not a happy one. The other children in the class were very rough and "crazy," according to his mother. Those who observed him in kindergarten felt that he had an attention deficit and that he was hyperactive, distractible, and impulsive. It was suggested that he be medicated, but his parents refused. Mike was difficult at home as well. He had an eye problem, myopia, and was supposed to wear a patch. Because he was so active, he refused to wear it and often ripped it off.

Mike's first and second grade experiences in his special class were better. He was involved in a reading and writing program and seemed much happier. Because he was having difficulty with reading, it was suggested that when he was mainstreamed back to my school, he repeat second grade.

Mike entered my school at the beginning of his second year in second grade. He was reading on a primer level. He was tested and classified as ADHD. As a result of this he was given an aide for twenty-five hours a week. Concerned about his behavior, his second grade teacher wanted him to work with the aide out of the classroom; thus, for the hours that the aide was with him, Mike worked in a small room with her. He was also scheduled to go out for skills in reading and for speech. It was during the trips to the skills room and the speech room that Mike took his time and wandered the halls. He was not in the classroom for much of the day.

Mike's third grade teacher had a different philosophy. She wanted him in the classroom, so he worked there with his aide and was not removed very often. Fourth grade was a different story again. For much of the twenty-five hours a week that Mike worked with a new aide, Joan, he was out of the classroom, in a small dark room. His attention span was very limited. For periods of fifteen to twenty minutes, he worked on specific word attack skills, filmstrips with audio cassettes, math games, and handwriting. Often, Joan and

Mike would read together, each reading a page aloud. He also left the class three times a week for reading skills but ran around the room and hid under desks before he could settle down. In skills he worked in a one-on-one situation with the skills teacher on computer games, word families, and isolated drills. In addition, he left the classroom to attend speech classes three times a week to work one-on-one with the speech teacher on articulation and on organizing his thoughts.

Although Mike liked his fourth grade teacher very much, he did not do much work. He would act up and was considered a behavior problem. Little was expected of him, and he was happy to run the film projector and take messages around the school. Again he wandered the halls, came in late from recess, and hid in the boys' room. When the class had reading once a week, he was placed in the low reading group, where he read a basal and did workbook pages.

Mike had few friends, perhaps because he was a year older than the other children, perhaps because he spent so much time out of the classroom with his aide and various specialists, perhaps because he was perceived as "different" by his peers. In fourth grade, however, he became friendly with Doug, a boy who had his own set of problems. Doug had no friends and was easily distracted, quite disorganized, and very disruptive because of his inappropriate behavior. Doug had been placed in my class, too, because it was felt that he would benefit from Mike's friendship.

Mike's Individual Educational Program (IEP) and the System

The first day of school I asked my students to write to me to tell me anything about themselves that they thought I should know in order to make their adjustment to me and fifth grade easier. Figure 14–1 shows Mike's letter.

I was interested that he printed his message. All the other children wrote

FIGURE 14–1. *First-day-of-school letter.*

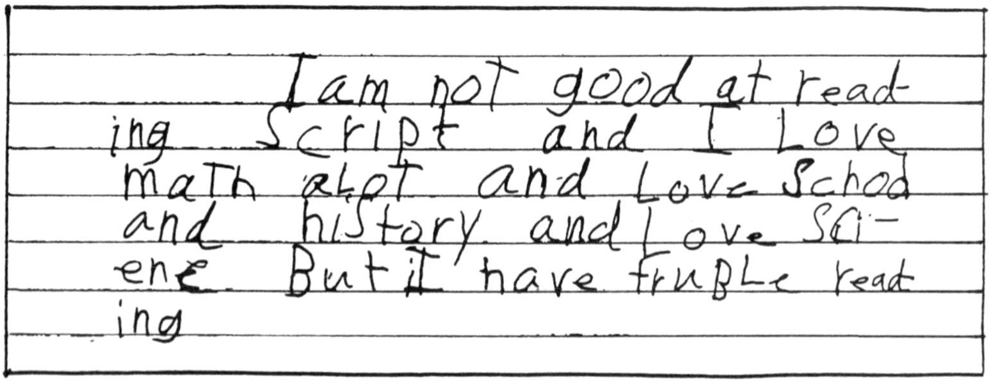

I am not good at reading Script and I Love math rkpt and Love Schod and history. and I ove Science But I have truBLe reading

in cursive. I also made note of his love for math, history, and science and hoped to build on these areas during the year. I wondered whether he would begin to feel more confident about reading once he became involved in reading workshop, where he could select his own books, read for an uninterrupted period of time, and respond to his reading with his own ideas in conferences and journals. It would certainly be a change from the basal reader and workbook he read once a week in fourth grade. I wondered, too, how he would respond to writing through the process approach, where kids selected their own topics, conferred with peers and me, made decisions about revision, and shared their work. I knew that he had done little writing in fourth grade because the teacher he had did not teach writing, though she occasionally assigned topics.

I looked forward to having Mike involved in a classroom community that emphasized reading, writing, speaking, and listening throughout the total curriculum. I felt that he would make progress as he learned to value his own ideas and developed confidence in his abilities.

Mike had been in my class for five days when I realized there would be problems not only with Mike but with the system. Upon receiving his schedule in my school mailbox, I realized that he would not spend as much time as I had hoped in my classroom. He was scheduled for an instrumental music lesson once a week and band for an hour every Friday. Based on his IEP (Individual Educational Program), he was to go to skills three times a week and speech twice a week. On certain days these special twenty-minute classes were scheduled back-to-back, so he would be gone for forty minutes on some days and for twenty minutes on other days. All these special classes were scheduled for him immediately after lunch, taking up the first part of the afternoon. It seemed he would once again work in a one-to-one setting on isolated skills.

This traditional view of learning posed a problem for me. I had discovered through my readings and my own case studies of students that they learn best when they are actively involved in their own learning; when they are immersed in a subject; and when they are reading, writing, speaking, and listening for a variety of meaningful purposes. I knew, too, the importance of creating a supportive environment that builds on students' strengths instead of dwelling on their weaknesses, an environment that gives children a chance to make decisions, to take risks, and to take responsibility for their learning. Within this environment, students come together as communities of learners to work together collaboratively and learn from each other as they develop hypotheses, and discuss and share ideas. I wanted Mike to be part of this environment, part of the classroom community of learners. In the past my students with special learning needs had flourished in this type of environment. Could Mike also thrive if he was removed from the class so frequently? Could the specialists work with me in the classroom with him and perhaps other children who had the same needs? How could I make Mike's time in the classroom count as quality time?

In the middle of September my principal, the skills teacher, and I went over Mike's IEP. I learned that he was above average in intelligence, that his math concepts were good, and that reading and speech/language skills continued to be areas of difficulty. It was also noted that writing was difficult for Mike because of his problems with handwriting and his fear of misspelling. The IEP stated that Mike needed to be involved in a structured setting, that he was easily distracted in a group situation and could learn better one-to-one. It listed the goals and objectives for the current year in each area of the curriculum based on Mike's deficits. The Committee on Special Education had assigned him twenty-five hours of aide time a week. In the morning he would have Joan, a well-trained, skilled aide who had been his aide in fourth grade; in the afternoon, he would have Beth, a new untrained aide.

After discussions with my principal and the skills and speech teachers, it was made clear to me that Mike would be removed from the class to work with the various specialists. That could not be changed because it was mandated by the state. When I asked about the programs and the approach the skills and speech teachers used with him, little information was forthcoming. It appeared that the three of us would work with Mike in our own way with little communication or connection.

I was faced with the dilemma of an educational system that attempts to address children's deficits through providing help in specific skills rather than whole learning. In such a system the classroom teacher, skills teachers, and aides all work in isolation instead of developing a unified approach to the child. The system thus fragments the educational program. A fragmented system can only work to create greater disorganization for an already disorganized child. This built-in systemic principle was and continued to be a source of frustration and concern in my work with Mike throughout the year.

I tried to rearrange my schedule so that Mike would be in my room for all, or at least some, of reading workshop. Since all my special classes—art, physical education, music—were in the morning, I had to schedule reading and writing in the afternoon in order to give children enough time for these areas. Mike would miss parts of reading on some days. He would not be able to hear me read aloud, be part of discussions about reading, or have the opportunity to share his ideas.

The Beginning

During the fall, Mike had problems in the class. He shouted out instead of raising his hand and talked to his friend Doug whenever he could. He got up from his seat frequently to sharpen a pencil, to smash a bug crawling on the window, and to go to the boys' room. He was unable to find his books and start assignments with the rest of the class, and he could not focus on his work. When he finally found his materials, he would get up from his desk and, with pencil and paper, head for Joan for help. He was ready to leave the room.

Because I had worked with Joan before, she knew my philosophy. Instead of taking Mike out of the room, we decided that when needed, she would work with him in the mornings at a table at the side of the room and take him out as little as possible. In the beginning she was at his side before he started any of his work to make sure he had the materials he needed and was focused on the lesson. I noticed that he was very dependent on her. In addition to helping him organize his work and move from one subject to another, she explained the homework to him. Sometimes she took him out of the room to the library to get a book for him to read so that he would be ready for reading workshop in the afternoon.

At the beginning of the year Mike showed little interest in class activities and did not participate in them. He did not appear to listen to our discussions of current events or the news articles brought in by his classmates. When he was offered a chance to give a news report, he agreed, but did not actually do it, seeming not to care. I told him that I thought he'd be able to find an article and suggested he bring in a newspaper for us to find one together. Finally, one day Mike brought in a newspaper and we found an article about a dog that he decided to use.

Then two days later Mike had his own article. He was very excited about the discovery of a two thousand-year-old corpse in Europe and wanted to share it for news. This was the first time that he had shown interest in a class activity. I suggested that he tell me about the article and then after reading it with Joan, he could write down all the facts. The next day he shared his information, but his interest in this discovery did not wane. Joan and I found articles about this event that added to his store of knowledge, and he continued to report on it for several months. Pleased that he was becoming involved in current events, I encouraged his interest by asking questions. It was the beginning of his speaking in class about the topic under discussion, the beginning of his raising his hand when he wanted a turn instead of shouting out, and the beginning of his interest in listening to the news reports of others and taking some responsibility for contributing his own. For the first twenty minutes of class he seemed able to participate and attend by himself.

Once we were involved in our regular academic routine, however, Mike needed support to focus and to get himself organized. Unfortunately, one of Mike's favorite subjects, math, was no longer easy for him because the fifth grade was involved in a new math program that emphasized the development of concepts and problem-solving. For much of the year Mike could not focus his attention and get started with the rest of the class. He often stared into space with his vacant look, or else he played with Scotch Tape inside his desk. Either Joan or I would help him begin, but often he had not heard or understood the initial lesson and we had to reteach it.

Many of the math activities involved working in groups or in partners, but Mike painfully discovered that his classmates chose to work with other children. He therefore worked with Doug whenever he had the opportunity. Unfortunately, this partnership did not work out well. Instead of working together on math, Doug also played with scotch tape, cut various designs out of paper with scissors, and twisted rubber bands. As much as Mike tried to focus on a math page or a math game, he became distracted by Doug and his antics. Even though he could ignore the inappropriate behavior of the other boys, Mike could not ignore Doug, whose behavior and attitude influenced him throughout the year. Perhaps the two boys bonded because they had no other friends. Perhaps part of Mike's attachment to Doug was his similarity in behavior;

Doug could mirror Mike's negative identity. Later on in the year when Mike took more responsibility, Doug served a different purpose. Mike realized and was pleased that he could complete his work and Doug could not.

When I placed Mike with other boys, he was able to work but usually stayed on the fringe, not participating. He'd had little experience over the years working with his peers and had usually worked with adults. Often, he'd return to Joan or she would take him from the group and work with him individually. He was able to complete more of his work in this setting.

Mike went to Joan immediately for help when we were involved in history or science activities that called for reading and writing. He was unwilling or felt unable to try any work on his own. Besides wanting to read with her, he seemed to feel that he needed her help in writing his ideas in his history or science journals. For the first few months of school, Mike spent the mornings doing his work with or near Joan.

The afternoons, however, were different. Beth had not worked with Mike before, nor had she worked with children with special learning needs. Mike came in at one o'clock and at the beginning of the year announced regularly that he was going to skills or to speech. He was usually wound up after lunch and recess and took a while to settle down. According to the routine I had planned for him, he was to copy his homework and then go to skills or speech. In the fall he seemed unable to do this. Despite my expectations, he did not think that he had to do homework because he had done very little in the past. Instead of copying, he ran around the room and played with Doug; then he went off to skills. When he returned twenty minutes later, he proclaimed his return and was more distracted than ever, seeming unable to adjust to the class routine. I wondered about the wisdom of taking an ADHD child out of a structured setting for twenty minutes and then sending him back into a class that had already begun; that meant he had to refocus and figure out what to do. I tried to begin reading workshop as late as I could so that he could be part of it from the beginning. But even though I waited for him, he could not attend to the mini-lessons and could not find the book Joan had helped him select. Beth would move in, taking him to her table, and together they would each read a page in his book. He could not or would not read on his own. At the end of the reading period, Mike did not participate in the group-share. Instead, he sat at his desk, staring into space.

Choices in Reading and Writing

Responding to reading is part of my reading program. Usually students respond by writing a letter to me at least once a week in reading journals. The first book Mike read in fifth grade was a short one that I had suggested, *The Ghost in Tent 19* (O'Connor & O'Connor, 1988). He read it with Joan and Beth, reading a few pages by himself. His first letter was his first and only letter written in script (see Figure 14–2).

I was glad to receive his letter and told him that I looked forward to a letter once a week. He looked shocked. "You do?" he exclaimed. "I don't think I can do that because I won't remember." I promised I'd remind him and hoped he would tell me his ideas about his book; however, throughout the year this proved a difficult task for him.

Mike had an easier time attending to routines during writing workshop, perhaps because he was there from the beginning and not taken out for special help. In the beginning of the year I taught mini-lessons with my own writing as a sample. Mike was interested because my story was personal—it was about my cats. I hoped that he would listen to, and learn from, his peers and me. During the first few sessions, though, Mike saw writing workshop as a block of unstructured time and used it to play and talk. When I began to have short brainstorming conferences with him, I realized that he thought he had no ideas, and I wondered how he had lost his ideas. Perhaps in the past he was not given choices and did not select his own topic. Perhaps in the past there was no respect for his ideas and he had been assigned a topic. Perhaps he had either worked with an aide or skills teacher who provided the ideas, spelled the words, or was the scribe for his dictated stories.

Eventually, Mike was able to select a topic that had meaning for him, but he did not come to the conference table, where groups of children and I share and respond to writing pieces. Instead, he went to Beth for help with spelling. She did indeed correct the spelling but, in correcting, she took away Mike's ownership by changing his words, crossing out his sentences, and writing in her own.

I was struck by the difference between Joan and Beth. Joan, who was trained to work with special learners, respected Mike's ideas and encouraged his efforts. She worked with the child. Beth, on the other hand, who was untrained and had little experience working with fifth grade children with special learning needs, did the best she could by relying on her own school

FIGURE 14–2. *First letter in reading journal.*

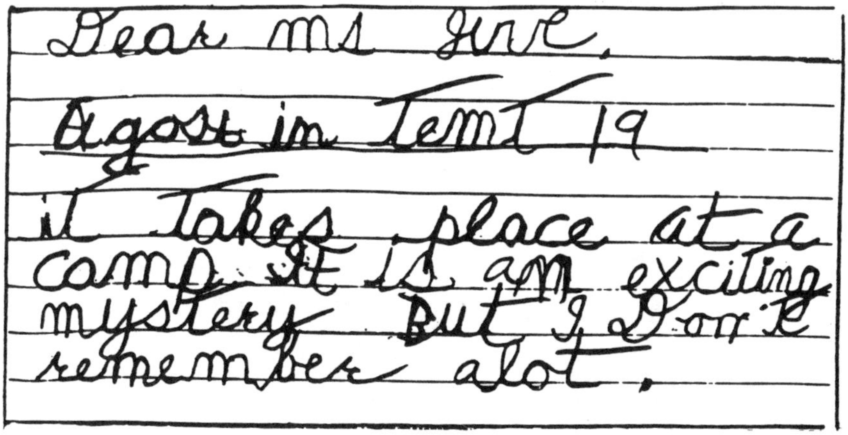

experiences. She worked on skills. In her desire to help Mike, though, did she increase his sense of helplessness by making him feel more incompetent?

Later in the fall Mike spent a few writing periods wandering around the room, trying to get close to Doug. It was during his roaming around the room that he passed near the conference table. Although he did not sit down, he stood by my chair, listening to a child reading a poem about Halloween. When the student finished, Mike decided to write a poem but was stumped for a topic. A child who had come to the conference table asked Mike if he could write a poem about the kinds of things that he liked to do. He told us, "I play Tag a lot with everybody." I asked whether tag might be a topic.

The next day Mike came back to me with a paragraph about tag. After he

FIGURE 14–3. *Mike's poem in November.*

Tag

Tag at Edgewood School
Brian was it,
Chasing, running, reaching
I was running too.
Then whoops!
I slipped and fell.
I was it,
chasing, running, reaching
to tag Dean.
Dean was it,
chasing, running reaching
to tag Timmy.
And Timmy got me.
The bell rang
No more
chasing, running, reaching.

read it, I asked him to underline all the important words or parts of sentences. When he worried that they wouldn't rhyme, I read some poems to him that didn't rhyme, and he read some himself.

Later Mike came back to me. He had discovered that some poems repeated the same words in different lines. I was excited at his discovery. "You could do that, too," I suggested. When he told me that chasing and running were activities that he did in Tag, I suggested that he repeat those words. Eventually, he took some of the words that he had underlined from his paragraph and after each child was tagged, he wrote "chasing, running" and later added "reaching" because "You have to reach out to tag them."

By the end of November Mike had finished his poem entitled "Tag," a poem he later evaluated as "loving the whole thing." (See Figure 14–3.)

Toward Personal Involvement in Learning

Although Mike was gaining some independence in writing, he was not making as much progress in reading. True, he showed an interest in reading some poetry that I gave him after he wrote his poems, and he wanted to read the Dr. Seuss books that I read to the class after the author's death. These selections, however, were suggested by me. Unable to select books by himself, he waited for Joan, the librarian, or me to give him a book. Joan and I decided to give him books from the Random House Stepping Stone series; these are short books at a second to third grade level. Even though the books were short and on his level, he still went to Joan to read if she was there or to Beth in the afternoon when he came back from skills and was unable to get himself settled after returning to the class late. He wrote a few letters in his reading journal. In response to *The Stories Julian Tells* (Cameron, 1986), he wrote:

> Dear MS. Five
> I say the Stories Julian tells
> is a vevy good Book.
> I Love the book
> bcacs it is by Ann Cameron
> and funny.

I wrote back to him:

> Dear Mike,
> I love all the Julian books.
> I like the way Ann Cameron writes. My
> favorite book about Julian is
> *Julian, Secret Agent.* Have you read it?
> I have it in the classroom. I wonder if
> you would like to read it.
> Sincerely,
> Ms. Five

As a result of that letter he looked through all my paperback books and found *Julian, Secret Agent* (Cameron, 1988). He read it with Joan and on a few rare days by himself. Later, Mike wrote:

> I Love the Book beceuse
> it is rell funng. thackyou
> for Letting me Borow it.

This was the first exchange we had through the journal. He wrote short letters to me sporadically about the fiction books he was reading with Joan, but he read my letters to him with interest—I think because I usually included something personal. Perhaps our communication and growing personal connection encouraged some of his reading. Perhaps my reading aloud to the class helped. Even though he could not sustain interest in the first book I read, he was very interested in the short story I read later and came to me often to tell me his predictions.

Later in the year the whole fifth grade was involved in a study of whales and ocean life, which integrated reading, writing, social studies, science, math, and computer activities. Mike did not become a participant at the beginning. The study used a series of videotaped episodes and expeditions. Students posed questions, were involved in much reading, and used data bases to find the answers. They recorded their information and reactions in science journals.

Mike had difficulty with these activities. He could not remember what he had seen on the videotapes or what he had discovered using maps of the ocean

FIGURE 14–4. *Science journal entry on navigation flags.*

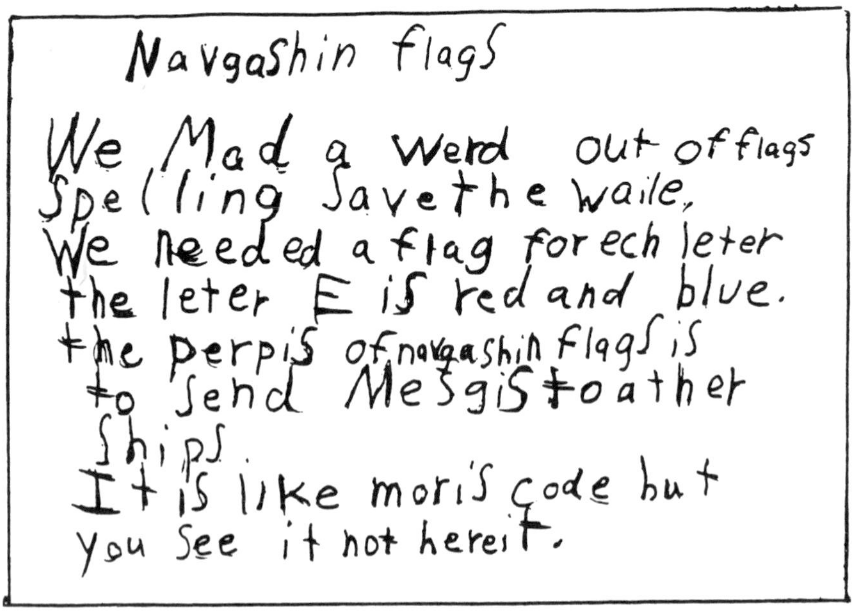
Navgashin flagS

We Mad a Werd out of flags
Spelling Savethe waile,
We needed a flag forech leter
the leter E iS red and blue.
the perpiS of navgashin flagS iS
to Send MesgiS to a ther
ShipS.
It iS like moriS code but
you See it not hereit.

floor. His main interest at first was in setting up the VCR and running and rewinding the tapes. However, once the students were given choices about hands-on activities they could explore and make, Mike became part of the learning community. He was able to record the activities he chose because they were meaningful to him. It seemed that when he was interested and personally involved on some level, he was able to write. Making navigation flags especially interested him (see Figure 14–4).

Collaboration in Assessment

In December I had to assess Mike's progress for his report card. I knew he was making slow but steady progress academically. I was concerned, though, that his involvement in the class was still through adults. Even though he had worked with groups of children in math, science, history, and writing, he did not realize the benefits of collaboration—that he could be involved in the sharing of ideas and that he could learn from his peers. Continuing his dependence on adults, he would often play with his pencil when he worked with classmates or would leave the group and wander around the room. He preferred to work with Joan or me. I feared that this dependence fostered his sense of helplessness. Perhaps it left him feeling ambivalent. Perhaps his need for people to tell him how to think and what to do reinforced his feelings of incompetence. I knew that I had to move him away from us gradually, making him less dependent while still providing support; but I did not force him to work with the other children. I hoped that it would happen at his own pace.

I was also concerned about his leaving the room to go to skills and speech because I had no idea what he was doing in these areas. Trying to discover something about the environment in which he worked and the activities and approach used, I decided to meet with the specialists. I wondered if we could coordinate our efforts so that our various programs were integrated in some way. This suggestion was not received enthusiastically, although the skills teacher said she would select a book for Mike to read. I hoped that Mike could read it during reading workshop and then continue to read it when he met with her. She seemed to agree to this arrangement. We both had realized that, whether Mike read an easier short book or a thicker book, he had the same problems with vocabulary and structural analysis. He was, however, learning to use the context to predict words that he didn't know.

Mike's reading evaluation conference seemed to be the time to encourage him to read the same book in class and during skills. I meet with all my students for a reading and writing evaluation conference before they receive their report cards. We look through their folders, discuss their work and progress, and talk about their responses to evaluation forms that I give them. When I met with Mike, he showed me a letter in his reading journal that described his improvement in reading:

> I improved by reading more Books with harder
> words and by extra reading at home

He told me that he wanted to read harder books, which meant that he wanted to read longer books. When I asked if there were any books that he had in mind, he had no ideas. I suggested a book that I knew had been a favorite with students in the past. I told him that he could read it when he went to skills, bring it back to read in class, and take it home to read each night. He was enthusiastic about this idea, although it turned out that he was not organized enough to carry it out.

When we discussed his progress in writing, he showed me his folder and told me he had written more during the first three months of fifth grade than he had written in all of fourth grade. Proud of his accomplishments, he revealed that he thought that writing a draft was easy. The only goal he wanted to set for himself was to improve in spelling. Spelling seemed to be a major concern at this time.

I asked Mike at the conference if he liked to work with his classmates in partners or in groups. He sadly admitted that he had no friends and that no one wanted to work with him. He told me that Doug always bothered him and got him in trouble. I suggested that he work with John, who seemed to be emerging as a kind, cooperative boy. In December when we changed seats, as we did each month, I moved Mike next to John. This turned out to be a good move because the two worked together on math, in history groups, and on science activities. Mike also gained some measure of acceptance from the other boys because of his friendship with John.

When I sat down to fill out Mike's report card, I had some thinking to do. I knew he felt good about many of his accomplishments; yet, in many areas he was not on grade level. Fortunately, my school's report card has five categories: excellent, good, satisfactory, improving, and unsatisfactory. In explaining to my students the meaning of each grade, I emphasize that "improving" shows that the student is working hard to learn. When I evaluated Mike, I checked "improving" in many areas and gave him a "good" or "satisfactory" check wherever I could. I wanted Mike to feel positive about his first three months of school, yet I wanted to be realistic. In reading, I added the words "on his level" next to comprehension, so that I would not have to deflate him with an "unsatisfactory." However, I did give him an "unsatisfactory" in completing homework and explained to him how he could improve. Written comments at the bottom of the page explained many of the checks in detail, as did a parent conference.

Becoming Part of the Classroom Learning Community

December and January flew by. The class was involved in a study of colonial America and the Revolution. We used a history text to provide some factual information, but most of their information came from trade books, films, and filmstrips. I also involved the class in many simulations and role-playing activities in connection with our study of history. This interested Mike, who enjoyed being part of what he considered a game; it also kept him part of the classroom community. Mike, who had spent most of his time reading the history book with Joan, began to stay in his seat when we began to read and discuss together. He even asked not to go to skills during our simulations. He was involved and discussed each activity with me after school or at recess. He was especially proud of his role as a representative to the Constitutional Convention. Joan and I discussed his ideas with him and helped him prepare and practice his speech. In this way he could be part of the class activity and do as well as his peers.

Immersed in colonial life, the students took a trip to a colonial manor where they ground corn, chopped wood, worked in a barn, and cared for the animals. Mike came to me one day, announcing that he was going to study colonial farming and that he was going to the library to get a book on farming. I was delighted that he had decided on a topic he wanted to explore and was now ready to select a book by himself. Perhaps when Mike was really involved, he could make choices and become an active learner.

Mike read many books about colonial farming with Joan and gradually began reading them by himself in reading workshop. Each day I had short conferences with him about his book, and I could tell that he was learning from his reading. I was very excited as I noticed his involvement in these books, and I hated to end the reading period because I wanted him to keep reading. Finding the illustrations of farm tools especially interesting, Mike came to me often to show me the tools and to tell me how they were used; later, in letters to me, he drew pictures of some of these farm tools. He had discovered that he could learn from illustrations. He wrote a longer letter to me in his reading journal:

> Dear Ms Five
> I lerned that farmers do not use a crop on
> a feld year after year and ever fuw years
> thay do not use the feld for a year.
> I like reading about farms. and I lerned
> that farmers have to clel the feld because
> the felds have alot of roks.
> from Mike

Not only was his letter longer, it seemed to me that it was full of his own learning and his own excitement about what he had learned. His enthusiasm was similar to his interest in the two thousand-year-old corpse. Noticing that he had signed his letter, I wondered if this was an indication of his growing self-esteem.

It was during this time that the miracle occurred. The class and I were about to read together from the history book. We usually read a few pages in partners, in groups, or as a whole class. When we read as a whole class, each person who wanted to read, read a paragraph. I usually read one, too. This time, since we were reading as a whole class, Mike took his book over to Joan, as he usually did, so that he could read it with her. We suggested that instead, he stay at his desk and read with the class. He returned to his seat, turned to the correct page, and followed along in the text. He then began to help the child who was reading aloud with some of the words. When Peter stumbled over a word or couldn't figure it out, Mike helped him by telling him the words. When Peter finished reading, Mike raised his hand to read the next paragraph. Stunned, I quickly skimmed the paragraph to see if there were any difficult words. Since it was a long paragraph, I didn't have time to check all of it. I decided that if Mike could take a risk, I could, too. I called on him, and he began to read the fifth grade history book. While Joan and I stared at each other and held our breaths, he read the paragraph well. Mike had trouble with a few words, but his new friend John, who sat next to him, helped him. When he finished reading the paragraph, he followed along with the next reader, mouthing the words. His hand was up to read again, but we went on to a discussion of some issues from the reading.

During the discussion Mike contributed his ideas twice. Other children agreed with him. Many children voiced their opinions, and Mike listened to their ideas and raised his hand to speak again. He was interacting with his classmates for the first time. I listened to them debate the issue they had created. Joan and I looked at each other frequently and smiled.

When the lunch bell rang, Mike was happy. Still full of ideas, he came to tell me about them. Talk was becoming more and more important to him, and because he was very excited, he had to tell me his thoughts. He told me he loved history and that he was teaching his mother all about colonial times and the Revolution. "I want to be a history teacher when I grow up," he said as he headed out the door to lunch.

From that day on, Mike was part of the class. He answered questions in math and discussed a question in his spelling homework. He began to do more of his homework, took greater responsibility for his assignments, and felt very bad when he did not do them or left them at home.

Growing in Self-Confidence

Mike's increased confidence was expressed in a variety of ways. He became a more active member of my community of writers. He came to the conference table to share the draft he was writing on colonial farming. He discussed with me which subtopics he thought would make good chapters. I made a number of suggestions, but he made the final decisions. I wanted him to feel in control of his learning and of his writing. Returning to the conference table often to listen to the drafts of classmates, he was especially proud when he could help Chris, who was also doing a report on farming. Mike gave him information and shared his book on farming tools. Often I encouraged them to read together.

When Mike completed his report, he had three short chapters, illustrations, and a cover. Joan and I helped him organize his report and put it together with a table of contents and a bibliography. He was proud when he shared a chapter from the report as the other children did. He selected the chapter that he wanted to read (see Figure 14–5). He always beamed when he sat in front of the class and received positive response from his peers. They especially liked his last line about recycling.

It was at this time that Mike began to respond to the writing pieces of other children. For months he had played with the Scotch Tape while they read their pieces. Perhaps he was listening, but he never responded. Now he sat without fiddling with some item. When the author of a piece was finished, Mike raised his hand and told the reader what he liked about the story. At first he made general comments that he had heard the other children say, but gradually he began to focus on vocabulary words that he liked and on similes that he heard. He was learning about writing by listening to the writing of his peers. He was now one of many children in the class who responded to the writing of others. Perhaps he realized the importance of response for himself and wanted to have others share that feeling, or perhaps he realized that he was now like the other students, part of the writing community.

Mike's confidence and excitement had another effect, making him more assertive in terms of his learning. He became upset if he had to go to skills or

FIGURE 14–5. *Mike's chapter on colonial farming.*

Chapter 1 What farmers planted

Colonial farmers planted corn, Tobacco, Wheat pumpkins, Squash, peas and carrots.
Farmers would have to clear rocks and Trees off The field when They made a new field.
They used The rocks To make Stone Walls and the Trees To make Their houses.
Farmers would not plant The Same crop in The Same field year after year be cause The plant Took minerals out of The Soil. Sometimes They would let The field lie fallow for a year, So The minerals would return To The Soil
They put corn in a mill which made flour and used The flour To make bread and cake. They used corn husks To fill in Their mattresses
They recycled every Thing and did'nt waste anyThing.

speech and miss part of the book I was reading, *My Brother Sam Is Dead* (Collier, 1985). Involved in the book, he joined in the discussion after each reading, making predictions and talking about the characters. He also had the opportunity to listen to and learn from his peers, making connections between the book, history, and his own experiences. If his schedule of skills classes got in the way and he became annoyed, I read the parts he had missed to him in the morning before school, and we would make predictions based on the book's title.

Then, during reading period, he told me that he did not want to read the book *Tales of a Fourth Grade Nothing* (Blume, 1972), which had been selected by the skills teacher. Perhaps this was an assertive statement of his wish to be like the other children and his growing sense that perhaps he could be. I suggested a book that some of the other boys were reading. After a long whispered conference with Chris about the particular book, Mike decided he would read it in class and in skills. I was glad that Mike sought the recommendation of a friend instead of accepting my suggestion. He took the book to skills that afternoon.

The next day the skills teacher told me that the book was too hard for him, that he did not know the vocabulary. Perhaps the skills teacher could not appreciate his new-found sense of potential—that he could be like the others— and wished to protect him from the experience of failure. Mike never brought the book back to class to read. When I asked him about it, he told me that he had to read the book with the skills teacher and could not read it in class. I asked if he could read the book with Joan. He told me he couldn't because he felt he was to read some books with Joan and some others with the skills teacher. "Can you read any by yourself?" I asked. He explained that he was supposed to read with the two adults because, "They're here to help me read." Clearly, Mike was conflicted about his own abilities. Could he read by himself, or did he need continued support from adults?

Mike was also asserting himself with Joan by talking back to her. He began to resent her insistence that he get his books out and start math with the rest of the class. He also seemed to resent her help and wanted to do his work on his own; he didn't think that he needed help. He became very frustrated when he realized that he could not do it all by himself and that he did, in fact, need her. Joan and I decided to let Mike start on his own, encouraging him to work with John at first if he had problems; then we would step in to help, if needed. Many times this plan worked well. His greatest difficulty at this time was getting himself organized in order to understand and start his work. Although he was motivated to learn and wanted more independence, he still needed support.

At this time, too, Mike seemed to have developed a greater sense of responsibility. He decided not to work with Doug on a science project because he was afraid Doug might not do the work. Instead, he made a fine electricity project with the help of his older brother. Besides trying to complete more of his work on time, he was also concerned about events in the classroom and the school. He seemed to be reaching out beyond himself and his formerly isolated world to become involved with his classmates in school activities. He took part with a small group in planning a surprise birthday party for me. He called the president of the PTA when he noticed some older boys climbing out of a window in the school during a weekend. He helped the band teacher set up chairs and put them away after rehearsals. And he volunteered to be one of our two class representatives to the school's Student Involvement Council. Mike went to the meetings without his aide and told me that he and Julie, the other representative, had a report to give. We planned a time and, even though it took Mike a few minutes to find his notes, he described in detail all the events discussed at the meeting. He conducted the class meeting very well by himself for twenty minutes. I was amazed. Julie said very little.

Mike also became playful during this time, expressing more of his thoughts and feelings. His personal connection with me became stronger. Often he would sneak up behind me when we were walking in the halls and tap me on the shoulder. He'd always laugh at my startled expression, no matter how many times he did this. He began bringing me apples each day because he'd noticed that I ate them at lunch. He showed interest in my running, talked about my cats, discussed the type of glasses he thought I should wear, and worried that I'd be mugged in the city.

As Mike's confidence increased, his ability to initiate his work increased as well. He was able to do much of his work each day but needed help in organizing his folders so that he wouldn't lose completed work. He became involved in science activities, initiated projects on his own, conducted and recorded the results of his tests, and wrote his ideas in his journal. I realized that when he became immediately involved in hands-on activities, he was better able to start and complete them. Again I noticed his excitement and enthusiasm. It seemed that whenever he made a personal investment in a subject, he wanted to read, write, and talk. And the success he experienced caused his excitement. All of this was happening in the regular classroom, which seemed to provide him with an environment he was able to use successfully.

Assessment and Reflection on Mike's Progress

In March I began giving the class my series of practice writing tests to prepare students for the state writing test to be given in May. The state tests required that the children write about two different assigned topics on two separate days. Because Mike was a classified student, his test score did not count in the scores of the whole class. However, I wanted him to be part of the class and to continue the expectations he had developed for himself. I was also curious to see how he would deal with an assigned topic that did not allow for conferences or for help with proofreading.

Mike enjoyed the practice tests. When we had our second reading and writing evaluation conference in March, he told me that he loved his poem "Tag" but that he also loved his writing tests. This time he was able to set two goals for himself: he wanted to write a story about Philadelphia, and he wanted to improve in proofreading. Spelling was not specifically mentioned. Perhaps it was no longer a major concern.

Mike told me in our reading conference that he had improved in reading because he could read faster and felt that he knew more words. He had read four books since January and twelve in all since the beginning of the year. He told me that he could recognize similes and liked to listen for them in the books I read aloud. He thought that he might use some similes in his own writing. He had made a connection between reading and writing.

I was pleased with Mike's progress. He seemed better able to focus on his work, could work for longer periods of time, and did not seem to be as helpless and dependent on adults as he was previously. There was more interaction with the other children, and he seemed to enjoy working with them in small groups. When I did his second report card, I was able to give him more "good" checks in work habits and personal and social development, oral communication, math, and science. There were more "satisfactory" checks and still many marks in the "improving" column.

By April, Mike was able to work much more independently. This was especially true in writing, an area difficult for him from the beginning of his school experiences. Now, when he took a practice writing test, he got to work immediately. He was always able to focus on the topic and was happy when he could include similes. He took risks using words he knew he couldn't spell, and he didn't come to me or to Joan for reassurance. He was able to work on his draft for two hours at a time before he got up to tell me he was going to proofread. I had been teaching him about using quotation marks because he had started to use dialogue in his writing and had wanted to know how and when to use them. When he proofread his practice tests, he showed me that he knew where to put the quotation marks. He wanted to do all the proofreading by himself and he especially wanted to check each spelling word he thought was misspelled. I was pleased at his growing independence as a writer.

At the same time Mike started to write in script. It just seemed to happen. I had not forced him, but I noticed he was practicing letters in script as the other children reviewed the letters. I complimented him on his handwriting and asked him why he decided to write in cursive. He smiled at me and said, "I don't know, I just wanted to." And I think that was the answer. He wanted to, he was ready, and he believed that he could.

In the spring I also noticed that he was reading more books on his own. We were studying the Westward Movement and once again the children were immersed in the topic through trade books, films, songs, music, historical evidence, and the stories I read aloud. Mike began to read books on the pioneers by himself. In fact, in the afternoons when we had reading and writing he was much better able to work by himself. One day he worked on a writing test all morning without any help; then, in the afternoon, he did some work on acid rain as he read, followed the directions, and answered the questions in his journal all by himself—something he couldn't have done in February. He spent the rest of the day reading another book about pioneers. I could only wonder what had happened and what caused the change.

Mike took the state writing test in May. I was not worried about him passing the test. In fact, he did very well, five points above the passing score of 8 (the top score was 16). He wrote in script and had fewer spelling mistakes than usual, even though he was not allowed to use any dictionaries. Telling me that he remembered how to spell some of the words that he had looked up on the practice tests, he said, "Guess what? I sounded them out." He told me, too, that he had put in a simile. The first few paragraphs of one of his tests showed his continuing growth in writing (see Figure 14–6).

In June, Mike wrote a fiction story about his first grade partner with whom he had worked during the year. At the end of his story he wrote "About the Author":

> Mike likes to watch tv and likes to read and write. His favorite subjects are history and science.

In our last writing and reading evaluation conference of the year, Mike decided that one of his practice tests was the best piece he had written because

FIGURE 14–6. *Beginning of state writing test.*

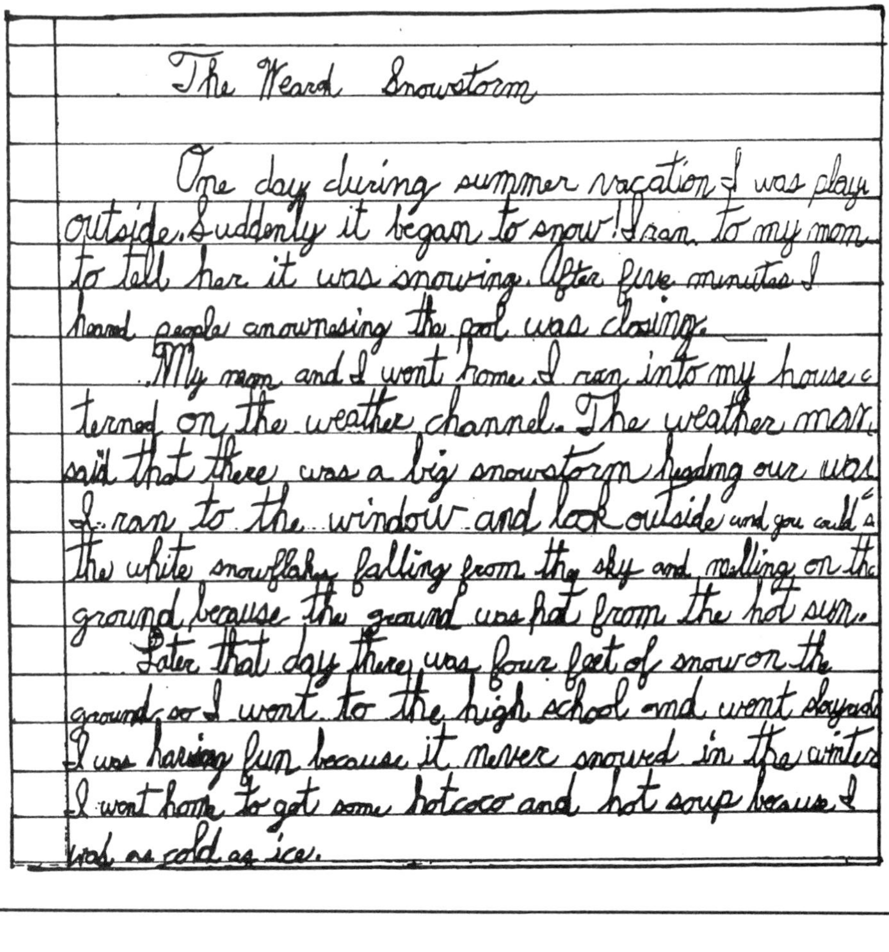
The Weard Snowstorm

One day during summer vacation I was playi outside. Suddenly it began to snow! I ran to my mom to tell her it was snowing. After five minutes I heard people anownsing the pool was closing.

My mom and I wont home. I ran into my house & terned on the weather channel. The weather man said that there was a big snowstorm heading our way. I ran to the window and look outside and you could s the white snowflakes falling from the sky and melling on the ground because the ground was hot from the hot sun.

Later that day there was four feet of snow on the ground, so I wont to the high school and went sleyadi I was having fun because it never snowed in the winter. I went home to get some hotcoco and hot soup because I was as cold as ice.

his spelling was "perfick." When he described his growth as a writer in fifth grade, he told me that he could now put in commas, similes, periods, and capital letters. "My spelling is better because by sounding out the letters, also by reading books." He added that he used to worry about spelling but that he didn't any more.

When we discussed reading, he told me he had read science fiction, contemporary fiction, and historical fiction. He felt that reading about colonial farming changed his thinking about the way people lived a long time ago. Telling me he had really learned a great deal about colonial times through the books he read, he seemed amazed by his discovery. I asked him how he had grown or changed as a reader, and he answered, "I learned to spell better." When I asked how, he told me that by reading more, he remembered the spelling of many words. Spelling seemed to be an issue that he felt he had conquered through reading and writing. Proud of the fact that he had read sixteen books during the year, he told me, "I read better every time I read."

The last week of school, Mike talked to me about the school year and how he felt it went by so fast. He wondered if I would miss him and the class. And then he took out his class yearbook. Turning to the Last Will and Testament delivered by the fifth graders before they went on to middle school, he read me his: "I am leaving my text books because I want other children to learn as much as I did."

Conclusion

How did Mike become a learner? How was an ADHD child able to function in a classroom setting? Did being pulled out for various specialists help or hinder his progress? I had to return to theories I had developed about special learners as a result of my readings, instruction I had received, and my work as a teacher researcher. Because of my case studies of children with special learning needs (Five, 1992), I knew that certain conditions were necessary to help these students develop into learners, and that these conditions applied to ADHD children as well: They need a supportive, structured classroom environment that involves them in using oral and written language; a cohesive community of learners; ownership of ideas; response from peers; time; and positive expectations for their success.

A structured, supportive classroom environment was necessary for Mike and others like him who have special learning needs. The environment promoted ownership. Ideas were accepted and respected. Perhaps Mike sensed this during the first half of the year. Being considered the expert on the two thousand-year-old man story reinforced his desire for more information. He was motivated to read and learn about this news item. And he wanted to talk, to share his information with the class. Talk became the vehicle that first connected him to the class community. I realized that if he was interested, he could focus his attention and wanted to learn.

ADHD children need a classroom environment that gives them the flexibility to learn through their own interests and express themselves in their own way—through talk, art, hands-on activities, and writing. Children like Mike often do not have many opportunities to develop and express their own ideas. Some aides and other adults who are concerned with teaching skills "help" these students form and express ideas in isolation. As with Mike in the past, these adults help students select topics to write about, subjects to study, vocabulary words to learn, and books to read, thus contributing to feelings of helplessness. Mike increasingly needed these people to tell him how to think and what to do. No wonder he had such difficulty expressing his wishes, initiating his work, and completing his homework assignments. Working with Mike in the classroom, Joan (an experienced, trained aide) was able to give him support when he needed it but also to empower him to have some control over his learning.

As Mike began to trust the class environment that freed him to pursue his interests (whether colonial farming, acid rain, or books on pioneers), he was able to move toward greater independence. ADHD children need opportunities to make a personal investment in learning and to feel that their ideas are respected. This enabled Mike to take his work more seriously and to accept more responsibility for completing assignments. He was willing to share his information through talking and writing and became very excited about his achievements. It is interesting that two of his deficits according to the IEP—speech and language—became areas of strength.

Ownership enabled Mike to value himself as a learner who had his own ideas. His self-esteem increased; he seemed better able to make decisions about his learning; and he became less dependent on adults to guide his learning. Mike was able to make choices; he could select his own subjects to study, topics for writing, chapters for his report, and his best writing pieces. The self-confidence he developed in writing spread to other areas of the curriculum. He began to record more of his ideas in his journals and became more involved in class activities. Becoming part of the class community of learners and receiving response from peers seems to help ADHD students focus their attention for longer periods of time.

The one area that Mike still found difficult was reading, although once he became a writer, reading became a more meaningful activity and not just one of decoding. He was able to select books and read on his own when he wanted to extend his knowledge; but when it came to selecting books to read for his own pleasure, he felt he couldn't do it. He remained convinced that he was supposed to read with Joan and the skills teacher. Perhaps the fact that he had been taken out of the classroom for skills in reading since second grade, when he could barely read, inhibited his growth as an independent reader. I can only wonder how his reading might have been affected if he had been able to become part of the reading community each day instead of arriving in the middle of reading workshop feeling even more disorganized and confused. Perhaps the fact that he continued to go to skills for reading may have contributed to his feelings of inadequacy in this area and may have prevented him from taking more risks to read on his own. Perhaps if there had been more communication between the specialists and me, we would have been able to coordinate our efforts, reducing for Mike's benefit the fragmentation of his schedule and the lack of consistency.

Mike's entrance into the class community of learners—the February "miracle"—occurred, I think, as a result of his greater self-confidence and his feeling that his talk, his writing, and his ideas were valued and respected. It also happened because he was immersed in the topic through various activities. I think that this is very important for ADHD children in the classroom because immersion provides them with many ways to learn and to express themselves. It also allows them to follow through on their own interests and helps them develop greater responsibility for their own learning.

Even though I felt that Mike became part of the class, I realized that it was easier for him to be an active learner if the whole class was involved in an activity. Perhaps this setting was more organized; there was more structure for the ADHD child. Mike enjoyed whole-group simulations, science activities, and math games. He became happy and very excited when he felt successful, but for most of the year he was not as successful when he worked with smaller groups of his peers. At times he lost interest when he worked with three or four boys. Perhaps his lack of experience prevented him from viewing this type of interaction as an opportunity for learning, or perhaps his disability made it difficult to focus on the ideas of a group of students, all of which were being expressed at the same time. There may have been too much input for this type of child. Perhaps he needed more structure within the small group.

Even though Mike had difficulties in some small-group settings, he was able to benefit from others. Collaboration with peers helped Mike develop new friendships and become accepted by more of his classmates. He began to be included in the group of boys in the class. This is especially important for ADHD children, who often have difficulties with social relationships.

Response from peers became important for Mike by the second half of the year. I think that before then, he had rarely experienced positive response from classmates for work he had done or for his ideas. In the beginning he always received response from adults; peers responded only to the sounds he made, his antics, and his shouting out. He wanted the class to laugh at him, to notice him. Soon he realized the pleasure of sharing his writing pieces and his ideas. He especially liked the times he called on the classmates who wanted to provide feedback on his writing pieces. This response helped him become better able to revise. And toward the end of the year Mike, too, was able to respond to their writings.

Time was an important factor. I had to give Mike time to become part of the class community. I could create the environment and provide encouragement, but I could not force a change in his attitude and in his feelings about his abilities. I had to be patient. It takes time for children with special learning needs to value themselves as learners with ideas. They need time to think, to take risks, to find themselves. Timing, too, is crucial; these special learners need to develop at their own rate and pace, not mine or that of other adults. Mike's entrance into the classroom community seemed like a miracle to me, but it happened when he was ready—in February, not in October. Children do not change quickly. They grow over time. And the classroom environment must allow that to happen.

When I reflect on Mike's progress, I think that one of the most important considerations for him and all ADHD children is the development of expectations. In September, I feel, Mike had few expectations for himself. He was satisfied with his work and relied on his aide to complete assignments. He took it for granted that he would not be able to succeed and do the same type of work that other children did. Removed from his classes in the past, he had not been involved in class activities. For many years he had worked in a one-to-one situation with an aide, a speech teacher, or a skills teacher. His IEP was based on his deficits—what he didn't know and couldn't do. The goals set for him were based on sets of isolated skills instead of focusing on the whole. When he was part of the class in some previous grades, he ran the film projectors and was often a behavior problem.

This year, I think, Mike began to see that he could do many of the same activities as his peers. Including him in all class activities, I encouraged him to do the assignments and projects that the other children did, even though he continued to need help with organization. He worked with the same fifth grade books and did much of the same class work and homework because I felt that he could do it. I had expectations for him, and he set expectations for himself. He became immersed in history and science activities, completed projects, set goals for himself, overcame his fears about spelling, became concerned about his class and school environment, wanted to serve as a class representative, and tried to take more responsibility for finishing homework and class assignments. In this classroom setting, Mike became more than a film projector operator. He became a more independent, motivated learner. All ADHD children need the kind of environment that allows them time, values ownership, and encourages response.

References

Blume, J. (1972). *Tales of a fourth grade nothing*. New York: Dutton.

Cameron, A. (1986). *The stories Julian tells*. New York: Random House.

Cameron, A. (1988). *Julian, secret agent*. New York: Random House.

Collier, C., & Collier, J. (1985). *My brother Sam is dead*. New York: Scholastic.

Five, C. L. (1992). *Special voices*. Portsmouth, NH: Heinemann.

O'Connor, J., & O'Connor, J. (1988). *The ghost in tent 19*. New York: Random House.

15

A Child with ADHD in a Middle School Reading Workshop: A Parent-Teacher Perspective

Marie Dionisio, with Linda Heath

The educational history of Andrew, a child with ADHD, is recounted by Marie Dionisio, his sixth grade reading teacher, in collaboration with his mother, Linda Heath.

A highly verbal child, Andrew nevertheless was first perceived as having attentional difficulties by his nursery school teacher, who described him as needing to listen and to concentrate more. By the third grade his self-esteem was faltering, and Linda took him for a comprehensive neuropsychological evaluation; the conclusion was that he probably had ADD, with hyperactivity. At this point he was treated not with medication but with more structure—both at home and at school. The highly structured traditional classroom did not help. In the fifth grade various kinds of support, including Ritalin, led to significant improvement and increased success for Andrew.

The heart of the chapter focuses on how Andrew then grew and flourished in Marie's sixth grade language arts classroom. In reading about Andrew, we see how the organization and routine of Marie's reading workshop complements the learning needs of children like Andrew, who have AD(H)D. The structure and predictability of the reading workshop assisted Andrew with his learning difficulties, while the opportunity to read self-chosen books made it easier for him to remain focused on reading—as did the Ritalin. The increasing depth of Andrew's journal letters about his reading offers an engaging and heartwarming portrait of his growth—and demonstrates how Marie's classroom and Linda's support functioned to nurture that growth.

Marie Dionisio is a teacher/researcher. She has authored several articles, including "Filling Empty Pockets: Remedial Readers Make Meaning" and "Responding to Literary Elements through Mini-lessons and Dialogue Journals," winners of 1989 and 1991 *English Journal* writing awards, and a chapter in *With Promise: Redefining Reading and Writing Needs for Special Students*, edited by Susan Stires (1991). For the past twenty years Marie has taught reading in Harrison, New York, and for the past thirteen years she has used writing and reading workshop approaches in her classroom. She has presented at both state and national conferences. She holds a master's in writing from Northeastern University and serves on the Commission on Curriculum of the National Council of Teachers of English.

Linda Heath graduated cum laude from Williams College, with a major in psychology. She holds a Massachusetts teaching certificate and is presently studying for a master's in elementary education at Manhattanville College in Purchase, New York. She has two sons, twelve and nine, who have been diagnosed as having an Attention Deficit Hyperactivity Disorder. A member of CH.A.D.D., a national support and advocacy group for parents of children with AD(H)D, Linda has been very involved with community volunteer work and has served as president of the PTA and PT Council.

Over the past eleven years, teaching and learning have merged for me. As a teacher-researcher, I continually learn from and with my students. As each new year begins, I look for a student who pulls at my professional interests and who will stretch my knowledge about how children learn. Andrew was one of those students. He has an Attention Deficit Disorder.

Open School Night gave me the opportunity to speak with Andrew's mother, Linda. Our conversation led us to discover a mutual interest in closely following Andrew's progress in sixth grade. We shared several concerns: How would Andrew adjust to the departmentalized program in our middle school? Would the movement of classes every forty minutes and the change of teachers for each class benefit or hinder him? How would he respond to the choices, freedoms, and responsibilities that the Reading Workshop atmosphere in my classroom would afford him? We decided right then to share our observations, discoveries, and concerns on a regular basis. The dual viewpoints of parent and teacher would surely provide a more complete picture and a better understanding of Andrew as a learner.

Background

A home rich in literary events is the perfect soil for the roots of a child's literacy. Andrew grew up in just such a home. Linda read to him daily, talked with him continually, surrounded him with books of his own, and exposed him to a wide variety of experiences. In our first meeting Linda told me: "I thought I had done all the right things. All the groundwork for success in school was there, so I expected that Andrew would do well."

Very verbal as a young child, Andrew was comfortable and confident with himself. Friends of the family often remarked on his extensive vocabulary and his ability to converse comfortably with everyone. It appeared that he would make an easy transition to school and to learning to read. In nursery school Andrew was given the part of the little red hen in the school play because he was the only child in the group who could learn the lines and deliver them with ease. In contrast to his verbal skill, Andrew had real difficulty with fine-motor tasks; still, his facility with language signaled success in academic pursuits. However, things did not turn out as expected.

Andrew's nursery school teacher reported, "Andrew needs to listen and concentrate more." This report was confusing to Linda, not what she had expected. In kindergarten his teacher observed, "Andrew is bright and inquisitive . . . his problem is that he is easily distractible . . . when I am teaching something new his attention is on other things." Linda's concern grew as the first grade reports continued: "Andrew has trouble internalizing directions . . . he daydreams and is distracted easily."

In first grade Andrew noticed that he wasn't keeping up with his peers, especially in reading. He couldn't understand why he was in the brown SRA level while his friends were in the aqua. Linda recalls him saying, "Hey, Mom, why am I only in brown when I could be in aqua? Joanie is in aqua. I can do everything she can do, can't I?" Andrew's discontent and confusion are evident in this remark. He couldn't understand why he was not reading as well as his peers; he knew that he could easily keep up with them orally. He even asked to go to school early in order to spend extra time on the SRA cards. The discrepancy between his perception of his abilities and the reality of his performance troubled him.

An interesting thing here is the open and trusting relationship between Andrew and his mother. He obviously knew that she would help him and would understand his feelings. He wasn't afraid of disappointing her or of losing her affection. Perhaps this trust and his verbal ability prevented the emotional difficulties that often plague children like Andrew.

Linda became concerned about the pattern of Andrew's behavior. The signal flags for ADD were there, but she didn't know how to interpret the code. His first grade teacher suggested that Andrew might be slightly hyperactive. Linda tried behavior modification at home. This had little impact on Andrew's ability to attend, either in school or at home, but the teacher did not suggest any further intervention.

By the end of second grade it was apparent to Linda that something was wrong. Again and again, Linda was told, "It's immaturity . . . he's bright but busy . . . he's a boy." Were these reasons or excuses? Linda's expectations of Andrew's school experience and the reality of those experiences did not fit. She said to me: "If you think you've done all the right things to prepare your child for school, and then things don't go well, what do you do? Do you just accept it, or do you keep looking for a way to help him?"

By this point Linda was closely monitoring Andrew's homework, structuring his time and sitting with him while he completed his work. Still she saw little or no improvement in his school work or in his ability to attend to tasks and sit still, even in the one-on-one situation at home. Andrew's difficulties seemed to disappear only with physical activities. At eight years old, he was swimming competitively, the youngest member of the team. Linda's inability to fix things for her son and her frustration with the lack of direction she received from his school weighed heavily on her.

"If he could only sit still . . . ," the teachers' voices echoed. Only Linda and her husband asked the obvious question, "But why can't he?" Despite frequent contact with the teachers, further intervention or diagnostic assistance was never suggested. Perhaps adults too easily accept the explanation that a young child *can* concentrate and sit still if only he wants to.

By third grade Andrew's self-esteem started to deteriorate. The third grade teacher reported that Andrew just couldn't stay tuned in to what was going on in class. Although his teachers continued to see Andrew as bright, with more potential than he was demonstrating, he began to lose confidence in his abilities because he recognized this discrepancy, too. The teacher referred Andrew to the school psychologist for counseling. Being pulled out of class to go to the psychologist was a real affront to Andrew. He complained to his mother, "Why do I have to go see that lady? There's nothing wrong with me. Why do you think there's something wrong with me?" It was his faltering self-esteem that finally spurred Linda on to seek a comprehensive neuropsychological evaluation at a private diagnostic facility.

The testing uncovered weaknesses associated with attentional and organizational difficulties. Among them were written expression, closure, following lengthy instructions, and comprehension of language with complex linguistic structure. According to the report, Andrew's weaknesses in both writing and reading tasks were especially characteristic of children with attention deficits. The report concluded:

> Andrew's evaluation profile and aspects of his developmental history are strongly suggestive of attention deficit disorder with hyperactivity. It is likely that his low self-esteem results from his attentional difficulty although unrealistic expectations may be contributing factors if authority figures in his environment have seen his difficulty settling down and focusing as volitional rather than beyond his control—which it truly is.

The results of this comprehensive evaluation provided an answer for Linda, an answer that made sense to her. She told me:

> Although I knew very little about attention deficit disorder, I felt I was beginning to understand why Andrew was having problems in school. The key words for me were that his behavior was not "volitional (but) beyond his control." I began to change my attitude about Andrew's learning style. It was clear that he needed help to learn to modify his behavior. With his evaluation in hand, I went to Andrew's school to ask how to proceed. I was told not to be too quick to label Andrew ADD. They thought that much of what Andrew was experiencing was maturational. I listened.

Yet three months later, when Andrew finished third grade, nothing had changed.

The neuropsychological report recommended that Linda explore the possibility of medication to control Andrew's attention deficit. The advice of a neurologist was sought, but medication was not prescribed. The report also suggested that Andrew, like other children with attentional difficulties, would thrive best with structure both in school and at home. Knowing this, Linda arranged for Andrew to be placed with a fourth grade teacher who was noted for structure. This classroom was indeed highly structured, with a teacher considered more "old school" in her approach to education. The students had few choices and little voice in the classroom. The assignments were teacher-directed, and there was little flexibility about when and how assignments were done. Andrew's slow work rate, which was commended in the diagnostic report, wasn't taken into consideration. He was penalized for not completing his assignments on time.

At the same time, Linda provided yet more structure to Andrew's life at home. Despite the additional structure, Andrew's difficulties at school remained. In June his fourth grade teacher wrote:

> Andrew is highly verbal and eagerly participates in all oral activities . . . he is reluctant to be self-motivated in daily written tasks . . . he does better when supervised . . . keeping him on an effective academic track has not been an easy task . . . hopefully, he will show more self-responsibility in fifth grade.

Linda still felt that there must be more that could be done to help Andrew. As his fifth grade year progressed, two incidents focused her feeling. The first was a comment from his teacher: "Andrew is a very capable boy, but he needs to exert some extra effort and concentration on his own initiative to reach his potential." And the reference to a "lack of motivation" was in direct contrast to the neuropsychological evaluation report. In the testing situation Andrew's attempts to channel his energy constructively by being a helper and his slower-than-expected work speed were seen as evidence of high motivation.

By this time Linda had learned a great deal about ADD. At one of our early meetings she recalled her feelings:

> What bothered me most was that Andrew was perceived by his teachers as lacking motivation in his school work. I sensed he was highly motivated to do well, but couldn't make it happen. This frustrated him enormously. From my perspective, it was Andrew's motivation to succeed that allowed him to achieve at all. Otherwise, I think he would have become a behavior problem.

The second incident was a conversation between Andrew and Linda. She remembered:

He asked me if he was stupid, and I, of course, responded with, "No you're not. Why would you ask such a question?"

Andrew said, "I guess I know I'm not stupid, but the kids in my class think I am. I know the answers, but I can't make them come out (of my head) fast when I need to, so they think I'm not very smart."

In her search for an answer, Linda had Andrew reevaluated. Once again, the diagnosis was ADD but without hyperactivity. The report stated:

> Andrew presents as a bright and engaging youngster whose attentional difficulties remain quite apparent. . . . Emotionally, Andrew appears to be doing somewhat better. . . . He is now aware of his attentional difficulties and seems to accept them without apparent embarrassment or self-consciousness. . . . Despite his ability to perform on grade level, his attentional difficulties continue to make it very stressful for him to sit through a full day at school. In addition, relative to his own intelligence, it is this examiner's impression that Andrew is underachieving.

This time Linda consulted a new neurologist who, after reviewing Andrew's Conners Rating Scale, strongly recommended Ritalin. Andrew thus began taking Ritalin in the spring of fifth grade. Linda worked more closely with his teacher to help support Andrew's special learning needs. An outside tutor was added to provide further support. By the end of fifth grade, Andrew was improving.

Linda reports that Andrew received the news of his diagnosis of ADD with a sigh of relief. It confirmed his feeling that he knew the answers but just couldn't get them organized in his mind fast enough to get them out. It wasn't his fault. And he wasn't stupid. Having a label helped in this case. It answered many questions for Linda, for her husband, and, most of all, for Andrew. Andrew finished elementary school on a high note because he understood why he couldn't pay attention, why he couldn't get the answers out of his head, and why he couldn't meet everyone's expectations of him. He knew that none of it was his fault. Best of all, he knew that there were strategies to help him deal with his attention deficit.

Middle School—The First Ten Weeks

This new optimistic Andrew is the one who entered my sixth grade language arts class. I didn't see the fidgety, inattentive boy described by the teachers in elementary school. Ritalin had controlled the impulsive movements and enabled him to focus. I didn't know it at the time, but the organization and routine of my reading workshop classroom also complemented the learning needs of an ADD child.

Linda told me that Andrew was in my first period class by design. She said:

> Andrew was scheduled to have reading early in the day because his neurologist and guidance counselor agreed he would be most alert and able to handle this type of task at the beginning of the academic day. The workshop approach to the teaching of reading was new to Andrew. Prior to sixth grade, Andrew's reading instruction was more traditional. He went through elementary school just before whole language and the reading/writing process became incorporated into the curriculum. Now in sixth grade he was being exposed to this type of learning environment.

Students in my class choose their own books from a variety of sources and according to their own interests and abilities. Presently my classroom library contains over six hundred paperback novels, nonfiction books, collections of poetry, and short stories. Every day the structure of the class is the same. It begins with a five-minute mini-lesson, a status-of-the-class check, twenty-five minutes of sustained silent reading, and a five-minute share session. Mini-lessons focus on the strategies that good readers use, present book and author talks, and model my own response to the adolescent novels I read (Atwell, 1987).

The structure is predictable; the rules are posted and consistent. From the first day my students know what is expected of them and what they can expect of me. Twenty minutes of reading are required as daily homework. A homework form is distributed on Fridays. The students record the title and author of the book they read for homework as well as the pages read. The form is to be signed and returned on the following Friday. Weekly, five new words from the student's reading must be entered in a vocabulary notebook. This work is due on the same day each week. One letter in a reading-response, dialogue journal is required each week. That letter must be written to me at least every other week (Atwell, 1987). Letters to peers are encouraged.

This structure and predictability assisted Andrew with his organizational difficulties. His weekly responsibilities were set from the beginning. The homework form, reading journal, and vocabulary notebook became tools for organizing his work. In those first weeks Andrew would often come to me for approval or assurance: "I have my homework sheet . . . . I read last night. . . . I wrote in my journal." Positive responses always brought a smile.

In an early meeting Linda remarked to me, "Andrew isn't certain he likes this new classroom format which, to him, requires more involvement on his part." In discussing this, we felt that his uncertainty was probably related to his fear of falling behind. In the same meeting we talked about the homework form; she commented, "It is the perfect organizing tool for an ADD child, and it also gives me, as a parent, a natural avenue to continue to stay involved in my child's reading progress."

Andrew's decisions about books were tentative. "Is this good?" was a frequent question during that time. My response would often be, "I read that book and really liked it" or "I think so because so many readers have told me it's good." After three weeks, his question became a statement, "I think this book will be good because the first sentence made me interested" or "I think this book will be good because I like adventure."

Within the structure of the reading workshop, Andrew had flexibility and choice. He chose his own books and what he would say about them in his journal letters. He did not have to answer any preset questions about what he read. At any time during silent reading, he could enter words in his vocabulary notebook and write letters in his reading journal. If he preferred, he could do this work for homework instead. These choices allowed Andrew the freedom to manage his time and to move within the classroom. If he needed to, he could browse the shelves for a book or go to the journal box. In the beginning he would often take advantage of these options and get out of his seat. Never disturbing anyone else, he would quietly look for a book or get his journal or a dictionary. Other children moved around in the same way, so he did not feel different anymore.

Linda had been concerned about how Andrew would handle moving from class to class every forty minutes and about how he would keep organized with a locker and seven teachers. Her concern proved unnecessary. The departmentalization was beneficial for Andrew. Every forty minutes he was able to move to a new room and attend to a new task! Actually, this schedule was much more suited to his attention deficit. He told her:

> I like changing classes and having different teachers. I know exactly what I will be doing every day and how long I have to be in a class. Also, it is nice to have different teachers because it doesn't get boring.

During that first month Linda asked Andrew about the Ritalin, wanting to know if he had noticed a change. He said, "I can read now!" He was able to remain focused on reading long enough to really enjoy it, a new experience for him.

On the first day of school I ask all my students to answer some questions about themselves as readers (Atwell, 1987). When he answered these questions, Andrew did not reveal his past difficulty with reading. He said that he had learned to read in preschool. His school records and his mother had painted a very different picture. He wrote, "I like to read" and "People read for fun and for something to do." In contrast, Linda reported to me that although Andrew always read what was required, he rarely read voluntarily. He indicated that he owned about eighty books and that he had read twelve during the previous year. I had the feeling that Andrew's responses were more indicative of the reader he wanted to be than of the reader he actually was. Linda confirmed my suspicions.

Andrew stuck with the first book he chose, finishing it by the end of the second week of school. His first journal letter had substance but was stiff. He appeared to be trying to answer questions (letters appear as written):

> Dear Ms. D,
>
> I just finished my book *Voyage of the Frog.* I enjoyed it a lot because it was exciting when he almost got thrown out of the boat. The reason he almost got thrown out of the boat cause the boom hit him because he was in the middle of a storm. Luckly he fell in the cabin. The reason why he went on the voyage was that he had to dump his uncles ashes where there was no civilization. He left from L.A. and end up at the Bay of Whales.

This letter took Andrew over fifteen minutes to write. He read it over several times before putting it in my mailbox, as he wanted so much to do it "right."

After that, he abandoned several books before settling on *Beatles Lightly Toasted,* a humorous story by Phyllis Reynolds Naylor. During the remainder of the first quarter Andrew read two more humorous and easy books. He also read *The Face on the Milk Carton,* by Caroline B. Cooney. This riveting contemporary novel about a teenager who discovers that she was abducted as a young child was the fall's hottest book. It was constantly mentioned by his classmates during share sessions. Andrew was still trying to keep up with his peers. This time he succeeded.

During the first quarter, Andrew had difficulty writing the required weekly journal letter. I suspected that he was nervous about fulfilling my expectations of a "good" journal letter. When I reminded him that he was behind in this requirement, he decided to write his letters at home every Friday.

While he was trying to catch up on missed journal letters, Andrew wrote two letters about *The Face on the Milk Carton.*

> Dear Ms. D
>
> I have started *Face on the Milk Carton* By C. B. Cooney. I am where she finds out her parents aren't really her parents but her grandparents. Boy, it's frightening when she has those daymares and nightmares.
>
> Andrew

> Dear Ms. D
>
> When I started to read *Face on the Milk Carton* it was hard to get into. But now it's hard to put down. I find her writing interesting because anywhere you stop it's a cliff hanger.

Andrew put his journal in my mailbox after the second of these letters. His difficulty with writing is apparent. I could almost hear the ideas that never made it from his head to the page. However, there was personal response in these letters. I had read *The Face on the Milk Carton* and responded enthusiastically as a fellow reader.

> Dear Andrew,
>
> Your letter (the one right above) is a great advertisement for *The Face on the Milk Carton.* When I read it, I couldn't put it down, either! I felt so scared for Janie. The world she knew was secure and predictable. Then it began to fall apart! What

could she count on now? I didn't know. The daymares only added to the crumbling of her world. Whom could she trust? She didn't know and neither did I!

Ms. D

Andrew stopped at my desk the next morning to tell me that he didn't know whom Janie could trust either and that he couldn't wait to finish the book. I responded: "I can't wait for you to finish, either. I want to know what you think of the ending." I had hoped that my letter would produce some extended journal dialogue between us, so I was thrilled with this very real conversation between interested readers. But this was the end of our exchange of ideas about the book. Andrew had moved on to another book before writing his next letter.

Toward the end of the first quarter, Linda remarked to me: "Andrew asks me to sit with him while he writes in his journal. I'm sure he feels that he needs my approval or my assurance that what he is writing is 'correct.'" I agreed. Andrew had struggled for so long to meet others' imposed standards that he had long ago stopped trusting his own ideas. I knew that I would have to gain his trust in order to help him trust himself as a reader and learner.

The first quarter ended about this time. Andrew had read five books during the first ten weeks. His journal letters had been tentative and he had difficulty remembering to write one a week, but there had been some subtle changes. He was more relaxed with himself, with me, and with the workshop classroom. I reminded myself and Linda that change takes time. We would both have to be patient.

At the end of each quarter my students engage in a self-evaluation. I believe that it is important to reflect on one's own work and to formulate goals for the future. As a teacher, I reflect on my own growth and share my reflections with my students. I ask them to do the same.

The self-evaluation consists of about five questions. The first is "What is the most important thing you have learned as a reader this first ten weeks of school? Why do you think this is the most important thing you've learned?" (Atwell, 1987). I want students to think about how they have changed and about the worth of the changes.

Andrew's response was that "when you tell your feelings about a book it helps to understand the book. I think it is the most important thing because it's hard to read a book and not wonder about what's going to happen." This answer indicated to me that Andrew was beginning to place some value on his own feelings about a book. He saw a connection between those feelings and understanding what he read. This important step for him wasn't evident in his journal, but it was on his self-evaluation.

The last question asks the students to formulate a goal or two for the next ten weeks. I also set a goal for each reader. Andrew wrote that he would like to work on "being able to read faster and read harder books." My goal for Andrew was to write a thought-filled journal letter *every* week.

I respond to the child's own evaluation of growth by writing comments on their sheets. Grades are also included. The final aspect of the quarterly assessment is a parent-child conference and a report to me. In his report Andrew wrote:

> Last night my mom and I had a conversation about how I'm doing in reading. We talked about how you taught us to use our short term memory more efficiently while reading. We also talked about my goal to do more journal letters. To help me to remember, we put a sign up to say that I will do them over the weekend.

On his report Linda added, "I'm so pleased you require the reading each night. Andrew does it very willingly, which compared to last year is an enormous change." The evaluation process highlighted two important changes: Andrew was beginning to put value on his own ideas, and he read more willingly.

When Linda and I met to talk about Andrew's first quarter, she remarked about how much she liked the idea of the parent-child conference. We had been talking about the importance of parental involvement in a child's education. I responded, "I loved your addition to Andrew's conference report."

She suggested, "Why not include the parents in the report? It's another way to keep them involved, and it will give you insight in some cases." I incorporated this great idea into the second quarter assessment.

The Second Ten Weeks

By the beginning of the second quarter, Linda and I agreed on our most important goal for Andrew. We wanted him to like reading enough to do it regularly. I knew from experience that this change would foster many others.

Andrew began reading a horror trilogy by Caroline B. Cooney at the start of the quarter. Horror was a new genre for him. It was also more difficult reading than the humor books he had read the first quarter. I was concerned that he might find horror too much of a leap, but I was wrong. He loved it. What's more, he and I had an eight-letter exchange of sustained dialogue about the first book, *The Fog*. This exchange illustrates an increase in Andrew's trust of himself and of me. It also opened the door to reading more deeply and trying books with more literary value.

> 11–15–91
> Dear Ms. D,
> I think *The Fog* is a great book. I like it because it has adventure and is a little hard to understand. I love the characters. They are fun and exciting.
> Andrew

> 11–18–91
> Dear Andrew,
> As long as you are enjoying *The Fog*, it is okay to be a little confused. To tell you the truth, I always have trouble understanding horror stories because the reasons why things happen in the story don't always make sense. Lots of sixth graders love reading horror so I guess they just ignore the parts that are a little hard to understand.
> Which character in *The Fog* do you feel most attached to? Why?
> Ms. D

11–22–91
Dear Ms. D,

I like the main character Christina the best because she seems like a real person. She has all the feelings of a real person. The book is very emotional through Christina. She doesn't listen to the principal when he makes her be friends with the person. When I read the book, I can feel the emotions and things that happen.

Andrew

This letter was a major change. Not only was Andrew continuing the conversation we began in the last letter, but also he was including a great deal more of his personal response to the character and story events. Many more of his ideas were making it to the page. I wanted to push him, but I held back and relied, as always, on modeling literary talk.

11–23–91
Dear Andrew,

Your letter really shows me you are involved in *The Fog*. Seeing and experiencing the story through the character, Christina, is allowing you to make decisions right along with her. I love reading when I can live the story with the character.

I don't know if I would want to be Christina because her life is too scary, but pretending to live her life through reading might be fun.

Do you think Christina made a good choice when she didn't listen to the principal about making friends with the person? Who is this person?

Ms. D

12–3–91
Dear Ms. D,

I like reading your letters. I think she made a mistake when she didn't make friends with Jonah. The person's name is Jonah. I don't really know if I would like to be Chrissie either because of all the problems. I think that Chrissie is right about Mr. and Mrs. Shevington trying to make Anya go out of her mind.

Andrew

At the end of my next letter, I wrote, "By the way, I really like your letters too!"

The literary talk in this group of letters represents several big steps for Andrew. He trusted himself and me, he tried different kinds of books, and he invested himself in the reading. The most important change was that he tolerated a minimal lack of understanding with the expectation that things would come together as he kept reading. This was a new reading strategy for him, and it enabled him to keep reaching for more difficult reading material.

Linda and I met during this time. She had seen the changes in Andrew's journal and other changes, too. She said to me, "Lately Andrew has been writing fewer journal letters at home. I think it's because he doesn't need my approval any more. He is writing to you and the personal feedback he receives from you is far more important and supportive than anything I could say as a parent."

Andrew had indeed taken a major step. He trusted himself as a reader and as a member of our community of readers and learners. He no longer needed approval from Mom or even from me. He was using his own ideas and responses to the books he read as his measure of success. More significantly, most days he read in class for the entire twenty-five minutes without moving! This is quite an accomplishment for an ADD child. We know that the internal desire alone is not enough to overcome the attentional difficulty. Undoubtedly Ritalin played a part, but there was something else that contributed to the change at this time. I believe that Andrew's ownership of his learning made the difference.

At the end of the second quarter, Andrew read *The Indian in the Cupboard,* by Lynne Reid Banks. Though he did not write any journal letters about this book, he did mention it on his quarterly evaluation sheet. Here is the question I asked:

> Reading books often allows us to discover something about ourselves, about others, or about life. What have you discovered about yourself, others, or life from a book you have read this quarter?

Andrew responded: "I have discovered that friends don't always get along and that you have to work at it. In *The Indian in the Cupboard* by Lynne Reid Banks, Omri and Patrick have this problem."

I was amazed by this statement. Andrew was now relating books, characters, and conflicts to real life. I had discussed this in mini-lessons during the latter part of the quarter but hadn't noticed Andrew stretching himself in this way. He usually participated eagerly in share sessions, especially the ones that tied to the mini-lesson topics, but he had not shared this. Later I discovered from Linda that Andrew had been having some friendship difficulties of his own. Perhaps his reading of *The Indian in the Cupboard* was timely, and that timing resulted in another step forward as a reader.

The Third Ten Weeks

Andrew was fascinated with Omri and decided to read the two sequels to *The Indian in the Cupboard*. During this time I observed two important changes in his letters. For the first time, Andrew made a recommendation to me. The ease and confidence that Linda described in the young Andrew resurfaced here.

> Dear Ms. D,
> I am now reading *The Return of the Indian*. I really injoyed *The Indian in the Cupboard* when Little Bear gets brought to life the first time. In this book I can feel Omri and his emotions. It's very interesting. I like it because I can understand it and get into it. If you like farey tails you will like this book. I want to finish the series soon, but I've got one more book to go.
> Andrew

When Andrew was near the end of the last of these books, *The Secret of the Indian,* he took the risk of writing to a peer for the first time.

Dear Ben,
    I've gotten to that part in *The Secret of the Indian* where Omri goes in the trunk. It wasn't anything I thought it would be. I really can't put this book down. It really is very interesting and I really enjoy it. Did you like the ending in it? I haven't read the end yet so just tell me if it was exciting, happy, sad, or boring. What books are you going to look at?

                                      Andrew

Ben was the optimum choice of a classmate with whom to talk about books. Because Andrew knew that Ben had read these three books and a wide range of others, Ben was a good resource for recommendations about books. Perhaps for Andrew, the most beneficial thing in Ben's letter is his own honest response to *The Secret of the Indian.*

Dear Andrew,
    I really loved reading *The Secret of the Indian.* I felt like I was Omri in the book. Sometimes my heart even stopped. The ending is one of the best parts of the book. It's really exciting and the ending is happy. Right now I'm reading *The Year Without Michael.*

                                      Ben

Andrew's confidence as a reader and as an equal and valued part of the literary community in my classroom is obvious. From this point on, his talk about books seemed more natural. He especially liked it when I had read the book he was reading.
    One of Andrew's third quarter goals was to read two new types of books in an effort to broaden his reading experiences. Wanting to try historical fiction, he asked me to recommend something. I suggested several books, from which he chose *Freedom Crossing,* by Margaret Goff Clark. It proved to be another milestone. He started this book near the end of the class period and became so involved that he was still reading after the bell rang! The next day he began writing the following journal letter during homeroom.

Dear Ms. D,
    I am injoying *Freedom Crossing* a lot. It's very scary and interesting when Martin gets into the secret room. I like it when they were going to town. Thank you for recommending *Freedom Crossing.*

                                      Andrew

At this point in the year, my journal dialogue with Andrew took on the tone of two readers sharing as equals. I think that this relationship fueled Andrew's risk-taking, pushing him to realize his potential. The next two letters illustrate this easy dialogue.

Dear Andrew,
    I'm so glad you are enjoying *Freedom Crossing.* I too got scared when Martin hid in the secret room. The hatred the townspeople had for runaway slaves is something I can not understand! No human being should be owned like property. Just wait until you see how scary things get as the kids try to help Martin escape to Canada!

                                      Ms. D

Dear Ms. D,
    It's even scarier when a slave gets caught. When everyone is running to the church, the people are shouting free the slave. I was very surprised when that happened. I can't wait to find out what happens and if it's Martin or not.

Andrew

This book pushed Andrew beyond surface involvement in reading. His letters didn't reveal the extent to which reading this book had affected his thinking, but his third quarter self-evaluation did. Actually, the third quarter was probably the time of biggest change for Andrew as a thinker. The confidence he gained as a reader spilled over into confidence in his own thinking and an openness to change, too. Notice the range and depth of thinking in this excerpt from his third quarter self-evaluation. My written comments are in italics.

What have you discovered about reading or being a reader these last ten weeks?

That every different book has a very different journal letter and that different books make your mind think differently to the same problems. *(This is a wonderful discovery. It shows how much you are thinking as you read and how you have grown as a reader.)*

Name a book that has taught you something and tell what that book taught you.

Freedom Crossing has taught me that people can change their opinion very quickly and people's emotion for someone change slower than people's opinion.

As a way of learning, do you prefer writing journal letters or answering comprehension questions? Give all your reasons.

I prefer journal letters because I can ask myself any questions I want but the comprehension sheet have questions for you and you don't have any freedom. *(I think freedom helps you to learn.)*

In the report on the parent-child evaluation conference, Linda wrote:

Andrew and I talked about how much he learned from the book *Freedom Crossing.* The insights that he came away with were wonderful. This book challenged his ability to begin to go deeper into a book's content. I loved his comment about emotions take longer to change than the changing of an opinion.

In this same report Andrew wrote, "I really enjoyed knowing how much my mother liked my statements in question 1 and 2. It is fun talking to my parents."

This seems like a casual remark, but it signals a change in the interaction between Andrew and Linda in regard to his school work, especially his reading. Before this, Andrew wanted his mother's approval; it was his barometer of correctness. And correctness was his major concern. Now, their interactions had taken on a new meaning. There was an exchange of ideas, with Andrew recognizing that his ideas had value of their own and that his mother saw their value.

Andrew's literary relationship with Linda continued to grow, but it had a solid footing to start. She told me:

I was once told that no matter what age your child, continue to read aloud with the child if he shows an interest. Andrew loved to be read to (it took the pressure away from him) and we enjoyed the time together. I tried to read with him twice a week. I would also occasionally read the books that Andrew was reading in school. I found this unstated reinforcement of his reading interest meant a lot to him. We would talk about the books and it gave me an idea of how his reading was progressing. Sometimes, *if it seemed appropriate,* we would even talk about how he read, or what strategies he might use to understand vocabulary or text.

Linda's involvement in Andrew's continuing literacy development gave him an edge, an edge that a child with ADD really needs.

The more Andrew relaxed with himself as a reader, learner, and thinker, the more his ownership grew and the more confidence he developed. Increased confidence resulted in his taking more risks. The most important result of all was an increasing ability to sustain his attention while reading and writing.

The Fourth Ten Weeks

When Andrew wanted to read harder books during the final quarter, he chose Madeleine L'Engle's *A Wrinkle in Time.* This is a difficult book because of its genre—science fiction—and because L'Engle's writing is linguistically complex. I was concerned that Andrew would experience his old difficulty with attention because of the linguistic complexity. Again, I was wrong! He loved the book. He wrote in a letter, "I think it would be awsem [awesome] to tesser because you could go anywhere." He clearly understood L'Engle's "tesseract" or "wrinkling of time" to travel through time and space. In the novel, tessering is explained in complex scientific detail.

While reading *A Wrinkle in Time,* Andrew continually spoke with Linda about the story events and the ideas they generated for him. His involvement and enthusiasm were so great that she decided to read the book herself. When she did, she recognized what had appealed to Andrew. This book had allowed Andrew, for the first time, to cross over the bridge from reality to fantasy and to believe in the fantasy. Because the characters and some of their problems were so real, the science fiction elements of the story became believable to him. L'Engle had carried Andrew into a fantasy world where everything felt real to him. He was amazed by this new literary experience. Linda and I were amazed, too.

The fourth quarter ended for Andrew with the realization of another of his personal goals. Since the second quarter he had wanted to read seven books in ten weeks. He did it in the fourth quarter! That made a total of twenty-one books in ten months. This was quite an accomplishment. The number alone had value for him, but that value increased a hundredfold when we looked at the titles of the books he had read and talked about the increased variety and difficulty of the novels he had chosen. I think he was surprised by how much he had accomplished and by how much change he saw in himself as a reader.

The fourth quarter evaluation is a final journal letter about how you have changed as a reader. Here is Andrew's final letter:

6–4–92

Dear Ms. D,

I have changed as a reader in many ways. One way is that I read faster. I am able to read more difficult books and I read a lot of different books.

These changes were caused by the minilessons everyday which help focus my reading. The other cause was having supervised time to read which inables me to read more books and by reading more, I learned to read faster.

I have discovered that there are a lot of things to read. Also books that are written well seem like I am the character in the book.

The character that influenced me the most was Laurie from *Freedom Crossing*. She taught me that it's important to like people for who they are and not what they are.

The most valuable thing I learned about myself as a reader is that if you don't expand your reading, you will never know what books are the best. My favorite book was *The Solid Gold Kid* by Norma Fox Mazer and Harry Mazer. It was very exciting and had lots of adventure.

I think journal writing has effected my reading because it lets me express my feelings about the books.

I had a very good year in reading and I owe it all to you. You're the best teacher I ever had.

Andrew

Indeed Andrew had changed as a reader and learner. The biggest change and the most influential was the rediscovery of confidence in himself and his abilities. He recognized that there were still things he needed to work on, but he now knew that learning is a lifelong endeavor and that everyone needs to work on something. Certainly the growth Andrew experienced would be a solid foundation for continued growth as a reader, writer, and learner.

Reflections

Linda and I had agreed to take time in early July to reflect on Andrew's progress and to try to determine what had helped him grow and change. We talked about her role as the educational advocate for her child. Without her commitment to identifying ways to help Andrew learn, his attention deficit may never have been diagnosed. Her response to me was simple:

> My concern for Andrew was no greater than that of any parent who sees her child unhappy, frustrated, and finding school to be a different experience from what one might have thought was possible. Andrew sought my help with his homework, and I tried to help him by monitoring his work, giving him ways to be better organized, and, most of all, encouraging him to plan ahead. For the most part, our working together was fine, but as in any parent-child relationship, we had our bumpy moments.

I had remarked to Linda numerous times about her role in Andrew's academic success. I still believe that her support and understanding, combined with the rich relationship they had, kept Andrew free of the emotional problems so often associated with ADD. The level of parental involvement I observed is unusual in the nineties, yet it is crucial for a child with an Attention Deficit Disorder.

Linda concurred. She too felt that the parent of an ADD child must be that child's advocate. She continued:

> Having two children with ADD was one of the reasons I decided to return to school and get my master's in teaching. I had taught long ago, but I was not up on the current trends in education and knew very little about learning disabilities. The course work has helped me as I tried to support my own children's needs. What I have learned is, as a parent, it is important to know your children and to work closely with the teachers to obtain the best support for, and understanding of, your child's needs.

Our reflections turned to the school setting. We were both interested in what learning environments, structures, and experiences made the difference for children with ADD. We agreed that the turning point for Andrew had been the middle school experience, where he felt better about himself as a person and as a learner. Generally, he was more comfortable with school than he had ever been. Departmentalization clearly had a positive effect because it divided the day into more manageable pieces for him. Specifically, he had grown and changed as a reader in many ways. We wanted to identify the specific elements contributing to the changes.

For the past ten years, the elements of time, ownership, and response (Giacobbe, 1986) have driven my teaching and enabled me to become a learner in my classroom. These elements were crucial ones for Andrew, too. Ownership is perhaps the most important of these elements. A child who is given choices and a voice in his learning is enabled as a learner. Ownership proved to be extremely important for Andrew, starting with the choice of books to read, extending to the ideas explored in journal letters, and reaching into his involvement in assessment.

I know that choosing his own books was important to Andrew's growth as a reader because it included the option of abandoning books that he found too difficult or just did not like.

Linda had very strong feelings about this aspect of the class. She said:

> What appealed to Andrew was he was given full control over the books he wanted to read. For an insecure reader, being given control over your own reading material lifts a tremendous weight from your shoulders. You don't have to worry whether the books will be too hard or too boring. Andrew could read books that interested him, that were comfortable for him to read and, most importantly, that he could finish at his own pace. Also, he was given the freedom not to finish a book once he started it. This encouraged him to take risks and pick up books that he thought would have been "too hard."

It is very simple to say that when children read according to their interests, they will become more involved in the reading. However, the effects of this simple idea are profound indeed. For Andrew, choosing his own books was the first step to increased self-esteem and growth as a reader. It enabled him to function within the limits of his attention deficit without being outwardly different from his classmates.

Response is at the center of my teaching. In the reading workshop, response to literature takes place in journal dialogues and in classroom share sessions. My letters to students are also my responses to their ideas as readers. In these letters I model my responses to literature, and I share my ideas.

Linda often remarked on the length and content of the letters I wrote to Andrew. She saw the journal as a very important aspect of the class. I certainly agreed. I know that Andrew came to value my letters, because he said so. When Andrew realized from my letters that I valued his ideas, he did, too, and his confidence grew.

Linda remembered that, in the beginning, journal letters were a challenge for Andrew. He had difficulty writing them on a timely basis. Later, things changed and so did Andrew. She recalled:

> After learning that the journal was a safe environment in which to express himself, and that he wasn't being judged on how "correct" his responses were, his journal writing changed. The teacher modeling was an excellent way for Andrew to observe how journal writing can be a dialogue that opens up new avenues of talk about books. There was no right or wrong way to comprehend the meaning of a certain passage. Andrew's thoughts were valued because they were his. I think that this had a great deal to do with his increased confidence about his letters and his reading.

Early in the year, Andrew remarked to Linda that he liked mini-lessons. At the time I didn't think much about that; but, as Linda and I reflected, we agreed that these short, highly focused talks about reading strategies, books, authors, and literary devices were manageable for Andrew. Linda commented, "Mini-lessons are just right. They fit the needs of an ADD child perfectly. They make one point and they're short, so Andrew was able to stay focused. They are always in context and usually, they can be applied immediately." I had known that mini-lessons worked well for most of the children in my classes, but I had never thought about how well suited they are to children like Andrew.

As previously stated, I include students in the evaluation process at the end of each quarter. This inclusion is further evidence of the child's ownership, and looking back at one's work is a valuable learning tool. Linda saw value in this as well. She said:

> Including Andrew in the assessment process fostered ownership and improved his attitude about reading, too. It gave him direct responsibility for his learning. It also formed a partnership between Andrew and you. The separate grade for effort is very important for a student such as Andrew because oftentimes ADD students put forth great effort with less to show for it. If this effort is recognized and documented, it is less likely that the ADD student will give up in frustration.

Andrew's responses to the questions on the third quarter self-evaluation are clear evidence of the positive impact that his involvement produced.

Clearly, several aspects of Andrew's sixth grade language arts experience met his special needs as a learner. Interestingly, I did not alter my classroom practices for Andrew in any significant way. Rather, the time, the ownership, and the response that helps every student also helped Andrew.

In my opinion, the collaboration between Linda and me contributed to Andrew's success as well. Because I was working closely with Linda, I continually questioned what was happening in the classroom. In one of our final meetings, Linda said:

> You have been one of those teachers that parents hope their child will have. You were always very accessible if I had questions or concerns about Andrew, and you were also very interested in what I had to say as a parent. You considered my ideas and even adopted one. I imagine that you are as open to student comments and input as well. For Andrew, your classroom was a safe and supportive environment in which to grow as a reader and writer.

Perhaps being a responsive teacher, giving learners choices and voices in my classroom, and having individual and personal dialogues with them in their journals provides a truly individualized learning environment, one that meets the needs of every child. It certainly met Andrew's needs; and, as a result, Andrew grew, Linda grew, and I grew.

References

Atwell, N. (1987). *In the middle: Writing, reading, and learning with adolescents.* Portsmouth, NH: Heinemann.

Banks, L. R. (1982). *The Indian in the cupboard.* New York: Avon.

Banks, L. R. (1987). *The return of the Indian.* New York: Avon.

Banks, L. R. (1990). *The secret of the Indian.* New York: Avon.

Clark, M. G. (1989). *Freedom crossing.* New York: Scholastic.

Cooney, C. B. (1989). *The fog.* New York: Scholastic.

Cooney, C. B. (1990). *The face on the milk carton.* New York: Bantam.

Giacobbe, M. E. (1986). Learning to write and writing to learn in the elementary school. In A. R. Petrosky & D. Bartholomae (Eds.), *The teaching of writing: Eighty-fifth yearbook of the National Society for the Study of Education,* (pp. 131–147). Chicago: University of Chicago Press.

L'Engle, M. (1973). *A wrinkle in time.* New York: Dell.

Mazer, N. F., & Mazer, H. (1977). *The solid gold kid.* New York: Delacorte Press.

Naylor, P. R. (1987). *Beatles lightly toasted.* New York: Atheneum Children's Books.

Paulsen, G. (1988). *Voyage of the frog.* Orchard Books.

Pfeffer, S. B. (1988). *The year without Michael.* New York: Bantam.

16

The Nature and Promise of Whole Language for AD(H)Ders and Other Special Needs Students

Constance Weaver

Most of the articles in the last three sections of this book have illustrated, in varying degrees, the nature of whole language classrooms. This is true even of some articles that never explicitly mentioned the term "whole language." But readers of this volume may still find themselves wanting a discursive explanation of whole language education. This seems all the more important since many classroom practices and instructional materials are labeled whole language nowadays, even though they reflect few if any of the principles that characterize a whole language philosophy of education.

This article explains that whole language is philosophy of education, not an approach nor a set of instructional materials. (Indeed, any curricular materials you can buy in a package are, by definition, not whole language). The discussion of whole language principles is followed by a description of some of the practices that commonly occur in whole language classrooms. Finally, the article describes results from research studies that have compared the effects of whole language teaching with traditional skills-based teaching. Bibliographies suggest starting points for further exploration of the topics introduced. The description of whole language principles should make it clear why whole language teaching is especially valuable for students with AD(H)D and others with special conditions and needs.

Most of the material for this chapter comes from the second edition of the author's *Reading Process and Practice* (Heinemann, 1994), though earlier versions of some materials have also appeared in *Theme Exploration* (1993) and *Supporting Whole Language* (1992), described more fully in the biographical sketch below.

Connie Weaver is a professor of English at Western Michigan University, where she teaches courses in the reading and writing processes, applied linguistics, and whole language education. Recent publications include *Reading Process and Practice: From Sociolinguistics to Whole Language* (second edition, 1994); *Theme Exploration: A Voyage of Discovery* (1993, written with Joel Chaston and Scott Peterson), *Supporting Whole Language* (1992, co-edited with Linda Henke), *Understanding Whole Language* (1990), plus two articles and a monograph on understanding and educating students with an Attention Deficit Hyperactivity Disorder. Connie's professional interest in ADHD stems from her son's being diagnosed at the age of sixteen as having ADHD.

With respect to special needs learners in general, Cora Lee Five writes: "These students' stories consistently reveal that they can learn and flourish together with their peers in a language-rich classroom, in an environment that allows ownership, provides time, and values response" (1992, p. 7). Her story of Mike in this book demonstrates such success, as do the other articles focusing on individual children in classrooms that are explicitly or implicitly "whole language" in their philosophical orientation.

The following whole language practices are especially critical for special learners, including those who have an Attention Deficit (Hyperactivity) Disorder:

1. Learners are treated as capable and developing, not as incapable and deficient.
2. Learners' strengths are emphasized, not their weaknesses.
3. Likewise, learners' unique learning abilities and strategies are valued.
4. Students' needs and interests partly determine the development of the curriculum.
5. Assessment is based much less on standardized tests than upon individual growth and upon the achievement of classroom-based goals, including goals for individuals that may have been established jointly by the teacher and the student, and perhaps the parent(s) as well. There is no rigid timetable for learning.
6. The teacher promotes the learning of *all* students by creating a supportive classroom community, giving students time (the whole school year) in which to grow, offering choices and ownership, providing response and structure, and gradually expecting and allowing students to take more responsibility for their work (Hansen, 1987).

In an environment where literacy events and other learning opportunities reflect such practices, special learners will usually have their best chance to flourish—as indicated by the references in Figure 16–1.

To better clarify the what, how, and why of whole language education, this chapter will first discuss in more depth some key principles of whole language education and the educational paradigm shift it entails. This will be followed by a brief characterization of some of the literacy and language events that are central to learning across the curriculum in whole language classrooms (Halliday, 1984). Finally, the chapter will summarize some of the conclusions that are emerging from the small but growing body of research that compares children's learning in whole language classrooms with their learning in traditional skills-based classrooms. Though so far none of the comparative research focuses on special needs students in general or AD(H)D students in particular, the success such children experience in whole language environments is amply documented by the case studies in this volume and others (Five, 1992; Stires, 1991; Doyle, 1990; and other references included in Figure 16–1).

What the comparative research helps clarify is that children in whole language classrooms are not merely succeeding on worksheets and standardized tests, as they may do in skills-oriented programs that claim success for special needs learners, such as Direct Instruction of the DISTAR variety (Tarver, 1992, and many references cited therein; Engelmann & Osborn, 1975; Engelmann, Osborn, Osborn, & Zoref, 1988). While at risk and special needs students are succeeding in accomplishing the limited aims of skills-based remedial programs, they are falling farther and farther behind classmates whose instruction

FIGURE 16–1. *Whole language for special needs and "at-risk" learners.*

Allen, J. B., & Mason, J. M (Eds.). (1989). *Risk makers, risk takers, risk breakers: Reducing the risks for young literacy learners.* Portsmouth, NH: Heinemann.

Allen, J. B., Shockley, B., & West, M. (1991). "I'm really worried about Joseph": Reducing the risks of literacy learning. *The Reading Teacher, 44,* 458–468.

Cutler, C., & Stone, E. (1988). A whole language approach: Teaching reading and writing to behaviorally disordered children. In M.K. Zabel (Ed.), *TEACHING: Behaviorally Disordered Youth,* Vol. 4, 31–39. Alexandria, VA (Educational Resources Information Center: ED 305 785)

Doyle, K. M. (1990). Listening to the sounds of our hearts. *Language Arts, 67,* 254–261.

Five, C. L. (1991). *Special voices.* Portsmouth, NH: Heinemann.

Hinnenkamp, B. (1991). Reading and writing with a special needs student: A case study. *Insight into Open Education, 23*(5), 2–6.

Lee, C., & Jackson, R. (1992). *Faking it: A look into the mind of a creative learner.* Portsmouth, NH: Boynton/Cook-Heinemann.

Rhodes, L. K., & Dudley-Marling, C. (1988). *Readers and writers with a difference: A holistic approach to teaching learning disabled and remedial students.* Portsmouth, NH: Heinemann.

Rigg, P., & Taylor, L. (1979). A twenty-one-year-old begins to read. *English Journal, 68,* 52–56.

Routman, R. (1991). *Invitations: Changing as teachers and learners K–12.* Chapter 14, "The learning disabled student: A part of the at-risk population." Portsmouth, NH: Heinemann.

Stires, S. (Ed.) (1991). *With promise: Redefining reading and writing for "special" students.* Portsmouth, NH: Heinemann.

Swenson, A. M. (1988). Using an integrated literacy curriculum with beginning Braille readers. *Journal of Visual Impairment and Blindness, 82,* 336–338.

Swenson, A. M. (1991). A process approach to teaching Braille writing at the primary level. *Journal of Visual Impairment and Blindness, 85*(5), 217–221.

Taylor, D. (1991). *Learning denied.* Portsmouth, NH: Heinemann.

White, C. (1991). *Jevon doesn't sit at the back anymore.* Richmond Hill, Ontario: Scholastic Canada.

And articles in the January 1982 issue of *Topics in Learning and Learning Disabilities* and the May 1991 issue of *Topics in Language Disorders.*

is more challenging and rewarding (Anderson & Pellicer, 1990; McGill-Franzen & Allington, 1991; Bartoli & Botel, 1988; synthesized in Weaver, 1994). In contrast, the vast majority of students in whole language classrooms and resource rooms are becoming enthusiastic and increasingly independent and self-confident readers, writers, and learners. In such classrooms and resource rooms, most AD(H)Ders and other special needs students succeed in achieving the kind of literacy and learning strategies needed outside of and beyond school, where worksheets and skills exercises don't matter.

Whole Language as a Philosophy of Education

As Dorothy Watson has expressed it, *"Whole language is a perspective on education that is supported by beliefs about learners and learning, teachers and teaching, language and curriculum.* . . . Whole language isn't a program, package, set of materials, method, practice, or technique; rather, it is a perspective on language and learning *that leads to the acceptance* of certain strategies, methods, materials, and techniques" (Watson, 1989, pp. 133, 134). In short, whole language education is far more than what the name would suggest.

Originally, however, the term was coined to reflect reading educators' concern for keeping language whole during literacy instruction—that is, for avoiding drill and practice on isolated bits and pieces of language (e.g. Y. Goodman, 1989; Watson, 1989). Research in language acquisition, in particular, had demonstrated that acquiring a language as a young child involves not merely (or mainly) habit formation, but adducing rules from the complex, authentic language children hear, in a sociolinguistic context where meaning is often clarified by intonation, gesture, other visual cues, and the situation (Brown, 1973; Lindfors, 1987; Halliday, 1975). Research into the nature of proficient reading (e.g. Smith, 1971, 1973; K. Goodman, 1973) had demonstrated that reading, too, is a complex cognitive process involving far more than the mere ability to identify words, though word identification has been the primary focus in both sight word and phonics approaches to the teaching of reading. Subsequent research on emergent literacy demonstrated that literacy develops most readily in contexts where children are encouraged to read and to write "whole" texts: to engage with authentic and meaningful language. Within the context of authentic literacy events, adults can support children in developing an increasingly sophisticated ability to deal with the parts of language, such as letter/sound relationships in reading and spelling conventions in writing.

From these roots in the late 1960s through the early 1980s, whole language has evolved into a full-fledged educational philosophy that reflects a substantive research base in such fields as cognitive psychology; psycholinguistics and reading; anthropology and education; and of course language acquisition and emergent literacy (Edelsky, Altwerger, and Flores, 1991). It also reflects the humanistic and Deweyan traditions that have characterized such earlier movements as progressive education and open education (e.g. Y. Goodman, 1989).

As a philosophy of learning and teaching, whole language is continually evolving, in response to reflective practice, theory, and research. Nevertheless, there are many principles that together form a core of beliefs characterizing the essence of a whole language philosophy. Most leading and long-time whole language educators would agree upon the principles discussed below, though doubtless they would describe them somewhat differently and include other principles as well (see references in Figure 16–2). For convenience, these whole language principles are grouped below into four overlapping categories: learning and the learner, the nature and development of the curriculum, teacher roles and functions in facilitating learning, and assessment and evaluation.

Learning and the Learner

Explicitly rejecting behaviorism as the primary model for significant human learning, whole language educators have been influenced by the work of cognitive psychologists and learning theorists who emphasize the roles of motivation and social interaction in learning (see Y. Goodman, 1989; K. Goodman, 1989). Their understanding of learning has also been strongly influenced by descriptions of language and literacy development in natural settings (e.g. Holdaway, 1979). Such observation and research has given rise to the following principles, which characterize a contructionist model of learning:

1. Learners construct meaning for themselves, most readily in contexts where they can actively transact (or interact) with other people, with books, and with objects and materials in the external world. The most significant and enduring learning, particularly of concepts and complex processes, is likely to be that constructed by the learner, not imposed from without. Or to put it somewhat differently, "Whole-language educators and their predecessors believe that learners ultimately are in control of what they learn regardless of what is being taught" (Y. Goodman, 1989, p. 114; also Emig, 1983).
2. When learning is perceived as functional to and purposeful for the learner, it is more likely to endure. That is, the most significant learning derives from whatever arouses the interest, meets the needs, and furthers the purposes of the learner in the here and now.
3. In order to engage themselves wholeheartedly in learning, however, learners must be confident that they will be safe from negative repercussions. They must be free to take risks without fear of being criticized, penalized, or declared wrong.
4. Though there are developmental trends among learners, learning is fundamentally idiosyncratic, even chaotic; the nature and course of each individual's learning is unique.
5. Individual learning is promoted by social collaboration: by opportunities to work with others, to brainstorm, to try out ideas and get feedback, to obtain assistance. Social collaboration also offers powerful demonstrations of how others work, learn, act, and so forth, which is particularly valuable in promoting the growth of those whose strategies are initially less successful. In short, learning is facilitated by and within a community of learners.

FIGURE 16–2. *Readings for understanding whole language principles.*

Articles

Altwerger, B. (1991). Whole language teachers: Empowered professionals. In J. Hydrick (Ed.), *Whole language: Empowerment at the chalkface* (pp. 15–29). New York: Scholastic.

Goodman, K. S. (1989). Whole-language research: Foundations and development. *The Elementary School Journal, 90,* 208–221.

Goodman, Y. M. (1989). Roots of the whole-language movement. *The Elementary School Journal, 90,* 113–127.

Gursky, D. (1991). After the reign of Dick and Jane. *Teacher Magazine,* August, pp. 22–29.

Monson, R. J., & Pahl, M. M. (1991). Charting a new course with whole language. *Educational Leadership, 48,* 51–53.

Newman, J. M., & Church, S. M. (1990). Myths of whole language. *The Reading Teacher, 44,* 20–26.

Pace, G. (1991). When teachers use literature for literacy instruction: Ways that constrain, ways that free. *Language Arts, 68,* 12–25.

Watson, D. J. (1989). Defining and describing whole language. *The Elementary School Journal, 90,* 130–141.

Books

Cambourne, B. (1988). *The whole story: Natural learning and the acquisition of literacy in the classroom.* Auckland, New Zealand: Scholastic.

Edelsky, C., Altwerger, B., & Flores, B. (1991). *Whole language: What's the difference?* Portsmouth, NH: Heinemann.

Goodman, K. S. (1986). *What's whole in whole language?* Richmond Hill, Ontario: Scholastic. (Available in the U. S. from Heinemann.)

Goodman, K. S., Bird, L. B., & Goodman, Y. M. (1991). *The whole language catalog.* Chicago: SRA.

Harste, J. C. (1989). *New policy guidelines for reading: Connecting research and practice.* Urbana, IL: National Council of Teachers of English.

Manning, G., & Manning, M. (Eds.). (1989). *Whole language: Beliefs and practices, K–8.* Washington, DC: National Education Association.

Short, K. G., & Burke, C. (1991). *Creating curriculum: Teachers and students as a community of learners.* Portsmouth, NH: Heinemann.

Stephens, D. (1991). *Research on whole language: Support for a new curriculum.* Katonah, NY: Richard C. Owen.

Weaver, C. (1990). *Understanding whole language: From principles to practice.* Portsmouth, NH: Heinemann.

The Nature and Development of the Curriculum

Several implications for curriculum follow from the aforementioned principles of learning:

1. Since learning proceeds best when learners engage in authentic literacy and learning experiences, the curriculum should consist not of worksheets and dittos but of opportunities to engage in the myriad kinds of reading, discussion, experimentation, and research that children and adults voluntarily engage in, outside of school. "Opportunities" implies a strong element of learner choice.

2. Since choice is an important factor in facilitating learning, the curriculum is in many respects negotiated among the teacher and the students. The teacher determines the parameters within which he or she and the children are free to make choices. Long-range curricular decisions may be made by the teacher and students brainstorming possibilities and together making choices, within the bottom-line parameters of the externally-imposed curriculum. Negotiation also occurs daily, in the give-and-take of the classroom. Students may suggest a better way to do something, or something better to do, and the teacher will often agree. Not all the initiation for change comes from the teacher (e.g. Weaver, Chaston, & Peterson, 1993).

3. Since learning opportunities need to be perceived as functional and purposeful by the learner, it follows that language itself must be kept natural and whole. This means that emergent readers will be helped to read rhymes, songs, repetitive and predictable stories, and environmental print, rather than the stilted, unnatural language known as primerese. They will read whole texts rather than the contextless bits and pieces of language that characterize worksheets and workbooks. Similarly, students will write authentic stories, poems, letters, and other pieces, not do assignments like "Write a story about the day you woke up as a pencil," copying a poem from the blackboard, or filling in the blanks or lines of a workbook page.

4. Direct and indirect instruction of the "parts" of language occurs in the context of the whole, and in the context of the students' need. For example: During shared reading or literature discussions, the teacher may demonstrate effective reading strategies, and during writers' workshop, the teacher may demonstrate effective strategies for drafting or revision or editing, in each instance adding ideas to the "class pot" (Calkins, 1986) for students to draw upon. At other times, for example, the teacher will show one or more students how to punctuate dialogue when the students have actually used dialogue in a story. Phonics skills are developed through writing and in the context of enjoying a rhyme or song, not through worksheet practice. To generalize: In whole language classrooms, the teacher will sometimes directly teach something to the whole class, if it seems relevant to what many of them are doing or might soon want to do as readers, writers, and learners. But at other times the teacher will work with a small group or an individual, particularly on a skill or strategy

currently needed by only a few students. Typically, instruction proceeds from whole to part, then back to the whole. That is, the part is considered only in the context of the whole: the authentic reading, writing, and investigating that students are doing.

5. Thus, direct teaching occurs not according to a predetermined scope and sequence chart, but mostly in direct response to the students' interests and needs, as determined by them and by the teacher's observations. Significantly, direct instruction also occurs between and among peers, as they help one another with reading and writing and learning. Much direct instruction occurs in response to the "teachable moment."

Teacher Roles and Functions in Facilitating Learning

Whole language principles of learning, characteristics of curriculum, and teacher roles all draw heavily from observational research into the acquisition of language and literacy and how such learning is facilitated (e.g. Laminack, 1991; N. Hall, 1987; various articles in Sampson, 1986; Newman, 1985; Harste, Woodward, & Burke, 1984; Teale, 1982; K. Goodman & Y. Goodman, 1979; Chapter 3 of Weaver, 1994). In fact, leading whole language educators have developed models of literary learning based upon the ways parents provide support for literacy development, in homes where adults frequently read books to children (e.g. Holdaway, 1979; Cambourne, 1988).

Just as parents do not teach the "rules" of spoken language directly, so they do not usually try to teach children rules for reading. They read to children, demonstrating what it means to be a reader; they guide and encourage the child's active participation in reading the story; they discuss the story with the child, encouraging strategies like prediction ("What do you think's going to happen?"); they respond to the child's "What's this?" when asked of pictures, words, and letters; and they repeatedly offer opportunities for such guided participation by acceding to requests of "Read it again!" Usually the child is not only allowed but encouraged to practice independently, retelling and later actually reading the book to him- or herself, or to a doll or the dog. Finally, the child, now a confident reader, will want to read the book to some other person—even though the child may mostly turn the pages and retell the remembered story as triggered by the pictures.

When whole language educators talk about the natural acquisition of literacy, what they mean is that literacy can best be fostered by using the means that parents have used, more or less naturally, to foster their preschoolers' development of literacy. Among the important implications for classroom instruction are these:

1. The teacher is, first of all, a role model. In order to foster students' development of literacy and learning, teachers must demonstrate that they themselves are passionate readers, writers, and learners. Teachers also need to demonstrate what it means to be risk takers and decision makers.
2. The teacher is also a mentor, collaborator, and facilitator. Often, the teacher

serves as a master to whom students are apprenticed, and from whom they learn such crafts as reading and writing and learning itself. The teacher demonstrates and discusses his or her own knowledge of the craft with students, while collaborating with them. For example, the teacher demonstrates and discusses reading strategies with students, helping them use and become consciously (metacognitively) aware of a growing range of strategies for constructing meaning and dealing with text. The teacher demonstrates and discusses writing strategies, teaches needed skills and strategies while conferring with students, and encourages peer collaboration and learning from one another. In general, the teacher offers learning experiences and choices, helps students consider and acquire the resources needed for their projects, guides students in learning valuable strategies and skills for carrying out their purposes, monitors their progress and responds to their needs: both the needs that the students articulate and those the teacher merely observes or intuits. The teacher also helps students perceive themselves and each other as sources of information, resources, and assistance.

3. Teachers are responsible for creating a supportive community of learners, in which everyone (including the teacher) is free to take risks and make decisions without fear of negative consequences, and in which everyone is supported by others. Within this community, teachers encourage collaboration in various ways, such as by brainstorming ideas, responding to each others' writings and other work, sharing resources, working together on projects, sharing expertise, helping one another, and collaborating to establish class rules and to resolve interpersonal difficulties that arise.

4. Teachers present themselves as learners rather than as ultimate authorities, and similarly they treat students as capable and developing, not as incapable or as deficient products. Such teachers model and encourage risk taking, and they respond positively to what their students can do, while issuing invitations and offering challenges to stimulate students' growth.

5. Teachers share responsibility for curricular decision making with students, thus encouraging them to take ownership of and responsibility for their own learning. By also encouraging risk taking and decision making without fear of negative consequences, teachers empower students to become independent, self-motivated learners and doers.

Though both implicit and explicit in the preceding discussion, it is perhaps worth emphasizing that one of the most important ways whole language teachers facilitate learning is by scaffolding (Ninio & Bruner, 1978; Bruner, 1983, 1986): They help learners do, or ask others to help them do, what they cannot yet do on their own; and they provide opportunities for children to do together things that none of them could do alone (Vygotsky's "zone of proximal development," 1962, 1978). By not only permitting but actually encouraging dependence on other learners, teachers make it easier for children to become and succeed as independent learners. Paradoxically, perhaps, collaborative learning experiences promote both cooperation and community, on the one hand, and individual and independent growth and ability, on the other.

Assessment and Evaluation

It should not be surprising that in whole language classrooms, assessment and evaluation reflect many of the aforementioned principles of learning and teaching:

1. Assessment is *collaborative*. The teacher evaluates the student, but the student also engages in reflection and self-evaluation. Assessment may also involve peers and/or parents. In particular, peers may evaluate each other's contributions to collaborative projects and learning, and/or to the class community in general. Parents may be invited to describe their child's strengths and needs as a learner at the beginning of the school year, then later invited to assess growth and suggest needs and goals (e.g. Barrs, Ellis, Tester, & Thomas, 1989). Furthermore, the various assessors can collaborate in assessing the individual. For instance, groups of students can talk about each others' strengths and suggest possible areas for improvement, and teachers can hold conferences in which child, teacher, and parent(s) together assess progress and determine learning goals. Or children can prepare for and conduct conferences with their parents (Anthony, Johnson, Mickelson, & Preece, 1991). Each contributor to assessment may provide a valuable and to some degree unique perspective—rather like the parable of the blind men and the elephant. We need *all* of these perspectives to begin to build an accurate picture.

2. Assessment is *complex and multi-dimensional,* based upon data of various kinds. Among other things, this means that those engaging in evaluation—teachers, students, and perhaps parents—look not just at *products* the learners have produced, but also at students' *processes* for reading, writing, and learning (and doing math, science, etc). For instance, one would look for growth in the range and flexibility of reading and writing strategies; growth in ability to extend these strategies into new genres of reading and writing and to refine or modify them accordingly; and/or growth in the ability to integrate various strategies to learn more effectively. Evaluators also look at changes in students' *perceptions* of themselves as readers, writers, and learners—in other words, the affective factors that most powerfully influence learning. Is the student coming to view him- or herself as a reader, writer, and independent learner? Is the student growing in the range of learning experiences that he or she enjoys and engages in wholeheartedly? Something else to consider are the *social aspects* of learning. Is the student growing in ability to work collaboratively with others? If so, in what ways? With each of these measures, growth is typically considered a major factor. As Kathryn Mitchell Pierce has suggested in personal correspondence, such ongoing assessment, with emphasis on growth, is like a videotape filmed over a substantial period of time, in comparison with standardized tests, which are more like single snapshots unrelated to one another.

3. Assessment is *contextualized,* drawing primarily upon information collected during the day-to-day activities of classroom life, rather than upon

scores from tests that are quite unlike normal learning experiences. Drawing upon data that are both rich and varied, assessment is thus ongoing and continuous, intertwined with learning and teaching. Recorded observations are an important part of teachers' contribution to evaluation, but so are various kinds of artifacts, including periodic performance samples (e.g. of writing or reading) and "think-alouds," in which the learner thinks and talks his or her way through a reading or writing experience, as well as data from conferences and interviews, inventories and questionnaires, dialogue journals and learning logs, and student-kept records of such things as books read, topics and range of writings, goals set and progress made, self-evaluation, etc. Projects of various kinds, and the processes involved in producing them, are another important source of data for assessment. (For an overview of such possibilities for assessment, see Chapter 10 of Weaver, 1990.) In other words, the teacher can draw upon a wide range of information for assessment, including (if desired) the students' own evaluations—or the data from students' self-evaluations can be kept and weighted separately, in the summative evaluation. Whole language classrooms invite many possibilities.

4. The summative evaluation is *weighted* appropriately, reflecting not only various viewpoints, kinds of goals, and kinds of data, but also a carefully conceived weighing among *individual-referenced assessment,* based primarily upon growth; *criterion-referenced assessment,* based upon the meeting of external expectations and the attainment of externally imposed goals; and *norm-referenced assessment,* based upon comparison with others, perhaps using whatever standardized tests may have been mandated. Often, whole language teachers keep individual-referenced and criterion-referenced assessments separate from the norm-referenced assessment (Edelsky & Harman, 1988). This is particularly true if the norm-referenced assessment consists exclusively of standardized test scores, which are best used (if they must be used at all) as part of an aggregate of data for an entire school.

Whole language teachers typically give significant weight to both individual-referenced assessment (growth) and to criterion-referenced assessment, with the balance between them determined by such factors as grade level. For instance, in evaluating preservice teachers in my university classes, I give more weight to criterion-referenced assessment than to individual-referenced, whereas the balance would be reversed if I were working with emergent readers and writers. (For an example of such weighted evaluation, see Cora Five's discussion on pp. 207–208 of how she evaluated Mike, a special needs learner. See also Anthony, Johnson, Mickelson, & Preece, 1991.)

5. Students and teachers evaluate themselves, each other, and the curriculum: that is, the classroom experiences that they have shaped and shared together. For example, students can consider how and how well they have contributed to the classroom community and/or to collaborative groups in which they have worked. They can also consider how their whole language learning differs from traditional instruction, compare the advantages and

C. Weaver

FIGURE 16–3. *Ends of a transmission-to-transactional continuum.*

Transmission	**Transactional**
Reductionist	Constructivist
Behavioral psychology	Cognitive psychology
Habit formation	Hypothesis formation
Avoiding mistakes prevents formation of bad habits	Errors necessary for encouraging more sophisticated hypotheses
Students passively practice skills, memorize facts	Students actively pursue learning and construct language
Teacher dispenses prepackaged, predetermined curriculum	Teacher develops and negotiates curriculum with students
Direct teaching of curriculum	Responsive teaching, to meet students' needs and interests
Taskmaster, with emphasis on cycle of *teach, practice/apply/memorize, test*	Mastercraftsperson, mentor: emphasis on demonstrating, inviting, discussing, affirming, facilitating, collaborating, observing, supporting
Lessons taught, practiced and/or applied, then tested	Mini-lessons taught as demonstration, invitation; adding an idea to the class pot
Performance on decontextualized tests is taken as measure of learning of limited information	Assessment from a variety of contextualized learning experiences captures diverse aspects of learning
Learning is expected to be uniform, same for everyone; uniform means of assessment guarantee that many will fail, in significant ways	Learning is expected to be individual, different for everyone; flexible and multiple means of assessment guarantee all will succeed, in differing ways
Adds up to a failure-oriented model, ferreting out students' weaknesses and preparing them to take their place in a stratified society	Adds up to a success-oriented model, emphasizing students' strengths and preparing them to be the best they can be in a stratified society

disadvantages, and offer suggestions for change. (These examples come from a real situation, documented in Weaver, Chaston, & Peterson, 1993.)

A Paradigm Shift

These principles of whole language should make it clear that no one can become a whole language teacher simply by using sets of materials labeled "whole language"; by getting ideas from a single inservice seminar or conference; or by experimenting with different activities. *One also needs to develop new ways of viewing students as learners and new ways of transacting with them and assessing their learning.* This new view is so radically different from the traditional views as to constitute a different paradigm, a different set of operating assumptions about learning and teaching.

The paradigm that underlies traditional skills-oriented instruction is often called a transmission paradigm, whereas the paradigm that underlines whole language instruction is often called a transactional paradigm. Alternative names are the mechanistic paradigm and a holistic paradigm respectively, as described in some articles dealing with the need for a paradigm shift in special education (Poplin & Stone, 1992; Heshusius, 1989).

Some key contrasts between these two paradigms are made explicit in Figure 16–3. According to behavioristic psychology, which underlies the transmission model, learning results primarily from habit formation and simple association; hence a great deal of time is spent practicing skills and memorizing information. It is true, of course, that rules can be practiced and isolated facts memorized, at least by some students. But such rules and facts are often forgotten soon after testing, and/or the "learning" is not transferred to situations for which it was intended (as, for example, punctuation rules taught in isolation are often not applied when students actually write). For one thing, the effective use or transfer of such skills seems to require high motivation. Cognitive psychologists point out that, given such motivation, people master complex processes and develop enduring concepts by repeatedly constructing hypotheses, testing them, and formulating new hypotheses (e.g. Smith, 1975, 1990). In other words, *humans construct knowledge for themselves, drawing from their experiences, and with (or without) the guidance and support of others.* This constructivist view of learning permeates curricular reforms in every major discipline, including math, science, social studies, and health education, as well as language arts. No wonder, then, that this tenet is central to a whole language perspective on learning and teaching. Indeed, one might broadly characterize a whole language teacher as someone who believes that humans fundamentally construct their own knowledge, and who works to increasingly activate that belief in the classroom. So defined, whole language teaching is obviously not confined to the language arts.

For convenience, Figure 16–4 organizes some of the contrasts between a transmission and a transactional paradigm into the four categories used in describing key principles of whole language; in effect, these lists constitute the extremes of a continuum. Some articles near the beginning of this book reflect more of the assumptions and practices from the transmission paradigm than

C. Weaver

FIGURE 16–4. *Continuum from transmission to transactional paradigm.*

Transmission model of learning	**Transactional model of learning**
LEARNING AND THE LEARNER	
Learner passively and often begrudgingly practices skills, memorizes facts, accumulates information	Learner actively and often enthusiastically engages in complex language and reasoning processes and the construction of complex concepts
Material practiced and learned is rarely perceived as functional or purposeful by the learner	Authentic experiences and projects are typically perceived as functional and purposeful by the learner
Uniform instruction reflects assumption that all learners learn the same things at the same time	Learner-sensitive instruction based on explicit assumption that all learners learn and develop uniquely
Lack of adult correctness generates negative feedback to what are considered to be errors in execution	Gradual approach to adult correctness is expected; learning is seen as best facilitated when learners are free to experiment and take risks without fear of negative feedback
Learning is seen as best facilitated by competition	Learning is seen as best facilitated by collaboration
CURRICULUM	
Curriculum is characterized by an emphasis on minimal skills and factual information	Curriculum is characterized by the kinds of learning experiences that lifelong learners engage in outside of school
Curriculum is divided into subjects, and subjects into skills and facts; language and literacy are taught as the mastery of isolated skills	Curriculum is integrated around topics and themes, with emphasis on developing language and literacy skills across the curriculum
Curriculum is determined by outside forces (curriculum guides and objectives, texts, and programs)	Curriculum is determined by, and negotiated among, the teacher and the students
Reading materials are characterized, at the earliest levels, by unnaturally stilted language ("basalese" consisting of basic sight words and/or phonically regular words)	Reading materials include, at the earliest levels, a wide variety of materials in natural language patterns, with emphasis on repetitive and predictable patterns
Beyond the primary grades, many reading selections consist of literature that has been altered, abridged, or excerpted from literary works	Beyond the primary grades, the range and depth of reading materials is increased, with emphasis on whole works of high literary quality as well as nonfiction prose
Direct teaching of skills occurs in isolation, according to a predetermined teach/practice/test format or program, with attention to mastering the parts of language	Direct teaching of skills occurs within the context of the whole learning experience and the learners' needs and interests (parts in context of the whole)

Transmission model of learning	Transactional model of learning
TEACHER ROLES	

Transmission model of learning	Transactional model of learning
Serves to dispense information, assign tasks, and evaluate work	Serves as a master craftsperson, mentor, role model, demonstrating what it is to be a literate person and a lifelong learner
Explains lessons and assignments; determines work to be done	Stimulates learning by demonstrating, inviting, discussing, affirming, facilitating, collaborating
Creates a climate wherein competition and comparison are encouraged	Creates a supportive community of learners wherein collaboration and assistance are encouraged
Treats students as incapable and deficient insofar as they have not measured up to preset objectives and norms	Treats students as capable and developing, honoring their unique patterns of development and offering invitations and challenges to growth
Rejects and penalizes errors, thus discouraging risk taking and hypothesis formation (thinking)	Responds positively to successive approximations, thus encouraging risk taking and hypothesis formation
Fosters dependence on external authority to determine what to do and how to do things, as well as to decide what is and is not correct	Shares responsibility for curricular decision making with students, thus empowering them to take ownership of and responsibility for their own learning

ASSESSMENT AND EVALUATION

Transmission model of learning	Transactional model of learning
Only the teacher assesses the student	Assessment is collaborative, involving not only the teacher but the student and perhaps peers and/or parents
Assessment is often limited to tests, with standardized tests given the greatest weight in evaluation and decision making regarding instruction and/or placement	Assessment is complex and multi-dimensional, with attention given not only to products (such as test scores and reading and writing samples), but also to processes and other affective factors
Assessment is decontextualized; that is, it bears little resemblance to normal reading, writing, and learning activities	Assessment is contextualized, reflecting the day-to-day authentic learning experiences of the classroom
Assessment is infrequent	Assessment is ongoing and continuous
Assessment is primarily norm-referenced and to some extent criterion-referenced	Assessment is learner-referenced (based on the individual learner's growth) as well as criterion-referenced
Both students and teachers are evaluated by students' performance on standardized tests and/or by students' attainment of externally imposed curriculum goals	Students and teachers evaluate themselves, each other, and the curriculum—that is, their shared learning experiences

later articles do—doubtless because that is what the authors have experienced as teachers, as psychologists, and/or as students. Other articles, particularly those from the last three sections of the book, reflect more of the transactional paradigm that characterizes whole language. The most obvious difference among these latter articles is the degree to which the students are involved in making decisions about their own learning and about classroom procedures. Or to put it another way, the most obvious difference is the degree to which the teacher shares responsibility and decision-making with the learners. To greater or lesser degree, this occurs as students and teachers engage in the literacy events and other learning opportunities that are common in whole language classrooms.

Literacy and Language Events in Whole Language Classrooms and/or Resource Rooms

What makes the following literacy and language events so valuable for special needs learners as well as others is the spirit in which they are introduced, undertaken, and monitored, as well as the way in which the processes and results are assessed in whole language classrooms and resource rooms. Or in other words, it is the teacher's underlying philosophy and knowledge that make the critical difference, not so much the activities per se.

I use the term literacy and language "events" to suggest that these are not exercises on isolated skills, nor even thematically-associated activities undertaken just for the sake of learning some specific skill or strategy (Altwerger, 1991). They are acts of reading, writing, and oral language undertaken for their own sake, because they are enjoyable, and because they encourage children to construct their own knowledge about literacy and language—to grow as readers, writers, speakers, listeners, and learners. Especially important, learners who seem less proficient than their classmates are equally valued for however they can engage in these events, not considered or treated as deficient. This is particularly obvious from the following characterization of the Shared Book Experience.

Shared Book Experience, or Shared Reading Experience

First developed in 1965 in New Zealand by Don Holdaway and a team of experienced teachers and consultants, the Shared Book Experience (SBE) derives from observation of the ways children often learn to read as a result of the bedtime story experience in the home (Holdaway, 1979). The teacher uses a "Big Book" that all the children in the group can see: a commercially published Big Book, a child/teacher-authored Big Book, or simply a chart of some sort, written in large print. A shared reading session begins with the *rereading of favorite selections* (rhymes, songs and poems, and/or stories), during which the teacher points to the words as teacher and children read together. After this choral rereading, the teacher may focus students' attention on particular aspects of print or particular reading strategies (parts in the context of the whole), or may simply ask children "What do you notice?" about the language or the print. Next, the teacher introduces and *reads a new story,* engages the children in discussing it, and reads it again. Children then have the opportunity to *reread the story independently* (using the big print version or individual copies), as well as to engage in related arts, crafts, drama, music, writing, and other activities.

Through the Shared Book Experience, children can learn many things, such as conventions of print, reading strategies, sight vocabulary, and letter/sound relationships. Each child participates in the rereadings and discussion however he or she can, and learns whatever he or she is ready to learn. Less proficient readers especially benefit because their less fluent reading goes relatively unnoticed among the group. The rereading of familiar texts gives them the opportunity to practice reading without being singled out for their lack of proficiency or fluency. In the Shared Book Experience—or any similar shared reading experience—reading becomes an enjoyable social activity, not a boring or humiliating seatwork task to be done independently. Children learn to read by reading together. (A fuller discussion of the shared reading experience can be found in Clark & Miller, 1992, and in Chapter 3 of Weaver, 1994).

Independent Reading

In whole language classrooms, students have many opportunities to read new as well as "old" materials independently, and often to *choose* what they will read. Not only do they choose what materials they will read, but they have opportunities to choose reading from among other learning alternatives. Even the least proficient of emergent readers is treated as a reader and is expected to read and enjoy at least the pictures of a book when time is specifically set aside for independent reading.

Paired Reading

Like independent reading, paired reading may take various forms. Students may choose buddies to read with, even if they're reading different books and mostly just reading silently together. They may be paired to read and discuss related but different books. A more proficient reader may be paired with a less proficient reader, to serve as consultant and perhaps even to help the less proficient reader develop more effective reading strategies. Students may read aloud to each other, or even in unison, perhaps with a less proficient reader echoing a more proficient reading buddy. These are just some of the possibilities.

Listening to Literature Read Aloud

Many teachers read aloud to students daily—even to high school and college students! This shared literature event creates a social bond as well as making reading enjoyable and meaningful. In addition, it helps develop listeners' grasp of syntax (e.g. Perera, 1986), vocabulary (Elley, 1989), and of course story structure and genre. "A story a day keeps the remedial program away." If that's not already a classroom motto, perhaps it ought to be. (See Trelease, 1989.) Of course, students too may read aloud: not to demonstrate how well they can or can't identify words, but for everyone's enjoyment. When reading aloud for this purpose, both adults and children may need to practice what they're going to read. Listening to literature on tape is a valuable complement to the live read-aloud. Nowadays, many book-tape combinations for all ages may be purchased at bookstores and borrowed from libraries.

Language Experience

What has come to be known as a language experience activity (LEA) involves dictating what one wants to write to a teacher or someone else who writes it down (or dictating into a tape recorder for later transcribing), then reading and repeatedly rereading the familiar text until it becomes easy to read (Van Allen, 1976; M. Hall, 1976, 1981). Language experience events are not as common in whole language classrooms as independent writing, because dictation can all too easily convince children that they are not yet ready to write for themselves. However, teachers may occasionally "do" language experience with children. Whether the language experience writing is based on a shared classroom experience or an individual's experience, typically, the teacher will write down a sentence dictated by each child: e.g. *Aaron said, "I put in peas and carrots"; Ye Jee said, "I like tomatoes."* Writing what the child dictates helps to give the child ownership over the writing, and makes it easier to remember when rereading. In turn, rereading familiar and enjoyable text helps the emergent reader internalize specific words, letter/sound elements, and conventions of print. In addition, reading dictated text and then rereading it again and again is one of the best ways for older students and adults to become readers, or more fluent readers (Rigg & Taylor, 1979; Meek, 1983; Routman, 1991). In short, this procedure works well with emergent readers of all ages, including those who are learning English as a second language (Rigg, 1989, 1990).

Guided Writing

In whole language classrooms, group writing more often takes the form of guided writing, rather than student-by-student dictation of sentences. That is, teacher and students together brainstorm, select ideas, compose and shape sentences, then reread, reconsider, and revise. Finally, they may edit what they've written and publish it—by adding it to a collection of class writings, by displaying it on the bulletin board or in the hallway, or by including it in a class or school newspaper. Such guided writing may be based upon field trips, classroom experiments, a book the class has shared—in short, almost any communal experience.

Modeled Writing

In modeled writing, the teacher demonstrates his or her own writing process by thinking out loud and writing a real piece as the children listen and observe. The kinds of writing that may be composed at the chalkboard (and copied by the children, if appropriate) include notices to go home, lists for parties, notes to lunchroom supervisors or janitors, and other practice items. By writing in front of the children, the teacher can demonstrate not only the writing process but the relationship between spoken words and written words, key letter/sound relationships, punctuation, and the like—as well as the concept that writing can serve various practical purposes.

Independent Writing

In whole language classrooms, even the youngest children—preschoolers and kindergartners—are encouraged to write independently. At first, their writings may consist merely of drawings, demonstrating their understanding that a visual image conveys meaning. Then they may progress to scribble writing, or prephonemic writing (e.g. Temple, Nathan, Temple, & Burris, 1993). The point, however, is that all students are treated as writers—even the least proficient of emergent writers. They become more proficient through exposure to books and print, through observing their more proficient peers writing and adults writing, and through direct help as well. As with reading, sometimes students are completely free to choose what they will write. At other times, they are expected to write in their dialogue journals, their reading journals or literature logs, or their learning logs; to experiment with certain forms and genres; and so forth. Nevertheless, choice plays a big part in what students write within whole language classrooms.

Journals and Learning Logs

Dialogue journals, reading journals or literature logs, and learning logs are such important aspects of learning in whole language classrooms that they deserve separate mention. A *dialogue journal* is, ordinarily, a journal in which student and teacher write back and forth to each other (Atwell, 1987). For example, Nancie Atwell initiated dialogue journals with the eighth graders in her reading class. They wrote letters to Atwell in response to the books they were reading, and Atwell responded with letters of her own; together, they discussed these and other related books (Atwell, 1987). In other words, they held literature discussions via journals. Some teachers call these journals "reading journals" or "literature logs" when they focus specifically on literary works, using the term "dialogue journal" more broadly, for writing back and forth about any subject. Similarly, *learning logs* are journals in which students respond to science or math or any other topic or subject. These logs may become dialogue journals if they are used transactively between teacher and student (Fulwiler and Young, 1982).

Literature Discussions

Increasingly, whole language teachers are discovering that perhaps the best way to develop children's reading strategies as well as their understanding and appreciation of literature is through discussion, particularly intensive small group discussions. Teacher and students can share reactions to the literature; make connections with other books and their own lives; discuss literary elements like characterization, symbol, and theme; and consider strategies for dealing with problem words and other elements of the text. Such discussion enriches understanding, as the group collaboratively constructs and reconstructs meaning (Eeds & Wells, 1989). The group may all read and discuss the same book, or they may read and share different but related books (e.g. Peetoom, 1993).

Choral Reading, Readers Theater, Drama, Storytelling

The oral and dramatic language arts also figure prominently in whole language classrooms (e.g. Heinig, 1994). Here are mentioned only some of the activities most obviously associated with literature and the literacy processes. Students have opportunities to perform literature through *choral reading,* with different parts of a literary selection assigned to different groups, who then read their part in unison, or chorus. Students may rehearse and read a script in *readers theater* format: The script is written much like a play, but the participants sit and read their parts (with appropriate facial expressions and perhaps gestures) instead of memorizing their lines and acting them out. Students may engage in *drama,* not only formal but informal: acting out key aspects of a story, for example, or acting out scenes in history, as the students think these events might have (or should have!) occurred. And they may engage in *storytelling,* after rehearsing a story for performance.

Observation and Experimentation

Observation and experimentation become literacy events when children record what they have observed. They may document the growth of a plant or a rabbit, for example, complete with graphs and learning log entries. They may predict the results of an experiment, write out the procedures for conducting it, and describe the results, comparing these with their predictions. Even the youngest of learners can engage in such literate documentation and response, using pictures or pictures with labels.

Research

Research involves reading, writing, speaking, and listening. In whole language classrooms, language and literacy are developed through and across the entire curriculum (Halliday, 1975, 1984). Even very young learners are capable of engaging in simple kinds of data gathering and recording.

Obviously, research as a regular part of classroom activity can and does encompass many of the other kinds of literacy events listed above. And clearly these do not exhaust the kinds of literacy events found in whole language classrooms; they are merely indicative of what often occurs.

Theme Study

Though the aforementioned literacy events can occur as separate experiences within the curriculum, many of them may naturally become part of *theme study*. Whole language classrooms are often characterized by in-depth exploration of a topic or theme, which naturally involves various reading and writing experiences as well as reading and the in-depth study of literature, research, the oral and dramatic language arts, and other arts (music, movement and/or dance, the visual arts). Topics typically derive from social studies and/or science. Depending upon the teacher's and students' purposes and interests, the topics may be relatively narrow (weather, family and friends, electricity, ecology and the environment) or relatively broad (change, contrasts, conflicts, compromise, cooperation, stability and change, conflict and resolution, similarities and differences). The broader the topic, the more opportunities for integrating the humanities, arts, math and the sciences, and social studies—and the greater the opportunities for students to gain proficiency in using language and to become increasingly literate and independent as learners. Also, the broader the topic, the more opportunities for engaging in cross-age or even whole school exploration of a common topic, or theme.

Discussions of Reading, Writing, and Research Strategies and Skills

Within the context of children's reading, writing, and researching, teachers help them develop the strategies and skills they need. For example, when a child has difficulty reading a particular word, the teacher may remind the child to use context and the initial consonant(s) to predict what the word might be, then look at the rest of the word to confirm or correct. When a child's writing demonstrates the need for a particular editing skill, the teacher may take that opportunity to teach the skill and help the child apply it. When children are researching topics of interest, the teacher may conclude it would be relevant to teach certain skills for locating and using various kinds of references that the children need. Whole language teachers know that children apply strategies and skills best when they have been learned in the context of their application (e.g. Freppon, 1988, 1991; Cunningham, 1990; DiStefano & Killion, 1984; Calkins, 1980). Therefore, they provide many opportunities to learn such strategies while the children are actually reading, writing, and researching: by demonstrating the teachers' own strategies; by providing mini-lessons for individuals, a small group, or the whole class; and by encouraging the sharing of strategies and skills as children discuss literature, each others' writings, and their ongoing research.

What Makes these Literacy and Language Events "Whole Language"

Of course many of these literacy and language events could be assigned as activities in a highly teacher-directed way, with follow-up exercises and tests that reflect a transmission paradigm rather than a transactional paradigm of education and learning.

What makes them "whole language" is the underlying philosophy: commitment to promoting students' ownership over their learning, and a concomitant trust in their ability to construct their own knowledge; facilitation and support of learning that is in large measure student-determined; direct instruction in the context of students' needs and interests; commitment to promoting individual growth rather than uniform mastery of a predetermined curriculum; and assessment that reflects these principles. When the aforementioned literacy and language events reflect such a philosophy of learning and teaching, they can justifiably be considered "whole language."

Figure 16–5 suggests some books that demonstrate how various teachers have actualized whole language principles and incorporated these kinds of literacy and language events in their classrooms. Such references are particularly valuable for teachers wanting concrete examples of how to apply whole language principles in their classrooms.

Research on the Effectiveness of Whole Language Education

Time and again, studies of individual children or small groups of children have demonstrated that they succeed much better in whole language learning/teaching situations than in traditional situations, whether the setting be the regular classroom, a special class or program, or a tutorial situation. Many of the naturalistic studies published prior to 1991 have been summarized in Diane Stephens' *Research in Whole Language: Support for a New Curriculum* (1991) and, more briefly, in Heald-Taylor (1989) and N. Hall (1987). These studies and various anecdotal reports suggest that whole language teaching succeeds with special learners in essentially the same way as it does with unlabeled students (e.g. Meek, 1983; Phinney, 1988; Rhodes & Dudley-Marling, 1988; Crowley, 1989; Doyle, 1990; Five, 1992; Stires, 1991; Chapter 14 in Routman, 1991; Chapter 12 in Weaver, 1994, especially the sections by Erdmann, Five, Dionisio, and Stone; and articles in the January 1982 issue of *Topics in Learning and Learning Disabilities* and in the May 1991 issue of *Topics in Language Disorders*). Other articles describing relevant research (some naturalistic, some experimental) are Shapiro, 1990, and Tunnel & Jacobs, 1989.

FIGURE 16–5. *Selected readings for understanding whole language practice.*

Atwell, N. (1987). *In the middle: Reading, writing, and learning with adolescents.* Portsmouth, NH: Heinemann.

Calkins, L. M., with Harwayne, S. (1990). *Living between the lines.* Portsmouth, NH: Heinemann.

Cordeiro, P. (1992). *Whole learning: Whole language and content in the upper elementary grades.* Katonah, NY: Richard C. Owen.

Crafton, L. K. (1991). *Whole language: Getting started . . . moving forward.* Katonah, NY: Richard C. Owen.

Fisher, B. (1991). *Joyful learning: A whole language kindergarten.* Portsmouth, NH: Heinemann.

Forester, A. D., & Reinhard, M. (1989). *The learners' way.* Winnipeg: Peguis Publishers.

Goodman, K. S., Bridges, L. B., & Goodman, Y. M. (Eds.). (1991). *The whole language catalog.* Chicago: SRA.

Harwayne, S. (1992). *Lasting impressions: Weaving literature into the writing workshop.* Portsmouth, NH: Heinemann.

Mills, H., O'Keefe, T., & Stephens, D. (1992). *Looking closely: Exploring the role of phonics in one whole language classroom.* Urbana, IL: National Council of Teachers of English.

Peterson, R. (1992). *Life in a crowded place: Making a learning community.* Portsmouth, NH: Heinemann.

Peterson, R., & Eeds, M. (1990). *Grand conversations: Literature discussion groups in action.* New York: Scholastic.

Pierce, K. M., & Gilles, C. (Eds.). (1994). *Cycles of meaning: Exploring the potential of talk in learning communities.* Portsmouth, NH: Heinemann.

Rief, L. (1991). *Seeking diversity: Language arts with adolescents.* Portsmouth, NH: Heinemann.

Routman, R. (1991). *Invitations: Changing as teachers and learners K-12.* Portsmouth, NH: Heinemann.

Weaver, C., Chaston, J., & Peterson, S. (1993). *Theme exploration: A voyage of discovery.* Richmond Hill, Ontario: Scholastic. (Available in the U. S. from Heinemann.)

So far, only a few research studies have focused on comparing the success of children in genuine whole language classrooms with the success of children in skills-based classrooms. (See Chapter 7 of Weaver, 1994, for an explanation of the qualifier "genuine"; or see Stahl & Miller, 1989, and the responses by Schickendanz, 1990, and McGee & Lomax, 1990.) All of these comparative research studies have dealt with children in the primary grades, and none (to my knowledge) has focused specifically on special needs students, though two studies have focused on students identified as being at risk of academic failure. Nevertheless, what has emerged from this growing body of research overwhelmingly suggests that whole language classrooms hold more promise for all learners than do traditional classrooms emphasizing the mastery of isolated skills and facts. In fact, in the comparative studies I've been able to locate, students in whole language classrooms have shown greater gains than those in traditional classrooms on every different kind of measure, standardized or otherwise.

The following generalizations are drawn mostly from the studies described in detail in Weaver, 1994, Chapter 7: Elley, 1991 (itself a summary of nine studies, including Elley & Manghubi, 1983); Kasten & Clarke, 1989; Ribowsky, 1985; Clarke, 1988; Freppon, 1988, 1991; Dahl & Freppon, 1992; and Stice & Bertrand, 1990; the two studies focusing on at-risk children are Stice & Bertrand, 1990, and Dahl & Freppon, 1992. Combining results from these studies, it seems reasonable to draw the following tentative conclusions, as long as we simultaneously consider them to be reframable as hypotheses subject to further testing.

1. *Children in whole language classrooms usually show equal or greater gains on various reading tests and subtests—or at least they did in these research studies* (though the differences in the aforementioned studies often were not statistically significant). For example, the whole language kindergartners in Ribowksy's study (1985) scored better on all measures of growth and achievement, including the tests of letter recognition and letter/sound knowledge. In the Kasten and Clarke study (1989), the whole language kindergartners performed significantly better than their counterparts on all subtests of the Metropolitan Readiness Test, including tests of beginning consonant sounds, letter/sound correspondences, and sounds and clusters of sounds in initial and final positions of words.

2. *Children in whole language classrooms typically develop greater ability to use phonics knowledge effectively than children in more traditional classrooms, where skills are practiced in isolation.* For example, in Freppon's study (1988, 1991), the skills group attempted to sound out words more than twice as often as the others, but the literature-based group was more successful in doing so: a 53 percent success rate compared with a 32 percent success rate for the skills group. Apparently the literature-based children were more successful because they made better use of phonics in conjunction with other information and cues. (For another relevant study, see Cunningham, 1990.)

3. *Children in whole language classrooms typically develop vocabulary, spelling, grammar, and punctuation skills as well as or better than children in more traditional classrooms.* (For example, see the 1991 Elley summary of studies on learning English as a second language; Clarke, 1988; and Stice & Bertrand, 1990, with regard to spelling. In addition, see Calkins, 1980; DiStefano & Killion, 1984; Gunderson and Shapiro, 1987, 1988.)

4. *Children in whole language classrooms are typically more inclined and able to read for meaning rather than just to identify words.* For example, when asked "What makes a good reader?", the children in Stice and Bertrand's study (1990) reported that good readers read a great deal and that they can read any book in the room. The children in the traditional classrooms tended to focus on words and surface correctness; they reported that good readers read big words, they know all the words, and they don't miss any words.

5. *Children in whole language classrooms typically develop more strategies for dealing with problems in reading.* For example, the whole language children in Stice and Bertrand's study (1990) typically described six strategies for dealing with problem words, while the children in traditional classrooms described only three.

6. *Children in whole language classrooms typically develop greater facility in writing.* For example, in the Dahl and Freppon study (1992), a considerably larger portion of the children in the whole language classrooms were writing sentences and stories by the end of first grade. The whole language children in the Kasten and Clark study (1989) were similarly much more advanced as writers by the end of their kindergarten year.

7. *Children in whole language classrooms typically develop a stronger sense of themselves as readers and writers.* Take, for example, the Stice and Bertrand study (1990): When asked "Who do you know who is a good reader?", *82 percent* of the kindergartners in the whole language classrooms mentioned themselves, but *only 5 percent* of the kindergartners in the traditional classrooms said "Me" (emphasis mine). During the first-grade year, when the children were asked directly "Are you a good reader?", 70 percent of the whole language children said yes, but only thirty-three percent of the traditional children said yes.

8. *Children in whole language classrooms typically develop greater independence as readers and writers.* In the Dahl and Freppon study (1992), for instance, passivity seemed to be the most frequent coping strategy for learners having difficulty in the skills-based classrooms. But in whole language classrooms, those having difficulty tended to draw upon other learners for support: by saying the phrases and sentences that others could read, by copying what they wrote, and so forth. The less proficient literacy learners still attempted to remain engaged in literacy activities with their peers. (See also item 5 above.)

It may be relevant to note that the whole language classrooms in these studies typically involved the Shared Book Experience, or something similar. That is, the teachers gave children support in constructing their own knowledge about print, books, words, letter/sound relations, reading strategies, and so forth. The teachers did not merely leave the children to figure out everything for themselves, as whole language teachers are sometimes said to do.

A growing number of research studies like these offer impressive evidence of the benefits of whole language education. To whole language educators, the fact that standardized test scores are about the same as or better than those in traditional classrooms is the *least* important result of these studies, though it may be politically useful with administrators who are reluctant to permit or promote whole language teaching because of their fear of lowered test scores. What whole language educators consider most important is the fact that whole language students are generally more proficient at reading and writing and more independent as learners. In addition, they have more positive concepts of themselves as readers and writers and learners.

Surely such success is what parents want most for their children, whether these children be unlabeled, labeled as gifted, or labeled as having an Attention Deficit (Hyperactivity) Disorder, a learning disability, or some other educationally handicapping condition. In whole language settings, all children can experience success at last.

References

Allington, R. L. (1991). The legacy of "slow it down and make it more concrete." In J. Zutell & S. McCormick (Eds.), *Learner factors/teacher factors: Issues in literacy research and instruction* (pp. 19–29). Chicago: National Reading Conference.

Altwerger, B. (1991). Whole language teachers: Empowered professionals. In J. Hydrick (Ed.), *Whole language: Empowerment at the chalkface* (pp. 15–29). New York: Scholastic.

Anderson, L. W., & Pellicer, L. O. (1990). Synthesis of research on compensatory and remedial education. *Educational Leadership, 48,* 10–16.

Anthony, R. J., Johnson, T. D., Mickelson, N. I., & Preece, A. (1991). *Evaluating literacy: A perspective for change.* Portsmouth, NH: Heinemann.

Atwell, N. (1987). *In the middle: Writing, reading, and learning with adolescents.* Portsmouth, NH: Heinemann.

Barrs,, M., Ellis, S., Tester, H., & Thomas, A. (1989). *The primary language record: A handbook for teachers.* Portsmouth, NH: Heinemann.

Bartoli, J., & Botel, M. (1988). *Reading/learning disability: An ecological approach.* New York: Teachers College Press.

Brown, R. (1973). *A first language: The early stages.* Cambridge: Harvard University Press.

Bruner, J. S. (1983). *Child's talk: Learning to use language.* Oxford: Oxford University Press.

Bruner, J. S. (1986). *Actual minds, possible worlds.* Cambridge: Harvard University Press.

Calkins, L. M. (1980). When children want to punctuate: Basic skills belong in context. *Language Arts, 57,* 567–573.

Calkins, L. M. (1986). *The art of teaching writing.* Portsmouth, NH: Heinemann.

Cambourne, B. (1988). *The whole story: Natural learning and the acquisition of literacy in the classroom.* Auckland, New Zealand: Ashton Scholastic.

Clark, J., & Miller, J. (1992). The shared reading experience. *Michigan Reading Journal, 25* (Spring), 16–21.

Clarke, L. K. (1988). Invented versus traditional spelling in first graders' writings: Effects on learning to spell and read. *Research in the Teaching of English, 22,* 281–309.

Crowley, P. (1989). "They'll grow into 'em:" Evaluation, self-evaluation, and self-esteem in special education. In K. S. Goodman, Y. M. Goodman, & W. J. Hood (Eds.), *The whole language evaluation book* (pp. 237–247). Portsmouth, NH: Heinemann.

Cunningham, A. E. (1990). Explicit versus implicit instruction in phonemic awareness. *Journal of Experimental Child Psychology, 50,* 429–444.

Dahl, K. L., & Freppon, P. A. (1992). *Learning to read and write in inner city schools: A comparison of children's sense-making in skills-based and whole language classrooms.* Final report to the Office of Educational research and Improvement. Washington, DC: U.S. Department of Education. (Grant No. R117E00134)

DiStefano, P., & Killion, J. (1984). Assessing writing through a process approach. *English Education,* 16, 203–207.

Doyle, K. M. (1990). Listening to the sounds of our hearts. *Language Arts, 67,* 254–261.

Edelsky, C., Altwerger, B., & Flores, B. (1991). *Whole language: What's the difference?* Portsmouth, NH: Heinemann.

Edelsky, C., & Harmon, S. (1988). One more critique of reading tests—with two differences. *English Education, 20,* 157–171.

Eeds, M., & Wells, D. (1989). Grand conversations: An exploration of meaning construction in literature study groups. *Research in the Teaching of English, 23,* 4–29.

Elley, W. B. (1989). Vocabulary acquisition from listening to stories. *Reading Research Quarterly, 24,* 174–187.

Elley, W. B. (1991). Acquiring literacy in a second language: The effect of book-based programs. *Language Learning, 41*(3), 375–411.

Elley, W. B., & Mangubhai, F. (1983). The impact of reading on second language learning. *Reading Research Quarterly, 19,* 53–67.

Emig, J. (1983). Non-magical thinking: Presenting writing developmentally in schools. In *The web of meaning: Essays on writing, teaching, learning, and thinking* (pp. 135–144). Ed. by D. Goswami & M. Butler. Portsmouth, NH: Boynton/Cook-Heinemann.

Engelmann, S., & Osborn, J. (1975). *DISTAR Language III: An Instructional System Kit.* Chicago: SRA.

Engelmann, S., Osborn, J., Osborn, S., & Zoref, L. (1988). *Reading Mastery VI.* Chicago: SRA.

Five, C. L. (1992). *Special voices.* Portsmouth, NH: Heinemann.

Freppon, P. A. (1988). An investigation of children's concepts of the purpose and nature of reading in different instructional settings. Unpublished doctoral dissertation, University of Cincinnati, OH.

Freppon, P. A. (1991). Children's concepts of the nature and purpose of reading in different instructional settings. *Journal of Reading Behavior, 23,* 139–163.

Fulwiler, T., & Young, A. (Eds.). (1982). *Language connections: Writing and reading across the curriculum.* Urbana, IL: National Council of Teachers of English.

Goodman, K. S. (1973). *Theoretically based studies of patterns of miscues in oral reading performance.* Detroit: Wayne State University. (Educational Resources Information Center:ED 079 708)

Goodman, K. S. (1989). Whole-language research: Foundations and development. *The Elementary School Journal, 90,* 208–221.

Goodman, K. S., & Goodman, Y. M. (1979). Learning to read is natural. In L. B. Resnick, & P. A. Weaver (Eds.), *Theory and practice of early reading,* Vol 1 (pp. 137–154). Hillsdale, NJ: Erlbaum.

Goodman, Y. M. (1989). Roots of the whole-language movement. *The Elementary School Journal, 90,* 113–127.

Gunderson, L., & Shapiro, J. (1987). Some findings on whole language instruction. *Reading-Canada-Lecture, 5*(1), 22–26.

Gunderson, L., & Shapiro, J. (1988). Whole language instruction: Writing in 1st grade. *The Reading Teacher, 41,* 430–437.

Hall, M. (1976). *Teaching as a language experience* (2nd ed.). Columbus, OH: Charles Merrill.

Hall, M. (1981). *The language experience approach for teaching reading: A research perspective* (3rd ed.). Newark, DE: ERIC Clearinghouse on Reading and Communication Skills and the International Reading Association.

Hall, N. (1987). *The emergence of literacy.* Portsmouth, NH: Heinemann.

Halliday, M. A. K. (1975). *Learning how to mean: Explorations in the development of language.* London: Elsevier.

Halliday, M. A. K. (1984). Three aspects of children's language development: Learning language, learning through language, and learning about language. In Y. M. Goodman, M. Haussler, & D. Strickland (Eds.), *Oral and written language development research: Impact on the schools* (pp. 165–192). Urbana, IL: National Council of Teachers of English.

Hansen, J. (1987). *When writers read.* Portsmouth, NH: Heinemann.

Harste, J. C., Woodward, V. A., & Burke, C. L. (1984). *Language stories and literacy lessons.* Portsmouth, NH: Heinemann.

Heald-Taylor, G. (1989). *The administrator's guide to whole language.* Katonah, NY: Richard C. Owen.

Heinig, R. (1994). Reading, literature, and the dramatic language arts. In C. Weaver, *Reading process and practice: From socio-psycholinguistics to whole language.* (2nd ed.). Portsmouth, NH: Heinemann.

Heshusius, L. (1989). The Newtonian mechanistic paradigm, special education, and contours of alternatives: An overview. *Journal of Learning Disabilities, 22*(7), 403–415.

Holdaway, D. (1979). *The foundations of literacy.* Sydney: Ashton Scholastic. Available in the U.S. from Heinemann.

Kasten, W. C., & Clarke, B. K. (1989). *Reading/writing readiness for preschool and kindergarten children: A whole language approach.* Sanibel: Florida Educational Research and Development Council. (Educational Resources Information Center: ED 312 041)

Laminack, L. (1991). *Learning with Zachary.* Richmond Hill, Ontario: Scholastic.

Lindfors, J. W. (1987). *Children's language and learning* (2nd ed.). Englewood Cliffs, NJ: Prentice Hall.

McGee, L. M., & Lomax, R. G. (1990). On combining apples and oranges: A response to Stahl and Miller. *Review of Educational Research, 60,* 133–140.

McGill-Franzen, A., & Allington, R. (1991). The gridlock of low reading achievement: Perspectives on practice and policy. *Remedial and Special Education, 12*(3), 20–30.

Meek, M. (1983). *Achieving literacy.* London: Routledge & Kegan Paul.

Newman, J. (1985). Insights from recent reading and writing research and their implications for developing whole language curriculum. In J. Newman (Ed.), *Whole language: Theory in use* (pp. 7–36). Portsmouth, NH: Heinemann.

Ninio, A., & Bruner, J. S. (1978). The achievement and antecedents of labeling. *Journal of Child Language, 5,* 1–15.

Peetoom, A. (1993). *ConneXions: Inviting engagement with books.* Richmond Hill, Ontario: Scholastic.

Perera, K. (1986). Language acquisition as a continuing process: The role of the English teacher. Paper presented at the Fourth International Conference on the Teaching of English, Ottawa, Ontario, May 13.

Phinney, M. Y. (1988). *Reading with the troubled reader.* Portsmouth, NH: Heinemann.

Poplin, M. S., & Stone, S. (1992). Paradigm shifts in instructional strategies: From reductionism to holistic/constructivism. In W. Stainback & S. Stainback (Eds.), *Controversial issues confronting special education: Divergent perspectives* (pp. 153–179). Boston: Allyn and Bacon.

Rhodes, L. K., & Dudley-Marling, C. (1988). *Readers and writers with a difference: A holistic approach to teaching learning disabled and remedial students.* Portsmouth, NH: Heinemann.

Ribowsky, H. (1985). The effects of a code emphasis approach and a whole language approach upon emergent literacy of kindergarten children. Alexandria, VA. (Educational Resources Information Center: ED 269 720)

Rigg, P. (1989). Language experience approach: Reading naturally. In P. Rigg & V. G. Allen (Eds.), When they don't all speak English: Integrating the ESL student into the regular classroom (pp. 65–76). Urbana, IL: National Council of Teachers of English.

Rigg, P. (1990). Using the language experience approach with ESL adults. *TESL Talk, 29*(1), 188–200.

Rigg, P., & Taylor, L. (1979). A twenty-one-year-old begins to read. *English Journal, 68,* 52–56.

Routman, R. (1991). *Invitations: Changing as teachers and learners K-12.* Portsmouth, NH: Heinemann.

Sampson, M. R. (Ed.). (1986). *The pursuit of literacy: Early reading and writing.* Dubuque, IA: Kendall Hunt.

Schickendanz, J. A. (1990). The jury is still out on the effects of whole language and language experience approaches for beginning reading: A critique of Stahl & Miller's study. *Review of Educational Research, 60,* 127–131.

Shapiro, J. (1990). Research perspectives on whole-language. In V. Froese (Ed.), *Whole-language: Practice and theory* (pp. 313–356). Boston: Allyn and Bacon.

Smith, F. (1971). *Understanding reading.* Hillsdale, NJ: Erlbaum. (4th ed., 1988).

Smith, F. (Ed.). (1973). *Psycholinguistics and reading.* New York: Holt, Rinehart.

Smith, F. (1975). *Comprehension and learning: A conceptual framework for teachers.* Katonah, NY: Richard C. Owen.

Smith, F. (1990). *To think.* New York: Teachers College Press.

Stahl, S. A., & Miller, P. D. (1989). Whole language and language experience approaches for beginning reading: A quantitative research synthesis. Review of *Educational Research, 59,* 87–116.

Stephens, D. (1991). *Research on whole language: Support for a new curriculum.* Katonah, NY: Richard C. Owen.

Stice, C. F., & Bertrand, N. P. (1990). *Whole language and the emergent literacy of at-risk children: A two-year comparative study.* Nashville: Center for Excellence, Basic Skills, Tennessee State University. (Educational Resources Information Center: ED 324 636)

Stires, S. (Ed.). (1991). *With promise: Redefining reading and writing needs for special students.* Portsmouth, NH: Heinemann.

Tarver, S. G. (1992). Direct instruction. In W. Stainback & S. Stainback, (Eds.), *Controversial issues confronting special education: Divergent perspectives* (pp. 141–152). Boston: Allyn and Bacon.

Teale, W. H. (1982). Toward a theory of how children learn to read and write naturally. *Language Arts, 59,* 550–570.

Temple, C., Nathan, R., Temple, F., & Burris, N. (1993). *The beginnings of writing* (3rd ed.). Boston: Allyn and Bacon.

Trelease, J. (1989). *The new read-aloud handbook.* New York: Penguin.

Tunnel, M. O. & Jacobs, J. S. (1989). Using "real" books: Research findings on literature based reading instruction. *The Reading Teacher, 42,* 470–477.

Van Allen, R. (1976). *Language experiences in education.* Boston: Houghton Mifflin.

Vygotsky, L. S. (1962, 1986). *Thought and language* (A. Kozulin, Trans.). Cambridge: MIT Press.

Vygotsky, L. S. (1978). *Mind in society: The development of higher psychological processes.* (M. Cole, V. John-Steiner, S. Scribner, & E. Souberman, Eds.). Cambridge: Harvard University Press.

Watson, D. J. (1989). Defining and describing whole language. *The Elementary School Journal, 90,* 130–141.

Weaver, C. (1990). *Understanding whole language: From principles to practice.* Portsmouth, NH: Heinemann.

Weaver, C. (1994). *Reading process and practice: From socio-psycholinguistics to whole language* (2nd ed.). Portsmouth, NH: Heinemann.

Weaver, C., Chaston, J., & Peterson, S. (1993). *Theme exploration: A voyage of discovery.* Richmond Hill, Ontario: Scholastic. Available in the U.S. from Heinemann.

Appendix A

United States Department of Education Memorandum on AD(H)D

Memorandum

DATE: September 16, 1991
TO: Chief State School Officers
FROM: Robert R. Davila
Assistant Secretary
Office of Special Education and Rehabilitative Services

Michael L. Williams
Assistant Secretary
Office for Civil Rights

John T. MacDonald
Assistant Secretary
Office of Elementary and Secondary Education

SUBJECT: Clarification of Policy to Address the Needs of Children with Attention Deficit Disorders within General and/or Special Education

I. Introduction

There is a growing awareness in the education community that attention deficit disorder (ADD) and attention deficit hyperactive disorder (ADHD) can result in significant learning problems for children with those conditions. While estimates of the prevalence of ADD vary widely, we believe that three to five percent of school-aged children may have significant educational problems related to this disorder. Because ADD has broad implications for education as a whole, the Department believes it should clarify State and local responsibility under Federal Law for addressing the needs of children with ADD in the schools. Ensuring that these students are able to reach their fullest potential is an inherent part of the National education goals and AMERICA 2000. The National goals, and the strategy for achieving them, are based on the assumptions that: (1) all children can learn and benefit from their education; and (2) the educational community must work to improve the learning opportunities for all children.[1]

---

[1] While we recognize that the disorders ADD and ADHD vary, the term ADD is being used to encompass children with both disorders.

This memorandum clarifies the circumstances under which children with ADD are eligible for special education services under Part B of the Individuals with Disabilities Education Act (Part B), as well as the Part B requirements for evaluation of such children's unique educational needs. This memorandum will also clarify the responsibility of State and local educational agencies (SEAs and LEAs) to provide special education and related services to eligible children with ADD under Part B. Finally, this memorandum clarifies the responsibilities of LEAs to provide regular or special education and related aids and services to those children with ADD who are not eligible under Part B, but who fall within the definition of "handicapped person" under Section 504 of the Rehabilitation Act of 1973. Because of the overall educational responsibility to provide services for these children, it is important that general and special education coordinate their efforts.

II. Eligibility for Special Education and Related Services Under Part B

Last year during the reauthorization of the Education of the Handicapped Act (now the Individuals with Disabilities Education Act), Congress gave serious consideration to including ADD in the definition of "children with disabilities" in the statute. The Department took the position that ADD does not need to be added as a separate disability category in the statutory definition since children with ADD who require special education and related services can meet the eligibility criteria for services under Part B. This continues to be the Department's position.

No change with respect to ADD was made by Congress in the statutory definition of "children with disabilities"; however, language was included in Section 102(a) of the Education of the Handicapped Act Amendments of 1990 that required the Secretary to issue a Notice of Inquiry (NOI) soliciting public comment on special education for children with ADD under Part B. In response to the NOI (published November 29, 1990 in the Federal Register), the Department received over 2000 written comments, which have been transmitted to the Congress. Our review of these written comments indicates that there is confusion in the field regarding the extent to which children with ADD may be served in special education programs conducted under Part B.

A. Description of Part B

Part B requires SEAs and LEAs to make a free appropriate public education (FAPE) available to all eligible children with disabilities and to ensure that the rights and protections of Part B are extended to those children and their parents. 20 U.S.C. 1412(2); 34 CFR SS300.121 and 300.2. Under Part B, FAPE, among other elements, includes the provision of special education and related services, at no cost to parents, in conformity with an individualized education program (IEP). 34 CFR §300.4.

In order to be eligible under Part B, a child must be evaluated in accordance with 34 CFR §§300.530-300.534 as having one or more specified physical or mental impairments, and must be found to require special education and related services by reason of one or more of these impairments.[2] 20 U.S.C. 1401 (a) (1); 34 CFR §300.5. SEAs and LEAs must ensure that children with ADD who are determined eligible for services under Part B receive special education and related services designed to meet their unique needs, including special education and related services needs arising from the ADD. A full continuum of placement alternatives, including the regular classroom, must be available for providing special education and related services required in the IEP.

B. Eligibility for Part B Services Under the "Other Health Impaired" Category

The list of chronic or acute health problems included within the definition of "other health impaired" in the Part B regulations is not exhaustive. The term "other health impaired" includes chronic or acute impairments that result in limited alertness, which adversely affects educational performance. Thus, children with ADD should be classified as eligible for services under the "other health impaired" category in instances where the ADD is a chronic or acute health problem that results in limited alertness which adversely affects educational performance. In other words, children with ADD, where the ADD is a chronic or acute health problem resulting in limited alertness, may be considered disabled under Part B solely on the basis of this disorder within the "other health impaired" category in situations where special education and related services are needed because of the ADD.

C. Eligibility for Part B Services Under Other Disability Categories

Children with ADD are also eligible for services under Part B if the children satisfy the criteria applicable to other disability categories. For example, children with ADD are also eligible for services under the "specific learning disability" category of Part B if they meet the criteria stated in §§300.5(b) (9) and 300.541 or under the "seriously emotionally disturbed" category of Part B if they meet the criteria stated in §300.5(b) (8).

III. Evaluations Under Part B

A. Requirements

SEAs and LEAs have an affirmative obligation to evaluate a child who is suspected of having a disability to determine the child's need for special education and related services. Under Part B, SEAs and LEAs are required to have procedures for locating, identifying, and evaluating all children who have a disability or are suspected of having a disability and are in need of special education and related services. 34 CFR §§300.128 and 300.220. This responsi-

---

[2] The Part B regulations define 11 specified disabilities. 34 CFR §300.5(b) (1)-(11). The Education of the Handicapped Act Amendments of 1990 amended the Individuals with Disabilities Education Act (formerly the Education of the Handicapped Act) to specify that autism and traumatic brain injury are separate disability categories. See § 602(a)(1) of the Act, to be codified at 20 U.S.C. 1401(a)(1).

bility, known as "child find," is applicable to all children from birth through 21, regardless of the severity of their disability.

Consistent with this responsibility and the obligation to make FAPE available to all eligible children with disabilities, SEAs and LEAs must ensure that evaluations of children who are suspected of needing special education and related services are conducted without undue delay. 20 U.S.C. 1412(2). Because of its responsibility resulting from the FAPE and child find requirements of Part B, a LEA may not refuse to evaluate the possible need for special education and related services of a child with a prior medical diagnosis of ADD solely by reason of that medical diagnosis. However, a medical diagnosis of ADD alone is not sufficient to render a child eligible for services under Part B.

Under Part B, before any action is taken with respect to the initial placement of a child with a disability in a program providing special education and related services, "a full and individual evaluation of the child's educational needs must be conducted in accordance with requirements of §300.532." 34 CFR §300.531. Section 300.532(a) requires that a child's evaluation must be conducted by a multidisciplinary team, including at least one teacher or other specialist with knowledge in the area of suspected disability.

B. Disagreements over Evaluations

Any proposal or refusal of an agency to initiate or change the identification, evaluation, or educational placement of the child, or the provision of FAPE to the child is subject to the written prior notice requirements of 34 CFR §§300.504-300.505.[3] If a parent disagrees with the LEA's refusal to evaluate a child or the LEA's evaluation and determination that a child does not have a disability for which the child is eligible for services under Part B, the parent may request a due process hearing pursuant to 34 CFR §§300.506-300.513 of the Part B regulations.

IV. Obligations Under Section 504 of SEAs and LEAs to Children with ADD Found Not to Require Special Education and Related Services Under Part B

Even if a child with ADD is found not to be eligible for services under Part B, the requirements of Section 504 of the Rehabilitation Act of 1973 (Section 504) and its implementing regulation at 34 CFR Part 104 may be applicable. Section

---

[3] Section 300.505 of the Part B regulations sets out the elements that must be contained in the prior written notice to parents:

1. A full explanation of all the procedural safeguards available to the parents under Subpart E;
2. A description of the action proposed or refused by the agency, an explanation of why the agency proposes or refuses to take action, and a description of any options the agency considered and the reasons why those options were rejected;
3. A description of each evaluation procedure, test, record, or report the agency uses as a basis for the proposal or refusal; and
4. A description of any other factors which are relevant to the agency's proposal or refusal.

504 prohibits discrimination on the basis of handicap by recipients of Federal funds. Since Section 504 is a civil rights law, rather than a funding law, its requirements are framed in different terms than those of Part B. While the Section 504 regulation was written with an eye to consistency with Part B, it is more general, and there are some differences arising from the differing natures of the two laws. For instance, the protections of Section 504 extend to some children who do not fall within the disability categories specified in Part B.

A. Definition

Section 504 requires every recipient that operates a public elementary or secondary education program to address the needs of children who are considered "handicapped persons" under Section 504 as adequately as the needs of nonhandicapped persons are met. "Handicapped person" is defined in the Section 504 regulations as any person who has a physical or mental impairment which substantially limits a major life activity (e.g. learning). 34 CFR §104.3(j). Thus, depending on the severity of their condition, children with ADD may fit within that definition.

B. Programs and Services Under Section 504

Under Section 504, an LEA must provide a free appropriate public education to each qualified handicapped child. A free appropriate public education, under Section 504, consists of regular or special education and related aids and services that are designed to meet the individual student's needs and based on adherence to the regulator requirements on educational setting, evaluation, placement, and procedural safeguards. 34 CFR §§104.33, 104.34, 104.35, and 104.36. A student may be handicapped within the meaning of Section 504, and therefore entitled to regular or special education and related aids and services under the Section 504 regulation, even though the student may not be eligible for special education and related services under Part B.

Under Section 504, if parents believe that their child is handicapped by ADD, the LEA must evaluate the child to determine whether he or she is handicapped as defined by Section 504. If an LEA determines that a child is not handicapped under Section 504, the parent has the right to contest that determination. If the child is determined to be handicapped under Section 504, the LEA must make an individualized determination of the child's educational needs for regular or special education or related aids and services. 34 CFR §104.35. For children determined to be handicapped under Section 504, implementation of an individualized education program developed in accordance with Part B, although not required, is one means of meeting the free appropriate public education requirements of Section 504.[4] The child's education must be provided in the regular education classroom unless it is demonstrated that education in the regular environment with the use of supplementary aids and services cannot be achieved satisfactorily. 34 CFR §104.34.

---

[4] Many LEAs use the same process for determining the needs of students under Section 504 that they use for implementing Part B.

Should it be determined that the child with ADD is handicapped for purposes of Section 504 and needs only adjustments in the regular classroom, rather than special education, those adjustments are required by Section 504. A range of strategies is available to meet the educational needs of children with ADD. Regular classroom teachers are important in identifying the appropriate educational adaptions and interventions for many children with ADD.

SEAs and LEAs should take the necessary steps to promote coordination between special and regular education programs. Steps also should be taken to train regular education teachers and other personnel to develop their awareness about ADD and its manifestations and the adaptations that can be implemented in regular education programs to address the instructional needs of these children. Examples of adaptations in regular education programs could include the following:

> providing a structured learning environment; repeating and simplifying instructions about in-class and homework assignments; supplementing verbal instructions with visual instructions; using behavioral management techniques; adjusting class schedules; modifying test delivery; using tape recorders, computer-aided instruction, and other audiovisual equipment; selecting modified textbooks or workbooks; and tailoring homework assignments.

Other provisions range from consultation to special resources and may include reducing class size; use of one-on-one tutorials; classroom aides and note takers; involvement of a "services coordinator" to oversee implementation of special programs and services, and possible modification of nonacademic times such as lunchroom, recess, and physical education.

Through the use of appropriate adaptations and interventions in regular classes, many of which may be required by Section 504, the Department believes that LEAs will be able to effectively address the instructional needs of many children with ADD.

C. Procedural Safeguards Under Section 504
Procedural safeguards under the Section 504 regulation are stated more generally than in Part B. The Section 504 regulation requires the LEA to make available a system of procedural safeguards that permits parents to challenge actions regarding the identification, evaluation, or educational placement of their handicapped child whom they believe needs special education or related services. 34 CFR §104.36. The Section 504 regulation requires that the system of procedural safeguards include notice, an opportunity for the parents or guardian to examine relevant records, an impartial hearing with opportunity for participation by the parents or guardian and representation by counsel, and a review procedure. Compliance with procedural safeguards of Part B is one means of fulfilling the Section 504 requirements.[5] However, in an impartial due

---

[5] Again, many LEAs and some SEAs are conserving time and resources by using the same due process procedures for resolving disputes under both laws.

process hearing raising issues under the Section 504 regulation, the impartial hearing officer must make a determination based upon that regulation.

V. Conclusion

Congress and the Department have recognized the need to provide information and assistance to teachers, administrators, parents, and other interested persons regarding the identification, evaluation, and instructional needs of children with ADD. The Department has formed a work group to explore strategies across principal offices to address this issue. The work group also plans to identify some ways that the Department can work with the education associations to cooperatively consider the programs and services needed by children with ADD across special and regular education.

In fiscal year 1991, the Congress appropriated funds for the Department to synthesize and disseminate current knowledge related to ADD. Four centers will be established in Fall, 1991 to analyze and synthesize the current research literature on ADD relating to identification, assessment, and interventions. Research syntheses will be prepared in formats suitable for educators, parents and researchers. Existing clearinghouses and networks, as well as Federal, State and local organizations will be utilized to disseminate these research syntheses to parents, educators and administrators, and other interested persons.

In addition, the Federal Resource Center will work with SEAs and the six regional resource centers authorized under the Individuals with Disabilities Education Act to identify effective identification and assessment procedures, as well as intervention strategies being implemented across the country for children with ADD. A document describing current practices will be developed and disseminated to parents, educators and administrators, and other interested persons through the regional resource centers, network, as well as by parent training centers, other parent and consumer organizations, and professional organizations. Also, the Office for Civil Rights' ten regional offices stand ready to provide technical assistance to parents and educators.

It is our hope that the above information will be of assistance to your State as you plan for the needs of children with ADD who require special education and related services under Part B, as well as for the needs of the broader group of children with ADD who do not qualify for special education and related services under Part B, but for whom special education or adaptations in regular education programs are needed. If you have any questions, please contact Jean Peelen, Office for Civil Rights; (Phone: 202/732-1635); Judy Schrag, Office of Special Education Programs (Phone: 202/732-1007); or Dan Bonner, Office of Elementary and Secondary Education (Phone: 202/401-0984).

Appendix B

Some Useful Addresses

A.D.D. WareHouse
300 Northwest 70th Avenue, Suite 102
Plantation, FL 33317
(305) 792-8944 FAX (305) 792-8545
Orders: 1-800-233-9273
This distributor sells books, tapes, and other products for understanding and dealing with AD(H)D.

Attention Deficit Disorder Association
PO Box 488
West Newbury, MA 01985
This organization publishes a newsletter called *Challenge*.

CH.A.D.D. [Children and Adults with Attention Deficit Disorders]
499 Northwest 70th Avenue, Suite 308
Plantation, FL 33317
(305) 587-3700 FAX (305) 587-4599
This support and information organization publishes a biannual publication called CH.A.D.D.ER and a monthly newsletter called *CH.A.D.D.ER Box*.

Index